Imperial Women

Imperial Women

A Study in Public Images,
40 BC - AD 68

Susan E. Wood

BRILL

LEIDEN • BOSTON • KOLN

This journal is printed on acid-free paper.

Design: TopicA (Antoinette Hanekuyk), Leiden

On the cover: Grande Camée de France, AD 49-54.
Sardonyx cameo. Cabinet des Médailles,
Bibliothèque Nationale de France, Paris, France.

Library of Congress Cataloging-in-Publication Data

The Library of Congress Cataloging-in-Publication Data
are also available.

ISBN 90 04 11950 7

© Copyright by Koninklijke Brill NV,
P.O. Box 9000, NL-2300-PA Leiden,
The Netherlands

PRINTED IN THE NETHERLANDS

For Evaline Smyth Wood

And for my colleagues
Janice Schimmelmon and John Cameron

"Sed quoniam res humanae fragiles caducaeque sunt, semper aliqui anquirendi sunt quos diligamus et a quibus diligamur: caritate enim benevolentiaque sublata omnis est a vita sublata iucunditas."

Cicero, *De Amicitia* 102

CONTENTS

PREFACE AND ACKNOWLEDGEMENTS

This book is intended for several audiences: primarily, for scholars and students of the history of Roman portraiture, but also for those, both scholars and laymen, who take an interest in the lives and social roles of women at other periods in history. Since not all of these readers may be trained in the classical languages, I have attempted to define Latin and Greek terms whenever they are used for the first time, to give English translations of all relevant inscriptions or passages from the ancient authors, and to keep the use of specialized English terms as accessible as possible. Because many researchers may wish to consult individual chapters rather than reading the entire volume, some material has been discussed under more than one heading. Works of disputed identification, in particular, must be often considered in relation to the portraits of more than one woman. Some repetition of information, therefore, has been inevitable; I trust that readers will understand the necessity for this organization.

The assistance of countless individuals and institutions has contributed to the research and writing of this volume. The Harvard University Art Museums permitted me to organize the small, in-house exhibition of coins at the Arthur M. Sackler Museum from which this project eventually developed; special thanks to David Mitten, James Loeb Professor of Classical Art and Archaeology and Curator of Ancient Art, to Amy Brauer, assistant curator, and to the keepers and staff of the Ancient Art Department. My colleagues at Oakland University, in the administration of the College of Arts and Sciences, in the Department of Art and Art History of the College of Arts and Sciences and in Kresge Library, have also given generous support and encouragement to my research. Special thanks to Barbara Sommerville of Kresge Library for her assistance in obtaining sources that were sometimes hard to locate. My colleagues Bonnie Abiko, Carl F. Barnes, John Cameron, Louisa Ngote, Janice Schimmelman and Tamara Machmut-Jhashi have offered constant support, encouragement, and advice over the years. The American Academy in Rome provided me with accommodations and access to its incomparable library during the summer of 1996, during which time the

Deutsches Archäologisches Institut of Rome also allowed me to use their photographic archives.

Whenever possible, I have attempted to study in person the objects that constitute the primary sources of information for this study, and this research has obliged me not only to visit numerous museums and collections but often to request special assistance from their curators, many of whom have graciously given me access to storage rooms or closed galleries, as well as supplying photographs and publication releases. The curators and staff of the Albertinum in Dresden, the American Numismatic Society, the Arthur M. Sackler Museum of Harvard University, the British Museum, the Capitoline Museums in Rome, the Castello Aragonese at Baia, the Hispanic Society of America, the Munich Glyptothek, the Musée du Louvre in Paris, the Musée Saint Raymond in Toulouse, the Museo Nazionale Romano (which now includes the Palazzo Altemps), the Museum of the Rhode Island School of Design, the National Archaeological Museum in Athens, the National Museum of Archaeology in Istanbul, the Ny Carlsberg Glyptotek in Copenhagen, Schloss Fasanerie bei Fulda, Schloss Wilhelmshöhe in Kassell, the Staatliche Münzsammlung in Munich, the Vatican Museums and the Würtembergisches Landesmuseum in Stuttgart all merit thanks for their generous cooperation. I owe a special debt of gratitude to Prince Heinrich von Hessen for permitting me to study an object in his private collection.

I wish in addition to thank the following individuals: Bessie Alexandris for her assistance in translating correspondence; Carmen Arnold-Biucchi of the American Numismatic Society; Elizabeth Bartman of New York, N.Y., to whom I owe special gratitude for her constructive criticism and for supplying me with typescripts of unpublished work; Bettina Bergman of Mt. Holyoke College, Nancy Bookidis of the Corinth Excavation of the American School of Classical Studies in Athens; Antonella Bucci of the American Academy in Rome Library; Francesco Burinelli of the Vatican Museums; Daniel Cazes of the Musée Saint Raymond in Toulouse; Magda Cima of the Capitoline Museums in Rome; Margaret Connors of the Hispanic Society of America; Robert Cro of Princeton University; Eve D'Ambra of Vassar College; Andreas Dobler of Schloss Fasanerie bei Fulda; Katrina Dickson of Emory University; Axel Filges of the Deutsches Archäologisches Institut in Istanbul; Renate Gerulaitis of the Department of Modern Languages and Literatures of Oakland University, who has also assisted me with correspondence in German; Catherine de Grazia-Vanderpool of the American School of Classical Studies in Athens; Vivan Hibbs of the Hispanic Society of America; Kate de Kersauson of the Musée du Louvre; Diana E.E. Kleiner of Yale University; Fred Kleiner of Boston University; Janet Larkin of the British Museum for her tireless assistance with numerous orders for photographs; Job Lisman of Brill Academic Publishers; Paolo Liverani of the Vatican Museums; William Metcalf of the American Numismatic Society; Bernhard Overbeck of the Staatliche Münzsammlung in Munich; John Pollini of the University of Southern California, H. Protzmann of the Dresden Albertinum; I. Raumschussel of the Dresden Albertinum; C. Brian Rose of the University of Cincinnati, who generously allowed me to see parts of the manuscript of his 1997 book before its publication; Meinolf Siemer of Schloss Fasanerie bei Fulda; Eric Varner of Emory University; Ute Wartenburg of the British Museum, and Rolf Winkes of the Center for Old World Archaeology and Art at Brown University.

If there are any individuals whose names I have omitted, I apologize and ask their indulgence; this project has lasted for over ten years, and many people have given me advice and assistance along the way. This brings me to my final expression of thanks, to my friend Henri Dees Millon of Kansas City, Kansas, for his encouragement and support, which often took the form of urging me to stop procrastinating and finish the manuscript. Credit is owed to all the persons named here; errors and omissions are my own responsibility.

Susan Wood
July 31, 1998

INTRODUCTION

A woman living in any city or town in the Roman empire would have known the faces of most members of the ruling family, even if she had never seen them in person. If her daily errands took her through a public forum, she might well see statues of the emperor and several of his relatives in the square, or on the porch of a temple fronting on the public space. If she had occasion to attend a hearing in a basilica, she might see such groups of likenesses set into niches or on pedestals along the walls; at the theater she might see their statues in niches of the *scaenae frons*, and if she made purchases at the market, the coins that passed through her hands would bear their profiles and names. On special yearly occasions, she might have entered a temple to pay her respects to some imperial figure who had died, been deified, and was now worshiped as a god or goddess, in a colossal likeness that would loom above her in the dim interior. She might even have been able to see painted or sculptural likeness of the ruling family without leaving home: if her family, or the family that she served, had some personal reason for gratitude or loyalty toward imperial figures, small busts of those individuals might have a place in the *lararium*, or family shrine, of the house along with figures of household gods and ancestors. Those familiar faces would include a number of women: the mother of the emperor, perhaps; his wife, if he was married, his daughters or sisters, if he had any—people with whom, thanks to both biology and social convention, she shared a number of very personal concerns, despite their difference from her in rank, fame and status.

If she was married, the married women of the imperial family would provide her with examples of appropriate ways for a wife to behave. Works of the visual arts would show her how they dressed and wore their hair, or—if their portrait heads were placed on torsos inspired by images of goddesses—to which goddesses they could appropriately be compared. She would learn from these portraits whether her society placed a higher value on physical beauty and fashionable appearance or on unassuming personal modesty: at some periods, the faces of these portraits might be ideally pretty and youthful, even if everyone knew that the women they represented had full-grown grandchildren, while at others, their representations might be uncompromisingly harsh, displaying realistic signs of age. Imperial women who had children might be represented holding their infants or standing near statues of their slightly older sons and daughters, a reminder to the female viewer that she shared with these prominent figures a concern for the well-being and future prosperity of her own offspring. If she was even partially literate, the inscriptions on coins that bore these women's portrait profiles would explain to her that they embodied the health of the empire, or the virtues of marital harmony, security, good fortune, constancy, and other such values. She might even have taken her wedding vows in front of a statue of the emperor's wife, who would thus be a witness by proxy to the legality of her marriage.

At the same time, our hypothetical observer of these statues and coins might learn, either by word of mouth or some other means, in what sort of behavior these women publicly engaged, and would understand that it was not inappropriate for a wife to present petitions to her husband about matters of public policy, to intercede with him on behalf of individuals, to lend money to people outside her own family, to make generous gifts of cash both to cities and to individuals, to undertake building projects in her own name and at her own expense, and still to be presented in public as the embodiment of a wife's traditional virtues. A woman who was fully literate, as many of the more well-to-do would have to be in order to begin the education of their sons, might for example have read a poem by Ovid in which he entreated his wife to plead with Livia for mitigation of the conditions of his exile.[1] Obviously, since Livia herself held no constitutional office and had no power to issue such an order, he expected that Livia in turn could present his petition to Augustus. He added in that poem the interesting observation that he expected Livia to deal with many such petitioners, and to have only rare and precious moments of leisure, advising his wife to choose carefully the most auspicious time to approach her.

The notion would be virtually inescapable for a Roman women that these imperial women were models that she should emulate, or *exempla*, to use the term that would come most naturally to the mind of a Latin-speaking person. Some of the lessons that she learned from these images, however, were negative: the statue of a woman

---

[1] Ov. *Pont.* 3.114–166.

who had fallen from official grace might quietly vanish from its usual place, never to return, or else perhaps to reappear with a heavily reworked face and an inscription that informed her that the portrait now represented someone else. If the offenses of the disgraced woman were serious enough, our observer might even see the likeness publicly vandalized, torn from its base and smashed, either on official orders or by angry citizens acting on their own initiative. If she lived in Rome itself in A.D. 62, she could have witnessed the astonishing spectacle of an angry mob knocking down the portraits of the emperor's new wife, and defiantly carrying on their shoulders likenesses of his former wife, whom he had convicted of adultery and sent into exile. If we wish to understand the lessons that she drew from those images and their fate, the sorts of behavior that they told her society would tolerate and what it would not, these portraits and their iconography are a fitting subject for scholarly study.

For many years, however, modern scholarship relegated the portraits of Roman women, literally and metaphorically, to the back of the book. Until the 1980's, the typical organization of most volumes of the great corpus of imperial portraits, *Das römische Herrscherbild*, was a long discussion of the portraits of a ruling emperor, followed by briefer sections devoted to his sons and male relatives, and finally to those of the women of his family. When Fittschen and Zanker began in 1983 to publish their immensely valuable catalogue of the Roman portraits in the Capitoline Museums of Rome, the volume on female portraits was the first to appear—and yet it was numbered as Volume III.[2] During the past two decades, however, concurrent with the growth of interest in women's history and gender studies, this picture has changed, and more and more scholars, not all of them women and not all of them ideologically feminist, have devoted historical, art-historical, and archaeological studies to the women of Roman antiquity. The year 1996 alone saw the appearance of Anthony Barrett's biography of Agrippina II, in a series of biographies that up until that point had been devoted only to the emperors; of C. Brian Rose's study of imperial family groups, in which the presence of women along with men demonstrated their significance in the transmission of dynastic power, and of Rolf Winkes's monograph on the portraits of Livia, Octavia Minor, and Julia.[3] In

---

[2] Fittschen-Zanker 3, 1983.
[3] Barrett, 1996; Rose, 1996; Winkes, 1995 (actually appeared in 1996).

the same year, the lives and experiences both of elite women and
women of all classes of Roman society were the subject of a major
loan-exhibition that originated at the Yale University Art Gallery
entitled *I Claudia: Women in Ancient Rome*; this exhibit included a major
section of portraits and coins of the imperial women.

When J.P.V.D. Balsdon published a book on Roman women in
1962, the idea of devoting a book-length study to such a subject was
quite novel; Sarah Pomeroy's *Goddesses, Whores, Wives and Slaves*, which
appeared in 1975, was one of the earliest such studies to approach
the material from a declared feminist point of view, and was prac-
tically revolutionary.[4] In the decades since, books have been devoted
to such subjects as the historical and archaeological evidence about
the career of Antonia Minor; to the relationships of fathers and
daughters in elite families; the lives of working women as documented in art from Ostia; and the laws that governed the lives and
social roles of women, to name just a few areas of interest. These
works of scholarship reveal that a surprisingly generous body of evidence about women in antiquity survives, even though scholars had
tended in the past not to focus their attention on it.[5] The majority
of these studies have dealt with elite women, and particularly those
of the imperial family, although Kampen has clearly demonstrated
that the visual arts can document the lives of working-class people
as well. The greatest volume of surviving material, however, records
the images, names and activities of women related in one way or
another to the emperor. It was, after all, their images that were
replicated for distribution throughout a huge empire, and that survive in multiple replicas and variants; their faces that would appear
on coins both of the official mint and of local authorities, and their
activities that historians like Suetonius, Tacitus, and Dio were most
likely to narrate in detail.

Paradoxically, of course, these women whose lives are so well documented were the most atypical of their society, in the degree of
privilege and influence that they enjoyed. However, their familial
roles, on a larger and more dramatically publicized scale, mirrored
those of women in other wealthy and elite families, and as we have
already seen, their portraits presented them to women like our hypothetical female observer as examples upon whom she should model

[4] Balsdon, 1962; Pomeroy, 1975.
[5] Kokkinos, 1992; Hallett, 1984; Kampen, 1981; Gardner, 1991.

her own behavior. Historians, on the other hand, who were generally writing long after these women and their powerful male relatives were safely dead and their dynasties defunct, often paint a virulently hostile picture of women like Livia and Agrippina II. The truth about these women's characters probably lies at some undeterminable point between the extremes of flattering official imagery and hostile literary tradition, but the standards to which these women were held, and by which they were judged, are informative and revealing of the social attitudes that applied to all women. The present study will examine the public images of the women of Rome's first dynasty, from the time of the power struggle that led to the establishment of the principate under Augustus to the death of the emperor Nero who was the last of Augustus's descendants to hold power. During this period of a little over a century, the likenesses of some dozen women of five generations will demonstrate the increasing public visibility of institutionalization of their roles in the ruling family, and the growth and development of the cults of women who had died and been deified. The decision to limit the study to the Augustan and Julio-Claudian periods has been dictated by the need to circumscribe the length of this study, rather than by the importance of this imperial family relative to later ones; women continued to play significant political roles in every succeeding dynasty, and their public images provide an equally important area of study. Fittschen has, indeed, devoted a monograph to the portraits of the Antonine women and the political significance of those likenesses.[6]

Since works of the visual arts tend as a rule to reflect official propaganda, it would be useful at this point to define the term "propaganda," and to discuss its meaning. Karl Galinsky, writing about coinage, art and literature at the time of Augustus, has recently challenged the validity of this word and concept when used to describe any favorable portrayal of the emperor, his families and his policies. Indeed many such portrayals were the work of poets or private patrons acting on their own initiative rather than on any official orders.[7] Spontaneous demonstrations of loyalty to a government or to a head of state are hardly an unusual phenomenon at any period in history. On the other hand, in order to set up a public portrait of an imperial figure, a patron from a provincial city would have

---

[6] Fittschen, 1982.
[7] Galinsky, 1996, 28–41 (re "propaganda" on coins); 229 (re literature).

needed to obtain a copy of an officially distributed portrait type: neither Augustus nor Livia (who as Ovid reminds us, was a busy woman) could pose for a new portrait every time some patron wished to honor them, and a sculptor who wished to produce an even minimally acceptable likeness would have needed some model to copy.

The existence of portrait types—that is, groups of objects that all recognizably reproduce the same prototype—is a fact established beyond serious doubt in the study of Roman portrait sculpture, although the degree to which the style and nature of the prototypes can be reconstructed on the basis of their surviving replicas remains problematic and controversial. When the subject first sat for her portrait, she could exercise some control over the appearance of that prototype: the arrangement of the hair, the facial expression, the degree of idealization or realism of the work. The subject, or her husband, father, or brother, presumably also had some say in choosing the artist whose style best suited official purposes and best conveyed the personae with which the emperor wished his family to be perceived. Some years later, the subject or members of the imperial family might wish to distribute a new prototype, to mark some important change in her status; on these occasions, the subject might give a new sitting for an official artist, but often, an artist could simply create a new prototype by modifying the old one. If the subject had died, and the occasion for the creation of the new prototype was her deification, he would obviously have had to rely on a combination of older portraits and his imagination. Once any prototype began to be copied and recopied, of course, other sculptors could adapt that original in many different ways over which the imperial family had no control, and probably little interest, unless in the course of their official travels they might happen to see some of these representations of themselves. Imperial family members probably never saw the great majority of their own likenesses. But whoever took the fairly expensive step of commissioning a statue, purchasing a cameo gem, or a glass phalera with representations of imperial family members (and for poorer people, a glass phalera was still an expensive display of devotion) probably wished to see the ruling family presented in a favorable manner, although that manner might have been rather different from the one that the subject herself would have chosen.

"Propaganda" took on a sinister meaning during the cold war, and was often used as an epithet to imply lies or distortions by an opposing government. The original meaning of the word, however,

is simply "that which must be propagated," and in its most benign
sense means what we in the current vernacular call "spin control."
The attempt to manipulate public opinion by creating a desired
appearance and persona is no modern phenomenon, although in our
media-saturated age, in which the consultants who design the public images of politicians are well-known celebrities or villains, historians naturally tend to give greater attention to the "public relations"
efforts of political figures in other periods. Throughout history, the
effort to present the ruler, his policies, actions, and family members,
in the most favorable possible light has always been a virtually
inevitable part of government. Any head of state, whether a monarch,
emperor, dictator or elected official understands that in the end, his
power does depend on the consent of the governed, since one way
or another, the governed can get rid of him if they want to. The
fates of the emperors Caligula, Nero, Domitian, Commodus and
Caracalla, to name examples from Roman history alone, amply document that fact. The desire to control one's public image by disseminating an appropriately dignified prototype to copyists is as natural
and inevitable as attempting to insist that "paparazzi" photograph a
public figure only in flattering circumstances. In most cases, then,
we are probably safe in assuming that a portrait intends to present
its subject in a favorable manner, and therefore to conform to some
socially accepted ideal.

What, then, was that ideal for women of the ruling dynasty? Let
us establish at the outset that Roman society was patriarchal in the
most literal sense of that much-overused word. The extended family, the basic unit of social organization, was under the control of
the senior male, or *paterfamilias,* who held authority over his children
and grandchildren for the entire duration of his life, no matter how
old they were, unless he officially granted them their independence.
He had the power of life and death over family members, although
few fathers of households exercised this latter right. It was, however,
their responsibility to oversee the punishment of children who had
committed crimes, in particular women of the family who had been
judged guilty of adultery. The power of life and death had another,
perhaps more common application: the *paterfamilias* had the sole right
to determine whether infants born into his family should be raised
or exposed.[8] The father-like power of political officials was consciously modeled on that of the head of a household, and reflected

---

[8] Gardner, 1991, 5–11.

in terminology such as "Patres conscripti," the conscript fathers, or members of the Senate. An individual who had performed some great service to the state could win the honorific title "Pater Patriae," Father of his Fatherland, as Cicero did by foiling the Catilinarian conspiracy, and this formula later became one of the standard titles of the emperors.

It was legally impossible for a woman to be the official head of a family, and by extension, in the thinking of most people at least of the Latin-speaking Western part of the empire, for her to be a head of state or to hold any position of officially recognized power. Greek-speaking people of the eastern part of the empire, of course, had another historical model: during the early years of the empire, many living people could still remember a monarchical system in which the daughters of kings might succeed to power if there should be no male heir, and might rule a kingdom not only in name but in actuality, as Cleopatra VII of Egypt had done. They would also remember, however, that Rome had won a decisive victory over Cleopatra that cost the independence of the last Hellenistic king-dom, and that Cleopatra had been portrayed ever since in litera-ture and official monuments as the archenemy of the Roman empire. Augustus made every effort to differentiate the nature of his power from that of a Hellenistic-style hereditary monarch.

There is no evidence that any of the women whose lives and images will be documented here, the women of Rome's first dynasty, ever questioned the validity of a patriarchal organization of society. Ideological feminism is a product of modern democracy, and did not exist in classical antiquity. Every female member of the Julio-Claudian dynasty seems to have accepted as a given that she must define her status and her public importance in terms of her rela-tionships to men, as for example Agrippina I did when, during a dispute with Tiberius, she reminded him that she was the grand-daughter of the deified Augustus, and entitled to respect on that account.[9] Her daughter Agrippina II, who came closer than any other woman in Roman history to demanding institutionalized recog-nition of her power, still claimed that power by virtue of her posi-tion as the mother of the ruling emperor. A number of these women did, however, have clearly documented personal or political agendas

---

[9] Tac. *Ann.* 4.52.

of their own, sometimes more or less the same as those of the men
in power, but occasionally not, and all of them either found or
attempted to find ways within existing social conventions to accomplish their goals. Some of them enjoyed astonishing success and
approval in the court of public opinion; others failed disastrously,
and the lives of some, like the elder and younger Agrippinae, demonstrate an intriguing mixture of success and failure. As Hallett has
amply demonstrated, a society that modeled its political system on
the organization of the family, and made the family structurally central to its system of government, also provided women with a means
to exercise their political wills by sharing a degree of power with
the men of their family.[10]

The blurring of the distinctions between the private and the public realm, the transmission of social status and of political authority
through birth and descent in an aristocratic social system or a dynastic system of government, naturally gives some importance to the
women who perpetuate those bloodlines. The wife of a living *paterfamilias* held the title of *materfamilias*, which gave her no specific legal
rights but which did reflect an institutionalized respect for her role
in the extended family. It is a fairly banal observation to note that
people in an intimate relationship can influence one another, whether
intentionally or not, and that anyone, male or female, will listen
more seriously to the opinions of a close family member than of a
stranger. Ovid obviously expected that Livia could use such influence
with Augustus, and some works of art and literature project such
behavior onto the gods as well. Works of funerary art, for example,
occasionally portray the goddess Proserpina gesturing toward and
pleading with her husband Pluto for mercy toward some deserving
mortal such as Alcestis or Protesilaos.[11] Not for nothing does Ovid

---

[10] Hallett, 1984, 12–13 and passim.

[11] For a fuller discussion of the role of Proserpina as intercessor, see Wood, forthcoming. Scenes of Proserpina interceding for the dead occur on the following two
sarcophagi:

Vatican, Museo Chiaramonti inv. 1195, sarcophagus of Caius Junius Euhodos
and Metilia Acte, *LIMC* 1¹ 535 no. 8, 536 no. 16, with full earlier literature, and
LIMC 1² pls. 401.8, 401.16, s.v. "Alkestis" (M. Schmidt); Blome 1978, 441–445;
Wood, 1978, 499–510 and 1993, 96–99, with earlier literature; Sichtermann and
Koch, 1975, 20–21 no. 8, pls. 16, 17.2, 18, 19; Calza, 197, 27–29, no. 31.

Naples, Church of Santa Chiara, marble sarcophagus with myth of Protesilaos,
Sichtermann and Koch, 1975, 65–66 no. 70, pls. 168.1, 171, and Blome, 1978,
445–449.

compare Livia both to Juno and to Venus, since both goddesses plead successfully with Jupiter on a number of occasions in the epics of Homer and Vergil.[12]

On the other hand, a woman asking her husband, father or brother for a favor possesses no power of her own, but only influence. Any political lobbyist knows the value of "access" to the holder of a public office, but also knows that access can only ensure that his point of view will receive a hearing, not that it will prevail. Feminists and anti-feminists alike find the concept of acting through another person ethically disturbing, and perhaps with good reason: "influence" implies a devious, indirect and unaccountable way of exercising one's will. In a modern democracy, opponents of the political agenda of a president's wife can reasonably point out, for example, that she has not herself been elected to any public office, and does not represent the will of the voters as her husband does. In a society like that of imperial Rome, on the other hand, men too usually owed their positions of power at least in part to accidents of birth into elite families; the argument that women should not likewise have used the power that came from their familial roles is somewhat harder to defend. Senatorial authors with lingering republican sentiments, however, found that exercise of influence shocking precisely because they distrusted the imperial system, its concentration of power into the hands of one man, and its hereditary transmission. Many ancient historians, most notably Tacitus, frequently represent the actions of women behind the political scenes as embodying capricious and unscrupulous abuses of those powers. Whether Tacitus was misogynistic in a pathological sense or not, he was fully willing to exploit prejudices against women to arouse the indignation of his readers.[13]

Pervasive and common as such prejudices may be, however, the range of attitudes among the public to the activities of these women was far more complex than one might infer from reading Tacitus. A commonly stated ideal of Roman society, as of many others, both ancient and modern, was that the male head of a household should

---

[12] Ovid, *Pont.* 3.117–118, 145. Verg. *Aen.* 1.228–296, 10.606–688; 12.808–840; Hom. *Il.* 4.50–72. See also Verg. *Aen.* 8.370–406, in which Venus obtains armor for Aeneas from her husband Vulcan.

[13] The literature on Tacitus's portrayal of women is enormous. For several recent studies, see Santoro L'Hoir, 1994, 5–25; Kaplan, 1979, 410–417; Barrett, 1996, 205–208.

make all decisions, and issue all orders, which it was the responsibility of his wife, daughters, and other female relatives to obey. It was also a goal probably very seldom fully realized, as one rather entertaining anecdote in Dio's Roman history vividly reveals. Augustus once advised a group of Roman senators who were complaining of bad female behavior that they should do as he did, and firmly establish the rules of the household that their women should obey. The senators reacted by demanding incredulously to know what sorts of instructions Augustus gave to Livia; taken aback by their questions, he finally responded with a few banal observations about regulating the manner of his wife's dress, appearance and public demeanor. Dio adds, in case the reader could still be in any doubt, that it was common knowledge that in this as in so many other matters of private morality, Augustus's words did not match his actions.[14] Another, later author, Macrobius, records a series of incidents that comically emphasize Augustus's utter failure to compel his daughter Julia to dress and present herself publicly in a properly modest manner. Julia chooses, in one of these stories, to pluck her grey hairs, rather than to age gracefully as a properly modest and sensible matron would, despite her father's sarcastic observation that it is preferable to be grey-haired than to be bald, and in another wears a dress of which Augustus disapproves, presumably because it is too frivolous or revealing. When she appears the next day in a more respectable garment that Augustus praises, she replies that she wore the other dress to please her husband rather than her father.[15] Naturally, a text written some five hundred years after the fact is hardly a trustworthy source for such intimate gossip about the imperial family, but the stories reflect the historical reality that Julia's behavior did not conform to Augustus's desired public image, and that Augustus's moral legislation had failed, even within his own family, to control female sexuality. By the time of Macrobius, much the same situation had arisen many more times in many more imperial households, thus inspiring the sort of repertory of jokes that Macrobius puts in the mouths of Julia and Augustus.

Yet if Julia's behavior clearly transgressed established Roman mores, Livia's did not. Dio's amused incredulity at Augustus's claim to control Livia did not imply criticism of the woman herself, or the ways

[14] Dio 54.16.4–5.
[15] Macrob. *Sat.* 2.5.5 and 2.5.7; Richlin, 1992, 65–91.

that she had used her political influence and economic power, for which Dio and several other sources praise her highly.[16] Although Roman convention gave ultimate authority over females to males, some institutions positively encouraged women to speak their minds: the ancient cult of the goddess Viriplaca for example, at whose temple wives and husbands who had some dispute could each express their points of view and attempt to reconcile their differences.[17] Valerius Maximus describes this custom in the past tense, as part of an admiring and nostalgic description of earlier and better times, perhaps implying that in his own time, during the principate of Tiberius, the habit of talking out disputes at the shrine of Viriplaca no longer existed. Yet the appearance of this reference is intriguing, occurring as it does among a list of ways in which Roman morals used to be higher, respect for marriage stronger, and the behavior of women better controlled. Maximus concedes that the old mores depended for their success on allowing women some luxuries, entrusting them with some freedom rather than strictly cloistering them from view, and granting them some opportunity to express their opinions.[18] As the name of the goddess Viriplaca might imply, the primary purpose of her cult was to make the husband happy, but Roman society also acknowledged that he could not accomplish this goal without accommodation to the needs of his wife.

For imperial women, then, as for women of all walks of life, the first and foremost means of accomplishing any goal was by persuading a man of her family to act on her behalf. There were a few other ways as well, more available to wealthy and aristocratic women than to those of other classes, that provided public respect and visibility. One of these was religious ritual: any man or woman who publicly performed the duties of the priest or priestess of an official cult enjoyed social prestige that could translate into political authority. During the late years of the republic, politically ambitious

---

[16] Dio's eulogy of Livia: 58.2.2–6. Similar observations about her use of power: Vell. Pat. 2.30–5; *S.C. de Cn. Pisone Patre* 115–118. Eck, Caballos and Fernández, 1996, 46–47, 222–228.

[17] Flory, 1984, 315; Val. Max. 2.1.6.

[18] Val. Max. 2.1.5: "ceterum ut non tristis earum et horrida pudicitia, sed [et] honesto comitatis genere temperata esset,—indulgentibus namque maritis et auro abundanti et multa purpura usae sunt—quo formam suam concinniorem efficerent, summa cum diligentia capillos cinere rutilarunt: nulli enim tunc subsessorum alienorum matrimoniorum oculi metuebantur, sed pariter et videre sancte et aspici mutuo pudore custodiebatur."

men who held priesthoods often called the public's attention to their
religious roles, as Augustus continued to do especially after receiv-
ing the title of *pontifex maximus*, which his adoptive father Julius Caesar
had also held before him, and which therefore, as he and his partisans suggested, should belong to him by inheritance as well as election.[19] Livia, who later became priestess of the cult of the deified
Augustus, and Agrippina II, as priestess of the deified Claudius, fully
understood the value of these religious titles. And finally, a woman
of personal wealth who controlled her own property had the power
to win friends and supporters through her euergetism, (that is, patronage of public works), and to demonstrate publicly her commitment
to various social causes. Not all women, of course, enjoyed such economic freedom, even if they belonged to very wealthy families: in
order to control her property, a woman needed to be liberated from
tutela (guardianship by a male relative).[20] Augustus's social legislation,
however, granted such freedom to free-born women who had borne
three children, and to freedwomen if they had four children after
manumission from slavery. A woman could also receive these rights
by fiat, whether she had enough children or not.[21] Long before the
passage of the law that established the *ius liberorum*, Octavian had in
35 B.C. already set a precedent for freeing some women from *tutela*,
by granting this privilege, along with several other extraordinary honors, to his sister and his wife. The suggestion that he did so as a
deliberate rebuke to Marc Antony seems very plausible: Antony was
openly cohabiting with a non-Roman woman and treating his legal
Roman wife badly, but it is striking that Octavian chose to honor
the women who in his propaganda embodied the virtues of traditional Roman matrons by granting them unprecedented freedoms.[22]
Both women, as we will see, made skillful use of their economic
independence in philanthropic activities and in patronage of art and
architecture. Activities like these—use of their influence to obtain
some official action, use of their personal wealth for euergetism and
charity, or participation in rites of the state religion—frequently provided the occasion for honors to these women in the form of public portraits. Cities of the empire usually set up statues or paintings
of members of the imperial family to express gratitude for their

---

[19] Fullerton, 1985, 479–480.
[20] On *tutela*, see Gardner, 1991, 14–22.
[21] Balsdon, 202; Gardner, 24, 197.
[22] Flory, 1993, 293–295.

patronage, which could take the form of financial generosity or of intercession with the emperor to obtain some political goal.[23]

We must, next, consider a few of the ways in which those representations achieved, or attempted to achieve, their desired effects. The objects to be examined in the present study include some fairly mechanical and unimaginative replicas of official types—although even they preserve at least some of the elements of the original, every detail of which must have been very carefully calculated by the artist and patron. Others, however, are sensitive and highly successful works, some of which may follow an official type with a fair degree of fidelity, but many of which probably reinterpret it quite freely, occasionally even endowing it with new meanings—as, for example, when a portrait from a woman's lifetime is replicated after her death to present her as a goddess, as in the cases of Drusilla I and Livia, or to rehabilitate her reputation, as in the cases of Agrippinae I and II. The overall form and style of a work will determine its first and strongest effect on the viewer: smooth surfaces, closed contours, relatively simple shapes, and quiet stance and gestures, for example, will have quite a different impact from intricate patterns of curls, strong contrasts of light and shadow, and more active and flamboyant poses. Throughout the Julio-Claudian period, portraiture of women tended to idealize the subjects to some extent, seldom showing more than the most subtle signs of advancing age even in portraits of women like Antonia Minor, who lived to the age of 73, and of Livia, who died at 86. Within the flattering conventions of the period, however, portraits in all media display a rich variety of formal devices.

Another method readily available to a portraitist for the characterization of his subject is visual allusion and assimilation. That an image can simultaneously resemble more than one person or thing is a fact understood by artists throughout history, and by the scholars who have later sought to interpret their work. Real family resemblances can be accentuated so as to call attention to blood-lines: thus, for example the portraits of Agrippina I from the time of her son's principate (e.g., figures 87–88, 91–92) tend to emphasize the long face and high forehead that Caligula inherited from her, while

---

[23] See Rose, 1997, 8; Rose describes the erection of a group of imperial statues as a form of gift-exchange, in which the local patron expresses thanks for "benefactions by the imperial family," either received or anticipated.

those of her daughter Agrippina II tend to stress the broad, square jaw, retreating lower lip and sharp chin that she shared with her father, the beloved Germanicus. (See in particular figure 95, in which the profile of Germanicus appears in close proximity to that of his daughter, and figures 136–140). Both siblings gained much political advantage by reminding the public of the memory of their parents, both of whom were regarded as political martyrs. In other cases, a portraitist could create a resemblance between people who were not related, by subtle manipulation of the features. Such assimilation in the portraits of married couples was a fairly common practice in Hellenistic and later in Roman imperial art, and is clearly visible in the coin portraits of Marc Antony, both on the issues that represent his Roman wife Octavia Minor and those on which he appears with Cleopatra (figures 2–3, 5, 7–8). This practice, of which the die-cutters may not even have been fully conscious, allowed the man and woman to appear as a visually harmonious pair, and so to suggest their marital concord. Assimilation could also serve to remind the viewer of family ties that existed only in legal, rather than in genetic relationships. The earlier portraits of Livia from the lifetime of Augustus (figures 24–27, e.g.), tend to show a woman with a long, oval face, but the most widespread and familiar type, the one probably disseminated late in Augustus's principate, after Livia's son Tiberius emerged as his heir, show a broader face, a wide forehead and more sharply tapering chin. (See figures 22–23). Livia's features remain recognizable, and most modern viewers agree in accepting the replicas of the later "Fayum type" as representations of the same individual as the early "Marbury Hall" and "Albani-Bonn" types. But the Fayum type also gives Livia a facial shape much closer to that of her husband Augustus, with his characteristically Julian triangular face, and in turn allows the creation of a fictitious resemblance of Augustus to his adoptive son Tiberius, with whom he has no blood relationship.

Portraits could subtly evoke other associations as well, with images of goddesses. Both imperial figures and private citizens could appear in portraits with the attributes and costume of a god or goddess, and portrait heads could appear on bodies copied from statue types originally created for deities. Such blatant associations were more appropriate for images of deceased persons than of the living, but it is not unknown for such quotations to appear in a likeness made during the subject's lifetime, particularly in works such as cameo

gems that were not intended for public display. Manipulations of
hairstyle and facial features could even introduce such references into
the face of the subject. Polysemy—the evocation of multiple meanings—has been documented in works of Roman sculpture ranging
from sophisticated public monuments like the Ara Pacis Augustae,
which were presumably made by the best artists available for patrons
who wished to spare no expense, to the more humble funerary monuments of private citizens, many of whom were freedmen.[24] It should
not surprise us, therefore, occasionally to find such visual allusions
in portraiture as well, as a means of characterizing or glorifying the
subject. Only recently, however, have such visual references received
intensive study in the area of Roman portraiture, for the obvious
reason that the first and most crucial task in the study of ancient
portraits must be iconography. As many images of historical individuals as possible must be identified to the satisfaction of most scholars before one can begin to put any portraits into a meaningful
historical context, since it is the identified portraits that give us the
chronological framework for the classification of anonymous works.
The second task, in the case of public figures, is typology: identification
of the various prototypes on which extant replicas depend.

Relatively few extant works of ancient portraiture come from documented archaeological contexts; in the majority of cases, context must
be inferred from the object itself, and must begin with identification
if possible, or dating based on stylistic analysis if the subject's identity is lost. The primary importance of identification has, inevitably
and understandably, often caused scholars to deliberately overlook
the intentional similarities to other images that the creator of the
portrait may have introduced into the work: it is the uniquely individual features that allow a type to be recognized. In the last decade,
however, several important studies have appeared that not only trace
the diverse sources of certain portrait images but analyze their intended
meaning and likely reception. Bernard Frischer's reconstruction of
the portrait of Epicurus, for example, documents the wealth of allusions to other images in that likeness, and its crucial, active role in
recruiting converts to the Epicurean philosophy. In a study more

---

[24] For a recent discussion of polysemy, a term already used by Servius in his
commentary on the *Aeneid*, see Galinsky, 1992, 457–475, esp. 473; on the variety
of responses to official art possible among the various religious groups of the Roman
empire, see Elsner, 1991, 52. On funerary monuments: Blome, 1978, 435–457, and
Wood, 1993, 96–99.

directly relevant to the present material Anne-Kathrein Massner has examined how the portraits of Augustus both incorporated references to other familiar works and themselves became prototypes to be quoted in official images of the Julio-Claudian dynasty.[25]

Because the great majority of sculptured portraits survive as heads or busts rather than complete statues, it will be necessary to concentrate in particular on the manipulation of the face and coiffure, although in the few valuable cases in which a full-length statue survives, costume, pose and gesture offer indispensable additional information. Since heads and faces were often worked separately from the rest of the statue, by portrait specialists, there is some justification for considering the head of a statue as a self-contained artistic conception. When examining visual quotations, however, there is one question that we must inevitably address: if such allusions were intended, how readily would they have been recognized and understood by the general public? Bluntly put, if propaganda was intended, would it have worked? Literary evidence implies that the contemporary audience for these portraits was very familiar indeed with the formal details of the divine images that the portraits sometimes quote. In St. Augustine's *City of God*, there appears a remarkable passage from a lost work of Seneca, in which the Roman philosopher contemptuously describes what he regards as the superstitious practices of uneducated people, and which incidentally reveals much about the role that works of the visual arts played in the religious lives and activities of ordinary people in the city of Rome:[26]

> But go to the Capitol, and you will be ashamed of the folly there disclosed, and of the duties which a deluded madness has assigned itself. One servant informs Jupiter of the names of his worshipers, another announces the hours; one is his bather, another his anointer,

---

[25] Frischer, 1982; Massner, 1982.

[26] "Huic tamen, inquit, furori certum tempus est. Tolerabile est semel anno insanire. In Capitolium perveni, pudebit publicatae dementiae, quod sibi vanus furor adtribuit officii. Alius nomina deo subicit, alius horas Iovi nuntiat; alius lutor est, alius unctor, qui vano motu bracchiorum imitatur unguentem. Sunt quae Iunoni ac Minervae capillos disponant (longe a templo, non tantum a simulacro stantes digitos movent ornantium modo), sunt quae speculum teneant; sunt qui ad vadimonia sua deos advocent, sunt qui libellos offerant et illos causam suam doceant. Doctus archimimus, senex iam decrepitus, cotidie in Capitolio mimum agebat, quasi dii libenter spectarent quem illi homines desierant. Omne illic artificum genus operatum diis inmortalibus desidet." St. Augustine, *De civ. dei*, 6.10, trans. Marcus Dods (New York, 1950), cited and discussed by Pékary, 1985, 117.

that is, he gestures with empty hands to imitate the act of anointing. There are women who are hairdressers for Juno and Minerva: while standing far away from the temple as well as from the image they move the fingers as if they were dressing the hair, and there are others who hold a mirror. There are men who summon the gods to give bond for them, and some who offer them lawyers' briefs and explain their case. An expert leading actor in the mimes, now a decrepit old man, used to act a mime each day in the Capitol—as if the gods would enjoy the performance of a player when men had ceased to do so. Every kind of artisan sits there to devote his time to the immortal gods.

The social and psychological phenomenon that causes rational people to treat images as though they were living beings has received a thorough recent study, with exhaustive documentation, in David Freedberg's *The Power of Images*,[27] and requires no further explanation here. For the understanding of an eclectic artistic tradition like that of the Roman empire, however, which frequently revived earlier styles, the passage is most significant in revealing how such eclectic images could have been created, and how directly they might have been understood.

Many of the cult images to which these worshipers offered their services as nomenclators, valets and hairdressers were either re-used original works of the Classical period, copies of such originals, or pastiches of Classical or Hellenistic style intended to convey a venerable aura of antiquity.[28] If Seneca's report is accurate, people examined these images not only in a spirit of reverence or aesthetic pleasure but with a very active and kinetic attention to form: a man who is pretending to bathe or anoint a statue (which he is presumably forbidden actually to touch) will pay some attention to its pose and composition in order accurately to mime the action of running his hands over the skin surfaces, while a woman who intends to arrange the goddess's hair will consider not only the appearance of the coiffure, but what series of steps one must follow in order to duplicate it. Some women may perhaps have mimed the creation of a contemporary fashion that they already knew how to achieve, making old Juno and Minerva a bit more *au courant*, but some may well

---

[27] Freedberg, 1989, passim.
[28] Zanker, 1988, 240–243; Pliny the Elder, *NH* 36.4.22–24 on statues in Rome by Praxiteles, 36.4.24–27 on works in Rome by Skopas, and 28–29 on Classical Greek statues in Rome of uncertain attribution.

have tried to imitate the coiffure that they saw on the statue. They
would thus have been able to create similar coiffures for themselves
or for other women, and certainly to recognize the allusion implied
if they saw that coiffure in another context. Such associations were
not lost on at least one witty and well-educated observer of the
Augustan period: Ovid cites a string of parallels in divine and heroic
iconography for the coiffures he recommends to enhance various
types of female beauty. He compares a coiffure with a simple middle part to the one worn by the images of Laodamia; another with
long locks hanging over the shoulders to that of Apollo as musician;
another with braided hair (which I take to mean a long braid down
the back of the neck) to that of Diana; and another with seemingly
accidental curls and tangles to the fetching disarray of Iole or Ariadne.[29]
Parallels that would merely be amusing in a private citizen could
lend more significant resonances to the publicly displayed likeness of
a woman of the emperor's family. The power of one type of image—
the cult statue—could then have lent power to another, the official
representation of a member of the imperial household. Quotations
of Classical styles and prototypes are sometimes quite blatantly present in their portraits, at other times entirely absent when historical
circumstances would make it advisable to avoid them, and often
somewhat ambiguously present in portraits that combine elements of
contemporary fashion with subtle visual allusions to divine images.

The final question that must concern us is who determined the
appearance of these portraits, who made decisions about style, about

---

[29] Ovid, *Ars Am.* 3. 135–144, 153–158:

Nec genus ornatus unum est: quod quamque decebit
   Elegat et speculum consulat ante suum.
Longa probat facies capitis discrimina puri:
   Sic erat ornatis Laodamia comis.
Exiguum summa nodum sibi fronte relinqui
   Ut pateant aures, ora rotunda volunt.
Alterius crines umero iactentur utroque:
   Talis es adsumpta, Phoebe canore, lyra.
Altera succinctae religetur more Dianae,
   Ut solet, attonitas cum petit illa feras . . .
Et neglecta decet multas coma; saepe iacere
   Hesternam credas; illa repexa modo est.
Ars casu similis; sic capta vidit ut urbe
   Alcides Iolen, "hanc ego" dixit "amo."
Talem te Bacchus, satyris clamantibus "euhoe"
   Sustulit in currus, Gnosi relicta, suos.

whether or not to assimilate one individual's appearance to another's, and whether or not to include elements that evoked divine or heroic images. The answer to this question must be in the plural: the patron of the prototype, the subject (not always the same person as the patron), the portraitist who created the prototype, the patrons who ordered copies of that type, for various different contexts, and the copyists who realized those copies in coin dies, on cameos, in painting or in sculpture, all contributed elements to the appearance of the finished object. The emperor himself presumably did not dictate every detail of costume and grooming to every member of his family, nor could he have determined the precise content and composition of every work of representational art produced during his reign, nor the design of every coin to leave the mint. He did, however, establish the agenda and set the tone that others were expected to follow, and in many cases probably enjoyed veto-power over any image too unorthodox or unacceptable. Pollini has rightly observed of numismatic images, ". . . the *princeps* or senate would, in any officially sanctioned work, bear ultimate responsibility for what was produced, if only by the tacit acceptance of it."[30] In costume and grooming as well, the emperor would establish by example the sort of image he expected his family to cultivate. Augustus, who was always acutely aware of public perceptions, usually dressed in clothing that had been made at home by the women of his family, thus cultivating an impression of his own unassuming modesty and of the domestic virtues of his wife, sister and daughter—two enormous but effective lies.[31]

The women of the imperial family also appear to have had some control over their own images; the anecdotes that Macrobius recounts about Augustus and Julia indicate that their dress and grooming sometimes did not conform to the wishes of the ruling emperor. Although Julia might be able to choose her own garments and hair-dressers, however, it was her father who ultimately controlled the officially sanctioned representations of her, and in the only securely identified images of her that survive—tiny profiles on coins and theater tokens—she wears the same severely modest *nodus* coiffure as her stepmother Livia.[32] (See figures 20–21). A contrasting situation,

---

[30] Pollini, 1990, 339.
[31] Suet. *Aug.* 73.
[32] Fullerton, 1985, 475, 476; *RIC*[2] I, 72, nos. 404–405, pl. 7.

but perhaps the other side of the same coin, is that of Trajan's wife
Plotina, a woman whose portraits do not fall within the chronological framework of this study, but whose manipulation of her image
is nonetheless relevant to consider in this context. Dio admiringly
recounts that Plotina turned before her first entry into the imperial
palace and announced to the assembled populace, "I enter this palace
such a woman as I would be when I leave."[33] The preceding dynasty
had been plagued by sexual scandal concerning both Domitian's wife
Domitia Longina and his niece (and alleged mistress) Julia Flavia;
Plotina, therefore, was determined to demonstrate from the first day
of her husband's principate that she would not let her new circumstances corrupt her.[34] Just as Trajan refused the title of "Pater Patriae"
when it was first offered to him, Plotina and Trajan's sister Marciana
both refused the title of Augusta, and both women receive great
praise from Pliny for their modest behavior, high moral standards
and harmonious relationship with one another (a situation that had
perhaps been conspicuously lacking between the two rival Augustae
of the family of Domitian).[35]

The visual arts present an impression wholly consistent with these
literary accounts of Plotina's character and role; ironically, however,
it appears that in her visual image at least, Plotina did change herself after entering the palace, although in the direction of more
emphatically asserting her modest character. If a recent identification

[33] Dio, 68.5.5.
[34] Domitian divorced Domitia on grounds of adultery, but later recalled her (Suet.
Dom. 3.1; Dio, 67.3.1–2; see also Suet. *Tit.* 10.2 on Domitia's character). Julia Flavia
died shortly after the remarriage; persistent rumors claimed that she had been pregnant by her uncle Domitian and had died as the result of an abortion (Juv. *Sat.*
2.29–33; Pliny, *Ep.* 4.11; Suet. *Dom.* 22). It was chronologically impossible for this
to be true, but the rumors persisted nonetheless; see Vinson, 1989, 431–50.
[35] Pliny, *Pan.* 83–84; on the refusal of the title of Augusta, see specifically 84.6–8.
The rumors that Domitia and Julia were sexual rivals for the affections of the
emperor Domitian may or may not have been true, but they may well reflect the
fact that they were rivals for status of the higher-ranking woman in the imperial
family. Julia, although younger, received the title of Augusta earlier, during her
father's lifetime, and in the early years of Domitian's reign was honored very highly
on coins: her portrait appears on the reverse of an issue of *aurei* that portray her
deified father on the obverse, while a concurrent issue honored the deified Vespasian
and Domitilla. Thus, Julia, although still alive, was placed in the company of three
deified members of her family, and in a position analogous to that of Domitilla, as
the daughter of a *Divus. BMCRE* 2, 312, no. 68, pl. 61, fig. 11, and p. 313, no.
69, pl. 61, fig. 12. For a discussion of these two issues, see Scott, 1936, 48, and
Daltrop, Hausmann and Wegner, 1966, 55.

proposed by Paul Zanker is correct, Plotina's earliest coiffure resembled that of Domitia Longina in that the hair toward the front of
her head was combed forward into a high crest of curls over the
forehead, while the rest was drawn back into a queue down the
neck, although already her portrait differs from those of the Flavian
era in showing curls that are more stiffly and severely lacquered into
place.[36] Soon, however, she abandoned this hairstyle in favor of a
simpler one, in which the hair still formed a crest over the forehead,
but was combed smoothly over some sort of frame, without the tiers
of decorative curls.[37] All Plotina's portraits, both sculptural and numismatic, show realistic signs of age, and a dour facial expression that
appears to modern tastes quite forbidding, but that probably conveyed the virtue of *gravitas*, or moral seriousness, quite well. Most
also show a deliberately dry execution, repeated so consistently in
most replicas that we can assume it was inspired by the prototype.
We appear, then, to see in Plotina a case of an imperial woman
who took an active and outspoken interest in the creation of her
own image—an image, however, that conformed well to Trajan's
agenda. A woman of the imperial family could, therefore, more successfully control her own image and presentation when working in
harmony with the goals of her male relatives.

One must consider as well the role of the anonymous artists and
technicians called upon to create these public images, a group that
in this case includes the valets and ladies' maids (most of them probably slaves) who dressed and groomed the imperial family as well
as the portrait sculptors responsible for casting those images into
monumental form. While the patron could establish the tone and,
to some degree, the content of public art, he required the services
of professional artists (some, in speaking of Roman culture, would
prefer the term "craftsmen" or "technicians") to achieve the desired
effect, and the creation of a desired image through fashion or grooming likewise often required such specialized assistance. Most of the
coiffures of Roman women, at least those that portrait sculpture
records, would have been impossible to create single-handed. Indeed,
the costly labor of the numerous ladies'-maids required to create the
spectacularly frivolous coiffure of the celebrated Busta Fonseca in
the Capitoline museum would have been one of the messages that

---

[36] Fittschen-Zanker 3, 7–8, no. 6, pls. 7–8.
[37] Wegner, 1956, 74–76; Fittschen-Zanker 3, 8–9, no. 7, pl. 9.

the work was intended to convey.[38] This coiffure, like the laboriously polished porcelain-like skin areas and the virtuoso drill work of the marble bust in which it appears, would have advertised the wealth and social status of the subject and her family.[39]

The process by which the image was then cast in monumental form remains controversial, despite a basic agreement among scholars as to some of the essential steps. The physical evidence of surviving imperial portraits proves beyond serious doubt that many works can follow the same few original types; it is the process by which they were replicated that remains problematic. Scholars of Classical-period Greek sculpture have recently attacked the very basis of "Kopienkritik," challenging in particular the existence of the "pointing machine" in antiquity and the assumption that a precise copy of an original was always necessarily desired or intended.[40] Many extant copies of Greek originals appear on the contrary to be free adaptations of an earlier work, while even those that recognizably replicate a still-extant original, such as the caryatids of the Erechtheion, deviate too much in proportions to be mechanically duplicated. In his study of copying methods, Pfanner has reconstructed a different, and far more plausible, system of mechanical sculptural replication, presenting abundant evidence in his catalogue of extant works with measuring *puntelli* for its use in imperial portraiture, although somewhat less among copies of Greek ideal sculpture.[41] His measured drawings of the profiles and cross-sections of extant replicas provide dramatic proof of the consistency of structure, mass, volume, and contour-line among replicas of the same type, despite their occasional differences in surface detail.

Despite the value of Pfanner's research on the methods of sculptural production, however, I must dispute his contention that no aesthetic concern whatsoever entered either into the creation of sculptural

---

[38] Museo Capitolino inv. 434, Stanza degli Imperatori 15. Most recent publication: Fittschen-Zanker 3, 53–54, no. 69, pls. 86–87, with full literature. I am indebted to Dr. Katherine Dunbabin, in her remarks as discussant for the costume panel at the 1989 AIA meetings, for some of these observations as to the importance of coiffure as status symbol.

[39] Pfanner, 1989, 227–228.

[40] On the weakness of the evidence for the pointing machine: Pfanner, 1989, 198–200. Touchette, 1991, elaborated on these problems. See also Ridgway, 1984, passim, and Hurwit, 1997, 587–591.

[41] Pfanner, 1989, 195–204, fig. 17, and 236–251 for a list of extant sculpture with measurement points that support his reconstruction; Touchette, 1991.

prototypes or into the marble-working techniques selected for their
production. Pfanner argues that many changes in style may have
been motivated by a desire to improve the process of production by
creating originals that could be easily and successfully copied. The
parallels in method that he points out between production of portraits and of architectural ornament, however, overlook the difference
in function and destination between those two types of objects.
Corinthian capitals and decorative friezes were the literally superficial
adornments of buildings in which they seldom any longer played a
significant structural role; the creative genius of Roman architecture,
as has long been recognized, lay in the shaping and manipulation
of space, through poured concrete in the Western empire and through
more traditional methods of stone-masonry construction and truss-
beam roofing in the East, but not in its use of the Greek orders.
Marble workers must have understood that fact. In column capitals,
furthermore, adherence to tradition, and uniformity—not only within
a building or complex, but within a city, and throughout an empire
seeking to assert its political unity—was a desirable goal that would
have discouraged any experimentation other than that which could
make production more efficient. Portraits, on the other hand, must
necessarily differ from one another in order to achieve their most
basic purpose: that of presenting an individual to his family, his community, or, in the case of imperial images, to an entire empire with
enough personal traits to be accepted by that audience as a likeness
of one identifiable person. Not even a photograph can achieve this
goal by mere mechanical replication of physical traits; some characterization, through facial expression, costume, pose, gesture, and—
last but by no means least—style of execution is required, and an
image will be considered a success or a failure depending on how
effectively it uses such devices to convey the patron's desired persona.

The portrait specialists who created the models in clay or wax for
faces of imperial statues knew that their works were to be replicated
by mechanical means, for broad distribution, and designed their prototypes accordingly; anything too difficult for a copyist to reproduce
would not have served its intended purpose well. Within the limitations imposed by these technical concerns and by the propaganda
goals of their patrons, they were however not only able but obliged
to exercise some degree of originality, if the portrait was to make a
desirably memorable impression on viewers. In female portraiture,
this task was made somewhat easier by the custom of wearing the

hair long and elaborately dressed; Fittschen's very valuable monograph on Antonine female portraiture has demonstrated how the
births of Faustina the Younger's many children required the creation of a corresponding number of new types for the empress, since
on each occasion the mother of the imperial heirs was honored with
an appropriately costly and impressive new image, and that the need
for variety thus imposed was met largely by varying the coiffure
rather than altering the treatment of the face.[42] The blandly pretty
faces of Faustina the Younger and many other Augustae may offer
relatively little insight into character or psychology, but external
features such as coiffure and dress offered an alternative means of
expressing ethos. Here, however, portrait sculptors were partly de-
pendent on the labors of even lowlier craftsmen, or more correctly,
craftspersons: the attendants, probably female and slaves, who created
those coiffures.

Finally, the image often underwent some mutations at the hands
of its copyist. Winkes's recent monograph on the portraits of Livia
has accomplished the Herculean task of sorting these many objects
into typological groups, but has also demonstrated beyond doubt that
within each type are a wealth of variations, some perhaps produced
by misunderstandings of the original as it was copied and recopied,
but many of them deliberate. One entire group of Livia's portraits,
a variant on her *nodus* coiffure in which narrow braids encircle the
sides of the head (figs. 21, 28, 29), appears to have been created by
artists of the Greek-speaking cities of Asia Minor, rather than to
have been an officially disseminated type, while another such variant, also found only in Asia Minor, takes her official "Marbury Hall"
type and embellishes it with a fringe of loose locks of hair along the
forehead.[43]

The creation of the images of empresses may be seen, in short,
as a complex collaborative process, originating with the wishes of
the patron who commissioned the prototype, and ending with the
labors of the copyist who produced the object that members of the
public in a given provincial city would see. Given the many levels
of interaction involved both in the creation and in the reading of a

---

[42] Fittschen, 1982, 38–43 on the coin portraits of Faustina II, 44–65 on sculptural typology; 66–68 for conclusions concerning the importance of coiffure and
such external features, as opposed to "character study."
[43] Winkes, 1995, 28, 35–38.

portrait, it is tempting to accept a deconstructionist interpretation of
Roman statues as works whose meaning no one, patron, subject, or
artist, really controlled, and to assume that the sculptors and copyists who produced these works were carried along powerlessly by
forces of technique, tradition, and economics.[44] I am in agreement
with Galinsky, however, that although some viewers, both ancient
and modern, may have missed intended meanings or read into works
meanings that their creators never intended, not all readings should
be equally privileged; emperors and the members of their families
had an urgent interest in controlling how they were to be perceived,
and in selecting the artists best able to manipulate those perceptions.
The fact that in some cases such manipulation did not work or was
not enough to maintain public good will toward the imperial household does not excuse us from the historical task of attempting to
understand what meanings were intended in Roman public sculpture. With these considerations in mind, let us proceed to a more
detailed examination of the public images of the women of Rome's
first dynasty.

---

[44] For such an interpretation of third-century portraits, see Balty, 1983, 301–315.
Unfortunately for his argument, one of the groups of portraits that he cites as replicas of a common prototype (pp. 303–306, figs. 1–6) may in fact not constitute a
replica series; see Wegner, 1979, 124–125. Another group of three portraits that
Balty believes to represent the same individual, although he concedes that they are
not replicas of a type, (pp. 312–315, figs. 17–19) may in fact represent three separate men whose portraits happen to have a coincidental similarity; certain facial
shapes and expressions tend to become popular at some periods of Roman sculpture, and these three portraits share one of the commonest facial types and facial
expressions of the third century A.D. The portraits in question are: Vienna,
Kunsthistorisches Museum; Rome, Museo Nazionale delle Terme, cat. no. 300, inv.
1244486; Vatican, Museo Gregoriano Profano inv. 10205.

CHAPTER ONE

OCTAVIA MINOR AND JULIA F. AUGUSTI

The women of Augustus's family figured prominently in his ambitions and political plans throughout his career. C. Caesar Octavian (later known as Augustus) was in this respect a typical product of his family- and class-conscious society. Marriage alliances were a common means of securing loyalty between powerful families, providing as they did the powerful incentive of protecting the interests of mutual grand-children. Romans considered the sacred bonds of father and son to be equally binding on fathers- and sons- in law.[1] It was to be expected, then, that Octavian would arrange marriages for his sister Octavia Minor that suited his political needs, and that since his only child was female, he would order her to marry the man he had chosen as heir to power, with the intention that her sons would eventually suc-ceed to the principate. Both literary and epigraphic evidence confirms beyond doubt that public portrait statues of both of these women once existed. It is frustrating for the modern scholar, therefore, that their portraits remain scarce and elusive. Most sculptures that scholars have attempted to identify as Octavia from the principate of Augustus lack the corroboration of contemporary coin portraits, since the only coins on which Octavia appears were minted earlier, during Antony's lifetime, in the cities and territories he controlled. From this earlier period, no sculptural portraits of Octavia have been identified with any certainty. For Julia I, the situation is even more frustrating: the only objects that definitely represent her are small objects such as coins, theater tokens, and gaming-pieces that give only a diminutive profile. No identifications of Julia's portraits in sculpture have yet met with wide acceptance, although several have been proposed.

The scarcity of the evidence for these women's portraits contrasts dramatically with the situation of Augustus's wife Livia, whose por-traits are so numerous, so diverse and so rich in their evolving forms that they merit a chapter to themselves. There are good historical

---

[1] E.g. Catullus 72.4.

reasons, however, for the discrepancy. First, Octavia enjoyed her greatest prominence in the earlier part of the reign of Augustus, when the emperor might have been cautious about embracing the custom of the publicly displayed statuary group of the imperial family that originated in the Hellenistic world and had associations with kingship.[2] Having attacked Antony for his adoption of Hellenistic royal practices, Octavian would also have needed to differentiate himself from his discredited rival for power, who had prominently flaunted the women of his family on coinage (figures 2–5, 7–10).[3] Portraits of Octavia unquestionably did exist, from the year 35 B.C. onward when the Senate formally voted this honor to her and to Livia, along with other important rights, but the scarcity of surviving inscriptions implies that such portraits were never plentiful. Of the 130 imperial statuary groups that Rose has catalogued, only two appear to have included portraits of Octavia, and in these cases, Rose has identified the surviving portrait heads on the basis of context and historical probability, since not a single surviving inscription attests Octavia's presence.[4] The very fact that the Senate had to authorize such portraits by a special decree suggests the unprecedented nature of such public honors to women, which in 35 B.C. served a very specific propaganda goal: they enabled Octavian to honor the respectable Roman wives of the triumvirs while implicitly rebuking Antony's bad behavior toward Octavia.[5] After the establishment of Augustus as *princeps*, portrait types of the male members of his family could legitimately be distributed and displayed, since the males generally held public offices that made such public presentation appropriate, but the presence of the women might have seemed too open a declaration of dynastic intentions. Although Augustus unmistakably did wish members of his own family eventually to inherit his powers, he was wisely reticent about expressing those plans, knowing that his power must rest on constitutional offices

---

[2] Balty, 1988, 31–37 on the Hellenistic origins of such groups; 34–38 on its gradual acceptance in the Greek east but relative absence from the Latin-speaking west until the reign of Augustus. Imperial examples: 39–46.

[3] See D. Kleiner, 1992, 357–367.

[4] Dio 49.38.1. Groups that may have included Octavia: Rose, 1997, 120–121, no. 49, pls. 125, 126 (group at Velia), and 128–129, no. 53, pl. 166 (group from Glanum). Lack of inscriptions for Octavia: *RE* 17 pt. 2 (1937), 1867, "Octavia," (M. Hammond); Hanson and Johnson, 1946, 399–400. Erhart, 1980, 126 n. 32, disputes this conclusion.

[5] Flory, 1993, 293–295.

and powers established under the traditions of the republic, which he claimed to have restored.[6] Such powers were not hereditary, but had to be conferred by the Senate, whose authority Augustus had to treat with respect. The fate of Julius Caesar, still a relatively recent memory, dictated such caution, especially during the early years of the principate, while Marcellus, the only son of Octavia, was still the likeliest heir to power. Octavia lost her status as the mother of the potential heir to power with the death of Marcellus in 23 B.C., at a time when she was probably too old to have any more children, and so although she continued to enjoy public honor, it was no longer so vitally important to keep her image in the public eye by the time imperial statuary groups became widely accepted. (See Appendix, chart no. 1, for the family tree of Octavia).

Julia, on the other hand, had three sons by her second husband Marcus Agrippa, and for a long period these children represented Augustus's main hope of succession by his own direct descendants. (See Appendix, chart no. 2). Julia, as the all-important link between Augustus and the two grandsons Gaius and Lucius Caesar that he adopted as his own sons, had therefore to be proudly presented along with them. Epigraphic evidence attests to the presence of her statues in public places, especially in the Greek-speaking east, where dynastic statuary groups had been a familiar and acceptable sight before the advent of Roman hegemony. Inscriptions attest her presence in at least eight and possibly nine imperial groups, all in Greece or Asia Minor, in some of which she appeared as the wife of Agrippa and in others with her last husband Tiberius.[7] In several dedications, she appeared with her all-important children, who must sometimes have been represented as babies in her arms.[8] This latter feature must have been a novel sight even in the Hellenistic east, but local donors evidently appreciated the significance of births in the imperial family, and celebrated them accordingly. Julia, however, fell dramatically

---

[6] *Res Gestae Divi Augusti* 1. For a recent commentary on the meaning of the restoration of the republic, see Galinsky, 1996, 42–79.

[7] Inscriptions attest statues of Julia I at Delphi, Ephesus, Megara, Thespiae, Lindos, Palaepaphus, Thasos, Sestus, and possibly Paros. Rose, 1997, 139–140, no. 70; 145 no. 76; 149–50, no. 82; 153–154, no. 87; 156, no. 91; 156–157, no. 92; 158–159, no. 95; 172–173, no. 112; 180, no. 122. See also Hanson and Johnson, 1946, 390–391, nos. 1–4, 6, 11. On the arch at Ephesus: Meriç, Merkelbach, Nollé and Şahin, 1981, no. 3006, pp. 6–9.

[8] Rose, 1997, 13, 149–150, no. 82.

from grace after her conviction for adultery in 2 B.C., after which time her portraits would certainly never have been replicated for public display again. Her behavior had been an acute embarrassment to the family of Augustus, violating as it did his own unpopular and excessively strict moral legislation, and thus leaving the imperial family open to gleefully vindictive ridicule.[9] Julia never, however, suffered a formal *damnatio memoriae*, and there would have been no official mandate to destroy her existing portraits. Local communities might, acting on their own initiative, have chosen to remove her likeness from display in some instances, but since none of the inscriptions bearing her name show signs of erasure, the works of sculpture that they accompanied may also have been spared. Some of her images, however, perhaps even most of them, might eventually have been recut. Roman patrons were often sparing with expensive materials, and the portrait of a discredited and embarrassing member of the imperial family could make a convenient source of raw material. But even in the cases of an official and thorough attack on the memory of a disgraced person, some objects usually survive the destruction. It seems incredible that at least a few portraits of Julia should not survive somewhere. Nonetheless, although various efforts have been made to identify surviving objects as portraits of Julia, no portrait types have yet been established for which there are no other plausible identifications. A few of the current theories about Julia's surviving portraits will be discussed below, but none are universally accepted.

Despite the scantiness of the visual information, however, let us consider the literary and numismatic evidence for the roles these women played in the public images of the imperial family, since their significance is too great to allow us to ignore them.

Biographical information: Octavia Minor

Octavia Minor, older sister of the future emperor Augustus, was born probably in or near 69 B.C. to Gaius Octavius and Atia.[10] (See Appendix, chart no. 1). At the age of about fifteen, she married Gaius

---

[9] On the *lex iulia de adulteriis coercendis*, see Gardner, 1991, 127–131 and Balsdon, 1962, 76–79; Ferrill, 1980, 339. See also Dio 54.16.3–4: Dio approvingly quotes the Senators as accusing Augustus of hypocrisy, in view of his own sexual promiscuity.

[10] Suet. *Aug.* 4.1. Plut. *Vit.Ant.* 31.1, claims that she was his half-sister and that

Claudius Marcellus, by whom she had two daughters and a son. While she was still married to Marcellus, her uncle Julius Caesar lost his daughter, the wife of his political partner Pompey the Great, and finding himself in need of a new marriage alliance with his friend, offered Octavia in marriage to Pompey.[11] The fact that such a match would have required her to divorce her husband with whom she had had children evidently did not trouble Caesar; a cavalier attitude toward existing marriages was typical both of his policies and later, those of Augustus and the Julio-Claudian emperors, who frequently ordered relatives, both male and female, to dissolve existing unions in favor of more dynastically desirable matches. In this case, however, Pompey evidently refused Caesar's offer, and Octavia remained married to G. Claudius Marcellus until his death. Her next marriage was to make her a crucial player in the politics of the second triumvirate and the ensuing civil war, but even before that time she had exercised influence with her brother in public matters: for example, helping the wife of a proscribed man to obtain clemency for him and his family.[12]

In 40 B.C., Octavian gave his sister in marriage to Marc Antony, in order to cement the renewal of their alliance with the treaty of Brundisium. Since the men had already made violent war on one another and since Antony already had a sexual relationship with Cleopatra VII of Egypt, the marriage had dim prospects. It is therefore an impressive tribute to Octavia's determination to serve the political interests of her brother that the match was surprisingly happy in its early years, during which Octavia lived with Antony in Athens where he was presiding over the administration of the eastern provinces, and that the marriage produced two children. Shortly after the birth of the second daughter in 37 B.C., Octavia successfully negotiated another peaceful settlement between the two rivals, during a tense confrontation, on the strength of their familial relationship through her.[13] During this period her portraits appear with Antony's on the

---

her mother's name was Ancharia, but Suetonius, the imperial archivist, was more likely to have access to the correct information.

[11] Suet. *Iul.* 27.1; *PIR* II (1897) 430, no. 45: *RE* 17 part 2 (1937) 1859–1860, s.v. "Octavia" (M. Hammond).

[12] Dio, 47.7.4–5.

[13] Plut. *Vit.Ant.* 31, 33.3–4, 35; App. *B.Civ.* V. 64, 76 (on the happiness of the marriage of Antony and Octavia), 93–95 (on her role in negotiations at Tarentum); Dio 48.54.1–5 (on the negotiations at Tarentum).

coins minted in Greek cities under his control such as Pergamon (figure 2). These coins remain our only secure evidence for identifying the likenesses of Octavia, and we must remember when studying them that they serve the propaganda needs of her husband, not of her brother.

Despite Octavia's role in securing the settlement of Tarentum, Antony parted from her shortly afterward on the pretext of protecting her and their children from danger during the Parthian war.[14] After sending Octavia back to his house in Rome, however, he began once again to cohabit openly with Cleopatra, to whom he referred in at least one formal letter to Octavian as his "wife," despite the fact that marriage of a Roman citizen to a non-citizen was legally impossible.[15] In 35 B.C., shortly after Antony had suffered a humiliating and expensive military defeat at the hands of the Parthians, Octavia traveled to join her husband in Greece with money and troops. Antony accepted the aid but sent her home without personally meeting her, one of many insults that helped Octavian to turn public opinion in Rome against Antony by contrasting Octavia's exemplary behavior toward her husband with her bad treatment at his hands.[16] In the same year, 35 B.C., Octavian obtained extraordinary rights and privileges for Octavia and for his own wife, Livia Drusilla: the right, as mentioned above, to be represented in public statuary, the right to control their own financial affairs, and the privilege of "*sacrosanctitas*," legal protection of their persons normally reserved for elected officials of a special type, the Tribunes of the People.[17] Octavian thus established a pointed contrast between Antony's behavior and his own respect for the legal, Roman wives of the triumvirs. The public statues of the two women would have provided the Roman public with a permanent, highly visible reminder of that respect.[18] It is possible, although not certain, that the Senate had to pass a decree granting these rights, a measure of the public respect and admiration for these women. The Senate was the political class most likely to suspect and fear monarchical ambitions; if such a body

---

[14] Dio 48.54.5–6, Plut. *Vit.Ant.* 36, App. *B.Civ.* V. 95.

[15] Suet. *Aug.* 69.2 quotes the letter in which Antony states of Cleopatra "Uxor mea est." In view of Suetonius's access to official archives, he probably quotes Antony's wording accurately.

[16] Plut. *Vit.Ant.* 53.1–2, 54.1–3.

[17] Purcell, 1986, 85; Dio 49.38.1–2.

[18] Flory, 1993, 293–295.

could vote to grant extraordinary rights to two women of the families of the triumvirs, they must have had compelling reasons to believe that the move was either appropriate or at least politically pragmatic.[19]

In 32, Antony officially divorced Octavia and sent agents to evict her from his house in Rome, an order she obeyed with dignity. This insult to his sister provided Octavian with the grievance he needed to seize and publicize Antony's will, in which Cleopatra and her children were named as his heirs, and to accuse Antony to the Roman public of monarchical ambitions.[20] After the ensuing war and the resulting suicides of Antony and Cleopatra, Octavia made a public show of magnanimity by raising all her stepchildren, including Antony's by Cleopatra.[21] Her hopes and ambitions for the future however were focused on her only son, the child of her first husband, the promising young Marcellus, whom Augustus honored highly in his triumph of 29 B.C. and to whom he married his only daughter Julia, a clear signal to the Senate and people that Marcellus would be his intended heir.[22] Marcellus's death in 23 B.C. was a blow from which Octavia never entirely recovered.[23]

Octavia remained a prominent member of the imperial family, but was no longer the mother of a prospective heir. Her presence in monuments and groups that celebrated the dynastic plans of Augustus was therefore less necessary than that of Livia or Julia, but as a model of behavior for Roman women, she continued to play a significant public role in the policies of Augustus. Octavia, like Livia, had enjoyed full control of her own property since 35 B.C., and used it to patronize building projects that benefitted the public, such as the Porticus Octaviae, a structure designed for both the enjoyment and the edification of the public.[24] This building housed a famous collection of paintings and statuary, in which at least one portrait statue of the patroness would logically have had a place.[25]

---

[19] *RE* 17 pt. 2 (1937), 1865, s.v. "Octavia" (M. Hammond).
[20] Dio 49.33.3–4; Plut. *Vit.Ant.* 57.2–3; 58.2–5. See Balsdon, 1962, 70, for a summary of the personal and political vicissitudes of Octavia's marriage to Antony.
[21] Balsdon, 1962, 71; Plut. *Vit.Ant.* 87.1.
[22] Suet. *Aug.* 63.1 and *Tib.* 6.4.
[23] Plut. *Vit.Ant.* 87.2; Verg. *Aen.* 6, 860–886, Suet. *Poet-Verg.* 1.32–33.
[24] Suet. *Aug.* 29.4. On the Porticus Octaviae, see Kleiner and Matheson, 1996, 32; on the similar Porticus Liviae and its significance for Augustan policy, see Flory, 1984, 309–330.
[25] *RE* 17 pt. 2 (1937), 1865–1866, s.v. "Octavia" (M. Hammond); Pliny *NH* 34.31; 35.114; 35.139; 36.15, 22, 24, 28, 34–35.

Since no identifiable trace of that great art collection now survives, the presence of Octavia's image must remain conjecture, but literary evidence records that the Porticus Octaviae also housed an older statue of Cornelia, mother of the Gracchi, and other famous mothers, both human and mythological, a fact that may suggest that Octavia herself was not only represented but placed in a context designed to emphasize her role as an example of Roman womanhood.[26] Not coincidentally, the Porticus Octaviae contained a temple to Juno.[27] Octavia's prominence, however, also had the same limits as that of Livia: she held no official titles and was never portrayed on the coins of the imperial or Senatorial mints during the principate of Augustus.

When Octavia died in 11 B.C. at the age of about 58, Augustus gave her a state funeral at which he himself and his stepson Drusus I both delivered eulogies.[28] Her body lay in state at the temple of the Divine Julius Caesar, which had dominated the east end of the forum since the massive remodeling of that public space in the early years of Augustus's principate. To honor her in this way linked her intimately with the glorious descent of the Julians, with the grief that the Roman people had earlier felt at the loss of Caesar, whose body was cremated on the spot where the temple later stood, and with the ultimate fate of Caesar in Roman religion, as the first mortal to be deified.[29] Octavia herself did not receive divine honors, but her funeral could hardly have helped but remind the public yet again of her brother's status as *divi filius*, son of the deified Caesar, as well as of Augustus's own impressive achievements, since the decoration in and around the temple celebrated Augustus's military and diplomatic triumphs over Egypt and Parthia.[30] The ceremony further allowed Augustus to remind the public once again of his *pietas*, toward his assassinated predecessor, whose death he had avenged at Philippi, and later toward Octavia, whose unjust treatment by Antony he had

[26] Flory, 1993, 292; Lewis, 1988, 198–200.

[27] Pliny, *NH* 36.24.

[28] Suet. *Aug.* 61.2; Dio 54.35.4–5; *PIR* II (1897) 430–431; *RE* 17 pt. 2 (1937) 1864, s.v. "Octavia" (M. Hammond). Suetonius puts the date of Octavia's death in 9 B.C.

[29] On the temple of Julius Caesar and the new rostra in front of it, see Zanker, 1972, 12–14; Seinby, 1995, 2, 337–38, s.v. "Forum Romanum (the Imperial Period)" (N. Purcell); Seinby, 1996, 3, 116–119, s.v. "Iulius, Divus, Aedes" (P. Gros).

[30] Zanker, 1972, 13–14 on the captured Egyptian ship's prows on the rostra of Julius Caesar; 15–17 on monuments to the Parthian triumph; Seinby, 1996, 3, 117, s.v. "Iulius, Divus, Aedes" (P. Gros). Dio 51.19.2 and 51.22.2–3.

also avenged at Actium—the spoils of which battle, in the form of captured ships' prows, decorated the speaker's platform of the temple of the Deified Julius Caesar from which Drusus delivered his eulogy. These observations do not imply that Augustus lacked genuine human affection for his sister, who was an admirable woman and a staunch political ally of her brother throughout her life, but in every aspect of his treatment of her and the other women of his family he was masterful at shedding glory on others in such a way as to bask in its reflected rays.

Biographical Information: Julia I

Julia I, the only child of Octavian (later Augustus), was born in 39 B.C. to his first wife Scribonia. (See Appendix, chart no. 2). Octavian's marriage to Scribonia had been a very unhappy one, and he divorced her shortly after the child's birth, claiming that he was unable to endure her perverse ways, by which he probably meant her objection to his own affair with Livia whom he promptly married.[31] Since children by law belonged to their fathers, Augustus and Livia raised the daughter in a very strict and traditional manner.[32] Considering the unorthodox circumstances of their own marriage, the austere behavior that they demanded from her and the severity with which they controlled any social contact with young men was incongruous, and eventually as unsuccessful as it was hypocritical, but Augustus had good reason to try to ensure that Julia would have no sexual contacts with any man he himself had not personally chosen to father the heirs of the Julian family.

Twice during Julia's childhood, Octavian betrothed his daughter to the sons of potential allies: to Marc Antony's son Antyllus, whom Octavian later executed after Antony's defeat at Actium, and then to Cotiso, the king of the Getae, another engagement never fulfilled.[33] Her first marriage was to her cousin Marcellus, Octavia's son, in 25 B.C.[34] This brief marriage, cut short by the untimely death of Marcellus two

---

[31] Suet. *Aug.* 62.2; Suet. *Aug.* 63.1, 69.1; *RE* 10 (1919) 896; Balsdon, 1962, 68.
[32] On the *potestas* of the father over his children, see Gardner, 1991, 142–144. On Julia's education, Suet. *Aug.* 64.2–3; Balsdon, 1962, 71.
[33] Dio 51.15.5; Suet. *Aug.* 63.2; *RE* 10 (1919) 896, "Iulia."
[34] Dio 53.27.5, Suet. *Aug.* 63.1.

years later, produced no children. Her second marriage to M. Agrippa, the brilliant general largely responsible for Octavian's victories in the civil wars and an important figure in his government, was at least dynastically a success, producing three sons and two daughters (see Appendix, chart no. 2). Augustus adopted Gaius and Lucius, the two older sons as his own, clearly designating them as his heirs, but allowed the youngest, Agrippa Postumus (born, as his name implies, after his father's death) to continue to bear Agrippa's family name.[35] The Roman legal custom of adoption that allowed Augustus to become the legal father of his own grandchildren may well have later prompted a crude witticism by his notoriously crude great-grandson Caligula about the nature of Augustus's relationship with his daughter. Suetonius reports that Caligula accused Augustus of incest with Julia, claiming that his own mother Agrippina I had been the product of this union, but like so many anecdotes about Caligula, this bizarre and obviously false assertion (coins and inscriptions from Caligula's reign clearly identify Agrippina I as the daughter of Agrippa) probably arose from a misunderstood joke, in this case an ironic observation on the oddities that legal adoption could introduce into a family tree.[36]

Agrippa's death in 12 B.C. left Julia a widow again at the age of only 27. Augustus's moral legislation required women of childbearing years to remarry promptly after the death of a husband, while his political needs required a marriage between his daughter and the adult male most eligible to rule the empire in the event of his own death.[37] After considering the various candidates best suited to succeed Agrippa in this role, therefore, Augustus ordered his stepson Tiberius to divorce his wife Vipsania Agrippina, to whom he was very happily married and with whom he had a son, in order to marry Julia.[38] Tiberius understandably resented this order and openly displayed his sorrow at being forced to leave his first wife, but complied with Augustus's wishes and lived with Julia long enough for the birth of one son. When the child died in infancy, however, the couple parted, evidently remaining married in name only from then on.[39] During this period of separation from her husband, if not ear-

[35] Suet. *Aug.* 64.1.
[36] Suet. *Calig.* 23.1. See Barrett, 1990, 216–218.
[37] Balsdon, 1962, 76–77.
[38] Suet. *Aug.* 63.2, *Tib.* 7.2–3; Dio 54.35.4; *RE* 10 (1919) 899–900, s.v. "Iulia."
[39] Suet. *Tib.* 7.3.

lier, Julia certainly entered into extramarital relationships that led to her downfall, conviction for adultery and exile in 2 B.C.[40] For five years of her exile she lived under severely restricted conditions on the island of Pandateria, then was allowed to move to a less harsh confinement at Rhegium on the mainland of Italy, but was never recalled to the imperial family. The final blows to her hopes of regaining acceptance came with the death of Augustus and the accession to power of her former husband Tiberius, a notoriously bitter and vindictive man who increased the severity of her house-arrest at Rhegium. After the assassination of her last remaining son Agrippa Postumus, she either committed suicide by starvation or was killed in this manner on Tiberius's orders.[41]

At least three ancient authors imply that Julia's offenses against Augustus consisted of more than sexual flagrancy. Pliny the Elder appears to indicate that the charges against her included conspiracy to assassinate her own father, Dio claims that at least one of her lovers acted out of ambition to seize the monarchy, while Tacitus implies that her long-time lover Sempronius Gracchus was likewise guilty not only of his relationship with a married woman but of abetting her political intrigues.[42] Julia, after her estrangement from Tiberius, probably wanted a divorce and a more congenial remarriage, but would have required Augustus's permission to obtain one, particularly in view of the political significance of her marriage to a potential heir to power. She therefore sent a letter to her father attacking Tiberius's character, and presumably attempting to portray him as an unfit heir to the principate. Gracchus, according to Tacitus, was the actual author of Julia's letter. After the exposure of Julia's conduct, Augustus contemplated executing his daughter, a punishment that could not legally have been imposed for adultery alone unless she had been taken *in flagrante* in her husband's house. This information suggests that he had reason not only to be ashamed of her actions but to fear them.[43] In fact, only one of the condemned persons did die: Iullus Antonius,

[40] *RE* 10 (1919) 901–902, s.v. "Iulia;" Vel. Pat. 2.100.2–5; Sen. *De Benef.* 6.32.1–2; Sen. *De Brev. Vit.* 4.5; Suet. *Aug.* 65.1; Plin. *NH* 7.45.149; Dio 55.10.12–16; Macrobius, *Saturnalia* 2.5.1–10.

[41] Tac. *Ann.* 1.53.

[42] Pliny *NH* 7.44.149; Dio 55.10.15; Tac. *Ann.* 1.53.

[43] Suet. *Aug.* 65.2; *RE* 10 (1919) 902, s.v. "Iulia" (M. Hammond). On the death penalty for adultery, see Gardner, 1991, 129.

the son of Marc Antony, who according to Velleius Paterculus committed suicide. Tacitus states that he was executed for adultery with
Julia, while Dio elaborates that Augustus had Antonius executed on
the grounds that he had designs on the monarchy, but both authors
were writing later than Paterculus, whose early account is perhaps
more trustworthy.[44]

Ferrill has recently reviewed the great volume of scholarship on
the fall of Julia, and has rightly cautioned that the evidence for Julia's
involvement in a political conspiracy is very scanty.[45] Pliny's reference
to Augustus's discovery of Julia's adultery and of plots of "parricide"
against him, for example, do not necessarily imply that it was Julia
who was responsible for the latter: "*parricida*" could perhaps refer to
any attempt on the life of a head of state, not necessarily of the literal "father" of the perpetrator.[46] On the other hand, the close juxtaposition in a single sentence of these two personal blows to Augustus
does imply that Pliny considered them to be connected. The incident
discussed above, when Julia collaborated with Gracchus to attempt
to turn Augustus against Tiberius, implies that her actions with her
lovers involved more than sex. That does not mean, however, that
the charges of adultery were falsely trumped up to conceal a more
serious offense. Ferrill suggests that modern scholars who regard
charges of adultery with skepticism must believe either that "they
regard the victims of the charge of adultery as innocent of that crime
or . . . simply assume that everyone in high station in Rome committed adultery and the emperor was free to make the accusation,
without fear of contradiction, against anyone he wished."[47] There is,
however, a third possibility: that for high-ranking women, adultery
and political conspiracy could be so closely linked as to be almost
one and the same offense.[48] Julia was the product of a society that
used sexual union, in its legally sanctioned form of marriage, as an
acceptable way of securing alliances. A natural if unintended con-
sequence of this institution would be to inspire women to use unsanc-
tioned sexual relationships in pursuit of their own ambitions, and to
secure the loyalty of powerful men through sex. It is natural to hope,

---

[44] Vell. Pat. 2.100.4; Tac. *Ann.* 4.44; Dio 55.10.15.
[45] Ferrill, 1980, 334–336, 344.
[46] Pliny, *NH* 7.45.149: ". . . luctusque non tantum orbitate tristis, adulterium filiae
et consilia parricidae palam facta . . ." Ferrill, 1980, 344.
[47] Ferrill, 1980, 336.
[48] See Barrett, 1996, 20–21.

with or without justification, that sexual union will produce genuinely closer bonds of affection; it is also possible for a thoroughly cynical person to seduce another party in order to gain a weapon of blackmail. Seneca describes Julia and her lovers as being bound by adultery as though by a sacred oath ("*filia et tot nobiles iuvenes adulterio velut sacramento adacti*").[49] Ferrill points out that this wording implies that there was, in fact, no such oath, but it also implies that the sexual bonds of the parties involved had the same force in securing their loyalty to one another.[50]

Whenever a prominent woman falls from grace for reasons that include sexual misconduct, human nature guarantees an exaggerated emphasis on the prurient gossip, often at the expense of other historically significant factors. Wildly exaggerated accounts of Julia's promiscuity circulated after her fall, just as they did about Messalina and Domitia after her.[51] Authors with a literary point to make that took precedence over historical accuracy accused both Julia I and Messalina of engaging in prostitution.[52] Modern historians are, therefore, not without justification in regarding the ancient accounts of Julia's behavior with some skepticism, although Ferrill is right to caution against the opposite extreme of accepting conspiracy theories as fact. The precise nature of Julia's conspiracy with her lovers, if there was one, is undeterminable on the available evidence: it has been theorized that she actually plotted to kill her father, or on the other hand merely sought to secure the rights of succession of her own sons against Tiberius, but the few scraps of information in the ancient texts are not enough to support either notion.[53] The emphasis that the ancient authors place on the location of her misconduct, however, is striking: Seneca asserts that she conducted her *stupra*, illicit sexual acts, in the Roman forum, on the rostrum (the very platform from which Augustus had introduced his legislation against adultery), and that she solicited clients for prostitution by the statue of Marsyas in the Roman forum, all landmarks associated with the most public

[49] Sen. *De Brev. Vit.* 4.5.

[50] Ferrill, 1980, 344.

[51] For a much later writer's account of Julia's character, see Macrobius, *Sat.* 2.4.31–2.5.8.

[52] Sen. *Ben.* 6.32.1, alleges that Julia prostituted herself in the public forum; Juv. 6.115–132 claims that Messallina habitually went in disguise to a public brothel, where she prostituted herself.

[53] For a summary of scholarship about Julia's conspiracy, see Balsdon, 1962, 86–87.

aspects of Roman government. Pliny and Dio also repeat the allegation that Julia's revelry took place in the forum: Pliny specifically mentions the statue of Marsyas, which she crowned with flowers, and Dio mentions the rostra. Whether these accounts are true, and whether, if true, the location of her revelry had any political significance to Julia and her lovers, the indignation that these authors express is most revealing of the angry reactions of males to her threatening conduct. Julia's nocturnal prowlings, according to all three of these authors, took her to places where a woman had no business to be.[54]

Throughout Roman history, the women who fare best at the hands of later historians are those who know how to exercise influence through their familial roles. One need only compare Julia's behavior during her estrangement from Tiberius with that of Octavia after her separation from Antony, then compare the glorious state funeral of the latter with the sad, obscure and undoubtedly very painful death of the former: the two women discussed in this chapter could not illustrate more vividly the contrast between the Roman concept of "good" and "bad" female behavior, which in both cases extended far beyond the bedroom. Octavia was no passive bystander in the power struggle between her brother and husband; on the contrary, Plutarch tells us that throughout her marriage to Antony and even after her estrangement from him she used all her influence with both Antony and Octavian to try to avert a civil war. Her lack of success in no way diminishes his admiration for her efforts.[55] Whether or not Plutarch' characterization of her is accurate, the behavior that he attributes to her as a mediator for peace, and her willingness to overlook her own legitimate personal grievances in the public interest, says much about the code of ethics that an honorable woman was expected to observe. Nor can she be regarded as a powerless or marginalized figure: the rights and immunities that she received along with Livia in 35 B.C. were a very public form of enfranchisement. Julia, on the other hand, stepped outside her roles both as wife and as loyal daughter when she formed sexual and political alliances with other men. In defying the power of her own father, Julia violated the most sacred bond of loyalty incumbent upon any Roman woman.[56]

---

[54] Sen. *Ben.* 6.32.1; Pliny *NH* 21.6.9; Dio 55.10.12.
[55] Plut. *Ant.* 35, 56.2, 57.3.
[56] See Hallett, 1984, passim.

The Numismatic Portraits: Octavia

During the period when Octavia lived with her husband Antony in Athens, her image appears on coins in all three metals from the mints of various Greek cities under Antony's authority. The precise provenance is sometimes difficult to ascertain, but most were probably Greek cities of Asia Minor, the heart of the old Hellenistic world, and an area that embraced the concepts of divine kingship. A public celebration of the ruler and his wife as a royal couple, and the dynastic intentions that such a presentation implied, were far more acceptable here than in Italy, with its historical fear and suspicion of royalty. Not one of these numismatic issues, however, identifies Octavia by name; we must infer her identity from context, and from the portrait-like, as opposed to ideal, features of the female profiles on these coins.

Octavia might not be the first Roman woman thus honored. Some attempts have been made also to recognize Antony's previous wife Fulvia in numismatic images. Coins from Lugdunum in Gaul, from a city in Phrygia that briefly bore the name of "Fulvia," and from the mint of Rome (Figure 1, e.g.), all apparently datable prior to Fulvia's death and Antony's marriage to Octavia, bear an obverse type of a female bust with wings that identify her as Victory. The figure also, however, wears a coiffure of the type fashionable in the late first century B.C. rather than one modeled on images of Classical or Hellenistic goddesses, and has unmistakably portrait-like features.[57] The Roman coins bear the names of two Roman mint officials, C. Numonius Vaala (figure 1) and L. Mussidius Longus, the latter of whom struck coins honoring all three of the triumvirs, but the provincial coins offer evidence that if the Victory on these coins does portray an actual individual, she might be a woman of Antony's family. One of the issues from Lugdunum in Gaul bears Antony's name on the

---

[57] Bartels, 1963, 12; D. Kleiner, 1992, 359–361.
   Coins from Lugdunum: Banti-Simonetti, *CNR* 2 (1973), 88–90, nos. 3–5; Sydenham, 1952, 189, nos. 1160, 1163; *BMCRR* 2, 394–395, nos. 40–45, pl. 103, fig. 10 (for *quinarii* with the "Victory" but without Antony's name on the reverse) and 396–397 nos. 48–51, pl. 103, figs. 13, 14 (for coins with Antony's name). *RPC* 512–513, p. 151.
   Coins from Fulvia in Phrygia: Bartels, 1963, 12; *BMCRR* 2, 499, n. 1; Furnée van Zwet, 1956, 2, fig. 3 and p. 4. *RPC* 3139–3140, p. 509.
   Roman mint: Crawford, 1974, 100, 522, no. 514/1, pl. 62; Banti-Simonetti, *CNR* 2 (1973), 87–88, nos. 1–2; Sydenham, 1952, 180, no. 1086; 181, no. 1095; *BMCRR* 1, 570, no. 4215, pl. 56.1; 575, no. 4229, pl. 56.10.

reverse, while the Phyrgian town that honored Fulvia with its change of name would logically also have honored her on its coinage.[58]

The female in all of these issues wears a small bun high on the back of her head and a large, full topknot above the forehead, formed by combing a broad section of hair forward along the middle of the head, sweeping it up at the hairline and then drawing it back again in a braided plait along the center of the crown. This coiffure appears in many public and private portraits of women of the late Republic and early empire, and is commonly known as the *nodus* coiffure, because it appears to correspond to the fashion that Ovid recommended for women with short, round faces, which he described as an "*exiguus nodus*" that could add height to the face. The name may or may not be appropriate; Kockel believes that Ovid was describing an older fashion, in which the wearer draws her hair up from the back of the head and twists it into a little topknot on the crown.[59] The term is so generally accepted, however, that it is easiest and clearest to continue to use the term *nodus* coiffure for the fashion in which hair is looped back over the forehead. This same fashion appears a few years later on the female profiles on Antony's eastern coins that must represent Octavia. In no other documented case does it appear on a purely ideal representation of a goddess or a personification. This "Victory," therefore, would seem also to have some human identity. Her face, moreover, invariably shows signs of middle age, most notably sagging cheeks and chin-line, and physical characteristics such as an arched nose and retreating lower lip that would not appear in an ideal image of a goddess or personification.

Many scholars, however, are skeptical of the identification of these profiles as Fulvia.[60] Grueber, who would date the coins of C. Numonius Vaala to 40 B.C. finds it unlikely that Fulvia should appear on Roman coins a year before Antony himself received this privilege, on the coins of L. Mussidius Longus and L. Livineius Regulus, whose term of office Grueber dates to 39 B.C. Grueber finds it even more unlikely that the busts of "Victory" that continue to appear on the coins of L. Mussidius Longus could still represent Fulvia at this late

[58] D. Kleiner, 1992, 360; Furnée-van Zwet, 1956, 4, fig. 1, no. 1.

[59] Ov. *ArsAm*. 3.139–140; Kockel, 1993, 37–38.

[60] Furnée-van Zwet, 3–4; Banti-Simonetti, *CNR* 2, 87, under no. 1; *BMCRR* 1, 570–571, n. 2, 573 n. 1, 575 n. 1. Sydenham, 1952, 180, no. 1086, 181, no. 1095, and 189, no. 1160, refers to the female only as "Victory," and does not mention Fulvia.

date, after Antony's remarriage to Octavia. Sydenham differs from
Grueber on the dates of these issues, pushing Vaala's term as moneyer back to 43 B.C. and Longus's to 42. Fulvia's presence on coins
of 42 would be somewhat more plausible, since she was still living
and still, despite their personal estrangement, an ambitious and powerful ally of her husband.[61] The dating of Vaala's coins to 43, however, presents another difficulty. Antony was at this time at war with
the Senate; indeed, coins from the mint of Rome were struck at
least partly to pay the troops fighting against him. Any honor to
Antony or his family on issues of 43 would be unthinkable. Crawford
argues that the evidence of coin hoards indicates a date later than
A.D. 42 for these coins, but apparently does not believe that the
winged figure represents any historical woman.[62] Could it be that
these portrait-like "Victories" represent different women on different
issues and at different times—that die cutters could adapt the same
basic formula to allude to Fulvia, to Octavia, to Octavian's first wife
Scribonia, or to various other relatives of the triumvirs, depending
on the highly volatile political circumstances of the day? The faces
all deviate from standards of ideal beauty enough to appear portrait-
like, but they differ somewhat from one another. Or, as Grueber suggests, could the coins struck under Antony's authority in Gaul and
Phrygia originally have represented Fulvia, but later been copied by
die-cutters in Rome who failed to understand the significance of
the contemporary coiffure and individualized face?[63] If the "Victory"
does bear the portrait features of one or more historical persons, she
should probably be regarded as a divine personification who subtly
resembles a living woman rather than as a deified portrait.

If these "Victories" do represent some living woman or women,

---

[61] Sydenham, 1952, 180. For coins with portraits of Antony that Sydenham dates
to the years 42–39: p. 182, nos. 1097, 1100. (L. Mussidius Longus); 182, no. 1103, pl.
28, and 1103a (L. Livineius Regulus); 184, no. 1118, pl. 28, and 1121 (P. Clodius,
dated to 41); 186, nos. 1141, 1144, pl. 28 (C. Vibius Varus, dated 39). On Fulvia:
Appian *Bell.Civ.* 3.51 (petitions Senators in 43 B.C. not to declare Antony a public enemy); 5.14, 19, 21, 33, on her conflicts with Octavian and others on behalf
of Antony's interests, 55 and 59 on her illness and death. Plut. *Vit.Ant.* 10.3–4 (on
her ambition and desire for influence with powerful men); 28.1 on her defense of
his interests against Octavian; 30.1–4, on her war against Octavian and death at
Sikyon. For a review of Fulvia's career and the portrayal of her character by the
ancient historians, see Barrett, 1996, 10–12.
[62] Bartels, 1963, 13–14; Crawford, 1974, 100, 742.
[63] *BMCRR* 1, 570–571 n. 2; D. Kleiner 1992, 360.

then Octavia's prominent role on Antony's coinage grows logically out of an existing trend particularly favored by Antony's partisans. When a female profile wearing the contemporary *nodus* coiffure appears after his remarriage in 40 B.C. on the coins of eastern cities under Antony's control, however, its identity as Octavia is far less ambiguous than that of the "Victory-Fulvia." First, the female bust never bears any attributes that would identify her as a goddess or personification; on the silver coins known as *cistophoroi* from Pergamon (figure 2), she appears along with sacred objects, but is not herself presented as a goddess, although such an association may be implied if not directly stated.[64] Several other issues, moreover, present the female in ways that make her identity virtually unmistakable. Silver *cistophoroi* from Asia (figure 3) join her in a jugate portrait with the profile of Antony, as do some bronze *asses*, the smallest Roman denomination of bronze coins, of ca. 36–35. At the same time as that issue of *asses*, bronze *tresses*, coins worth three *asses*, show her facing jugate portraits of Antony and Octavian. (Figure 10). In all these issues, she is in the company of living men, and is therefore presumably also a mortal. The jugate portrait, in Hellenistic coinage and glyptic art, is common for images of royal couples or for persons bound by close bonds of family, so that Antony's wife would appear behind him on the Milesian coins (figure 3), while the bronze *tresses* represent Antony and Octavian as brothers-in-law, facing the woman who establishes their connection and who was instrumental in negotiating their latest treaty.[65]

Let us examine the formats of these coins in more detail. Two issues of *aurei* (gold coins) juxtapose Antony's portrait on the obverse with that of Octavia on the reverse. One, which unfortunately survives only in a single, but very fine, specimen (figure 4), has no

---

[64] Pergamene cistophoroi: Banti-Simonetti, *CNR* 2, 96–100, nos. 8–16; Sydenham, 1952, 193, no. 1197, pl. 29. *BMCRR* 2, 502, nos. 133–134 pl. 114.1 and 2. *RPC* 2201, p. 377, attributed to Ephesus.

[65] Milesian *cistophoroi*: Banti-Simonetti, *CNR* 2, 100–104, nos. 17–23/6, Sydenham, 1952, 193, no. 1198, *BMCRR* 2, 503, nos. 135–137, pl. 114, figs. 3 and 4. *RPC* 2202, p. 377.

Asses with jugate portraits: Banti-Simonetti, *CNR* 2, 114–115, nos. 41–42/9; Sydenham, 1952, 198, nos. 1258, 1264; 199, no. 1268; *BMCRR* 2, 513, 516, 519 nos. 164–171.

Tresses of Antony, Octavian, and Octavia: Banti-Simonetti, *CNR* 2, 119–120, nos. 1–3/3; Sydenham, 1952, 197, no. 1256; 198, nos. 1262, 1266; *BMCRR* 2, 511, 515, 518, no. 154, pl. 115.3, for *tresses*.

Hellenistic cameos with jugate portraits of royal couples: see Oberleitner, 1985, 32–34; Megow, 1985, 456–466; 473–475.

inscriptions on the reverse at all, only a circle of dots framing the portrait bust. The other (figure 5) has inscriptions on both the obverse and reverse, but they consist solely of the titles of Antony; none identify the woman.[66] The unique *aureus* now in Berlin (figure 4) represents a woman with a short, slender neck, delicate bone structure, high cheekbones, a small, pointed chin, and a coiffure similar but not identical to that of the "Victoria-Fulvia." Octavia wears her bun lower on the back of the head, just above the nape. The hair around her face forms a broad roll of waves swept out and back, and a small strand escapes from the coiffure at the nape of her neck. Her features in this coin bear an unmistakable family resemblance to those of Octavian as he appears in contemporary coinage.[67] This issue is probably the earlier of the two, since the obverse inscription identifies Antony simply as "Triumphant general, Triumvir for the restitution of the republic" (M. ANTONIUS IMP.III.VIR.R.P.C., "Marcus Antonius imperator, triumvir rei publicae constituendae"). The more plentiful coins (figure 5) give a longer series of titles, requiring the extension of the inscriptions onto the reverse, and describe Antony as "augur, triumphant general for the third time, consul designate for the second and third time, triumvir for the restitution of the republic." (M.ANTONIUS.M.F.M.N.AUGUR.IMP.TER, obverse, and COS.DESIGN.ITER.ET.TER.III.VIR.R.P.C, reverse).

This issue would, therefore, be a little later than that of the unique Berlin aureus, datable 38 to 37 B.C., and Octavia's image has undergone a metamorphosis since the issue from immediately after her marriage to Antony. The arrangement of hair has been simplified slightly: it is now drawn straight back from the face instead of forming a roll of full waves around the face, and the bun is worn a little higher in back. Octavia may really have altered her coiffure, or die cutters may have simplified it for their own convenience; both possibilities are entirely plausible. More surprisingly, her face and neck

---

[66] Unique *aureus* from De Quelen sale: Crawford, 1974, 101, 531, no. 527/1, 743, pl. 63; Banti-Simonetti, *CNR* 2, 95, no. 7; Sydenham, 1952, 193, no. 1196; *BMCRR* 2, 499.

Aurei with inscribed reverses: Crawford, 1974, 101, 534, nos. 533/3a and b, 743, pl. 63; Banti-Simonetti, *CNR* 2, 93–94, nos. 1–6; Sydenham, 1952, 193, nos. 1200–1201; *BMCRR* 2, 507–508 nos. 144–145, pl. 14, figs. 7, 8. For a discussion of the portraits on both issues of *aurei*, see Winkes, 1995, 67–68, 69–71, fig. 16; Bartels, 1963, 15 and D. Kleiner, 1992, 362.

[67] E.g. an *aureus* of 42 B.C. from Rome, struck by L. Regulus, with obverse portrait of Octavian, Sydenham, 1952, 182 nos. 1104 and 1104a, pl. 28.

now appear fleshier, her chin larger and more prominent. Pose and
presentation have become a little more flamboyant, her head held
more proudly upright on a thick, column-like neck sometimes emphasized with necklaces or "venus rings," and several loose locks of hair
at the nape of the neck now form decorative little curls. Octavia
might have gained some weight after the birth of her daughter by
Antony, but it is most unlikely that her bone structure would have
changed. The shift in her appearance from the earlier to the later coin
probably reflects instead a common artistic convention: the assimilation of the appearance of one person to another. The message of the
portraits on these coins is the harmony of the couple, visually reinforced
by their close resemblance. Thus, Octavia acquires a thick neck and
protruding jaw like those of her husband, just as Cleopatra later
does on the *denarii* (silver coins worth 10 *asses*) that represent Antony
on the obverse and the queen of Egypt on the reverse (figure 7).[68]

Smith has rightly pointed out the dichotomy between Cleopatra's
somewhat more attractive "Hellenistic style" portraits on her own
Ptolemaic coins (figure 6) and the "Roman" verism of the harsh
profiles on Antony's coins. These "Roman" style portraits of Cleopatra
appear both on Antony's Roman *denarii* and his *tetradrachms*, a Greek
denomination of silver coins worth 4 drachmas, from Antioch (figure
8). The latter portray the queen as a Roman client in a style that
matches that of Antony's profiles on the obverses. Surprisingly, however, Smith fails to note one of the most striking effects of these
Roman-style portraits of Cleopatra: their close resemblance to Antony
not only in style but in actual physical features. The coins that represent Cleopatra alone (figure 6) show a short, slender neck and a
long nose with a pendulous tip, but a straight bridge. The *denarii*
(figure 7) and *tetradrachms* (figure 8) on which she accompanies Antony
give her a large nose with a distinct bend similar to that of Antony's
broken nose, and a tall, thick, columnar neck also like Antony's.[69]

Silver coins with portraits of Octavia emanated from at least one,

---

[68] *Denarii* of Antony and Cleopatra: Crawford, 1974, 102, 539, no. 543/1, 743,
pl. 64; Banti-Simonetti, *CNR* 2, 125–127, nos. 1–6; Sydenham, 1952, 194–195, nos.
1210, 1210a, 1210b, pl. 29. Erhart, 1980, 125, also notes the phenomenon of assimilation of Octavia's portraits to Antony's.
[69] Smith, 1988, 132–134, pl. 75, figs. 21–22 (coins of Cleopatra alone) and 23–24
(coins of Cleopatra with Antony). On the phenomenon of assimilation in these portraits, see Pollini, 1986, 217. On the political significance of the denarii of Antony
and Cleopatra see D. Kleiner, 1992, 365–367.

and possibly two mints in Asia Pergamon and of Ephesus. (Figures 2 and 3). Both follow the format known as *cistophoroi*, a type of coinage issued by several cities of the old kingdom of Pergamon from at least the second century B.C. onward. These coins derive their name from the objects represented on them: the *cista mystica*, or cylindrical basket of sacred objects of the cult of Dionysus, and other attributes and familiars of the god. Earlier issues from the time of the independence of the kingdom of Pergamon usually displayed the *cista*, with a serpent emerging from under its lid, on the obverse, framed by a wreath of ivy, and a pair of entwined serpents with upraised heads on the reverse, but after Pergamon and its territories became part of the Roman province of Asia, the coins also incorporated references to the new authority.[70] During Antony's hegemony over these regions, his portrait, crowned with the ivy wreath of Dionysus, replaced the *cista* within the garland of ivy and grape clusters on the obverse, while the sacred basket moved to the reverse, between the two rearing serpents. Since Antony identified himself with the god Dionysus, the association of his portrait with these emblems would have seemed especially appropriate both to Antony and to the local minting authorities of the respective cities.[71] On the Pergamene coins (figure 2), Antony's profile appears alone on the obverse, while Octavia's bust, in a smaller format, hovers above the basket of sacred implements on the reverse, framed by the pair of serpents. The inscription on the reverse is, as on the *aurei*, a continuation of Antony's nomenclature and titles which begin on the obverse. Octavia's identity must be inferred from context. The reduced scale of her images here would seem at first glance to subordinate her importance to that of Antony, but on the other hand, her association with the sacred objects implies her identification with the divine consort of the god Dionysus, her husband's alter ego. The traditional bride of Dionysus in mythology would be Ariadne, a mortal raised to semi–divine status by her marriage with the god, but these coins might have suggested to their viewers a more contemporary religious and political reference: Antony, during his stay at Athens, had conducted a symbolic "sacred marriage" of his own patron god Dionysus with Athena, the patron of Athens as well as

---

[70] Mørkholm, 1991, 36–37, 171–173, pl. 41, figs. 616–617; Head, 1910, 534–537.
[71] Plut. *Vit.Ant.* 60.3, Dio 48.39.2. Antony was called "Διόνυσος νέος," New Dionysus.

of Pergamon where these coins were struck.[72] Since Octavia bears
no divine attributes, however, any identification of her either with
Ariadne or with Athena would be implied rather than openly stated.

The small scale of Octavia's busts does not allow for much subtlety of representation, but her coiffure here is the same shown on the
Berlin *aureus* (figure 4), with a *nodus* above forehead, a braid along
the crown and a small bun low on the back of the head, just above
the nape. The specimens illustrated by Banti and Simonetti display
a variety of treatments of the features, some more resembling the
unique Berlin *aureus* with their slender necks and delicate features,
while others show more assimilation of Octavia's appearance to
Antony's, most notably in the strong jaw and tall, thick neck.[73]

The other issue of *cistophoroi* from Miletus (figure 3) appear to give
Octavia a more prominent status by moving her to the obverse, in
a jugate portrait with Antony, although her face, as is conventional
in jugate portraits of females with males, is behind his. The reverse
shows, once again, the basket of sacred implements between a pair
of entwined serpents, but this time the object above the *cista* is a
little full-length figure of Dionysus. Antony, on the obverse, again
wears the ivy crown of Dionysus, but the larger wreath around the
flan does not appear this time, probably because the larger format
of a jugate portrait did not allow enough room. Instead, a simple
circle of dots frames the two profiles. But the identification of Antony
with Dionysus remains unmistakable, and his closer association with
the image of his wife makes the conclusion inescapable that she
should be read as the god's consort, either Ariadne or Athena.

In a jugate portrait, obviously, only the front of the face of the
person in the background can be seen, but since Octavia once again
wears a *nodus*, it is safe to assume that these portraits follow the standard format. Whether we can yet speak of an officially disseminated
portrait "type" such as later exists during the Roman empire is debatable, but Antony's images repeat certain distinctive features such
as the thick neck, prominent jaw and long, broken nose with great
consistency, and some official model of his wife's portraits was pre-

---

[72] Flory, 1988, 356; Dio 48.39.2 on the "sacred marriage" of Dionysus and Athena.
[73] Banti-Simonetti, *CNR* 2, 96–100. Examples that resemble the Berlin *aureus*: nos. 8,
12, 12/3, 13/2, 13/4, 14/6, 15. Specimens that show clear assimilation to Antony:
9, 10, 10/1, 11, 12/2, 13, 13/1, 14, 14/3, 14/4, 14/5. The remainer show a range
of features between profiles that clearly differ from Antony's portraits and profiles
that clearly resemble him. *RPC* 2201, p. 377, attributed to Ephesus.

sumably also available to die cutters. In jugate portraits, however, the impulse toward assimilation of the two faces must be powerful and perhaps not even in the artist's conscious control: having committed themselves to a format that dictates more or less parallel contours, the die-cutters will tend to make the necks of the same length, and give foreheads, noses and chins roughly the same shape. The better-preserved specimens of this issue show an effort to differentiate Antony's broken nose from the smoother line of Octavia's, but her forehead and nose, like his, are generally drawn in a single line, with either no indentation or very shallow indentation at the root of the nose. Her nose, like his, is long, slightly arched, and has a pendulous tip. Some specimens show an effort to indicate that Octavia's neck is a little shorter than Antony's by beginning his profile at the base of the neck and hers just below the collarbone, thus allowing the faces and throats to parallel one another while suggesting the woman's more petite stature, but others dispense with this refinement and show the necks as being of the same length.[74] Virtually all the jugate portraits give Octavia a jaw similar in shape to her partner's, although a few dies compromise between the appearances of the couple by softening and idealizing Antony's features rather than exaggerating Octavia's.[75]

Jugate portraits of Antony and Octavia also appear on some issues of bronze *asses* probably datable to about 37–35 B.C.[76] Other issues of the same time, which have larger flans that allow for a greater variety of compositions, portray the couple in a remarkable new format, facing one another on the obverse.[77] These issues include both bronze *sestertii*, coins worth 2½ *asses*, (figure 9) and *dupondii*, bronze coins worth two *asses*. If neither profile is relegated to the reverse or partially obscured behind the other, then the two are presented as nearly equal, although the husband's placement on the proper right (the viewer's left) still establishes his higher status. The instinctive

---

[74] Examples that show Antony and Octavia with necks of differing lengths: Banti-Simonetti, *CNR* 2, 100–104, nos. 17 through 17/4; 19/2, 19/3, 20, 20/1, 23/3.

[75] Banti-Simonetti, *CNR* 2, 101–103, nos. 17/5, 21/1, 21/2, appear to minimize Antony's characteristic large jaw. *RPC* 2202, p. 377.

[76] Refs. supra, n. 65.

[77] *Sestertii*: Banti-Simonetti, *CNR* 2, 105–106, nos. 24–26, 109, nos. 33, 111–112, nos. 37–38; *BMCRR* 2, 510, 515, nos. 151, 517, nos. 152–153. Sydenham, 1952, 197, nos. 1255, 198 nos. 1261, 1265.

Dupondii: Banti-Simonetti, *CNR* 2, 106–107, 27–29/1; 110, 34–35; 113, 39–40/1; *BMCRR* 2, 512, 516; Sydenham, 1952, 197, nos. 1257, 198, nos. 1263, 1267.

tendency of most people to read from left to right will ensure that
the figure on the left of a composition will appear to "go first."
Although the precise provenance of these coins is difficult to ascertain, the fact that they bear the names of the minting authorities on
the reverse, in accordance with Roman custom, suggests a site in
Italy during one of Antony's brief trips there, most probably the
occasion in 37 B.C. when the triumvirs met at Tarentum and worked
out their agreement with the aid of Octavia.

The All the reverse types of these coins have naval themes: the *sestertii*
(figure 9) represent a chariot drawn by four hippocamps in which a
couple stand facing and apparently embracing one another. Antony
and Octavia here appear to be identified with another divine couple, this time Poseidon and Amphitrite.[78] The *dupondii* have a reverse
type of two galleys, one just visible behind the other, and the *asses*
with the jugate obverse portraits have a single galley on the reverse.
Ships and naval power played a key role in the settlement between
Antony and Octavian at Tarentum: Antony had made a threatening show of force by sailing to Italy with three hundred ships, but
in the end traded one hundred of his galleys for two legions of men
for his Parthian campaign, while Octavia secured an additional gift
of twenty light ships from Antony for her brother, and a promise
of one thousand more soldiers for Antony from Octavian.[79] The conclusion seems inescapable, therefore, that these bronze coins refer
specifically to the agreement of Tarentum and Octavia's key role in
it. Three more issues of *tresses* (figure 10), signed by the same minting authorities, L. Atratinus, L. Bibulus, and M. Oppius Capito,
make the connection even more explicit. On the obverses of these
coins, jugate portraits of Antony and Octavian (the latter, significantly,
relegated to the background) face the bust of Octavia, while three
galleys appear on the reverse.[80] The number of galleys probably
refers to the coin's denomination, since the *dupondii* have two galleys
and the *asses* one, but the designers of these *tresses* seem to have
made a point of including three significant images on both sides,
since there are portraits of the three key individuals on the obverse.

The quality and preservation of these bronze coins is too poor to
allow many conclusions about the style or physical features of the por-

---

[78] D. Kleiner, 1992, 363.
[79] Plut. *Vit.Ant.* 35.1–4.
[80] Refs. supra, n. 65.

trait profiles. Octavia still wears her characteristic *nodus* coiffure, however, and her face generally shows the same tendency to assimilate
her appearance to Antony's that we have observed on the *aurei* and
silver *cistophoroi*. The tall, thick and columnar neck is particularly
noticeable in the *sestertii* (figure 9), *tresses* (figure 10) and *dupondii*, on
which the image is larger and is not obscured behind another image
in the foreground. However poorly Antony may have treated Octavia
in the following years, the coins issued by the cities under his control or by his followers during the years of 40 to 37 B.C. present
her with respect and honor. Her prominence on the *cistophoroi* and
aurei might be motivated only by her role as the link that cemented
the treaty of Brundisium in 40 B.C., but the bronze coins minted
after the agreement at Tarentum in 37 appear to present her as a
powerful individual in her own right.

Octavia: The Problem of her Sculptural Portraits

The coins of Antony from before the civil war tell us much about
Octavia's political significance, but are less reliable for her actual
physical appearance. The phenomenon of assimilation, discussed at
length above, demonstrates that the creation of accurate likenesses
was not a high priority for these die-cutters. Since she never again
appears on coins after her husband's death, all theories about the
identification of her portraits in other media have had to rely on
the evidence of these early numismatic profiles, supported in some
cases by historical probability and archaeological context.[81] Scholars
can at least be certain that she wore the *nodus* coiffure, but since
Livia wore the same coiffure for many years, the differentiation of
the two women in sculptural replicas has long presented problems.
Many portrait heads and busts once believed to be Octavia, such as
a handsome basalt head in the Louvre, have since been reattributed
to Livia.[82] (Figures 24–25). Further complicating the matter is the
fact that Julia wears the same sort of coiffure on her coins and
tokens. The *nodus* coiffure was, indeed, a very popular fashion that

---

[81] Winkes, 1995, 67–73; Rose, 1997, 60–61.
[82] Winkes, 1995, 71, 206–207, no. 215 (Winkes questions the antiquity of the
Louvre head); Arias, 1939, 76–81, pl. 18; de Kersauson, *Louvre* 1, 1986, 98–99, no.
43, with recent literature on the controversy over the identification as Livia or
Octavia.

appears on funerary busts of many private individuals. The presence
of this fashion is not by itself, therefore, sufficient evidence to associate
any sculptural portrait with either Octavia or Livia; some external
support, such as the existence of at least several true replicas, or its
discovery in the context of an imperial family group, is necessary
before any such object can be taken as an imperial rather than a
private portrait.

The two most convincing identifications of Octavia in sculpture,
therefore, are a bust from Velletri (figures 11–13) and a fragmentary
marble head from Smyrna (figures 14–15), now in the Athens National
Museum, that matches it point for point in details both of coiffure
and of physiognomy.[83] The existence of two true replicas from widely
separated geographical locations proves convincingly that the portrait type represents a woman of empire-wide significance, while the
provenance of one (figures 11–13) from the hometown of the Octavius
family in Italy strongly support the inference that that woman was
Octavia.[84] The coiffure, furthermore, closely resembles the one that
Octavia wears on the aurei of Antony from 38–37 B.C., while the
physical features and profile line correspond well to those of Octavia
on the De Quelen aureus (figure 4), although the coiffure of that
coin, with its lower-set chignon, differs slightly from that of the sculptural type. Some of Antony's aurei with inscribed reverses, including the specimen illustrated here (figure 5) also strongly resemble the
Velletri and Symrna portraits.[85] One more argument in favor of the
identification is the physical similarity of this woman to Augustus, a
family resemblance that sculptors would have had good reason to
emphasize, especially in Octavia's portrait statue of 35 B.C. That
statue, with its powerful political message, may well have been the
prototype for these two replicas. The high and full form of the *nodus*

---

[83] A. Velletri bust: Museo Nazionale Romano delle Terme, inv. 121221. Marble
bust, h. 39.5 cm., of head 21.1 cm. Felletti Maj, 1953, 51–52, no. 80; *MNR Sculture*
Vol. 1 part 1 (Rome, 1979), 340–342, no. 203 (V. Picciotti Giornetti). On the
identification, see Winkes, 1995, 68–69, fig. 15, and p. 210, no. 226. Kleiner,
Sculpture, 1992, 39, fig. 17; Bartels, 1963, 15; Poulsen, 1946, 20–22 fig. 16; Marella,
1942, 31–82.

B. Portrait from Smyrna: Athens, National Archaeological Museum no. 547. Fragmentary marble head, h. 23.5 cm. Winkes, 1995, 68, 208–209, no. 221 with earlier literature.

[84] Suet. *Aug.* 1 for the origins of the Octavii in Velitrae (ancient Velletri).

[85] *BMCRR* 2, 507, no. 144, Vol. 3 pl. 114, no. 7, Banti-Simonetti, *CNR* 2, 93, no. 1.
On the similarity of the bust to numismatic profiles, see Kleiner, *Sculpture* 1992, 39.

as it sweeps up above the forehead indicates a date in or near the time of the triumvirate for the creation of this type, since private funerary reliefs indicate that this is the older form of the fashion. Women of the first century A.D. apparently preferred a smaller and more horizontally oriented *nodus*, of the type that many of Livia's portraits display (see figures 22–23, e.g.).[86]

Just how the head from Smyrna (figures 14–15) was originally displayed is impossible to reconstruct, but the Velletri bust (figures 11–13) is more informative: the cutting of its base indicates that it was inserted into a herm.[87] This format is somewhat more honorific than a simple bust, and more appropriate for public display, although not as common as statuary for the representation of an imperial figure.[88] It is, however, a format that would allow relatively close, eye-level observation, and the sensitive, skillfully nuanced modeling of the face rewards such examination. The slender, gracefully lifted neck and calm, serious facial expression lend the subject an air of dignity, while the slight hooding of the outer corners of the eyes create a hint of melancholy, a mood entirely appropriate for the loyal but unappreciated wife of Marc Antony, and therefore exactly the sort of characterization for Octavia that partisans of Octavian and his cause would prefer. The delicate beauty of the face may or may not accurately reflect the woman's own appearance, but surely would cause most viewers to wonder why Antony could prefer Cleopatra, whose likenesses, even those in the more idealizing Hellenistic style (figure 6), represent a woman with much harsher features.[89] It is possible that viewers in at least one setting could compare and contrast likenesses of those two women readily, if, as Flory suggests, the statues of Octavia and Livia that were dedicated in the year 35 stood

---

[86] Kockel, 1993, 44–46. Kockel establishes a relative chronology for the form of this coiffure on the basis of reliefs that depict more than one woman: in these cases, when two or more women wear a *nodus* coiffure, those of the older women tend to be higher and fuller, those of the younger women smaller: e.g., a relief in the Palazzo dei Conservatori, Museo Nuovo inv. 2231, Kockel, 1993, 119–120, no. F1, pls. 31a; 32a–d; 33a–b.

[87] Marella, 1942, 33–34, figs. 1, 3; Felletti-Maj, 1953, 51, no. 80; *MNR Sculture* 1 pt. 1, 340; Bartels, 1963, 15.

[88] On publicly displayed herm-portraits of females, see Sande, 1992, 43–58; on herm format, Stähli, 1992, 147–172. The herm format was favored for portraits of literati and intellectuals rather than political figures, but could be used for public or for private display.

[89] Winkes, 1995, 73, expresses a similar reaction, noting that ancient literary sources also praise Octavia's beauty.

in the temple of Venus Genetrix. Julius Caesar had earlier dedicated a golden statue of Cleopatra in the same shrine.[90]

At the same time, however, the Velletri bust expresses the *ethos* of the ideal Roman matron that Octavia, according to her brother's propaganda, represented, in contrast to the allegely "libidinous" queen of Egypt. The *nodus* coiffure is deceptively simple in appearance; it is in fact a fashion that probably required the long labors of at least one or two ladies' maids, since it involves making two parts in the hair, combing a long section forward and then twisting it back across the crown, and also making several smaller braids that are wrapped around the chignon to fasten it into place. This, then, is the coiffure of a woman of high rank and wealth, yet also a very orderly fashion that brings the unruly forms of nature under control. On each side of the nape of the neck, however, a long and thick lock escapes from the coiffure that trails down almost to Octavia's shoulders, and introduces a note of warm spontaneity into the image, the sort of humanizing touch that the best sculptors of the Augustan era frequently used to make an image of any sort more approachable and appealing.[91] These shoulder-locks will have a long life in the iconography of other women of the Julio-Claudian family; this is their earliest appearance in a public portrait type. The careful finishing of the Velletri bust in back leaves little doubt that the rear of the head was meant to be seen, and that the sculptor of this replica devoted some care to these details.

Publicly displayed replicas of this portrait type may be relatively rare, in comparison with those, for example, of Livia, but objects made for private possession help to supplement that picture. At least three surviving gems match Octavia's sculptural portraits very closely; one is a precise replica of the Velletri type, and the other two show closely similar coiffures and virtually identical features.[92] The number of objects, again, is not large in comparison to the representation of some other imperial figures on gems, but sufficient to attest to the esteem in which some private citizens evidently held Octavia.

---

[90] Flory, 1993, 295–296. On the statue of Cleopatra: App. *BCiv.* 2.102; Dio 51.22.3.

[91] See Galinsky, 1996, 150–152, for similar observations about the processional friezes of the Ara Pacis Augustae.

[92] Winkes, 1995, 209, no. 222; p. 210, nos. 224 and 225; Vollenweider, 1974, 226, pl. 166.1–4. Vollenweider also suggests identification as Octavia for several gems that depart a little more freely from the type.

Winkes also recognizes another portrait type for Octavia that survives in only one sculpture, a work in the Von Bergen collection, but does have an exact replica in a glass cameo.[93] The coiffure here differs somewhat from that of the Velletri type, but the face shows such strong physical similarities that the case for recognizing it as the same woman is plausible. Here, the *nodus* consists not of a single loop of hair swept up from the forehead, to form a slightly asymmetrical crest, but has a more complex trefoil shape, formed by a braid at the center that begins at the hairline and is drawn up over the broader roll of hair. This type would, according to Winkes's chronology, be an even earlier portrait type than that represented by the Velletri bust, dating perhaps to the period when Octavia's marriage to Antony still appeared to be a success, since its style resembles that of many of her coin profiles. In particular, it shares with them the strongly emphasized and prominently lifted chin that helps to assimilate Octavia's appearance to that of her husband.

In the absence of other life-sized replicas, it is not possible to draw too many conclusions from this work about the style of its "Antonian" prototype, but there is a similar portrait that may be a variant on this type, although not a true replica, that Von Heintze has also recognized as Octavia.[94] (Figures 16–17). This work shares the trefoil-shaped *nodus*, and a similar, although not identical, treatment of the hair on the sides of the head. Because the back of the head is broken away, the bun is lost, but the pattern of strands that sweep up from the nape of the neck suggest that it was placed high on the occiput, as in the Velletri and Von Bergen busts. Whether or not the physiognomy is close enough for this work to represent the same individual as the Velletri type, however, is debatable. The frontal views of the heads are similar, but again, not identical. (Figures 11, 14, 16). They share slightly hooded upper eyelids and eyebrows that slope downward toward the temples, giving the face a seemingly pensive expression, and all three have slightly prominent, low-set ears,

---

[93] Marble bust in private collection, measurements not available. Winkes, 1995, 67–68, fig. 14, and pp. 214–215, no. 228, with earlier literature; Winkes also recognizes a replica of this type in a glass cameo in Geneva. Winkes, 1995, 209, no. 222; Vollenweider, 1974, 226, pl. 166.1, and 1967, Vol. 2, 194, no. 204, pl. 62.1.

[94] Fragmentary marble head, h. 14 cm., of face 10.6 cm. Von Heintze, *Fulda*, 1968, 19–20, 97, no. 13, pls. 20, 21, 110a. Winkes, 1995, 221, no. 266. Winkes is dubious of any imperial identification for this head, which he lists under the portraits attributed to Julia ("Benennung als Iulia unsicher").

a physical feature that also characterizes some of the likenesses of Augustus. On the other hand, the cheeks of the Schloss Fasanerie head appear fleshier, the bone structure less pronounced, and the overall impression of the face more child-like. (Figure 16). In profile view (figures 13, 15, 17), the similarities are more compelling. The foreheads and noses have a similar shape, although the chin of the Schloss Fasanerie head is less prominent. The smaller scale of the Schloss Fasanerie marble would easily explain all these deviations, since smaller works by their nature must receive a somewhat more freehanded execution than a one-to-one measured replica of a prototype. This little head would furthermore have most probably been a private possession, preserved in the lararium of a private citizen who had some personal reasons for devotion to the woman it represents, and in this format, we can expect to find more freedom in the interpretation of a prototype than in works made for public display. A pair of small bronzes of Augustus and Livia (figures 32–33) from Neuilly-le-Real, to be discussed in the following chapter, likewise take considerable liberties with the standard prototypes of both the emperor and his wife. If the bronzes did not bear identifying inscriptions, the identity of the Livia might be in doubt, and its place in the typology of Livia's portraits remains problematic.[95] If the Schloss Fasanerie marble (figures 16–17) does represent Octavia, then, it provides evidence of her popularity with the public that ancient authors attest; her presentation as the embodiment of the virtues of a Roman woman seems not merely to have been her brother's official line of propaganda but a widely shared public perception.

Some observers have also recognized Octavia in a marble head from an imperial group found at Béziers (figures 18–19) and in a bust in Copenhagen that resembles it closely enough to be a replica of the same prototype.[96] Here, both provenance and the existence

---

[95] Winkes, 1995, 37–38, 146, no. 73. Winkes classifies this as a replica of Livia's "Zopftyp," yet the distinguishing feature of that type, the braids that encircle the sides of the head, do not appear in this bronze, which defies classification into any of the types or groups that Winkes has catalogued. See Chapter 2 for a further discussion.

[96] Toulouse, Musée Saint-Raymond inv. 30004, marble head and neck made for insertion, h. 35 cm. Rose, 1997, 126–128 and pl. 159; Balty, 1996, 199, no. 138 (as Julia f. Augusti); Balty and Cazes, 1995, nos. 3, 54–59, figs. 19, 43–48, 51; Boschung, *JRA* 1993, 44–45, no. Ba; Clavel, 1970, 466–467, figs. 46–47; V. Poulsen, 1946, 9–10, fig. 7; Gross, 1962, 109–110; Bernoulli, 2¹, 1882–86, 113, no. 16, fig. 13; Espérandieu 1, 1907, 341–343, no. 528. For a more extensive discussion, see Wood, 1996–97, 1–19. On inv. 30004, see 4–7 and figs. 16–17.

of copies support an imperial identification: the Béziers portrait comes from a public place, a building on the forum of the ancient colony in Gaul, where it was excavated along with eight other portraits of members of the Julio-Claudian family, including securely identified likenesses of Augustus, Livia (figures 39–40), Agrippa, Tiberius, Germanicus, and Drusus II.[97] The group also includes a portrait of a child, possibly Gaius Caesar, the son of Agrippa and grandson of Augustus, but more probably one of the sons of Germanicus or Drusus II, and a problematic portrait of a woman whom some identify as Antonia Minor (figure 67), but who does not match the portrait typology of any known imperial woman.[98] This assemblage came to light amid the remains of a Roman building that was, unfortunately, never scientifically excavated, but that, given its close proximity to the forum, must have been some public structure such as a temple or basilica.[99] Information about the original placement of the Copenhagen bust is flimsier, but it seems to have come from Caere, along with portraits of Livia and Tiberius purchased at the same time, and may have belonged to an imperial group in the theater there that ranges in date from Tiberian to Claudian.[100] The Béziers group likewise must span some years, from the lifetime of Augustus

Copenhagen, Ny Carlsberg Glyptotek cat. 619, marble bust, h. 40 cm. Poulsen, *Portraits* 1, 76–77, no. 41, pls. 68–69; Erhart, 1980, 126–127 figs. 15–16.

[97] Rose, 1997, 126–128, no. 52; Balty, 1996, 196; Balty and Cazes, 1995, 8–12; Clavel, 1970, 464–499 figs. 41–60; Belhomme, 1841–1847, 277–295. Belhomme quotes two items from *L'indicateur de l'Herault* of April 12 and 19, a contemporary account of the discovery, pp. 279–282. Rose questions whether all of these portraits were in fact found together, since *L'indicateur de l'Herault* specifically mentions the discovery of only eight. However, this publication was a weekly newsmagazine for the general public, not a scholarly publication, and the omission of some information from a news item about the discoveries at Béziers is not at all surprising.

[98] Portrait of the child: Musée Saint Raymond inv. 30 008, marble, h. 27.5 cm., of face, 17.5 cm. Balty, 1996, 200, no. 139; Balty and Cazes, 1995, nos. 4, 62–69, figs. 20, 52–53, 57, 59, 61; Clavel, 1970, 468–469, figs. 51–52; Poulsen, 1946, 12, no. 6. Clavel identifies this portrait as Lucius Caesar, citing the arguments of a number of earlier authors, but concedes (p. 493) that Gaius Caesar, the older of the two brothers, had special connections to the city of Béziers. Balty proposes an identification as Agrippa Posthumus, represented in 12 B.C. at the age of one year old or less!

Problematic female portrait: Musée Saint Raymond inv. 30 005, marble, h. 25 cm. Balty 1996, 205, no. 144; Balty and Cazes, 1995, no. 9, 104–109, figs. 25, 98–99, 102, 105–6; Clavel, 1970, 472, 493, figs. 58–60; Poulsen, 1946, 9, figs. 8; 10, no. 4; 24. Polaschek, *Antonia*, 1973, 38–39, n. 62. See below, Chapter 3.

[99] Belhomme, 1841–47, 277–295; Balty and Cazes, 1995, 123; Cazes, 1994.

[100] Rose, 1997, 61, pls. 43–44; *Caere* 2, 83–85, no. 11, figs. 78–81; Poulsen, *Portraits* 1, 76–77, no. 41.

to the principate of Tiberius.[101] The portrait of Augustus belongs to one of his earliest types, and could have been set up early in his principate, at the time when Octavia enjoyed her greatest prominence as the mother of his prospective heir Marcellus.[102] The woman represented in the Béziers (figures 18–19) and Copenhagen portraits wears a *nodus* coiffure like those of Octavia's coin profiles, and she clearly cannot be Livia, who is represented by a different head at Béziers, and whose face in all of her likenesses differs considerably from the face represented here.[103]

There are, however, other possible candidates for identification with this portrait type besides Octavia: some that have been proposed are Atia, the mother of Octavian, Julia, the daughter of Augustus, or Vipsania Agrippina, the first wife of Tiberius and mother of his son Drusus II.[104] Of these, the identification with Julia today enjoys the greatest favor, and has largely supplanted that of Octavia Minor in the current literature.[105] The merits of this identification will be discussed below; suffice it here to observe that the rejection of the identification as Octavia is probably correct. The subject certainly cannot be the same as that of the Velletri type (figures 11–15): her bone structure is heavier, the eyes wider set, her lower face broader, her mouth wider and more full-lipped. In profile view, the forehead is rounded rather than straight. Unlike the Velletri bust and the related

[101] Clavel, 1970, 494–495, argues that the group must have been set up at a single date late in the principate of Augustus or early in that of Tiberius. Most more recent studies agree, however, that the portraits of Augustus and Agrippa must be earlier than those of Tiberius, his sons, and the portrait of Livia, which belongs to a Tiberian type. See Rose, 1997, 126, 128; Balty, 1996, 196; Balty and Cazes, 1995, 121–122.
[102] On the typology of the Béziers portrait of Augustus, see Balty and Cazes, 1995, no. 1, 38–40; Boschung, *Augustus*, 1993, 25–26, 107; Clavel, 1970, 465, 473–475 figs. 41–43.
[103] Toulouse, Musée Saint-Raymond inv. 30006, h. 50 cm. Balty, 1996, 204, no. 143; Balty and Cazes, 1995, 96–101, no. 8, figs. 24, 88–89, 93, 95, 97; Clavel, 1970, 465–466, 476–477, figs. 44–45; Poulsen, 1946, 8, figs. 6, 10–12, no. 5. See Chapter 2, n. 143, for fuller references.
[104] Bartels, 1963, 18, 23–24; M. Fuchs in *Caere 2*, 84. Fuchs notes that Poulsen, *Portraits* 1, 77, lists seven portraits of the same woman, but that they are not true replicas of a type, a conclusion with which I agree. See also Giuliano, 1957, 31, no. 34, pls. 13, 60, on one of Poulsen's proposed "replicas."
[105] Balty, 1996, 199, no. 138; Balty and Cazes, 1995, 58; Rose, 1997, 61, 126–128, no. 52. The identification of Toulouse Musée Saint Raymond 30 004 as Julia is the one currently given by the museum label. Winkes, however, does not include this portrait type at all in his recent corpus, either under "Octavia" or under "Julia," even in his list of mistaken attributions: see Winkes, 1995, 209–223.

sculptures, furthermore, this work demonstrates virtually no physical resemblance with Augustus.

A number of unique sculptured heads have also been identified as Octavia, on various grounds ranging from the context of their archaeological discoveries to wishful thinking. Two of the former merit consideration: a head from Glanum in France, and one from Velia in Italy, both of which were found in proximity to portraits of other Julio-Claudians.[106] The Glanum head came to light outside a temple that faced onto the forum of the ancient city, along with another marble head that unquestionably represents Livia.[107] There were two females of the imperial family with whom Livia could logically be paired: her sister-in-law, as in the statue dedications of 35 B.C., or her stepdaughter Julia, as many surviving inscriptions attest, but the coiffure of the other head from Glanum presents problems for either of those two possible identifications. Here, there is no braid drawn back along the crown of the head; instead, the hair from the *nodus* is divided into two plaits that encircle the head like a diadem, while the hair behind those braids on the sides of the head is parted into melon-like segments. The chignon rests low on the back of the head, in contrast to the Velletri (figures 11–15) and Von Bergen types, which wear the chignon quite high. The sculptor represented all these details with great care, since the head was evidently meant to be visible from all sides, and they do not match any of the variants on Octavia's coiffure that her coins or securely identified sculptural portraits attest.

The head from the much larger sculptural assemblage at Velia likewise shows braids wrapping around the sides of the head, and a chignon that not only rests low on the back of the head but hangs down toward the nape of the neck. This latter work comes from an assemblage of ten portraits, most of them recognizable as members of the imperial family, all of which were found within a single building that appears to have belonged to a medical association. This group must have taken its form over several generations, since the

---

[106] Glanum head: Saint-Remy-de-Provence, Depot, marble, h. 26.5 cm. Winkes, 1995, 223, no. 281 and Rose, 1997, 128–129, no. 53, pl. 166, with earlier literature.

Velia head: Marina di Ascea, Soprintendenza Archeologica, marble, h. 31 cm., of head 21.8 cm. Winkes, 1995, 218, no. 253; Rose, 1997, 120–121, no. 49, pls. 125–126, with earlier literature.

[107] Portrait of Livia from Glanum: Saint-Remy-de-Provence, Depot, marble, h. 22.5 cm. Winkes, 1995, 169, no. 91, and Rose, 1997, 128–129, no. 53, pl. 167.

figures represented range in date from the principate of Augustus to
that of Claudius. Here again, since the Augustan phase of the group
includes likenesses of Gaius Caesar, Lucius Caesar, and Livia, the
unidentified female could logically be either Julia I, the mother of
the two young men, or their aunt Octavia. Yet the coins of neither
of those women show this specific variant of the *nodus* coiffure. Julia's
coins and tokens from Rome (figure 19) all show the version of the
nodus coiffure in which a single braid runs from front to back along
the crown of the head.[108] Some of Julia's provincial coin profiles do
appear to show braids encircling the head, but they never show the
long, thick escaping strands that trail from the chignon down each
side of the neck in the Velia sculpture.[109]

Women can, of course, wear variations on their favorite hairstyles,
and copyists could and did frequently embellish or alter official prototypes, as the more abundant and securely identified portraits of
Livia will attest. Both the Glanum and the Velia heads, however,
also display physical differences from the Velletri type that are more
difficult to explain. The Glanum head shares with both replicas of
that type elements of the profile line, such as a high, straight forehead, a nose with a slightly arched bridge, and retreating lower lip.
In frontal view, it also shows slightly hooded eyes, a narrow nose
and small but gracefully formed mouth. The lower face, however,
appears broader and fleshier than that of the Velletri head, and the
eyebrows, rather than sloping downward, have a strong upward flare
toward the temples, a treatment that gives the face a look of energy
and authority quite different from the pensive mood of the Velletri
type. The proud lift and turn of the head, and the upward direction of the gaze, complement the bolder treatment of the features,
suggesting that the intention of the artist in this public work is to
characterize the woman as a figure of formidable character and dignity. Given the great variety of Octavia's coin profiles, none of these
variations is unthinkable in her likenesses, but combined with the
anomalous hairstyle, they add up to serious evidence against the

---

[108] Winkes, 1995, 223, no. 281, lists the Glanum head as "fälschlich Iulia genannten
antiken Bildnisse" on the grounds that its coiffure does not match her coin portraits, and the Velia head, p. 218, no. 253, under "fälschlich Octavia genannten
antiken Porträts" for the same reason.

[109] Coins of Livia and Julia from Pergamon: Sutherland and Kraay, 1975, pl. 29,
nos. 1229–1234; *BMC Mysia* 139, nos. 248–249, pl. 28, fig. 6; Cohen, 1880, 1,
180; Gross, 1962, 35–36, pls. 4, 6–8.

identification. The Velia head likewise shares some similarities of profile line with the Velletri type, but has a much longer face, with a heavier and more rectangular jaw-line. Not only does it differ from the Velletri type, but it differs so much from the Glanum head as to raise doubts whether both could represent the same woman: the Velia head has more prominent, heavy-lidded eyes, and a much broader mouth than the sculpture from Glanum.

But if the Glanum and Velia portraits do not represent Octavia or Julia, who else could they be? Scholars of portraiture have tended to assume that discovery of a portrait head in the same archaeological context as identifiable imperial likenesses constitutes conclusive proof of imperial rank, but this may not always be a justified inference. We should perhaps consider the possibility that portraits of prominent local citizens could sometimes have stood in the same general vicinity as imperial statues—not, obviously, in the same groups, but perhaps in different parts of the same buildings or public spaces— and that statues could often find their way, through deliberate disposal, concealment in times of emergency, accidental falls, or re-use as building materials, into a deposit of fragments that did not originally belong together. As Rose observes, the two female portraits from Glanum differ from eachother enough to suggest that they were not set up at the same time or in the same type of setting: the Livia is left unfinished in back, as though destined to stand in a niche where the back of the head would never be seen, but the other female head is fully finished, as though intended to stand in the open. In view of the fact that the two heads came from an open public square rather than a building, then, it is possible that they belonged to two separate dedications of statuary, and happened to be found together by chance. The proximity of the Velia heads is more difficult to explain, since they were clearly located within a specific structure, the cryptoporticus of a semi-public building, but again, it is not impossible that a group of imperial portraits and likenesses of prominent local citizens might have been housed under the same roof, although not in immediate proximity to each other, and that when the building collapsed in ruins, those statues might have fallen into the same lower level of the structure, or that in late antiquity, portraits from the "pagan" past could have been removed from display and placed indiscriminately together in the basement levels of buildings.[110] Portrait

---

[110] A statue of Julia Domna from Ostia appears to have been deliberately buried

statues of prominent private citizens who paid for the construction
of public buildings, like Eumachia of Pompeii or the Nonius family
of Herculaneum, could and did appear in those buildings. Although
there is no direct evidence that imperial groups appeared in those
same structures, it is entirely possible that such statues originally
stood in the Porticus of Eumachia, and were later salvaged by the sur-
vivors of the disaster of A.D. 79.[111] Livia in particular would have
been a very likely subject for representation, since the building appears
to have been modeled on the Porticus Liviae in Rome, and Eumachia
may well have been self-consciously modeling herself on the first lady
of the empire with this dedication.[112] Eumachia's own statue stood
in a more protected area in a cryptoporticus that was less accessible to the diggers, but appears to have been aligned with the niche
that probably held Livia's statue. The private citizen would never
have appeared in direct proximity with statues of gods or members
of the imperial family, but her portrait could stand within the same
building as theirs. The excavation of a portrait with recognizable
likenesses of the imperial family, then, may constitute strong evidence that it too represents an imperial figure, but without the additional evidence of replicas or comparison with coin profiles, such a
provenance is not sufficient evidence by itself of imperial status.

The most reliable information for Octavia's public images, then,
comes from the two replicas of the Velletri type (figures 11–15), and
prior to 35 B.C., from coin profiles. One thing is clear from these
works: although she might by implication and by juxtaposition be
identified with Ariadne, Athena, or Amphitrite, such divine associations do not extend to her personal costume or appearance. Her
hairstyle in all these likenesses is the strictly contemporary *nodus*.
Visual allusion, when it is present in her images, emphasizes only
family connections, to her husband or to her brother. That fact, in turn,

---

in late antiquity, probably to protect it from destruction: see D. Kleiner, *Sculpture*,
1992, 326, 327, fig. 291, 354 with literature; Bieber, 1977, 166, figs. 740–41; Calza,
1977, 50–51, no. 63, pls. 49–50.

[111] Nonius family group at Herculaneum: On the Balbus family group: Deiss,
1985, 158–66; Barker, 1908, 155–57, figs. 12, 14. On the female statues: Polaschek,
1972, 162–164; Bieber, 1977, 150, pl. 116, figs. 683–687.

Building of Eumachia at Pompeii: Mau, 1902, 110–118, figs. 45–50, statue of
Eumachia, pp. 112, 445–46, fig. 255; MacDonald, 1986, 165, fig. 149; Richardson,
1988, 194–98, fig. 31. On the statue of Eumachia, see Hanfmann, 1975, 83–84,
no. 52, with earlier literature. The statue is more ideal than portrait-like, but the
inscription establishes its intended identity.

[112] Kleiner and Matheson, 1996, 33–34.

casts a surprising light on the propaganda and policies of Antony, whom Octavian accused of adopting a decadently "eastern" mode of life, and of aspiring to Hellenistic-style kingship.[113] The ivy wreath and Dionysiac emblems on his cistophoroi from Asia could indeed suggest the quasi-divine status of a monarch, but the uncompromising verism of his own portraits and, later, those of Cleopatra, and the relatively modest presentation of Octavia should caution us against accepting too readily the conventional wisdom that Antony lost the battle for the "hearts and minds" of the Roman people through his flamboyantly Hellenistic behavior and policies. How directly he controlled the decisions of mint-masters in Pergamon and Miletus is difficult to ascertain, but if he gave explicit permission for the coin types on which he wears an ivy crown, he was perhaps displaying more respect for local customs and beliefs than personal megalomania.

In identifying himself as "New Dionysus," he was far from alone among his contemporaries, as he himself pointed out in an aggrieved letter to Octavian in which he accused the latter of having taken part in a costume-banquet at which he and the other guests impersonated the twelve gods.[114] A recent analysis of that notorious party has suggested that it was none other than Augustus's marriage banquet, at which he, his bride Livia and her former husband enacted a comic and undoubtedly rather blasphemous parody of the *amours* and adulteries of the gods.[115] Octavian had at least the discretion to do this in private among like-minded friends, although the story leaked out and caused considerable indignation. His portrayal of himself as the defender of traditional Roman values against the "eastern" decadence of Antony and Cleopatra, however, succeeded only because he won the war, not vice versa.

Coin Portraits: Julia

Only one issue of coins from the mint of Rome unquestionably bears the likeness of the emperor's daughter Julia.[116] (Figure 20). One other issue from the same year may introduce her features into a profile

---

[113] Plut. *Vit.Ant.* 54.3–6, e.g.

[114] Suet. *Aug.* 69.2–70.2.

[115] Flory, 1988, 352–359.

[116] Banti-Simonetti, *CNR* 8, 243–245, nos. 1–4; *RIC* 1² 72, nos. 404, 405, pl. 7; *BMCRE* 1, 21, no. 106, pl. 4, fig. 3.

of the goddess Diana, but this hypothesis remains controversial and unconvincing.[117] Local coinages of the Greek east are, as usual, more receptive than the official mint in Rome to an open acknowledgement of Julia's role in Augustus's dynastic plans, and so she appears in larger and more detailed profiles on coins of Pergamon (figure 21), Ephesus and, possibly, of north Africa in association with the likenesses of Augustus, of her first husband Marcellus, her second husband Agrippa, and her stepmother Livia.[118] The Pergamene coins (figure 21) bear inscriptions that explicitly identify Livia with Hera and Julia with Aphrodite, thus associating the entire imperial household with Hellenistic traditions of divine kingship. The identification of Julia with Aphrodite, the equivalent of the Roman Venus whom the Julians claimed as ancestress, emphasizes Julia's role as the mortal *genetrix* of the Julian line, and probably refers specifically to the recent births of her sons.[119] None of these coins, from Rome or from the provinces, give much secure information about her appearance beyond the fact that she, like the older women of her family, wore the *nodus* coiffure. They are, however, useful evidence for her role in official propaganda and ideology.

One of Augustus's reforms aimed ostensibly at the restitution of the Roman republic was the revival of the mint of Rome, which once again issued gold and silver coins bearing the names of the responsible officials from the years 19 through 12 B.C.[120] These officials continued to produced coinage in bronze in the smaller denominations until 5 B.C.[121] During the period of the civil wars, Roman coins had been struck wherever they were needed for the payment of the warring armies, and frequently bore the names only of the triumvir under whose authority they had been minted, not of the city or the subordinate official in charge of monetary policy. The

---

[117] Banti-Simonetti, *CNR* 8, 177–180, nos. 1–4; *RIC* 1² 72, no. 403 pl. 7; *BMCRE* 1, 21, nos. 104–105, pl. 42, fig. 2; Winkes, 1995, 77.

[118] Coins of Livia and Julia from Pergamon: Sutherland and Kraay, 1975, pl. 29, nos. 1229–1234; *BMC Mysia* 139, nos. 248–249, pl. 28, fig. 6; Cohen 1, 1880, 180; Gross, 1962, 29–30, pl. 4, figs. 6–8. *RPC* 2359, p. 402.

Coin of Julia and Agrippa from Ephesus: Cohen 1, 1880, 180.

Coin, possibly from north Africa, with reverse type of confronted male and female heads, possibly Marcellus and Julia: Banti-Simonetti, *CNR* 3, 183–184, nos. 1 and 1/1.

[119] De Grazia-Vanderpool, 1994, 285. Rose, 1997, 13, 25.

[120] *RIC* 1² 31–34, 61–74, nos. 278–419; *BMCRE* 1, 1–28, nos. 1–133; Fullerton, 1985, 473.

[121] *RIC* 1², 74–78, nos. 420–468; *BMCRE* 1, 28–50, nos. 134–270.

restoration of the authority and dignity of the offices of the *tresviri monetales*, the three elected officials in charge of coinage, was therefore a highly symbolic reestablishment of a more democratic tradition, but as with so many of Augustus's revivals of republican practices, he used it for his own aggrandizement. Virtually every issue of coins from the reestablished mint of Rome refers directly or indirectly to Augustus, his policies, his political accomplishments, or his status as the son of the deified Caesar. The *tresviri monetales*, rather than the emperor himself, undoubtedly had the most direct say in determining the types of these coins: the rich variety of types and images, which change with every year and from moneyer to moneyer within any given year indicate that these officials, like their Republican predecessors, either chose or were required to differentiate their issues clearly from one another and that this necessity caused them to invent types with a considerable degree of originality.[122] These ambitious young men, all presumably hoping for eventual Senatorial careers, obviously understood however that a patriotic emphasis on the achievements of the head of state could only help them, while it is most unlikely that any coin could have been allowed to leave the mint if it somehow failed to reflect official policy.[123]

The *aurei* and *denarii* of 13–12 B.C., among the very latest issues from the mint of Rome under Augustus, introduce a new theme: the intended heirs of Augustus, Gaius and Lucius Caesar, and their parents Agrippa and Julia I. Fullerton has analyzed the significance of these issues in detail, and so no more than a brief summary of his conclusions is necessary here.[124] Events in 13 B.C. converged to make dynastic plans a pressing concern for Augustus, when the death of Agrippa left him without an adult male associate capable of immediately assuming the burdens of leadership in the event of his own death. Gaius and Lucius would succeed to power eventually according to his plans, but they were both still very young children. Augustus could not assume, therefore, that his intentions would be self-evident to the Senate, which had conferred all of his powers and offices on him and had the power either to confer them on or withhold them from future claimants to authority. It was now of vital importance to make his plans for Gaius and Lucius unmistakably clear in every

---

[122] C.V.H. Sutherland in *RIC* 1², 32–33.
[123] Pollini, 1990, 339.
[124] Fullerton, 1985, 473–483 pls. 55–57.

medium available: in ceremonial events like the "Trojan games," in which Gaius Caesar, although he was very young, participated, and in public monuments like the Ara Pacis that celebrate the imperial family with an ostentatious emphasis on its children.[125] The repetition of pairs of mythological children in the east and west friezes of the same monument—the two children in the lap of the personification on the east facade (figure 31), the twins Romulus and Remus, the two young camilli who assist Aeneas at his sacrifice to his household gods—could hardly help but remind a Roman viewer that the emperor was blessed with two male heirs of his own blood, as well as with two adult stepsons, his wife's children, both of whom were capable generals and had already been groomed for succession.[126] By ordering Julia to remarry to Tiberius in 12 B.C., Augustus made it clear that if necessary, Tiberius was to succeed him in the immediate future, although Gaius and Lucius would, according to his plans, come to power when they were old enough.

The medium most able to reach a large, widespread audience with all these messages was coinage, and so on an issue of *denarii* of 13–12 (figure 20), we encounter perhaps the clearest statement of dynastic intention in any medium. Augustus' own portrait appears on the obverses of these coins, bareheaded and accompanied by one or more of the priestly implements that mark his newly acquired status as chief priest, *pontifex maximus*, of the state religion.[127] Some of the coins place the *lituus*, or crook-like priest's staff, behind his head; others add the *simpulum*, or water pitcher for ritual purification. One, the coin on which only the *lituus* appears, bears the simple inscription *Augustus*: just one title, but his single most important one.[128] The other (figure 20) identifies him as "*Augustus Divi F[ilius]*," Augustus the son of the Deified [Julius Caesar].[129] In both cases, he bears the

---

[125] Dio 54.26.1 on the Troy games; Fullerton, 1985, 481. Although I disagree with Fullerton's acceptance of the identification of the two long-haired boys wearing torques as Gaius and Lucius Caesar, I agree that the emphasis on children in the Ara Pacis, on the coins of the same year, and in the Troy games constitute a coherent program. For a recent discussion of the problem of identifying Gaius and Lucius Caesar on the Ara Pacis, see Pollini, 1987, 21–28. I agree with Pollini that the long-haired children are probably not Romans but foreign princes, and that the child of the north frieze, figure no. 37, is probably Gaius Caesar.

[126] See Spaeth, 1994, 89–90.

[127] On Augustus's assumption of the office of Pontifex Maximus in 13 B.C., Suet. *Aug.* 31.1; *Res Gestae Divi Augusti* 10.2.

[128] *RIC* 1² 72, no. 404; *BMCRE* 1, 21, no. 106, pl. 4, fig. 3. On significance of the title "Augustus:" Suet. *Aug.* 7.2.

[129] *RIC* 1² 72, no. 405; *BMCRE* 1, 22, nos. 108–109, pl. 4, fig. 5.

marks primarily of his human status, as "first citizen," but the issue of coins that mention his status as Julius Caesar's son calls attention to his glorious lineage, and by extension, that of his own child and grandchildren. On the reverses of these two issues appear three tiny busts, lined up facing to the right. In the center is a woman with the *nodus* coiffure flanked by two young boys. Above the woman's head hovers the oak crown, one of the honors granted to Augustus. It is the military decoration awarded to a soldier who has saved the life of a fellow Roman citizen in battle, but in Augustus's case the award had a broader meaning, honoring him as the savior of the state, of not just one fellow citizen but all of them, and it became one of the permanent insignia of his power, and that of subsequent emperors.[130] Here, it is the badge both of Augustus's power and of the moral authority that justifies it, and its placement over the head of his daughter expresses, in the simple and compact language of coin-type imagery, the transmission of that power through his daughter to his grandsons and chosen heirs.

Both these issues bear the name of the moneyer C. Marius of the Tromentina tribe (C.MARIUS TRO III VIR). This same man also issued *denarii* with a reverse type of the goddess Diana with her divine attributes, a diadem and quiver of arrows, but also with features that differ enough from ideal type to appear very portrait like. Those features, with the long, slightly arched nose, thin lips and small chin, closely resemble those of Augustus on the obverse of the same coin, prompting the conclusion by many that the face must be that of Augustus's daughter Julia, who naturally displays a family resemblance to her father which die-cutters and portraitists in all media would wish to emphasize.[131] The identification, however, presents several problems. First, while the face has portrait-like features, the coiffure is not the *nodus* that appears on Julia's bust on the issue on which she appears with her two sons, or on provincial coinages. "Diana" wears her hair drawn down severely alongside the face,

---

[130] Corona Civica: Dio 51.19.5; *Res Gestae* 34.2. Coins from Spain and of Rome associate the oak crown with the words OB CIVIS SERVATOS, sometimes abbreviated O C S ("For saving citizens"): *RIC* 1^2 43, nos. 29a, 29b, 30a, 30b; 44, nos. 40a, 40b; 47, nos. 76a–79b; 62, nos. 278–279; 63, no. 302. *BMCRE* 1, 2, nos. 5–6, pl. 1, figs. 3–4; 7, no. 35, pl. 1, fig. 18; 26, no. 126 pl. 4, fig. 15; 29, no. 134, pl. 18, fig. 1; 30, nos. 139–140, pl. 18, fig. 2; 57, no. 314, pl. 5, fig. 19; 58, no. 317, pl. 6, fig. 2; 60, nos. 330–331, pl. 6, figs. 10, 11; 66, nos. 376–378, pl. 8, figs. 6, 7; 67, nos. 381–383, pl. 8, figs. 8–9.
[131] Fullerton, 1985, 476–477; Banti-Simonetti, *CNR* 3, 177–180, nos. 1–4; *RIC* 1^2, 72, no. 403; *BMCRE* 1, 21, nos. 104–105, pl. 4, fig. 2.

then pulled back to a small, tight bun (a fashion not dissimilar to those of women of the first century B.C.), but no *nodus* over the forehead. There is an ornament over her forehead that produces a similar visual effect, but it is clearly a jewel or flower of some sort attached to her diadem, not part of her coiffure.[132] The hairstyle displays another oddity, a sort of flap or loop of hair hanging down over the ear that almost resembles the ear-flap of a hat, and gives the goddess's hair the appearance of an artificial wig. Another problem is the nature of the goddess Diana in Roman religion: a virgin goddess of the wild countryside. Julia, whose primary claim to public importance was her fertility, would have been a somewhat incongruous object of identification with Diana. Fullerton suggests that the choice alludes specifically to her husband Agrippa, who first distinguished himself against Sextus Pompeius at the battle of Naulochos, a battle in which he and Augustus claimed to have been protected by their patron goddess Diana. The identification of the wife of one and daughter of the other with their mutual divine patron would thus emphasize the multiple connections of these two men, through their accomplishments, their alliance, their public merit, and their familial bonds.

There is another explanation of the portrait-like "Diana" that I find somewhat more convincing: that the goddess bears the features not of Julia but of Augustus himself.[133] The goddess would thus become "Diana Augusta," not the emperor in the form of the goddess but the goddess subtly assimilated to the emperor. The difficulty for the die cutter of combining a man's well known portrait features with a female coiffure might explain some of the oddities of the coiffure, in particular its wig-like quality.

We are left, then, with only one clear official image of Julia I on coins from the capital city: the tiny bust on the issues in which she appears with Gaius and Lucius Caesar (figure 20). These images are too small to have legible portrait faces, but they do at least demonstrate that Julia wore the same modest, neatly controlled coiffure as the women of the older generation of her family, Octavia Minor, and Livia, under whose strict discipline she had been raised. She wears her chignon somewhat lower than they do, hanging down over the nape, but appears to share with them the braid drawn back

---

[132] Winkes, 1995, 77, makes a similar observation.
[133] Pollini, 1990, 353–355.

along the center of the crown.[134] The tiny scale of the busts does
not allow for the observation of any other distinguishing details. The
evidence for her association with any divinity on coins produced
under the direct authority of the emperor remains highly questionable. Even on the Pergamene coins that name her "Julia Aphrodite,"
(figure 21) her portrait wears the *nodus* coiffure: the die cutters could
inscribe any divine epithets they pleased, perhaps, but for the face
of the emperor's daughter, the only prototypes available to them
portrayed her in a strictly mortal guise. Her portraits and those of
Livia on the obverse do show some effort to individualize the two
women: on the best preserved specimen available for study, in the
British Museum, both women have rather low foreheads and sharply
jutting noses, rather than the idealized profile of goddesses and
personifications in which the forehead and nose form a single line,
an elegant simplification rarely seen in nature, while Livia's mature
age is subtly suggested by her slightly fleshier chin line.[135] Livia
appears to wear either braids or a fillet around her head, just behind
the soft roll of waves around her face, and an escaping strand of
hair at the nape of the neck, while Julia's coiffure lacks these elements. Both women wear the *nodus* coiffure, but this time without
the braid drawn back along the crown of the head; instead, the hair
from the topknot seems to be divided into two segments and drawn
down around the face.

In addition to coins, Julia's likenesses, with identifying inscriptions,
appear on a few other objects of similar nature. In Rome, some
small, lead theater tokens have been discovered that show a woman
with a profile strikingly similar in shape to that of Augustus, and
wearing the same *nodus* coiffure that appears on the tiny busts of
Julia on the coins of 13–12 B.C. Here, the braid that runs from
front to back along the crown is much more clearly visible, and
braids around the side of the head just as clearly absent. The inscription (IU)LIA AUGUSTI identifies her as Julia the daughter of
Augustus, which the family resemblance would bear out.[136] A bone
gaming token from Oxyrhynchos, now in Alexandria, likewise represents a woman wearing a *nodus* coiffure, and on its reverse the

[134] Winkes, 1995, 77.
[135] *BMC Mysia* 139, no. 248, pl. 28, fig. 6. *RPC* 2359, p. 402.
[136] Winkes, 1995, 220, no. 264; Grimm, 1973, 279, n. 4 with earlier literature,
pl. 87.2; *EAA* 3 (1960) 921, fig. 1150, s.v. "Giulia." (C. Pietrangeli).

inscription ΙΟΥΛΙΑ. The features of this little object, however, are too simplified and idealized to offer much assistance in reconstruction Julia's appearance, or even in determining which woman who bore the name of Julia it represents. The subject could also be Livia, who assumed the name Julia Augusta in A.D. 14, after Augustus adopted her in his will into the Julian family, and Winkes attributes this little token to her, rather than to Augustus's daughter, on the grounds that the long locks of hair that hang to the shoulders have closer parallels in Livia's portraits.[137]

Julia: the Problem of the Sculptural Portraits

At present, the most widely accepted identification of Julia in sculpture is the portrait type discussed above that survives in two replicas, one from Béziers (figures 18–19), the other apparently from Caere. This type, briefly discussed above, therefore merits renewed examination here. Both surviving replicas represent their subject as a mature woman, with plump cheeks and "Venus rings" across her throat, although according to the conventions of Augustan and Julio-Claudian sculpture, no lines interrupt the skin surfaces of the face. She has a rather broad, squarish and large-boned face, slightly hooded eyes, and a wide, full-lipped mouth. All of these features give her portrait a pronounced resemblance to that of Agrippa, whose portrait appeared with her in the Béziers group. As the wife of Agrippa, Julia's portraits might conceivably have been assimilated to his in much the same way that Octavia's were to Antony's, and as Livia's later would be to those of Augustus.[138] In the case of the emperor's daughter, however, we must ask ourselves to whom her portraits are most likely to have shown a resemblance. Her most vital role in the imperial family was as the bearer of Augustus's bloodline, and as the mother of his prospective heirs. Would the artists who created her official prototype, and the copyists who duplicated them, have minimized that resemblance in favor of assimilation of her likeness to that of Agrippa? If so, then their treatment of her portraits would

---

[137] Winkes, 1995, 38, 81, no. 1, with earlier literature; Grimm, 1973, 279–282, pls. 86–87, for identification as Julia.

[138] Balty, 1996, 199, no. 138, and Balty and Cazes, 1995, 58, cite the "stylistic" resemblance of this head to the portrait of Agrippa in the same group as evidence for identification with Julia.

have differed dramatically from their representations of her sons Gaius and Lucius Caesar, whose images are so closely modeled on that of Augustus that controversy still continues as to whether some types represent Gaius Caesar or Octavian as a young man.[139] The woman, furthermore, looks considerably more mature than the standard images both of Augustus and of Livia, whose official portraits rarely seem to show an age beyond the early thirties. One would expect portraits of other members of the emperor's immediate family to follow the same idealizing convention. Otherwise, if the Béziers and Copenhagen replicas are faithful to their type, we are left with the odd mental image of portrait groups in which the emperor's daughter would have appeared to be older than both her father and her stepmother.

The lack of family resemblance to Augustus is one point against the identification of this head as Julia. Another is its close technical affinities to a portrait of Livia in the same group (figures 39–40) that belongs to a type of the time of Tiberius.[140] The portraits of both women are carefully finished in back, unlike some of the male portraits in the same assemblage, and share technical details of finishing like the form of the tool-marks on the insertion plugs that originally connected them to statues. If these two works are contemporaneous, however, the problematic head cannot be Julia, whose presence would be possible only before 2 B.C.

In my opinion, although it remains a minority point of view, there is a strong case to be made for identification of the Béziers type as Vipsania Agrippina, the daughter of Agrippa by his first marriage, the first wife of Tiberius, and the mother of his son Drusus II.[141] Prior to her death, during her second marriage to Asinius Gallus, it would have been less than tactful to include Vipsania Agrippina's image in official groups, where it would have constituted an embarrassing reminder that Tiberius had given her up unwillingly and had reason to resent her remarriage. After her death in A.D. 20, however, she could have been included without offense to anyone as an honored ancestor, the mother of Drusus II and grandmother of Tiberius

---

[139] Galinsky, 1996, 166–169; Pollini, 1987, 59–75. On the assimilation of all Julio-Claudian males to Augustus, see Massner, 1982, passim.

[140] Winkes, 1995, 48, 181, no. 104, with earlier literature; Freyer-Schauenburg, 1982, 220–224, on the dating of this head and its replicas.

[141] Bartels, 1963, 23, first advanced this identification; my own reasons for accepting it will be discussed in more detail in chapter 4. See also Wood, 1996–97, 5–7.

Gemellus, and have taken an appropriate place near the statue of her
father Agrippa. She, along with Livia, would demonstrate the lineage
of Drusus II, the son of Tiberius who could trace his ancestry through
his mother to Augustus's great general Agrippa. The female portrait
in question displays telling resemblances not only to Agrippa, but to
the portrait of Drusus II in the same group, and to the child that
may be his son Tiberius Gemellus, but she shares none of the characteristic features either of the Julians or of the Claudians.

The major objection to this identification is the existence of another
type with a very different coiffure that may represent Vipsania Agrippina (figures 72–73). A head of this type came to light in the Old
Forum of Leptis Magna, where inscriptions attest the existence of a
Julio-Claudian family group of the year A.D. 23 in which the two
young princes who had recently died, Germanicus and Drusus II,
appeared side by side in chariots, accompanied by their mothers and
wives.[142] Vipsania Agrippina was definitely present in that group, and
the head of a woman with severely straight hair, parted simply in the
middle and drawn back to a low bun at the nape, has a good claim
to be her image. The existence of another replica from Russellae
confirms that the subject must have been a woman of the imperial
family.[143] Although the Leptis-Russellae type differs in coiffure from
the Béziers-Copenhagen portraits, however, the physical features show
no discrepancies, and the two types could well represent the same
woman at different times in her life. Both represent a woman with
a rather heavy bone structure, hooded eyes, a wide, fleshy mouth
with distinctive folds of flesh at the corners, and severely straight
hair, a rather unusual feature in Roman portraiture. The more old-
fashioned *nodus* coiffure, perhaps, belongs to portraits of the time of
her marriage to Tiberius; that with the middle part, from her later
marriage to Asinius Gallus. The identification of these two types
need not, then, be mutually exclusive.

Boschung has recently attempted to revive the identification of the

---

[142] On the group at Leptis Magna: Aurigemma, 1940, 22–26 on dating and reconstruction of the form of the group, 66, figs. 45–46 on the head identified as
Vipsania Agrippina; Trillmich, 1988, 51–56, on the epigraphic evidence for dating
precisely to the year 23, shortly after the death of Drusus II. See Chapter 4 for
more extensive discussion.
[143] Boschung, *JRA* 1993, 58–59, no. Ma. The Rusellae group is unpublished, but
I am most indebted to the curators and staff of the Museo Nazionale di Grosetto
for permitting me to examine it.

Béziers-Copenhagen type as Octavia, and to attribute to Julia another of the portraits in the Béziers group, the head cited above that most scholars recognize as a Tiberian portrait of Livia (figures 39–40).[144] This proposal, however, remains a minority opinion. None of Julia's coin or token likenesses represent her hair parted in the middle, but coins of Livia from the principate of her son Tiberius do, as does her earlier relief portrait on the Ara Pacis (figure 30). Some of the replicas of this type are quite idealized, but others, *pace* Boschung, do conform well with the physiognomy of Livia's earlier portrait types.

De Grazia-Vanderpool, finally, has recently made a plausible case for recognizing Julia in a fragmentary marble head from Corinth, where her image might have accompanied a statuary group of very fine quality that definitely included Augustus with his two grandsons.[145] The version of the *nodus* coiffure that this portrait wears, so far as it is preserved, is almost identical to that of the one securely identified type of Octavia, a style that would be a little old-fashioned for Julia, but not impossible for her: the hair is drawn up from the forehead in a soft, full topknot, then swept across and tucked under a little to the proper right of the middle of the head. The hair around the face is drawn back in soft strands indicated by S-curves incised on the marble; unlike Octavia's portraits, this head also seems to show a thin fillet that encircles the head just behind this area of waves. The face itself has some individualizing features like the long, thin nose with a slight bend high on the bridge, and its slightly hooded upper eyelids, but the proportions of the long, fleshy oval face with its full, pouty lips look suspiciously like those of ideal Classical sculpture, to which local craftsmen may have added a contemporary coiffure and a few individualizing features based on scanty knowledge of the subject's actual appearance. The possibility also cannot be ruled out that this is a provincial, rather free replica of Octavia's Velletri-Smyrna portrait, although the differences in the

---

[144] Boschung, *JRA* 1993, 44–45, no. Ba (Béziers-Copenhagen type) and 49–50 figs. 17–18, no. Ea on the type he attributes to Julia. The latter is the type identified and discussed by Freyer-Schauenburg, 1982, 209–224 and Winkes, 1995, 48–49.

[145] De Grazia-Vanderpool, 1994, 285. Photographs of this portrait are unfortunately not yet available for publication, but will appear in De Grazia-Vanderpool, forthcoming 1999. This is the only sculptural portrait of Julia that Winkes accepts as a secure identification: Winkes, 1995, 221, no. 265. On the portraits of Gaius and Lucius Caesar from Corinth, see Pollini, 1987, passim, esp. 56–57, 83–84, 99, no. 14, 107, no. 38.

treatment of the mouth and chin do not allow for a certain identification of it as a member of that type. No other exact replicas of
the Corinth head have, to my knowledge, been discovered. We have
not, therefore, identified a portrait type for Julia as yet, but only
one object that may have been intended to represent her.

   To say that the problem of Julia's sculptural images is frustrating
is to put it mildly. Surely they must have existed, and in large enough
numbers for some to have survived, but where are they? The surviving inscriptions may at least offer us some guidance on where to
look, since all of them come from sites in the Greek-speaking east.
The museums and excavation sites of these areas may eventually
yield evidence that will allow the recognition of Julia not just in one
isolated image but in a coherent portrait type. We are left in the
meantime, however, with the conclusion that embarrassment and
sympathy for the imperial family could have been an even more
powerfully destructive force than an officially mandated *damnatio memoriae*, a punishment that Julia never received. No one would have
been legally obliged to destroy her images, but thrifty patrons looking for re-usable material would have had every motive to appropriate and recut them, where other members of public groups would
have been protected from such mistreatment by respect for their
memories and reputations. Julia was the first, although certainly not
the last, Julio-Claudian woman whose sexual and political conduct,
when finally exposed, proved her public image of respectable matronly
virtue to be a fraud, and centuries after her death she was still the
object of jokes that showed how her conduct undermined and thwarted
her father's patriarchal authority.[146] The absence of her sculptural
images speaks volumes of the nature of male power in the Roman
family—and of its limits.

---

[146] Macrobius, *Sat.* 2.4.31–2.5.8; Richlin, 1992, 65–91.

CHAPTER TWO

LIVIA

Biographical Information

Livia Drusilla was the wife of the emperor Augustus, the mother of his successor Tiberius, great-grandmother of Gaius "Caligula" Caesar, grandmother of Claudius, and great-great grandmother of Nero. In purely genealogical terms, she, even more than Augustus, can be seen as the founder and ancestor of the Julio-Claudian dynasty. (See Appendix, chart no. 3). Furthermore, though she died during the principate of Tiberius, all these future emperors but Nero would have known her and been influenced by her powerful personality, and all would have had reason to celebrate her as part of their family tree. Livia's numerous and richly diverse portraits did not owe their prominence, however, solely to an official line of propaganda emanating from the ruling emperors. She seems to have enjoyed the genuine affection of many people and provincial cities throughout the empire, many of which bestowed honors on her that had not yet received official sanction. The evidence that the visual arts offer of her popularity stands in contrast to her harsh portrayal in written histories, especially in the *Annals* of Tacitus.

Both Livia and Octavian (later Augustus) had been married before their marriage to one another, but precipitously divorced their respective spouses when they met in 38 B.C.[1] The couple was too impatient even to wait for the birth of Livia's second son by her husband, Ti. Nero Drusus, but began to cohabit immediately, while Livia was still pregnant. Octavian may have had political as well as personal motives for this match, which provided him with an ally from one of Rome's noblest families, and one for whose intelligence and political skill he demonstrated respect throughout their marriage. The couple may well have had the full cooperation and acquiescence of the first husband of Livia, Ti. Nero, who apparently even "gave

---

[1] On Augustus' marriages: Dio 48.34.3; Suet. *Aug.* 62.2 and 69.1; Tac. *Ann.* 1.10.

away" the bride at the celebration of their marriage, and then took
part in a comic parody of the loves of the gods in which Octavian,
dressed as Apollo, stole away Juno from her husband Jupiter.[2] Their
unorthodox conduct provided Marc Antony with a counter-charge
to Octavian's accusations of immoral behavior with Cleopatra, and
scandal-mongers with ammunition even many years later.[3] Despite
its indiscreet beginning, however, the marriage remained stable, and
apparently happy for the remaining fifty-two years of Augustus's life.
It is of course pointless to speculate on the private emotions of persons in antiquity, but the relevant point for a study of public images
is that Augustus and Livia succeeded throughout their married life
in presenting an appearance of marital concord. Even though Livia's
earlier marriage was common knowledge, two Augustan poets even
write of her as a sort of honorary *univira*, a woman who has been
married only once and therefore enjoys special ritual purity: Ovid
observes that no husband but Augustus would have been worthy of
her, while Horace describes her, while she performs sacred rituals,
as "a woman rejoicing in only one husband."[4] Augustus' last words
as recorded by Suetonius were an affectionate farewell to Livia:
"Livia, nostri coniugii memor, vive ac vale!" ("Livia, live mindful of
our marriage, and farewell"), although Tacitus's very different account
of Augustus's death might imply that this quotation, a carefully composed hexameter verse, is one of those "last words" concocted after
the fact for the benefit of the living.[5] The one disappointment of
their marriage was their failure to produce heirs, since Livia's only
pregnancy by Augustus ended in miscarriage. Despite the sterility
of their marriage, however, Augustus remained married to Livia, although divorce was widespread and carried no great social stigma—
a testimony, perhaps to the value Augustus placed on Livia's political
partnership.[6] Augustus, although he would clearly have preferred a

---

[2] Flory, 1988, 343–359. See in particular 345–346, on Octavian's motives for
the match and those of Ti. Nero for cooperation.

[3] Suet. *Aug.* 69.1–2; Tac. *Ann.* 1.10; Flory, 1988, 348–352 on the origins of Tacitus'
version in the propaganda of Antony.

[4] Hor. *Carm.* 3.14.5: "unico gaudens mulier marito..." Ov. *Trist.* 2.161–64:
"Livia sic tecum sociales compleat annos/quae, nisi te, nullo coniuge digna fuit,/quae,
si non esset, caelebs te vita deceret/nullaque, cui posses esse maritus, erat..." Ovid
here seems to rationalize their earlier divorces on the grounds that only Augustus
and Livia were good enough for each other, and that their current marriage is the
only true one for either of them. On the religious status of the *univira*: Dion. Hal.
Ant.Rom. 8.56.4; Gardner, 1991, 50–51; Flory, 1984, 318.

[5] Suet. *Aug.* 99.2; Tac. *Ann.* 1.5.

[6] Suet. *Aug.* 63.1; Bartman, 1998 and forthcoming.

Julian heir, eventually chose his stepson, Livia's son Tiberius as successor to the *imperium*.[7]

During her husband's lifetime, Livia played the role of "first lady"
as familiar today as in antiquity, by setting a public example of
acceptable female behavior. She, along with Octavia and Julia, spun
and wove clothing that Augustus frequently wore in public as a proud
demonstration of the domestic virtues of the women of his household,
and she won praise from a number of writers for her chastity.[8] Livia
and Augustus evidently saw no contradiction between this official
image and her open involvement in political matters, nor did people
of many regions of the empire, who honored Livia as the archetypal
good wife, almost as the divine personification "Concordia." Couples
in Roman Egypt, for example, sometimes signed marriage contracts
"in the presence of Julia Augusta"—not, presumably, the woman herself, but her statue, which thus functioned almost as a cult image.[9]
Surviving documents on papyrus prove the existence of this practice
in Egypt, and it may well have existed also in other areas where
the climate is not so conducive to the survival of fragile writing materials. Dio implies that some senators were amused at Augustus's
efforts to portray Livia as the model of an obedient wife, but archaeological and artistic evidence attests that many people did accept
this official image at face value.[10]

It is of course impossible to know how and to what ends Livia
may have wielded her influence privately, but her authority received
some public acknowledgment as well: early in their marriage, Augustus
granted her the same rights, of *sacrosanctitas* and of control over her
financial affairs, that he gave to his sister Octavia.[11] She, like Octavia,
used those financial resources for acts of euergetism that complemented
Augustus's public policies, and the projects that the two women spon-
sored complemented each other in their themes.[12] Two documented
examples of her patronage involve the establishment or restoration
of temples, a skillful use of the one area of Roman life—religious

---

[7] Suet. *Tib.* 23.
[8] On Augustus's homespun clothing, see Suet. *Aug.* 73. On Livia's *pudicitia*, see
Flory, 1984, 321: Flory quotes Ov. *Pont.* 3.1.114–116 and 4.13.29; Val. Max. 6.1.,
and Hor. *Carm.* 3.14.5. To these one might also add Dio 58.2.4–6; Dio praises
both her chastity and her claim of tolerance toward her husband's occasional
infidelities.
[9] Flory, 1984, 319.
[10] Dio 54.16.4–5.
[11] Dio 49.38.1; Purcell, 1986, 85.
[12] Bartman, 1998 and forthcoming.

ritual—in which women could legitimately play a public role. One such project was the construction of the Porticus Liviae, which housed a small shrine to Concordia.[13] Just as the sculptures displayed in Octavia's portico had celebrated good mothers of history and mythology, then, Livia's building complex evidently celebrated good wives, and the virtue of marital harmony, which the moral legislation of Augustus encouraged. By building this porticus on the site of a lavish private residence that had come into possession of the imperial family by inheritance, she also displayed the public spiritedness, in preference to personal wealth and luxury, that Augustus considered crucial to restoring the republic.[14] Livia also paid for renovation of the old temple of Fortuna Muliebris, a cult that had been established to honor the patriotic actions of two other women of early Roman history with whom she perhaps wished to compare herself.[15] The mother and wife of the exiled general Coriolanus, accompanied by a delegation of Roman women and children, had averted disaster from Rome by persuading him to give up his attack on his own city. Two Augustan authors, Livy and Dionysius of Halicarnassus, both narrate this episode in detail and with great rhetorical flair, leaving no doubt that the story and its connection with the cult of Fortuna Muliebris was thoroughly familiar to Romans of the period.[16] The behavior of Veturia and Volumnia and of the women who accompanied them had in one sense been highly unorthodox, in that they left the seclusion of their homes to address a man publicly on public issues, but in another, they had done what society expected, invoking their familial relationships to Coriolanus, and exercising their personal influence with him for the greater good of the state.[17] Dionysius emphasizes that their delegation had the blessing of official male authority, but Livy, most significantly, states that it did not matter whether they acted on their own initiative or by public decree,

---

[13] Flory, 1984, 309–330; Kleiner and Matheson, 1996, 32–33.

[14] Flory, 1984 (supra n. 8), 309, 327–330; Kleiner and Matheson, 1996, 32; Galinsky, 1996, 98.

[15] Flory, 1984, 318; Purcell, 1986, 88.

[16] Livy, *AUC* 2.40.1–12; Dion. Hal. *Ant.Rom.* 8.39–62. Both authors mention the foundation of the cult of Fortuna Muliebris (Livy, *AUC* 2.40.12; Dion Hal *Ant.Rom.* 8.55–56), and Dionysius makes a point of mentioning that the fame of Coriolanus had survived five centires and was still very well known in his own day (*Ant.Rom.* 8.62.3).

[17] Dionysius twice mentions the unusual and, by normal criteria, unseemly behavior of the women: *Ant.Rom.* 8.39.1 and 8.44.2.

since the outcome of their actions benefitted the state and averted danger where male virtues on the battlefield had failed.[18] These women also shared some accomplishments and virtues with Augustus in that they ended a destructive civil war, displayed the quality of *pietas*, and inspired in Coriolanus both justice and clemency. The three virtues of *pietas, iustitia* and *clementia* were the cooperative and communitarian values that complemented the more aggressive quality of *virtus*, and it was precisely these four virtues for which the Senate honored Augustus on the golden shield that they set up in the Senate house.[19] A woman could not, by definition, possess *virtus*, which derives from the word *vir* and implies specifically manly courage, but Veturia and Volumnia had impressively demonstrated the other three, while Livia sought to display and inspire these feminine virtues through her patronage of relevant cults.

Religion might be a traditionally accepted area of activity for women, but Livia ventured as well into some very untraditional ones. It was a matter of record in the archives available to Suetonius that Livia sometimes made formal petitions to her husband, for example, in requesting the right of citizenship for a tributary Gallic city, a request that Augustus refused.[20] He did, however, grant the province freedom from tribute, and on other occasions, Livia's pleas on behalf of her provincial clients may have been more completely successful. She was the personal confidante of the Jewish princess Salome, on whose behalf she intervened on at least one recorded occasion in a dispute with her brother, King Herod, about an arranged marriage. On that occasion, Salome eventually accepted Livia's advice to comply with Herod's wishes, something that equally formidable woman was willing to do because she trusted Livia's good judgment, which had served her well on other occasions.[21] Since Livia traveled with Augustus throughout the empire, she could and probably did cultivate many

---

[18] Dion. Hal. *Ant.Rom.* 8.43.3–7; Livy *AUC* 2.40.1–2: "Id publicum consilium an muliebris timor fuerit, parum invenio: pervicere certe, ut et Veturia, magno natu mulier, et Volumnia duos parvos ex Marcio ferens filios secum in castra hostium irent et, quoniam armis viri defendere urben non possent, mulieres precibus lacrimisque defenderent."

[19] Galinsky, 1996, 80–88.

[20] On the Gallic city, Suet. *Aug.* 40.3. Tac. *Ann.* 1.3 speculates at the nature of her secret machinations, but of course could have known nothing about them beyond hearsay.

[21] Josephus, *AJ* 17.10 and *BJ* 1.566. On the friendship and personal correspondence of the two women, *BJ* 1.641, 2.167.

such personal and political friendships.[22] Tacitus implicitly condemns
Livia's involvement in provincial affairs as a pernicious usurpation
of male authority, and a dangerous precedent for imperial women
who followed her, but the reaction of provincial cities seems to have
been quite the opposite: the honors that they lavished on her, in the
form of statues, inscriptions, titles and even cults prior to her official
consecration reflect gratitude and appreciation.[23] Livia could and evidently did present petitions to Augustus on behalf of private individuals as well, since Ovid believed that if his wife appealed to her,
Livia could alleviate the conditions of his exile. He obviously expected
the emperor's wife to deal with many such petitioners, since he warns
his own wife to choose her time carefully, avoiding a moment either
when Livia is too busy, or is enjoying a rare moment of leisure. His
assumption that wives can appropriately act both on behalf of and
through the men of their families and that a man can without embarrassment openly request such an action is most revealing of Roman
social attitudes.[24]

Augustus seems to have regarded his consultations with Livia as
sufficiently important to merit the preparation of carefully worded
written statements, "so that he would not say either too much or
too little by speaking ex tempore," just as he did for public speeches
and conferences with other important individuals.[25] His correspondence to her also reflects her active role in dynastic decisions, a clear
case in which her private role as *materfamilias* intersected with public affairs.[26] In Livia's case, we may almost speak of a woman who
enjoyed real power as well as influence, although she enjoyed it by
virtue of her familial role. The distinction exists in Latin as well as
in English: power that an individual holds by virtue of his or her
moral stature and exercises publicly and honorably is "*auctoritas*,"
while influence behind the scenes, secret and lacking in accountability, is "*potentia*," and is regarded with suspicion. In the poem

---

[22] Tac. *Ann.* 3.34.
[23] Santoro L'Hoir, 1994, 12–17; Winkes, 1995, 52, for a list of the honorific
inscriptions to Livia from cities along the itinerary of Augustus's travels in the east
in 22–19 B.C., a trip on which she evidently accompanied him.
[24] Ov. *Pont.* 3.114–166. See in particular lines 129–144, on choosing an appropriate time for the request.
[25] Suet. *Aug.* 84.2, "Sermones quoque cum singulis atque etiam cum Livia
sua graviores non nisi scriptos et e libello habebat, ne plus minusve loqueretur ex
tempore."
[26] Suet. *Claud.* 4.1–6.

consoling Livia on the death of her son Drusus I, the anonymous author explicitly praises her for a public and ethical use of her power.[27]

At no time during her husband's life did she hold any sort of official title, an honor which would probably have seemed too much like a blatant declaration of intention to found a dynasty. Augustus, like his successor Tiberius, had to strike a very delicate balance between acknowledging the fact of his autocratic rule and maintaining the appearances of a republic in which he was only "first citizen."[28] By the time he wrote his will, however, Augustus felt sufficiently confident of his authority to adopt Livia into the Julian family and grant her the title of "Augusta."[29] After his death, Augustus was deified, and Livia—or Julia Augusta, as she was now properly called— became the priestess of his cult, a title that gave her the right to be accompanied by a lictor when performing her priestly office.[30] Tiberius, himself seeking to avoid the appearance of monarchical ambitions, firmly vetoed efforts by the Senate to confer further titles on his mother, such as "Mother of her Country" (Mater Patriae) or "Parent of her Country."[31] In spite of his efforts, however, "Mother of her Country" seems to have become a popular title, even if it lacked official sanction.[32] Tiberius's actions could have been motivated partly by resentment of her power, but are more likely to reflect intelligent reticence about accepting honors that would appear too extravagant. Tiberius also refused such honors to himself, probably recognizing that for every member of the Senate who wanted him to have it, another might privately resent it.[33] To be sure, he lacked the skill of Augustus at manipulating and responding to public opinion, but had greater subtlety than his successors, notable among them Caligula and Nero, who not only accepted but demanded such honors and paid the price for their insensitivity.

[27] Purcell, 1986, 80–81, and *Consolatio ad Liviam* 47–50, quoted by Purcell 80–81 and 98 n. 11. On "potentia," see Levick, 1990, 53.

[28] See Tac. *Ann.* 1.11–13 on the maneuvering of Tiberius after Augustus's death to avoid offending lingering republican sentiment.

[29] Tac. *Ann.* 1.8; Suet. *Aug.* 101.2. See Gross, 1962, 11, on titles and nomenclature of Livia.

[30] Dio 56.46.1–2.

[31] Tac. *Ann.* 1.14.

[32] Dio 58.2.3.

[33] Suet. *Tib.* 50.2,3; Tac. *Ann.* 2.87.

In A.D. 22, Livia fell seriously ill, which in view of her advanced age was hardly surprising, but made a remarkable recovery, in thanks for which the Equestrian order dedicated a statue to the goddess Equestrian Fortuna.[34] The coins of the same year that identify her with "the imperial good health," (*Salus Augusta*), make refer to this recovery, but probably also have a broader meaning. (Figure 34). *Salus*, as Winkler has recently pointed out, does not refer to the personal health of an individual, the term for which is *valetudo*, but to the well-being of the state.[35] Another issue of the same year represents a mule-drawn carriage, or *carpentum*, accompanied by the inscription *SPQR IULIAE AUGUST[ae]* ("The Senate and the People of Rome to Julia Augusta") that has often been interpreted as referring to the ceremonies of thanksgiving for her recovery.[36] It could, however, have another meaning: in A.D. 22, Livia also received an important new honor, the right to sit with the Vestal Virgins at public games. It is possible that at the same time she received another privilege, formerly reserved only for the Vestals: the right to transportation within the city by *carpentum*.[37] Tiberius did not give his mother the full rights of an honorary Vestal, a step that his successor Caligula would take when honoring the living women of his family, but granting Livia comparable privileges implied that she, like the Vestals, was a guardian of the survival of the Roman state, and established the precedent on which Caligula later built.

When the Augusta died at the age of eighty six in A.D. 29, on the other hand, Tiberius' behavior was so unceremonious that it was widely interpreted to signify contempt for his mother's memory. His refusal to deify her is understandable, in view of the fact that such an honor was unprecedented for a woman, but neither did he execute her will, nor even attend her funeral, leaving the delivery of the eulogy to her great grandson Gaius "Caligula."[38] During the last three years of her life, the Augusta could not often have seen her son, since he lived in retirement in Campania, and did not even return to visit his mother during her last illness. Tacitus reports

[34] Tac. *Ann.* 3.71.
[35] *RIC* 1², 97 no. 47; *BMCRE* 1, 131, nos. 81–84, pl. 24, fig. 2; Gross, 1962, 17–21, pl. 2.2–3. On interpretation, see Winkler, 1995, 40–44, 48–49.
[36] *RIC* 1², 97 nos. 50–51, pl. 12; *BMCRE* 1, 130–131, nos. 76–78, pl. 23, figs. 18–19; Sutherland, 1974, 151, fig. 273; Winkler, 1995, 53–54; Winkes, 1995, 24.
[37] Tac. *Ann.* 4.16.4; Flory, 1984, 321; Winkler, 1995, 53–54.
[38] Tac. *Ann.* 5.1–3; Suet. *Calig.* 10.1, 16.3; Dio 58.2.1–3.

rumors that the emperor's withdrawal from Rome was prompted by
desire to escape from her domination. Tacitus himself is skeptical of
this explanation, preferring to attribute the emperor's decision first
to the intrigues of Sejanus, and then later to a desire to hide his
own cruel and immoral conduct.[39] As with all personal and emotional matters, the reports that Tiberius and Livia were in conflict
during her last years are unproveable by their nature, but the rumor
that Tacitus reports does reflect public awareness of Livia's real
power. It was common knowledge that the emperor owed his position to her, and that even very late in life she had a degree of personal authority that he would find it difficult to oppose.

Dio adds the information that the Senate admired the ways in
which she had used that authority, since many quite literally owed
their lives to her intercessions with Augustus and Tiberius, while her
financial assistance had enabled many people to raise their children.
In an era when exposure of unwanted infants was a common practice, helping a family to support a child could likewise mean that her
generosity made the difference between life and death. The Senate
therefore voted honors to her in spite of the emperor's opposition.[40]
The recently discovered copies of the senatorial decree condemning
Cn. Piso confirm Dio's accounts of her philanthropy: the Senate
explicitly thanks the emperor's mother for her beneficial acts toward
men of all social orders, and states that her generosity has earned
her the right to make requests of the Senate, although they praise
her for using that right sparingly. Velleius Paterculus eulogizes her
in very similar terms when he mentions her death, acknowledging
the fact of her power and asserting that she used it only for beneficial
purposes.[41] The honors that the Senate granted her included a full
year's official mourning and the construction of an arch in her memory, something unprecedented for a woman. Tiberius prevented the
latter extravagance by offering to pay for it himself and then "for-
getting" to carry out the project, but did, as Dio grudgingly admits,
patronize some "images"—presumably meaning public statues—of
her at the same time that he attended to her state funeral and burial
in the Mausoleum of Augustus.

---

[39] Tac. *Ann.* 4.57.
[40] Dio 58.2.2–6.
[41] Vell. Pat. 2.130.5; *S.C. de Cn. Pisone Patre* lines 115–118. Eck, Caballos and
Fernández, 1996, 46–47, 222–228.

During the principate of Caligula, Livia's memory enjoyed great honor, but not until the reign of Claudius was Livia apotheosized, as "Diva Augusta," undoubtedly because Claudius felt it was time the Claudian branch of the family had a divine ancestor of its own.[42] Even after the fall of the Julio-Claudian dynasty, at least one of the Augusta's protegés, the short-lived emperor Galba, still remembered her kindly and honored her on coins.[43]

These are the basic facts, as far as can be verified, of Livia's remarkable career, but her reputation, thanks largely to Tacitus, is far more colorful. Tacitus's first mention of her in the *Annals* is a sinister innuendo that she somehow contrived the deaths of Augustus's grandsons Gaius and Lucius Caesar.[44] Nearly every reference that follows connects her with allegations of abuse of power or rumors (usually narrated in indirect discourse, and attributed to no specific source), of assassination plots. The portrait of a ruthlessly ambitious woman that emerges from his account is as darkly compelling as Sir Thomas More's portrayal of Richard III of England; small wonder, then, that Livia, like Richard, has fired the imaginations both of attackers and of impassioned defenders in the scholarship and literature of subsequent generations.[45] On the side of Livia's defenders is the argument that even in Tacitus's day, there was no real evidence that many of the deaths of which she was accused were anything but natural, or that the "conspiracy theory" concerning the death of her grandson Germanicus had any validity. The sudden death of a healthy young man would inevitable arouse suspicions, but poisoning is notoriously difficult to establish even by modern forensic methods, and so naturally lends itself to the sort of malevolent rumor that can never be proven or disproven. Ironically, the traditional role of women in Roman society, as in so many societies, as caregivers to the sick left females particularly vulnerable to charges of poisoning if a patient should fail to survive. Poisoning, therefore, is

---

[42] Suet. *Claud.* 11.2.
[43] *RIC* 1², 240–241 nos. 142–143, 150–153, pl. 26; *BMCRE* 1, cciv, and 309–310, nos. 3–13, pl. 52, figs. 2–6. Livia here appears as a little full-length, standing figure holding a patera and scepter, with the inscription "Diva Augusta," the deified Augusta. On Livia's patronage of Galba: Suet. *Galba* 5.2.
[44] Tac. *Ann.* 1.3.
[45] Balsdon, 1962, 90–96. One of the most memorable fictional interpretations of Livia is that of Robert Graves in his novel *I Claudius*, the version of her character perhaps best known to most modern readers including those well versed in Classical history and philology.

one of the commonest elements in the stereotype of the ambitious woman in the writings of Roman historians—"woman as poisoner" is the dark side of "woman as nurturer."[46]

The most notorious alleged murder with which Livia's name was connected was that of Germanicus. The Senate convicted Cn. Piso of charges that certainly included the murder of Germanicus, but were also far broader: first and foremost, Piso was accused of and convicted for *maiestas*, treason against the power of the emperor Tiberius. The suicide of Piso before the conclusion of the trial inevitably left unanswered questions about his guilt or innocence and the possible involvement of higher officials in his alleged crimes, but although Tiberius had several good reasons to want Germanicus out of the way, no proof ever emerged that he had actually given orders for the assassination, or that if he did, his mother had been involved.[47] On the other hand, Livia did make one intervention in that case, after the fact, that incriminated her in the eyes of the supporters of Germanicus. Many incidents recorded about the Augusta indicate that she was a force for clemency and moderation, both with her husband and with her son, but her most notorious exercise of such a plea for clemency, recently confirmed by discovery of new epigraphic evidence, was her request that Piso's wife be pardoned for her alleged role in the murder of Germanicus.[48] This act of loyalty to her old friend Plancina convinced the supporters of Germanicus and of his widow Agrippina I that Livia was a party to his murder.

In the context of Livia's other official and semi-official acts, the request was not unusual: on one occasion during her husband's lifetime, her timely intervention had saved the life of a senator mistaken

[46] On the death of Germanicus and accusations of poisoning: Tac. *Ann.* 2.69–72, 2.82; Suet. *Calig.* 1.2. Suetonius describes some physical evidence, none of which sound especially convincing, such as the claim that when Germanicus's body was cremated, his heart did not burn, a symptom of poisoning. On the difficulty of proving poisoning, see Barrett, 1996, xiv–xv. Bartman, 1998, commented on the traditional role of women as caregivers of the sick and the consequent ease with which they could be accused of poisoning a patient who did not survive.

[47] The two most thorough ancient accounts of the trial are those of Tacitus, *Ann.* 3.12–18 and the official decree, the *Senatus Consultum de Cn. Pisone Patre*. At least six copies of the latter, all from Spain, survive. For publications and interpretations see: Eck, Caballos and Fernández, 1996, full reconstructed text of decree pp. 38–51; Eck, 1993, 189–208; Flower, 1997.

[48] Tac. *Ann.* 3.15, 3.17; *S.C. de Cn. Pisone Patre* lines 109–120, Eck, Caballos and Fernández, 46–47, 222–228; Eck, 1993, 199; Rowe, 1994; Flower, 1997.

for a would-be attacker; she had, on another occasion, persuaded Augustus to pardon L. Cinna and other members of an abortive conspiracy, had supported Julia the daughter of Augustus in exile, and later counseled moderation toward the provocative behavior of Agrippina I.[49] Contrary to the implication of Tacitus that Livia secured the pardon by acting behind the scenes in an unaccountable and therefore unprincipled manner, there was nothing furtive or secretive about her intervention on Plancina's behalf.[50] On the contrary, the widely copied and distributed *Senatus consultum* that records the conviction of Piso and the decision to show mercy to his son and wife specifically states that Tiberius asked the Senate to show mercy to Plancina at the request of the Augusta.[51] Whether such openness demonstrates a clear conscience or astoundingly arrogant boldness must remain in the realm of speculation, but Ockham's razor (a principle inimical to conspiracy theories of all sorts) would tend to suggest the former.

Livia's characaterization in Tacitus has become so entrenched in popular fiction and entertainment that it is easy to forget that in his own day, it was he who was the revisionist, presenting as a villainess and "harsh mother" of the Roman state a woman whose public image as the ideal wife and mother many people had enthusiastically accepted both during and after her lifetime.[52] Tacitus's description of Livia as a *gravis mater* may contain as well a sexual innuendo, playing on the double meaning of *gravis* as "pregnant," and alluding to Livia's marriage to Octavian while still carrying the son of her previous husband. Tacitus, as Galinsky observes, sets this image in opposition to the more widely accepted depiction of Augustus as *pater patriae*, the father of the state, thus using the very familiar slur of "feminization" to challenge the legitimacy of a regime. The authors and poets who praised both Augustus and Livia, however, were independent-minded men who could not have been coerced into parroting a "party line," nor could donors in provincial cities

---

[49] Sen. *Clem.* 1.9.6; Dio 55.14–22.2 (pardon of Cinna); Tac. *Ann.* 1.13, 4.71, 5.3.

[50] Tac. *Ann.* 3.15: ". . . ut secretis Augustae precibus veniam obtinuit, paulatim segregari a marito, dividere defensionem coepit." Shortly afterward, however, in *Ann.* 3.17, he quotes Tiberius as openly citing his mother's appeals to the Senate in requesting the pardon.

[51] *S.c. de Cn. Pisone Patre* lines 109–120, Eck, Caballos and Fernández, 1996, 46–47, 222–228; Eck, 1993, 199. On the distribution of the Senatus consultum, see in particular pages 202, 204–208.

[52] Galinsky, 1996, 77–78. Tac. *Ann.* 1.10.

in the empire be compelled to honor Livia with statues, representations on coins, or ceremonial honors such as the above-mentioned solemnization of marriage contracts in the presence of her portrait.[53] Both representations of her, as an avatar of traditional feminine virtues and as a ruthless political schemer are probably gross oversimplifications of a complex personality. Livia appears to have shared with her husband a combination of genuine idealism and public-spiritedness with shrewd and sometimes cynical pragmatism. Her presentation of herself as the stereotypically obedient wife while openly participating in political decisions may seem contradictory, but not hypocritical, since she never attempted to conceal the latter activities, which were a matter of public record in inscriptions and official decrees.

Let us give the final word on the subject of her character to someone who knew her very well, her great-grandson Caligula, who referred to her as a "Ulixem stolatum," a Ulysses in a *stola*. The common translation "Ulysses in petticoats" misses the force of Caligula's witticism, which blends a backhanded compliment to her sometimes devious cleverness with genuine respect: Ulysses was, after all, a sympathetic hero despite his human flaws, usually fighting for good ends and just causes, while "stolatum" is an honorific term, since the *stola* was the garment of a matron of Roman citizenship, a garment with social significance comparable to that of the toga for a man.[54]

The Portraits

Livia, as we have seen, presented herself as the archetypal Roman matron, yet enjoyed very atypical powers and opportunities. Her paradoxical image must have presented visual artists with a formidable challenge. Romans who could remember the war against Cleopatra would never have tolerated any representation of Livia

---

[53] See Galinsky, 1996, 10–41, on the "mutuality" of the relationship between the authority of Augustus and expressions of that authority in art and poetry. Galinsky rejects the idea that all such art was mere official "propaganda." On the circumstances under which a local donor would sponsor a public group of imperial portrait statues, see Rose, 1997, 8–10. Rose sees these groups as primarily part of a "gift exchange," an honor that the local donors give to the imperial family either in thanks for or in anticipation of some favor.

[54] Purcell, 1986, 79; Sensi, 1980–81, 59–60. On Caligula's remark: Suet. *Calig.* 23.2; Barrett, 1990, 22.

that suggested the official status of a queen, but on the other hand, she was as much a public figure as her husband. Though Livia is known to have been honored with numerous portrait busts and statues, and to have appeared on a major public monument—the Ara Pacis Augustae—during the lifetime of Augustus, (figures 30, 53), references to her on coinage are very subtle and discreet.[55] It is possible that little full-length figures of a seated female figure on reverses of some Augustan and Tiberian *aurei* and *denarii* represent the first emperor's wife, since a very similar figure appears many years later on *dupondii* of Claudius honoring the deified Augustus and his more recently deified wife. Here, the same seated female figure appears with an inscription that explicitly identifies her as "Diva Augusta."[56] The Augustan *aurei* and *denarii* that bear this reverse may have appeared at about the same time as other issues with reverses that honor Livia's son Tiberius, who by then had emerged as the clear heir to power, so that an identification of the seated figure as Livia could perhaps be inferred by association. The Tiberian coins, similarly, are apparently contemporaneous with issues honoring the Deified Augustus, the adoptive father of Tiberius, and simultaneous commemoration of his mother, who by then also had died, might have been appropriate.[57] But neither the Augustan nor the Tiberian coins bear inscriptions that identify this figure, either as a living woman or as a goddess. She sits on a low-backed chair, holding a scepter in her right hand and an object in her left that sometimes appears to be a branch, sometimes a bundle of corn-ears. In the latter case, she would presumably represent Ceres, but when the attribute more resembles an olive branch, she may instead be Pax. On some of the Tiberian coins, the figure holds an inverted spear, rather than a scepter, which would also support an identification with Pax. Both associations would be appropriate for Livia, who was identified with

---

[55] Gross, 1962, 10.

[56] Augustan *aurei* and *denarii* with seated female figure: *RIC* 1² 56 nos. 219–220, pl. 4; *BMCRE* 1, 91 nos. 544–546, pl. 14, figs. 8–9. Winkes, 1995, 19–20, fig. 1; Gross, 1962, 12–13, pl. 1.1. Tiberian coins of 36–7 with similar reverse: *RIC* 1², 95 nos. 25–30, pl. 11; *BMCRE* 1, 124–127 nos. 30–60, pl. 22, figs. 20–26, pl. 23, figs. 1–9; Gross, 1962, 14–15, pls. 1.2–3. Claudian *dupondii* that identify the seated female figure as "DIVA AUGUSTA:" *RIC* 1² 128 no. 101; *BMCRE* 1, cli and 195, nos. 224–225, pl. 37, fig. 7.

[57] Augustan *aurei* and *denarii* of A.D. 13–14 with reverses honoring Tiberius: *RIC* 1² 56 nos. 221–226, pl. 4, *BMCRE* 1, 87–88 nos. 506–512, pl. 13, figs. 1–6. These

Ceres in numerous statues and inscriptions, and possibly also with Pax on the Ara Pacis Augustae. In the Claudian coins of the Diva Augusta, the larger flan of the *dupondius* allows more certainty: the objects in her outstretched hand are unmistakably ears of grain, and the long vertical object in her right this time is a torch.

The inference on the basis of the Claudian coins that the earlier images of a seated female also represents Livia, however, is tenuous. Both sculptors and die-cutters at the time of Claudius could easily have adapted a standard image of Ceres, with whom Livia had by then long since been identified, to represent the new *diva*, while coins could confer a new identity on this figure with the inscriptions. It is somewhat more likely that an enthroned and veiled figure of "Pietas" on the bronze *asses* of Tiberius represents Livia in her new capacity as priestess of the deified Augustus; again, no inscription identifies the figure on coins of the Roman mint, but this time, contemporary provincial issues do associate the same figure with the name "Iulia Augusta." Here again, however, we cannot be certain whether the die cutters of Rome intended the same meaning as the provincial die-cutters who adapted the image for their local issues.[58] If any of these full-length figures on Augustan or Tiberian coins did represent Livia, which is possible but not certain, then ancient viewers, like modern ones, would have had to deduce that meaning as we do, by associations with other coins and objects, since the inscriptions would have given them no help. Only once during Livia's lifetime did her name, without her portrait, appear on a coin struck at the mint of Rome; on another, the "Salus Augusta" issue, her portrait appeared without her name, although the title of the personification obviously alluded to her. (Figure 34).[59] Not until her deification by Claudius did any overt representation of her, with an unambiguous identifying inscription, appear.

Provincial mints, on the other hand, especially those from Greek states accustomed to Hellenistic kingship, did not hesitate to portray

---

reverses appear with the obverse of Augustus, laureate, facing right, with the inscription CAESAR AUGUSTUS DIVI F PATER PATRIAE, the same obverse that appears on the coins with the reverse of the seated female figure holding the scepter and corn ears. Tiberian coins with reverses of the deified Augustus: *RIC* 1² 95 nos. 23–24, pl. 11; *BMCRE* 1, 124 nos. 28–29, pl. 22, figs. 18–19.

[58] *RIC* 1² 96 nos. 33–36, pl. 11; *BMCRE* 1, 128 nos. 65–69, pl. 23, figs. 14–15; Winkes, 1995, 22–23; Gross, 1962, 15, 47, pl. 1.4–5.

[59] *RIC* 1² 97 nos. 50–51, pl. 12; *BMCRE* 1, 130–131 nos. 76–78 pl. 23, figs. 18–19.

Livia and identify her by name. The best and most numerous examples come from Egypt, the province under the emperor's direct control and therefore one that had a special relationship to the imperial household.[60] The legends on some provincial coins even give Livia titles and honors specifically denied to her by Tiberius: coins of Leptis Magna call her "AVGVSTA MATER PATRIA(E)," while one remarkable issue from Colonia Julia Romula in Spain calls her "Iulia Augusta Genetrix Orbis"—"Mother of the World."[61] The latter title was more extravagant even than that unsuccessfully offered to her by the Senate, and particularly surprising in coming from a western province rather than a Hellenistic city. It also implies an identification of Livia with Venus Genetrix, mythological ancestor of the Julians, and a goddess whose cult was of immense political importance to the dynasty.[62] Here, as in so many cases, we see a clear example of autonomy on the part of some local mint official: expressions of loyalty to the Roman state and the imperial family were not always dictated from above. Local patrons could and often did apply their knowledge of the official propaganda of Augustus and Tiberius, but developed it in their own ways.[63]

In the major arts, public representation of women in the context of family groups became established somewhat earlier than on coinage, partly because private families appropriated this Hellenistic royal custom before the imperial family did so, thus paving the way for its acceptance. In coinage, which is by nature the prerogative of governments, no such mechanism existed for the imperial imitation of private practise. A group of bronzes from Cartoceto, evidently datable to the late Republic, included two female statues along with two equestrian male portraits who appear to be members of some distinguished family, thus illustrating that the women of such a family could be honored with public images.[64] Although Augustus was initially cautious about the adoption of a practice that could imply aspirations to royal power, the public eventually grew accustomed to

---

[60] Gross, 1962, 22–24; Winkes, 1995, 19–20 fig. 2.

[61] *BMCRE* 1, cxxxvi; Winkes, 1995, 22; Gross, 1962, 55; Mikocki, 1995, 28–29, 168 no. 121, pl. 28. *RPC* 73, p. 80 and 849, p. 209.

[62] Mikocki, 1995, 28–29.

[63] See Rose, 1997, 74. On the "reciprocity" between the imperial family, artists, and private patrons in the development of imperial ideology and imagery, see Galinsky, 1996, passim, esp. pp. 10–41.

[64] Balty, 1988, 31–46; Pollini, 1993, 423–446.

seeing such sculptural groups of local elite families in their basilicas, markets and other such public places, thus eventually allowing the imperial family as well to adopt the practice without violating existing and accepted traditions. Livia's image figures prominently as part of the imperial family group, in a composition designed to present and justify Augustus's dynastic plans, on the reliefs of the Ara Pacis Augustae (figures 30, 53) as well as in numerous statuary groups datable throughout Augustus's principate. Imperial portraits could also be privately owned, as in the case of several cameos, small bronze busts and life-sized marble busts that will be considered below, in which case their function, as part of a private lararium or a collection of *objets d'art*, and their message, as a demonstration of patriotic and personal allegiance, could be quite different from those of officially sanctioned and publicly displayed likenesses.

Despite the absence of Livia's portrait profiles from coins of the official mint until the one issue of A.D. 22–23, the labors of several generations of scholars, notable among them Walter Hatto Gross, Vagn Poulsen, and Paul Zanker, have allowed the fairly secure identification of many of her portraits in sculpture and other media such as gems. Most recently, Rolf Winkes has published a thorough and immensely valuable corpus of all surviving portraits of Livia, analyzing her portrait types, her characteristic coiffures, and the rich variations on these types in extant objects.[65] The portraits fall into two major categories: those that represent Livia wearing several variations on the *nodus* coiffure, and those that show her hair parted in the middle and drawn back around the face in soft waves. Within the former group, Winkes and Zanker both recognize four distinct portrait types, while those with the middle part have several variations. The prototypes with the *nodus* certainly date to the lifetime of Augustus, while with one significant exception, all surviving works that display the middle part belong at the earliest to the principate of her son Tiberius, but portraits of both groups continued to be produced throughout her life and long after her death.

The images of Livia are far too rich, however, to analyze solely in terms of her officially disseminated types. As Winkes clearly demonstrates in his recent study, every group of objects traceable to an identifiable prototype includes both works that appear to follow the

---

[65] Winkes, 1995, 19–63. Catalogue of portraits pp. 80–207.

prototype faithfully and those that modify that original in a variety
of ways, some perhaps unintentional, others quite deliberate.[66] In the
process of making copies from copies, mistakes and simplifications
could creep into a series of replicas, just as they do in recensions of
manuscripts, but in many cases, copyists may have felt free to adapt
rather than mechanically reproducing an official prototype. The latter phenomenon is most clearly visible in the portraits datable after
the death of the Augusta, and especially in those from after her
deification. Although controversies will inevitably continue for many
years over the identifications and typological classifications of specific
objects and coin profiles, her iconography at least in its broad out-
lines is well understood. The sheer volume of surviving objects, both
inscriptions and works of the visual arts that represent this woman
attest to the ubiquity of her image both in public and private settings.

When and how did her images become so widespread and familiar? At least a few evidently existed even before Octavian secured
sole power in 31 B.C., since Livia and Octavia both received the
honor of public statues along with "sacrosanctity" in 35 B.C. In the
eastern Mediterranean, her earliest known representation in a sculptural
group occurred not long after 31 B.C.: an inscription records that
statues of her and of Octavian (not yet honored with the title Augustus,
or its Greek equivalent Σεβαστός) stood in the sanctuary of Eleusis,
where Octavian became an initiate of the rites of Demeter and
Persephone in 31.[67] That patrons at Eleusis should honor one of its
most distinguised initiates with a statue is hardly surprising, but the
presence of his wife as well is striking and most suggestive. She would
surely not have been with Octavian at the time of his initiation,
which took place soon after the victory at Actium and before the
final conclusion of the civil war, yet the local patrons evidently
regarded both members of the couple as having a special relationship with the sanctuary. The identification of Livia with Demeter
that later occurs so often in inscriptions and in visual representations may have its origins at this early date, in the creation of that
relationship, and perhaps with Augustus's shrewd recognition of the
political value of the beloved goddesses. When he revisited Greece
in 19 B.C., Livia definitely was traveling with him, and could con-

---

[66] Winkes, 1995, 25–50.
[67] Rose, 1997, 140–141, cat. no. 71, with earlier references. Initiation of Augustus:
Suet. *Aug.* 93; Dio 51.4.1.

ceivably have been initiated at the time, since Augustus is known to have attended the ceremonies again. No source records whether Livia became an Eleusinian initiate, but it would have been rather surprising if she had failed to do so even though she was with Augustus at Eleusis.[68] The rites at Eleusis had profound personal meaning to their initiates, who apparently witnessed the reenactment of the myth that celebrates Demeter not only as a giver of fertility but as the archetypal good mother. Demeter's association with the wife of the first citizen, the *exemplum* for Roman womanhood, would have had an obvious appeal to patrons throughout the empire seeking ways to express their loyalty and affection.

The portrait profiles of Livia that sometimes appear on provicial coins are not reliable enough to fix identifications of Livia in the major arts, but at least inform us that she wore several variants of the "nodus coiffure."[69] (Figure 21). Where her sculptural representations occur in groups with other members of her family, context and historical probability, taken together with the evidence of her coin likenesses, has allowed recognition of her portraits. Such a group of three marble busts, from Arsinoë in Egypt, proved to be the "Rosetta Stone" that allowed the deciphering of Livia's iconography, since these three marble busts, all of high quality, included securely identifiable likeness of Augustus, of Tiberius, and of a woman who possessed striking physical resemblances to Tiberius (figures 22–23). She must obviously represent his mother Livia, the dynastic link between the two men.[70] That portrait, in turn, allowed the recognition of numerous replicas of the same type, and of other portrait types of the same woman. The essential features of the coiffure are these: a segment of hair in the middle of the forehead is rolled forward from the middle of the crown and then up from the hairline to form a broad, rather flat topknot, somewhat different in shape from the higher, more asymmetrical crest of Octavia's *nodus* (see

---

[68] On Augustus's second visit to Eleusis: Clinton, 1989, 1507–1509; Dio 54.9.10. If Livia was initiated in 19 B.C., it is possible that historians neglect to mention the event because it was eclipsed by a far more unusal and shocking occurrence, the suicide of another new initiate, Zarmaros, in the presence of the emperor.

[69] Winkes, 1995, 19–24, figs. 2, 3, 7; Gross, 1962, 22–42, "Bildnisse Livias auf Lokalen Prägungen Augusteischer Zeit."

[70] Copenhagen, Ny Carlsberg Glyptothek no. 615. Poulsen, *Portraits* 1, 65–71, no. 34; Gross, 1962, 87–91, pls. 15–16; Rose, 1997, 188–89, cat. no. 129, pls. 237–240; Winkes, 1995, 115 n. 41. On the typology of the portrait of Livia and its replicas: Fittschen-Zanker 3, 1–3, no. 1. Johansen, 1994, 96–7, no. 36.

figures 11–15), then drawn back in a broad, flat braid along the top of the head. The rest of the hair is rolled back at the sides to form a soft aureole of waves that frame the face, then combed smoothly to the base of the skull where it is bound into a tight chignon, encircled by small braids, worn low on the back of the head but slightly above the hairline at the nape. A few small wisps are allowed to "escape" from the coiffure, thus tempering the severity of the fashion: at the temples, in front of the ears, and at the back of the neck, but these strands are short and, in most sculptural representations, shallowly carved.

The securely identified types of Livia's portraiture display three variants on this style: one (known as the Albani-Bonn type) with a larger *nodus* and fuller hair around the face (figures 24–25), another— the most widely replicated Fayum type—with more tightly bound hair, but a few soft wisps escaping at each side of the *nodus* that are carved in shallow relief on the forehead, and the third, the Marbury Hall type (figures 26–27), even more severe, with the hair at each side of the head pulled back tightly into two twisted plaits that run back toward the chignon behind each ear. Vagn Poulsen placed the creation of these three types in this order, in which others, including Zanker, have followed him.[71] Kockel's study of private tomb monuments offers support to this chronology, since it demonstrates that a higher and fuller topknot seems to be an earlier version of the fashion, while the smaller roll of hair above the forehead became more popular in subsequent years.[72] Winkes, however, argues that the Marbury Hall type (figures 26–27), which Livia's profiles on the coins from Alexandria appear to follow, is probably the earliest, the Albani-Bonn type (figures 24–25) somewhat later, and the Fayum type the latest portrait created for Livia during Augustus's lifetime.[73]

In addition to the modifications of the coiffure that Winkes has analyzed in such thorough detail, there are two more strong arguments in favor of this chronology: the subtle transformation of Livia's features, and the shifts in artistic style that the works display. The Marbury Hall and Albani-Bonn types tend, as a rule, to show Livia

---

[71] Poulsen, 1968, 21; Winkes, 1988, 556–557. See Fittschen-Zanker 3, pp. 1–2, and note 3, pp. 2–3, for a complete list of the extant replicas of each type.

[72] Kockel, 1993, 42–46.

[73] Winkes, 1995, 32, 63; see also Winkes, 1988, "Spanish Image," 76–78.

with an oval face, although with a small, pointed chin, but the Fayum
group more strongly emphasizes her broad forehead and triangular
lower face.[74] The faces of men and women often do tend to become
broader as they grow older, and so, within the idealizing conventions
of Augustan portraiture, this change could reflect Livia's maturity,
and her "matronly" status as the mother of Tiberius. More impor-
tantly, however, it has the effect of assimilating her features to those
of Augustus, who also has a broad, triangular face. The tendency
of portraitists to assimilate the appearance of wives to their husbands
is a common phenomenon in Roman art, already evident in the
portraits of both Octavia and of Cleopatra, but in the case of Livia,
after the adoption of her son Tiberius as heir, it served a particularly useful political purpose, by allowing portraitists in turn to assimilate Tiberius's appearance to hers and to that of Augustus, creating
the impression of a family resemblance between an adoptive father
and son who had no actual genetic relationship.[75] If we accept the
hypothesis that Livia's Marbury Hall type is the earliest and the
Fayum type the latest of her portraits from Augustus's lifetime, we
can also observe a trajectory in the development of their styles very
similar to those of her husband's portraits: the Marbury Hall replicas
tend to be rather harsh and unflattering, and ironically, to make
Livia appear much older than she would really have been. This characteristic of the Marbury Hall type probably accounts for the chronology adopted by Poulsen and Zanker, but as Bartman has more
recently observed, the mature and respectably matronly appearance
of those earlier likenesses conforms well to the tastes of republican
Rome, while the far more beautiful and idealized Fayum type, with
its large eyes and serene expression, more closely matches the classicizing taste reflected in Augustus's Primaporta type.[76]

    There also exist a group of portraits that display a variant on this
coiffure in which two small braids are wrapped around the sides of
the head like a diadem. (Figures 21, 28–29). These braids can appear

---

[74] Winkes, 1995, 31, 33, 39, 44, on the physiognomic characteristics of the three
types.
[75] Bartman, 1998 and forthcoming, has made similar observations.
[76] Bartman, 1998 and forthcoming. Note in particular the replica of this type
from Ampurias in Spain, now in Barcelona, Museo Arqueológico, which shows particularly harsh signs of age; cf. Winkes, 1995, 84 no. 5, and Winkes, "Spanish
Image," 1988, 75–78.

either instead of or in addition to the broad plait that runs from front to back along the crown.[77] The earliest datable examples are Pergamene coins of the latter years of Augustus's lifetime, works which conveniently confirm by their inscriptions the fact that the intended subject is Livia, and thus prove that she could be represented wearing this variation of the *nodus* coiffure.[78] (Figure 21). The identification of sculptures with this hairstyle can sometimes be more problematic, since they vary too much from one another to be described as true replicas of a type, and might in some cases represent private citizens whose portraits happened, either by pure coincidence or by stylistic influence, to resemble those of the Augusta. One of the most handsome members of this group, for example, is a portrait bust from Asia Minor, now in Copenhagen (figures 28–29), that represents a woman who does indeed share Livia's triangular face, large eyes, gracefully arched eyebrows, small mouth, and thin lips. In profile, she displays the overbite so typical of the Claudians.[79] On the other hand, a bust, as opposed to a full length statue, is a format more appropriate for private portraiture than for public dedications, although the group from the Fayum demonstrates that this format could occasionally be used in public settings.[80] The Pergamene coins, however, offer justification for the identifications of this and related works.

All of the coins and two marble portraits of this group come from Asia Minor, which would tend to suggest that this variant on Livia's coiffure was a local creation by portraitists who for some reason chose to depart from and embellish on the more austere official typology. Some marble carvers who reproduced official types were unimaginative technicians, as the evidence of their work demonstrates, but some, though by no means all, possessed the skill and will not only to reproduce but to interpret their prototypes. Provincial marble carvers also embellished Livia's better established types with

---

[77] Winkes, 1995, 35–38; Winkes, 1988, "Bildnistypen," 556; Fittschen-Zanker 3, pp. 1–2, note 3, number 4a–e.

[78] Gross, 1962, 28–29, pl. 4, 6–8.

[79] Ny Carlsberg Glyptotek, Copenhagen, cat. 616: Winkes, 1995, 35–37, fig. 11, and pp. 115–116, no. 40; Gross, 1962, 103–104, pl. 21; Poulsen, *Portraits* 1, 1962, 71 no. 35, pls. 55–56; Inan and Rosenbaum, 1979, 62 no. 7 pl. 6; Fittschen-Zanker 3, 1–2, note 3 no. 4a. Johansen, 1994, 94–5 no. 35.

[80] Rose, 1997, 73 and passim. Rose's exhaustive documentation of imperial portrait groups demonstrates that the format of choice for public portraits was the full-length statue.

wisps of hair along the forehead that soften the severity of the *nodus* coiffure, a variant well attested in finds from Greece and Asia Minor but very rare in the Latin west.[81] If some short-lived official proto-type for Livia with the braids around the sides of the head was dis-seminated from the capital, it found its most enthusiastic acceptance in the Eastern provinces, but these portraits are far likelier to have been local creations.

Most of the extant sculptures that follow these portrait types from Livia's lifetime are often described as "classicizing." This term is use-ful, although not perhaps ideal; let us examine just what it means in these cases. The sculptural portraits of Livia are dominated by gracefully curved but strictly closed contours, smooth, tightly controlled surfaces, an engraved and linear treatment of the hair that suggests no unruly softness of texture, and a blandness of facial expression that gives little hint of inner life. From the time when his "Primaporta" type was created, portraitists never represent Augustus as looking any older than he did at the time of his accession to power, and since the same idealization naturally had to extend to his wife and relatives (who would otherwise have looked incongruously older than their *paterfamilias*), the skin surfaces of Livia's Albani-Bonn and Fayum-type portraits are not interrupted by the lines, wrinkles, and com-plexity of textures that the normal ageing process must have introduced into the real woman's appearance.[82] This is a style that suggests con-trol of nature and emotion while still representing its subject as an attractive and eternally youthful woman: the embodiment of the good wife, who is desirable but chaste.

The *nodus* coiffure of the more securely established types is as notable for what it is not as for what it is. As observed in the pre-vious chapter in relation to Octavia's portraits, it bears no obvious resemblance to any Classical or Hellenistic statuary, whether of god-desses, personifications, or Hellenistic queens. In the passage about hairstyles from the *Ars Amatoria*, this coiffure is one of the few for which Ovid was unable to cite a Classical parallel.[83] The sculptural

---

[81] Winkes, 1995, 28, 94 no. 17, 106 no. 33, 172 no. 98, 174 no. 99; Inan and Rosenbaum, 1966, 60–61, no. 11, pl. 7, 3–4; Inan and Rosenbaum 1979, 61–62, nos. 5–6, pls. 4.2, 5.

[82] Winkes, "Spanish Image," 1988, 75–78, argues that a harshly veristic portrait of a gaunt older woman whose coiffure conforms in precise detail to Livia's "Marbury Hall" type represents the emperor's wife, but freely interprets her official type so as to reflect republican style and ideals.

[83] Ov. *Ars Am.* 139–140.

style of these works, then, is "classicizing" in the sense of coldly elegant form and flattering treatment of the subject's appearance, but
the portraits do not incorporate specific visual references to works
of the Classical period. Livia's portraits are not "Classicizing" with
a capital C in the same sense, for example, as the Primaporta statue
of Augustus, which unmistakably quotes the Doryphoros of Polykleitos,
not only in stance and proportions but also in its smoothly combed
locks of hair.[84] For the women of the imperial family, a coiffure that
was fashionable during the Republic would do, a conservative choice
that might subliminally reassure the viewer of Augustus's respect for
Republican traditions and of his determination not to turn his family into a Hellenistic-style dynasty, even though the harsh verism of
that period that was still evident in Livia's earliest portraits had since
been abandoned.

By the time of Augustus, however, the *nodus* coiffure was not the
only choice available; Ovid, as we will recall, recommended selecting
the most flattering from among several possibilities, although he recommended the *nodus* for women with short and plump facial types.
Since Livia's portraits consistently depict a round-cheeked woman
with a tapering chin, the motive behind her choice might not have
been much different from that of the fashion-conscious young women
to whom Ovid addressed his advice. The simpler coiffure with the
middle part, however, resembled not only that of Laodamia, as Ovid
observed, but of many Classical goddesses, perhaps too much so for
comfort in view of Augustus's political agenda, and his refusal of
any overtly divine honor to himself.[85] Another possible advantage in
favor of the *nodus* coiffure might also have been the possibility of
weaving into the braid along the crown the *vitta* that marked the
status of a married woman, although since all extant replicas have
lost their paint it is difficult to be sure whether these braided bands
of hair included ribbons of fabric or not.[86] There can, at any rate,
be no question in the viewer's mind as to the *ethos* embodied in all
these portraits: the empress is attractive but modest and serious,
avoiding both frivolity and excessive self-promotion in her personal
appearance.

---

[84] Kähler, 1959, 13; Fittschen-Zanker 1, 3–6, no. 3, on the "Primaporta type,"
and 1–3, nos. 1–2, on the earlier "Octavian" type; Galinsky, 1996, 24–25.

[85] Ovid, *Ars Am.* 3.138; Suet. *Aug.* 52.

[86] Sensi, 1980–81, 60, 78–79, 86–87.

There is however a striking and datable exception to the rule of Livia's modestly matronly coiffure in her portraits from Augustus's lifetime: her relief representation on the Arà Pacis Augustae (figures 30, 53). It is debatable whether any of the highly idealized female figures in the processional friezes are true "portraits," but they unmistakably stand for specific women of the imperial family. Livia here wears not only the simpler coiffure with a middle part, but long, cascading waves of hair that hang from behind her ears to below her shoulders. Her head is veiled and turned at a three-quarter angle to the viewer, so that these long locks are not readily visible from the figure's principal viewpoint, but despite the cautious reticence of their inclusion they are unambiguously represented.

There is evidence that some of the panels of the south frieze have been reworked by the neoclassical sculptor Carradori, and any study of their sculptural style must approach them with according caution.[87] It is unlikely, to judge from the present state of the relief, that the Livia originally wore a *nodus* coiffure, since the hairline as it now appears, despite the damage to the center of the forehead, clearly shows the contour of waves spreading outward from a central part. There is no room below the laurel crown for a *nodus*; if the coiffure has been recut, then so has the entire head, a possibility that the proportions of the head to the body and the proximity of the figure to its neighbors appear to rule out. A drawing in the Codex Ursianus in the Vatican, made before the panels were sent to Florence and reworked by Carradori, seems to confirm that the figure wore her hair parted in the middle and drawn back smoothly, without a *nodus*, although it is impossible make out in this drawing whether the figure wore shoulder locks.[88] It is, then, possible but unlikely that the shoulder-locks could have been added to an existing image by modifying folds of the veil on each side of the neck. Again, there are no telltale signs of such modification, and no particular motive for Carradori to have altered a relatively hidden detail well below the highest projections of the relief. Assuming that the coiffure now visible is the original one, it gives Livia an unmistakable similarity to Classical and classizing goddesses, most notably that of the figure on the east facade of the same monument variously identified as Saturnia

---

[87] Conlin, 1992, 210–211. See also Koeppel, 1992, 216–217, for problems with the present condition of the reliefs.
[88] Conlin, 1992, 209–210, fig. 1a.

Tellus, Ceres, Venus, and Pax Augusta (figure 31).[89] Since plausible
cases can be made for every one of these candidates, it is difficult
to escape Galinsky's conclusion that the figure is a deliberately composite, polysemous image.[90] Ancient observers must, however, have
understood her to have some name, for which I tentatively prefer
the identification as "Pax," the personification to whom the altar
was dedicated, but in whose image the allusions to Venus and to
Ceres are conspicuous and fully intentional.[91] I shall refer to the
figure provisionally as "Pax," but with quotation marks to remind
the reader that this is a hypothesis.

This figure turns more frontally toward the viewer and is far less
modestly clad, but shares with Livia the veil drawn over her head
and the vegetal crown; that of Livia consists only of olive leaves,
while that of "Pax" includes flowers and grain, but both figures are
veiled and garlanded. Livia and Augustus are the only two mortal
figures on the Ara Pacis to share this arrangement of veil and garland, ornaments that establish a relationship between both of them
as well as with the goddess.[92] The loss of paint unfortunately prevents
us from knowing the color of the garments, but the garment drawn
over Livia's head may well have been purple, the *tutulus* that identified
her rank as a *materfamilias*.[93] In addition to the information it gives
us about Livia's "real life" role, however, the parallel that it creates
between her and "Pax" adds another level of meaning to the figure
of Livia. The allegorical figure incorporates clear visual references
in her filmy, provocatively slipping drapery, to Venus Genetrix,
mother both of the Roman people and of the Julian line.[94] She also,

---

[89] See Winkes, "Bildnistypen," 1988, 558–560 for a similar observation. For recent
effort to establish the identification as Pax, with earlier literature on the problem,
see de Grummond, 1990, 663–677. For identification as Ceres: Spaeth, 1994,
65–100.

[90] Galinsky, 1992, 457–75; passim, esp. 458–463.

[91] Spaeth, 1994, 91 discusses the close relationship in literature and the visual
arts between Ceres and Pax. She is arguing for the appropriateness of an image
of Ceres on an altar of Pax, but the same arguments could as well explain why
an image of Pax on her altar should bear such a noticeable resemblance to the
standard iconography of Ceres.

[92] Bartman, 1998 and forthcoming.

[93] Sensi, 1980–81, 61–63 and 73–74. On the form of the *tutulus* as a purple veil
worn over the head: Bonfante, 1986, 160 fig. IV–94, 25; Wood, 1995, 478.

[94] On the sculptural type of Aphrodite generally believed to have provided the
prototype for the Roman cult image of Venus Genetrix: *LIMC* 2, 34–35, nos.
225–240, s.v. "Aphrodite" (Robert Fleischer); *LIMC* VIII, 196–198, nos. 1–29, s.v.
"Venus" (Evamaria Schmidt). Schmidt notes however that several other types have
also been identified as replicas of the cult statue of the temple of Venus Genetrix:

as De Grummond has recently observed, resembles the statuary type generally identified as Kephisodotos' Eirene with the child Ploutos (figure 99).[95] The coiffure of the latter, like that of the Augustan personification, is parted in the middle, and drawn back softly from the face to the nape of the neck, while several long curls emerge from behind the ears to fall to the shoulders on each side of the neck. Flowing, golden hair is a distinctive attribute of Demeter/Ceres (e.g., the Demeter of Knidos, figure 98), an argument that Spaeth has advanced for recognizing the Ara Pacis figure as Ceres, but the close similarity of the iconography of Peace to that of Demeter/Ceres could allow the argument to apply equally well to either.[96] The Eirene of Kephisodotos, who carries the infant son of Demeter in her arm, symbolic of the hope that Peace will nourish and protect the prosperity that Demeter grants to humanity, bears a fully intentional resemblance to that goddess.[97]

The parallels of the male mythological figures with contemporary figures in the processional friezes have long been recognized as part of the program of the Ara Pacis: the pose of the sacrificing Aeneas closely matches that of Augustus on the south frieze, both of which a viewer standing to the south-west of the monument could see at the same time, as Pollini has demonstrated.[98] Rose has more recently pointed out the similarities of Aeneas's *camilli* to the child whom he identifies as Gaius Caesar in the north frieze.[99] Viewed in this context, the somewhat more reticent parallels between the allegorical

---

see *LIMC* VIII, 216 no. 257, a marble relief from Sperlonga, which shows a diademed bust of Aphrodite with a small Amor hovering above her right shoulder, and several reliefs that likewise show a draped figure with a small Amor: *LIMC* VIII, 222, nos. 328–330, 332.

[95] De Grummond, 1990, 667–668.

[96] Spaeth, 1994, 69. *HymnHomCer.* 1: the very first words of the Homeric hymn identify Demeter as "ἠΰκομον."

[97] On the Eirene of Kephisodotos: most complete replica in Munich Glyptothek 219. *LIMC* III (1986), s.v. "Eirene" (E. Simon), 702–703. Vierneisel-Schlörb, 1979, 255–273 no. 25; Robertson, 1975, 384, pl. 125a. De Grummond, 1990, 667, fig. 6; Bieber, 1977, 30 n. 19.
Note in particular the similarities in treatment of hair and face of the Eirene to those of the Demeter of Knidos: British Museum 1300. *LIMC* IV (1988), s.v. "Demeter" (L. Beschi), 859 no. 138; Robertson, 1975, 462–3, n. 39, pls. 143c, 144a, with full earlier references.

[98] Pollini, 1987, 298.

[99] Rose, *AJA* 1990, 463–467 and figs. 11–12; Pollini, 1987, 21–25; Simon, 1967, 18, 21. Although the identifications of the children on the Ara Pacis remain a hotly constested issue, I agree with Rose and Pollini on the identification of this child, rather than the long-haired boy next to Agrippa on the south frieze, as Gaius, and prefer Simon's identification of the long-haired children as barbarian princes.

figure and that of Livia take their part in a complex system of visual
associations between the imperial household and mythological or
divine beings, an allusion made far richer by the associations that
the allegorical figure in turn evokes with divine images in Classical
sculpture.[100]

Why should the empress, whose images during her husband's lifetime were otherwise scrupulously mortal rather than goddess-like,
suddenly receive such heroizing treatment on the Ara Pacis? Events
in 13 B.C. had converged to make dynastic concerns of paramount
importance to Augustus, but his wife was not, at that point, the
mother of Augustus's chosen heirs.[101] His young grandsons Gaius
and Lucius Caesar were the imperial family's hope for perpetuation,
and Augustus's adoption of them as his sons was as close to an overt
declaration of his dynastic intentions as political circumstances would
permit. It is to Gaius and Lucius Caesar that the insistent repetition
of pairs of babies or young children throughout the monument presumably allude: the twins in the lap of "Pax," the infants Romulus
and Remus, and the two camilli in the Aeneas panel.[102] Livia, however, also had two sons, who by 13 B.C. were young men. Augustus,
despite his affection for and pride in his daughter's children, was
probably realistic enough to recognize that in an era of high infant
mortality, his grandsons might predecease him, in which case his
stepsons would be the next logical successors. His wife's fertility was
therefore as important in the dynastic imagery of the altar as that
of the Julians. Augustus had already groomed Tiberius for the role
of successor in the years 27 to 25, although he gave first preference
to his nephew Marcellus, and he continued to honor Tiberius and
Drusus I even after the births and adoptions of Gaius and Lucius
Caesar. Tiberius appears close behind his mother, while Drusus I,
with his own wife and son, follow a little further along.[103]

---

[100] Spaeth, 1994, 88–90 notes the similarities between "Pax" (the figure she
identifies as Ceres) and Livia; I arrived independently at a similar conclusion.
[101] Specifically, the return of Augustus and Agrippa to Rome and establishment
of the Pax Romana, and Augustus's adoption of Gaius and Lucius Caesar, followed
by the death of Agrippa, which suddenly left Augustus without an experienced contemporary in his family who could if necessary assume power, and made his two
young grandsoms Gaius and Lucius Caesar the heirs apparent. See Fullerton, 1985,
477–478, 480–482.
[102] See Spaeth, 1994, 89–90. This is, again, a conclusion that Dr. Spaeth and I
have reached independently.
[103] Suet. *Tib.* 6.4, on the honors to Tiberius and Marcellus in 27 B.C.; Tac.
Ann. 1.3.

Aside from the concrete issue of the imperial succession, the Ara Pacis presents the family of Augustus and Livia symbolically as an example of the virtues Augustus wished to promote in his legislation concerning marriage and sexual morality: the prominence of children throughout the monument would remind Roman citizens that the imperial family had contributed to the birth-rate that Augustus sought to encourage, while the parallels of Augustus with Pater Aeneas and Livia with the beautiful, maternal personification on the east facade present the imperial couple as a symbolic father and mother of the Roman state.[104] In 13 B.C., Augustus was *Pater Patriae*, and although Livia never officially held any corresponding title, observers of the south frieze of the Ara Pacis could easily draw the inference that if he was the father of the state, then his wife must be its mother.[105] As we have seen, some provincial cities bestowed such titles on her without official blessing. One title that belonged indisputably to her was that of *materfamilias* of the imperial family. Her real domestic and political responsibilities involved playing a maternal role to children other than her own. Not only was she the stepmother of Augustus's daughter and adoptive sons, but she was in charge of the rearing of hostage children whose inculcation with good Roman virtues and a sense of Roman citizenship would presumably one day make them loyal subjects of the empire, and perpetuators of the Augustan Peace. The child directly in front of Livia on the Ara Pacis has often been identified as one of these hostage princes, and although the identification remains controversial, there is much good evidence to support it.[106]

Finally, in addition to her domestic responsibilities, Livia and her villa "Ad Gallinas Albas" at Primaporta played an important ceremonial role in the celebrations of military triumph, since it was a laurel grove at that villa that provided the crowns of the triumphators throughout the Julio-Claudian period, until a very portentous blight killed all the trees shortly before the fall of Nero. The legend

---

[104] On Augustus's moral legislation, and his use of the imperial family as an example of fecundity, Suet. *Aug.* 34; Bartman, 1998 and forthcoming. On the laws of 19–18 B.C., Hor., *Car.Saec.* 57–61; Balsdon, *Roman Women* 75–79.

[105] On the title of Pater Patriae, Suet. *Aug.* 58.1.

[106] Bartman, 1998 and forthcoming; Purcell, 1986, 87; *Res Gestae Divi Augusti* 32. On the possible identities of the non-Roman children in the procession: Rose, *AJA* 1990, 453–461; Pollini, 1987, 22–23; Simon, 1967, 18 and 21. For the opposing view, see Zanker, 1988, 217–218.

of the origins of that laurel grove and the dramatic omens connected with it, as Bartman has recently demonstrated, smoothly interweave the appropriate virtues of male aggression and female domesticity into a whole necessary for the success of the Pax Romana.[107] The fact that the Ara Pacis was dedicated on Livia's birthday, January 30, 9 B.C., was surely significant.[108] A later, Tiberian inscription likewise associates Livia with Pax by adding her title of Augusta to the name of the goddess Diana Pacilucifera, and Livia may also appear in the guise of Pax on Augustan and Tiberian coinage of Rome, although as noted above, the identifications of these seated figures holding olive branches and inverted spears are not certain beyond doubt.[109]

The sculptors of the frieze have therefore departed entirely from Livia's established portrait types for sculpture in the round and created a new image for her, a decision perhaps encouraged by the fact that the copying technology that allowed such efficient and accurate duplication of a fully three-dimensional image was far more difficult to apply to a face in relief, especially one turned at a three-quarter angle to the viewer. The sculptors would therefore have been obliged to work free-hand rather than from measurements, a procedure that could in cases such as the female figures have liberated them entirely from the tyranny of an official prototype.[110] Here, then, is the earliest appearance of a coiffure that was to become very common in Livia's portrayals after the death of Augustus, but significantly, hardly any examples of this type in sculpture in the round can be dated earlier than the time of Tiberius.[111] Winkes dates the creation of the prototype for these sculptures to the late Augustan period, on the evidence of the Ara Pacis, but the type did not receive widespread distribution until later.

---

[107] Suet. *Galba* 1; Bartman, 1998 and forthcoming.

[108] Simon, 1967, 8, 18; Torelli, 1982, 50; Gross, 1962, 73; Purcell, 1986, 93.

[109] Purcell, 1986, 92–93. Inscription: Ehrenberg and Jones, 1955, 95 no. 130: "[Dianae] Pacilucife[rae Aug]ustae sacrum [pro salut]e Ti. Caesaris [Augusti] P. Licinius P.l. [. . . . . . .] Philosebastos [d.s.] p.f.c." On the coins with reverses of Livia (?) as Pax, see Gross, 1962, 12–14, pl. 1, 1–5.

[110] Pfanner, 1989, 217–218.

[111] Winkes, 1995, 49 and 63. Of the 31 replicas of this type that Winkes identifies, he dates only one, in Tunis, to the late Augustan period, on stylistic rather than external evidence: see pp. 44–49, 186, no. 109. The crescent diadem of the statue in Tunis, however, suggests a possible later date.

There are, however, a few highly problematic objects that, if they are genuine and correctly identified, must belong to the lifetime of Augustus, in which Livia's contemporary coiffure, the *nodus*, is embellished with the long, Classicizing shoulder locks reminiscent of divine images. These long locks are very different both in scale and in nature from the little wisps that soften the hairline in Livia's more standard portrait types. One such work is a small bronze bust from Neuilly-le-Real, one of a pair with a bust of Augustus, inscribed on its base LIVIAE AUGUSTAE ATESPATUS CRIXI FILIUS V.(otum) S.(oluit) L.(ibens) M.(erito). (Atespatus, the son of Crixus, fulfilled this dedication to Livia Augusta, gladly and deservedly.)[112] (Figures 32–33). It would appear that Atespatus, whether individually or on behalf of his community, was grateful to both members of the imperial couple, possibly due to Livia's good efforts on behalf of Gallic clients.

Both imperial portraits appear to introduce signs of advancing age into the faces—in Livia's case, gaunt cheeks and pouches under the eyes, in Augustus's, a heavily lined forehead—that almost never appear in public portraits of the imperial couple, while the inscriptions are equally anomalous. Livia's name is given in the form of "Livia Augusta," a combination of names that she never bore at any one time in her life: she did not receive the title of Augusta until Augustus's death, when his will adopted her into the Julian *gens*, making her name properly "Julia Augusta," not "Livia Augusta." For these reasons, the Neuilly-le-Real busts were long dismissed as clumsy forgeries, but their authenticity has recently and quite convincingly been defended by De Kersauson, who points out that these were not public monuments but private possessions, probably venerated in the lararium of Atespatus, and that a private patron in the provinces need not concern himself either with the legally correct forms of nomenclature or with officially sanctioned iconography. Nor for that matter did the bronzecaster feel obligated to observe the established style of the official prototypes: the long locks added to the coiffure complicate

---

[112] Paris, Musée du Louvre, Br. 22, Inv. N 3253. Bronze bust, h. 21 cm., of head 10 cm. Winkes, *Livia* 37–38, and 146 no. 73, with full literature; De Kersauson, *Louvre* 1, 1986, 94–97 nos. 41–42; Fittschen-Zanker 3, 2, no. 1, note 4; Gross, 1962, 85–86. Gross summarizes the arguments against the authenticity of the busts, and the possibility that if the busts are antique, the inscriptions may be modern additions; Zanker is noncommittal but seems to favor accepting the authenticity of the busts. Boschung, *Augustus*, 1993, 134, no. 55, agrees in accepting the busts as genuine, as does Winkes.

the contours of the bust of Livia, just as the facial furrows of both works tear into the smooth, reflective metal, interrupting the closed surfaces that urban artists preferred. The work's pendant, the bronze of Augustus, conforms most closely in its arrangement of locks of hair to the Forbes type, the replicas of which tend to present the *princeps* in a somewhat more unflattering manner than the Primaporta type, showing gaunt cheeks and a slightly haggard expression, features clearly visible in this little bronze.[113] This replica, however, also shares features with the earlier, and more flamboyant, "Octavian type," with its dramatically twisted neck and intense expression, which in this replica causes the forehead to disintegrate into a mass of furrows. Photographs create a deceptive impression of old age in the face of this little bust: the wrinkles of the forehead seem intended to convey muscular contraction rather than the ravages of time, but the shiny texture of the bronze calls emphatic attention to these lines and exaggerates their effect. One would not go so far as to call these two bronzes "Baroque," but they are far less smoothly closed and controlled than, for example, the Copenhagen marbles from Arsinoë (figures 22–23). Works like the latter suggest a coolly rational source of authority in political life, while the Neuilly-le-Real busts appear to employ both the stark verism of the republic and the Hellenistic emotional devices invented to portray divinely granted charisma.

Another work of provincial provenance, the fragment of the sheath of a sword, likewise presents Livia wearing a *nodus* coiffure with shoulder locks that have been carefully rendered as flowing along her shoulders, above the lines of her drapery. The wife of the ruling emperor here appears as the center of a triad, the other two members of which are her sons Tiberius and Drusus I, to whom the owner of this piece of decorative military equipment no doubt was displaying his allegiance. The work must therefore presumably date to the lifetimes of both young men, and thus to the lifetime of Augustus, to whom the two generals were connected through his marriage to their mother Livia. For this reason, presumably, the maker of this object selected a more goddess-like version of her official portrait, and combined it with a strikingly honorific placement in the center of the group, facing directly outward, while the two lateral figures direct their attention toward her. A similar placement will later be

---

[113] De Kersauson, *Louvre* 1, 96, no. 42. Boschung, *Augustus*, 1993, 134 no. 55 on the typology of the bust.

seen in provincial coins that represent Drusilla, the first Roman woman to be deified, after her consecration (figure 84).[114]

The Neuilly-le-Real bust of Livia differs considerably from the figure on the Ara Pacis in its combination of a strongly characterized, individual face and contemporary coiffure with the blatantly goddess-like element of the shoulder-locks. The little face on the sword-sheath, perhaps because of the limitations of scale, shows a more blandly ideal face, but a similar variation on the coiffure. This sort of cult of semi-divine personality was more tolerable in the provinces and in works that expressed the political allegiances of private patrons, than in the officially sanctioned public image of the emperor's wife. At the other extreme of reinterpretation, there is a bust of Livia from Ampurias that, like the Neuilly-le-Real bronze, introduces emphatic signs of advancing age into a face of the "Marbury Hall" portrait type, but does not embellish it with goddess-like elements. Most of the replicas of this earliest and frumpiest of Livia's portraits make her look mature, but those elements were evidently not enough for the local Spanish copyist, who has here presented her as an old woman. The effect here is one of verism in the Roman republican tradition, a style that, as Winkes argued, survived in Spain despite its lack of favor in the official sculpture of the capital.[115]

These idiosyncratic adaptations of the official image in a provincial and/or private context may find a parallel in another recent and controversial identification of Livia in one of the tiny, painted portrait medallions from the villa at Boscotrecase.[116] Here, if Anderson's identification is correct, Livia is paired with her stepdaughter Julia, and both wear the *nodus* coiffure with long, wavy shoulder-locks. The private patron would, according to this hypothesis, be none other than Agrippa himself, the husband of one and son-in-law of the other, displaying in the privacy of his home the proof of his familial connection to the imperial household in a manner more heroic than would have been acceptable in public. Whether or not Agrippa was indeed the owner of the villa, it is not improbable that some wealthy

---

[114] Bartman, 1998 and forthcoming; Winkes, 1995, 97 no. 20, with full earlier literature. On the coins from Apamea in Bithynia that represent the deified Drusilla, see below, Chapter 5, n. 34.

[115] Winkes, 1995, 26, 84, no. 5, and Winkes, "Spanish Image," 1990, 75–76.

[116] Anderson, 1987, 127–135; Kleiner and Matheson, 1996, 35–36, fig. 6. Winkes, 1995, 198 no. 134 and 221 no. 269, lists the Boscotrecase medallions under "Benennung als Livia unsicher," and "Benennung als Iulia unsicher" respectively.

private citizen might have chosen to display his affection and loyalty toward the imperial family in this manner, as Atespatus in Gaul
did. It is not insignificant that the closest parallel Anderson cites for
the "Livia" medallion is a fine cameo-gem with a portrait of Livia's
"Marbury Hall" type. Although this is the most severe and probably
the earliest version of her *nodus* coiffure, the escaping wisp at the
nape of the neck of this replica is large enough and long enough
almost to reach the shoulders. This, too, was a small and privately
owned object, not a public monument.[117]

This painted medallion-portrait, and the bronzes that belonged to
Atespatus, were works definitely datable to the lifetime of Augustus,
but their characteristic features will appear again, both in works evidently made for private possession, like a marble bust now in Copenhagen, and works whose scale and execution suggest public display.
Already at this relatively early period, we see evidence, particularly
in the Gaullic bronzes, of genuine and spontaneous affection for Livia,
and a willingness to deviate from her official likenesses in the direction of more goddess-like presentation. When Livia did eventually
become a *diva*, some of the heroizing devices that made their way
into her official public images were, therefore, already in existence,
and indeed, well established in art from the private sphere.

Portraits of Julia Augusta from the Principate of Tiberius

Despite Livia's alleged conflict with her son Tiberius, and the documented fact of her physical separation from him in the last years
of her life, her image remained vitally important for his dynastic
claims to power. She represented his only connection to the family
of the deified Augustus, and her presence was therefore essential in
the public art intended to legitimize his claim to power and that of
his son Drusus II. Of the public statuary groups that Rose has catalogued, the greatest number that include Livia date to the time of
Tiberius, slightly outnumbering those from the lifetime of Augustus.[118]

---

[117] Paris, Bibliothèque Nationale, Musée des Médailles, Bab. 232a. Winkes, 1995,
144, no. 69, with full earlier literature; Anderson, 1987, 132–133, fig. 7; Megow,
1987, 252 no. B11, pl. 2, 6. See also Bartman, 1998 and forthcoming, on the greater
stylistic freedom possible in cameo gems than in public sculpture.
[118] Rose, 1997, catalogues 25 Tiberian groups, 24 Augustan, 4 Caligulan and 6
Claudian groups in which Livia appeared: see concordance, pp. 191–197.

The first recognizable likeness of Livia on coins of the Roman mint appears on *dupondii* of the year A.D. 22–23, one of a group of three related issues with a very specific propaganda message. (Figure 34). At a time when the position of Drusus II as heir seemed relatively secure, and his twin sons seemed to offer the promise of dynastic continuity into another generation, these three issues of coins link Tiberius with his mother and son in an elegantly effective manner.[119] All three *dupondii* share the format of an inscription with names and titles on the reverse and a female personification on the obverse. The two with the obverses of "*Iustitia*" and "*Salus Augusta*" bear the titles of Tiberius, while those of Drusus II appear with "*Pietas*," a virtue appropriate both to a loyal son and to a man worthy to rule the empire. Although Livia is not identified by inscription, the portrait-like features of the "*Salus Augusta*"—the arched nose, small mouth and soft chin-line—become more striking by their juxtaposition with the ideal features of the *Iustitia* and *Pietas*, in whose company, however, the softer and simpler coiffure allows her to look as though she belongs. Her hair is now parted in the middle, drawn down and then back to the nape in full waves around the face and smoother strands toward the back of the head, and is fastened in a tight chignon at the base of the skull like the one she wore earlier with the *nodus*. This is similar to the fashion that she wore on the Ara Pacis, except that here there are no long shoulder-locks but only small wisps of loose hair along the neck. The fashion remains austere and modest, maintaining closure of line and smoothness of surface, and suggests a tight control over the potentially unruly forms of hair in its natural state. Livia, however, is now more than a respectable matron, although she is still that.

Various unconvincing efforts have been made to identify the *Iustitia* and the *Pietas* as portraits of other living women of the imperial family, or as portraits of Livia, but only the *Salus* head is in any way individualized, and it alone of the three lacks the obviously divine attribute of a crescent diadem.[120] Livia, as noted earlier, had recovered

---

[119] *RIC* 1², 97 nos. 43, 46, 47, pl. 11; *BMCRE* 1, 131, nos. 79–84, pl. 24, figs. 1 and 2; 133, no. 98, pl. 24, fig. 7; Winkes, 1995, 22–23, figs. 4–5. On the dynastic meaning of these three issues, see also Winkler, 1995, 48–49.

[120] Gross, 1962, 18–19; Fittschen-Zanker 3, 3–4, no. 3; Mikocki, 1995, 28, 167–168 no. 199; Winkler, 1995, 46–47. Zanker and Winkler agree with Gross that only the *Salus* coins bear portrait faces. Mikocki, however, also tentatively accepts the identifications of the busts of *Pietas* and *Iustitia*: Mikocki, pp. 25–26, 27–28, 164 no. 94,

from a major illness in the year 22; as the almost incredibly hardy matriarch of a dynasty with four living generations, she was particularly well suited to personify the good health of the entire imperial house and, by extension, the empire.

Some sculptural portraits of Livia conform to the same type as the profiles of *Salus Augusta* on the *dupondii* of 22/23, and therefore can be dated with reasonable security to the same period; these portraits will be discussed below. A new type, however, rarely supplanted an earlier one completely, since some copyists might not have access to the newer type, while in other cases patrons of conservative tastes might prefer the better-established and more readily recognizable likeness. The portraits of Livia wearing the *nodus* coiffure, therefore, continued to be replicated, but in some cases at least the copies identifiably belong to the principate of Tiberius because of their archaeological context, their presentation of the Augusta in the guise of priestess of her deified husband, or by the presence of attributes of Ceres.

Archaeological context establishes the date of a colossal head of Livia from the Temple of Augustus and Roma in the old forum of Leptis Magna, since her portrait appeared here in a family group that, according to the inscriptions on the temple and on two of the statue bases, was set up in A.D. 23 or soon afterward, while the Augusta was still alive. (Figure 35).[121] The scale of the figure establishes beyond doubt, however, that she and the current emperor Tiberius are beings of a far more awe-inspiring status than that of other members of the imperial family in the group. The latter included Germanicus and Drusus II, the two heirs of Tiberius who had both

---

pl. 21; 166, no. 109, pl. 26. See also Kokkinos, 1992, 90–95. Kokkinos attempts to identify all three profiles as Antonia Augusta, and to relate them to her role in foiling the conspiracy of Sejanus, but this interpretation requires a redating of the issues, and a rejection of the evidence of the consular date given in the inscriptions.

[121] Tripolis Museum, from Leptis Magna, marble head, hollowed out in back, h., chin to crown 68 cm. Aurigemma 1940, 50–56, figs. 32–34; Poulsen, 1946, 45–46 fig. 37; Gross, 1962, 106–109; Bartels, 1963, 31–32; Fittschen-Zanker 3, 2 n. 6n, under no. 1; Kreikenbom, 1992, 179 no. III 36, with full literature, pl. 11a; Rose, 1997, 182–184, cat. no. 125, pl. 221; Winkes, 1995, 181 no. 105. On the inscriptions that establish the date: Aurigemma 1940, 21–27; Trillmich 1988, 51–60. Aurigemma believed that the group must date to the lifetime of Germanicus, who appeared in a life-sized figure in the associated chariot group, but Trillmich, reinterpreting the Latin inscriptions on the bases, establishes that the group must be no earlier than A.D. 23, the last year of the life of Drusus II, and probably constitutes a posthumous honor to both young princes.

suffered untimely deaths. They appeared in chariots, accompanied by their wives and mothers, all of whom appeared in life-sized scale. But overlooking this group, which probably stood on the platform of the temple, on a porch visible to passers-by in the forum, were four enormous figures, of Augustus, Dea Roma, Tiberius, and Julia Augusta (Livia). The inscription indicates that this whole group was set up at the same time; the differentiation of scale, therefore, places the living emperor and his living mother on a closer footing to the gods than to the young men whose deaths the group commemorated.

The colossal statues were probably acrolithic: the heads are hollowed in back to lighten the massive load, which suggests that bodies of some lighter and less costly material had to support them, while the scale relative to that of the temple suggests that they were probably represented sitting down, on thrones, rather than standing. Their backs must have been placed against the wall of the pronaos, since the heads were obviously never meant to be seen from behind.[122] The image of Augustus was the largest: the surviving head measures 92 centimeters from chin to crown, approximately the same scale as the fragmentary head of Dea Roma, but 24 centimeters larger than that of Livia and 18 centimeters larger than that of the living emperor Tiberius. The status of the deified emperor compared to that of his living relatives was still maintained.

Nonetheless, the presentation of the Augusta on a scale more than twice life-size marks a significant change in the nature of her image. Indeed, of the eleven colossal portraits of Livia that Kreikenbom has recently catalogued, not one can be dated before the death of Augustus.[123] In every case, either archaeological context or the use of the later coiffure, the type attested on the *Salus Augusta* coins, establishes a date no earlier than the principate of Tiberius. In the head from the Leptis Magna group, the portrait type with the *nodus* coiffure receives a very free, and quite dramatic, interpretation: the enlarged eyes have a dramatic upward gaze, enhanced by the twist and turn of the neck, while the rippling waves of hair around her face, have a looser and more artfully disorderly appearance than in the primly tidy portraits of Augustus's lifetime. Deeply carved grooves separate the strands, both in the *nodus* and in the hair drawn back

[122] On the reconstruction of the group and its placement: Aurigemma, 1940, 24–25; Gross, 1962, 107; Rose, 1997, pls. 217 A and B.
[123] Kreikenbom, 1992, 179–186 nos. III 36–46.

over the ears, and create a rising and falling surface very different
in effect from the smooth surfaces with their shallowly engraved
strands of replicas such as the bust from Arsinoë (figures 22–23).[124]
Some of these features, like the exaggeration of the size of the eyes
and the deep carving of the strands of hair could be dictated by the
scale, which requires bold treatment in order for forms to read clearly
from a considerable distance above eye-level, but the colossal portraits of Augustus and of Tiberius in the same group display a far
more restrained treatment, and greater fidelity to established prototypes. The sculptor of Livia's head, in contrast, seems to have felt
the need to use the devices of Hellenistic royal portraits in order to
express the Augusta's new status. Not every city and colony of the
empire treated her image quite so extravagantly during her lifetime,
but the local patrons of Leptis Magna seem to have felt a special
affection for Livia, whom they honored with at least three extant
colossal statues, and one more life-size statue that does not survive
but that, according to the inscription on its base, was dedicated to
the "DIVAE AUGUSTAE."[125]

Epigraphic evidence indicates that during the period of her widowhood, Livia first began to be explicitly identified as "Ceres Augusta."[126]
At least one and possibly two of these inscriptions appear on statue
bases, indicating that the works of sculpture they supported probably translated these epithets into visual terms with the attributes of
the goddess Ceres. Some of the surviving statues that display these
attributes probably date to her lifetime, although certainty on that
score is often difficult, since we must often rely on the notoriously
subjective evidence of style.[127] In at least one case, however, a likeness

[124] Bartels, 1963, 31–32.
[125] Standing colossal statue of Livia as Cybele, from the temple of Ceres-Tyche
near the theater of Leptis Magna, Tripolis Museum, inv. 26, h. 310 cm. Winkes,
1995, 184 no. 107; Mikocki, 1995, 156 no. 37 pl. 14, with earlier literature; Kreikenbom, 1992, 180–81 no. III 39, pl. 11c.
Enthroned statue of Livia with diadem and *infula*, also from the Old Forum:
Aurigemma, 1940, 70–74 figs. 47–50 (as Antonia Minor); Kreikenbom, 1992, 185
no. III 45, pl. 11d, with literature; Winkes, 1995, 182–183 no. 106.
Inscribed statue base: Aurigemma, 1940, 32 fig. 16.
[126] Fittschen-Zanker 3, 3–4, no. 3; Mikocki, 1995, 19, 151 nos. 1–4, *CIL* XI, 3196;
CIL X, 7501 = *ILS* 121; *CIG* II, 2815; *CIG* II, 3642 = *IGR* IV, 180. The interpretation of the latter two is controversial; they may refer to Julia Domna. *CIL* X,
7501, however, unambiguously identifies Julia as the wife of the deified Augustus
and mother of Tiberius Caesar Augustus, thus allowing the inscription to be dated
to the principate of Tiberius.
[127] See Winkes, "Bildnistypen," 1988, 560–561.

of the Augusta as Ceres appears in a context that allows its dating to the time of Tiberius: not a monumental sculpture, but a small object made for private possession. This sardonyx cameo, now in Florence, represents Tiberius and Livia in a jugate portrait, the former laureate, the latter wearing a garland of poppies and corn ears behind a crescent diadem.[128] (Figure 36). Although the coiffure is of the "Marbury Hall" type, the most severe of Livia's hairstyles, she here has a long and thick escaping lock that cascades far past the shoulder, and helps, along with the floral crown, to equate her with "golden haired Demeter." Despite the partial concealment of her profile behind that of her son, the gem-cutter went to some pains to make these attributes legible, while emphasizing the family resemblance in the parallel lines of her profile and that of Tiberius. The use of an early portrait type of Livia suggests a date for this gem fairly soon after the succession of Tiberius to power. The *stola* that the gem-cutter has carefully represented is the costume of a living woman, and the mark of her status in this world, another indication that this is a lifetime portrait, rather than a posthumous image.

Winkes has raised the interesting, and most plausible, suggestion that the identification of Julia Augusta with Ceres was not a matter of officially dictated propaganda, but a spontaneous idea, perhaps most popular with provincial patrons, as an alternative to the official title of *Mater Patriae* that Tiberius refused to allow her to accept.[129] Mikocki's recent study of the identifications of Roman imperial women with goddesses confirms that the identification of Livia with Ceres was both one of the earliest and one of the most enduringly popular of such associations, first for her and later for many other Julio-Claudian women, a fact that suggests both official tolerance and enthusiastic public reception of the representation of a living woman with such attributes.[130]

More valuable in official propaganda than the association with Ceres was the role of the Augusta as priestess. The cult of the living emperor's dead and deified predecessor was one of the most powerful weapons in the political arsenal of Tiberius, and one that,

---

[128] Sardonyx cameo in Florence, Museo Archeologico inv. 1453, h. 5.5 cm. Winkes, 1995, 103 no. 28; Mikocki, 1995, 157, no. 40, with earlier literature, pl. 2; Megow, 1987, 179–180 no. A 49, pl. 10.10.

[129] Winkes, "Bildnistypen," 1988, 560–561.

[130] Mikocki, 1995, 18–21, 141, 151–158 nos. 1–45.

like so many patriotic appeals to love and nostalgia, had a distinctly
dark side. Tiberius often used sacrilege against the divine Augustus
as a charge against political enemies, both individuals and communities.[131] Yet despite the brutal abuses of Tiberius, and his blatant
hypocrisy in feigning personal modesty while using the memory of
the deified Augustus as a weapon against enemies, the power of the
title "*Divi Filius*" and the potency of the image of the immediate
predecessor as an object of religious worship proved very effective
in buttressing claims to political legitimacy. The cult of recently
deceased emperors remained a keystone of dynastic imagery throughout the imperial period, even when, as in the case of Septimius
Severus, a claimant who came to power after a period of civil war
had to manufacture a fictitious dynastic connection for himself.[132] In
this aspect of the cult of the imperial family, the role of the late
emperor's widow as priestess of her deified husband became crucial,
and therefore, just as one might expect, Julia Augusta appeared both
in monumental sculpture and in smaller, privately owned works, as
priestess of Divus Augustus.

An especially fine surviving example of the former, in the Vatican
was found in the basilica at Otricoli, apparently near a nude statue
of the deified Augustus toward which her prayerful gesture was presumably directed.[133] (Figure 37). The statue is heavily restored, but
although most of the *nodus* is modern marble, the fragments of the
original coiffure support the accuracy of this restoration; the work
therefore, follows the prototypes of the lifetime of Augustus, but the
archaeological context, gesture and pose allow for a secure dating
of the work after his death. There is no evidence that the statue of
Livia ever had any divine attributes: it is the Augusta's upturned
gaze and gesture, arms outspread with the hands raised, that convey

---

[131] Tac. *Ann.* 4.36 (punishment of Cyzicus for neglecting the worship of the Deified
Augustus); Suet. *Tib.* 58; *S.C. de Cn. Pisone Patre* lines 68–70; Eck, Caballos and
Fernández, 1996, 42–43, 186–188.
[132] Dio 76.7.4–8.3.
[133] Rome, Vatican, Sala dei Busti, from Otricoli, marble, h. 211 cm. Winkes,
1995, 39–41, 164–65, no. 88; Rose, 1997, 97–98 no. 25, pl. 89; Dareggi, 1982,
18–21 figs. 30–31; Amelung, *Vatican* 2, 538–541, no. 352, pl. 70; Poulsen, *Portraits*
1, 67 no. 5, under cat. no. 34; Helbig 1², no. 183, pp. 134–135 (H. von Heintze);
Bieber, 1977, 197–198, fig. 807; Fittschen-Zanker 3, 2, under no. 1, n. 6, o. Statue
of Augustus apparently found in same location: Rose, 1997, 97–98, cat. no. 25, pl.
88; Dareggi, 1982, 12–14 figs. 19–20; Helbig 1², no. 19, pp. 15–16 (H. von Heintze);
Lippold, *Vatican* 3¹, 162–164, no. 565.

her role and status, while her costume is contemporary rather than Classicizing. She wears, over a light tunic, a heavier, sleeveless dress with braided shoulder straps, the *stola* of a Roman matron.[134] Her importance, this statue clearly tells us, consists entirely in her relationship to her deified husband, the connection so crucial to the claim of Tiberius, but there are formal elements in the choice of figure type that change the characterization of the woman herself: the expansive gesture that breaks the smooth contours, emphasized by stretched folds of drapery between the arms that break the placid verticals of the folds of her *stola*, and the gaze that directs the figure's energies outward and heavenward. Although the style of carving still has the classicizing coolness of the Augustan period, this is not a tightly closed and self-contained object but one, like the much earlier Primaporta Augustus, that interacts with visible or invisible figures in the space around it, though not, like that more commanding male image, with the viewer. Some efforts have been made to identify the prototype of this and related statues of Roman priestesses as a Greek original of the late-classical period, an era during which extant votive reliefs attest that this praying gesture was a well-established formula. Bieber has plausibly suggested however that the freestanding statuary type for draped, female *orantes* is an original creation of the first century after Christ, invented in response to the new need for an image of an imperial priestess of an imperial cult, and that the prototype may have been some prominently displayed portrait of Livia, conceivably in bronze or some valuable material, of which the Vatican marble may be a direct copy.[135]

Another extant sculpture may combine Livia's role as priestess with an identification as Ceres: a somewhat poorly preserved and heavily restored statue in the Louvre that, like the Florence cameo and the Vatican statue, still wears the *nodus* coiffure.[136] (Figure 38). Here, the overall effect is even less cool and self contained: the floral crown that she wears interrupts the contour of the veiled head and disintegrates the marble around her face into a maze of light and shadow. Since the statue in its present state may be a pastiche of

---

[134] Bieber, 1977, 195–196; Zanker, 1988, 165. For a detailed description of the drapery of the Vatican statue, see Amelung, *Vatican* 2, 538.

[135] Amelung, *Vatican* 2, 539–541; Helbig[2] no. 183, p. 135 (H. von Heintze); Bieber, 1977, 198.

[136] Paris, Musée du Louvre Ma 1242 inv. MR 159. Winkes, 1995, 148–150, no. 74; De Kersauson, *Louvre* 1, 1986, 102–103 no. 45, with earlier literature.

pieces that do not belong together, it is not certain whether the original composition included references to Fortuna, although such references would be most appropriate, given Livia's special relationship to the cult of Fortuna Muliebris and the dedication of thanks for her recovery at the temple of Fortuna Equestris.[137] It is, at any rate, clear that the portrait head of Livia combines the floral crown of Ceres with an attribute that belongs not to the Olympian or the mighty chthonian goddesses, but to living or recently deceased women: the beaded woolen *infula* that hangs from the floral garland inside the veil. Many observers take this attribute to allude to her role as priestess of Augustus, since the emblem often appears on portraits of women performing a sacrifice and evidently acting in a priestly capacity.[138] The significance of the infula may be somewhat broader and less specific than this interpretation allows; it is a general mark of sanctity that can adorn altars or sacrificial beasts, as well as humans, but one of its meanings, though by no means the only one, was the identification of the wearer as a priestess.[139] A private citizen from Pompeii, for example, wears this emblem in a statue that clearly depicts its subject as a sacrificing priestess, about to pour an offering from the *patera* in her outstretched hand, and she, like the Louvre statue of Livia, wears a floral garland as well as the beaded infula around her head.[140]

The Tiberian portraits of Livia discussed so far all follow the portrait types with the *nodus* coiffure, but the "Salus Augusta" coins (figure 34) demonstrate that the middle part, previously attested only on the Ara Pacis, now enjoyed widespread dissemination. In life-sized sculpture, a number of extant replicas correspond closely to the "Salus" coin profiles, so much so that many scholars including Zanker, in the Capitoline catalogue, find it convenient name this series of portraits the "Salus-Typus."[141] A more accurate term, however, might

---

[137] Tac. *Ann.* 3.71. On her restoration of the temple of Fortuna Muliebris: Flory, 1984, 318.

[138] This detail is partly restored, but sufficient original marble fragments of it exist to prove that the restoration is correct. Gross, 1962, 106–107, De Kersauson, *Louvre* 1, 1986, 102.

[139] For a fuller discussion of the *infula* and the controversies that surround its interpretation, see Rose, 1997, 77, and Wood, 1995, 478, n. 79–84 for earlier literature.

[140] Naples, Museo Nazionale di Archeologia, inv. 6041. Rumpf, 1941, 22, no. 2, with earlier literature, pl. 2c.

[141] Fittschen-Zanker, 3–4 no. 3; Gross, 1962, 106–131 on the portrait types of Livia as Julia Augusta and Diva Augusta.

be "adoption type," since as Freyer-Schauenburg has argued, the most logical time for its creation would have been just after the death of Augustus, when Julia Augusta, as we should now refer to Livia, became a member of the Julian family and chief priestess of the deified emperor.[142] At least four closely related marble heads, all of Tiberian date, closely match these coin profiles: in Kiel, in the Metropolitan Museum in New York, in Cherchel, and in the group from Béziers, now in Toulouse (figures 39–40).[143] The Kiel and New York heads are fairly portrait-like and similar in their physiognomy to replicas of the earlier type, those from Béziers and Cherchel somewhat more idealized, but the variations fall well within the range of interpretation that one might expect in replicas of a single type.[144] The provenances of the Kiel and New York heads are, unfortunately, unknown, but the head in Toulouse belonged to a sculptural group in or near the forum of Colonia Urbs Iulia Baeterrae in Gaul, while the Cherchel head must come from a north African provenance. Although both are of high technical quality, they are "provincial" in the sense that they are copies of copies, produced far from the centers of artistic production, and both of these replicas display a tendency to move toward a more flattering and attractive interpretation of the prototype, especially when the subject is female.

---

[142] Freyer-Schauenburg, 1982, 209–224.

[143] Freyer-Schauenburg, 1982, 209–224; Winkes, 1995, 48–49. Winkes, p. 102 no. 26 identifies a fifth replica, in Cordoba.

Kiel: Marble head, h. 32.9 cm., Kieler Antikenssammlung inv. B536. Freyer-Schauenburg, 1982, 209–224, figs. 1–6; Winkes, 1995, 112–113 no. 38.

New York: Fragmentary marble head, 25.1 cm., of face 16.3 cm. Metropolitan Museum, inv. 18.145.45; Freyer-Schauenburg, 1982, 212, figs. 16–19; Winkes, 1995, 140 no. 64.

Cherchel: Marble head in the Museum of Cherchel, h. 33 cm. Freyer-Schauenburg, 1982, 212, n. 3 with full earlier literature, figs. 13–15; Winkes, 1995, 101 no. 24; Bartels, 1963, 56, 104 n. 451.

Toulouse: Musée Saint Raymond inv. 30 006, marble, h. 33 cm., w. 24.5 m., dia. 25 cm., h. of head 19 cm. Published: Rose, 1997, 126–128, cat. no. 52, pl. 161; Balty, 1996, 204 no. 143; Winkes, 1995, 181 no. 104; Balty and Cazes, 1995, no. 8, 96–101, figs. 24, 88–89, 93, 95, 97; Boschung, *JRA* 1993, 49–50, figs. 17–18; Freyer-Schauenburg, 1982, 210, figs. 7–12; Salviat, 1980, 48, 54, 70–72, photos pp. 48, 49, 53, 70, 74; Clavel, 1970, 465–466, figs. 44–45; Gross, 1962, 110; Poulsen, 1946, 8 figs. 6, 10–12 no. 5; Wegner, 1939, 225; Espérandieu I, no. 528 fig. 5; Belhomme, 1841–1847, 291, pl. 15 n. 3 (as "Faustina the Younger").

[144] Boschung, *JRA* 1993, 49–50, has recently questioned the identification of this type, reassigning the Toulouse head inv. 30 006 to Julia the daughter of Augustus, but I believe that when viewed as a group, the four sculptures look enough alike to be accepted as replicas of a common type, and that the less idealized examples conform well to the earlier portrait types of Livia with the *nodus* coiffure.

All four share a coiffure that dispenses with the "nodus" over the forehead and substitutes a middle part, but retains the small, tight chignon at the base of the skull. Here, as in the older type, the hair at the back of the head is combed down smoothly, but around the face forms a fuller area of soft waves that rise in considerably higher relief than the rest of the hair, flowing down around the face so as to frame the features. These waves partly overlap the tops of the ears, then twist into narrow, tight coils behind the ears that run back toward the chignon. This last feature is a direct survival from the earlier coiffure, in which the hair behind the ears received the same tidy and restrained treatment, and the chignon itself, which has a horizontal division, matches that of the Fayum type. For this reason, Winkes identifies this group of replicas as hybrids of two prototypes, but since they are consistently earlier in date than the members of his "core group" of portraits of Livia with the middle part, they might rather be described as transitional.[145] The elderly Augusta is most unlikely to have posed for this new portrait; rather, sculptors evidently created it for her by modifying the older type, with surprisingly successful results. The middle part has a more classicizing effect than that of the *nodus* coiffure, since it retains the smoothly controlled and closed contours of the latter while approximating Livia's image more closely to that of Greek images of goddesses of the fifth and fourth centuries. Above the forehead, the waves puff up to form a sort of crest that has the same effect as the nodus in lengthening Livia's short, round face. The similarity of this arrangement to a *nodus* coiffure is particularly striking in profile, a telling detail, since copyists measuring from an official prototype are likely to reproduce the profile contour with particular accuracy. Here, perhaps, we can catch the master sculptor in the act, so to speak, of making a pastiche of two official coiffures, the older and more established to which he and the prospective viewers were more accustomed, and the newer one, with the simpler middle part, that acknowledged the new status of the Augusta. Whether or not any or all of the statues to which these heads belonged represented Livia as a priestess is, unfortunately, impossible to ascertain without the survival of the

---

[145] Winkes, 1995, 44–46 and 48–49. Winkes lists six replicas of the "core group," all of which he dates to the principate of Claudius, while all five replicas of the Kiel type he dates as Tiberian.

rest of the figure, but the fact that none of the heads are veiled suggests that perhaps she was not.

Only one, the Béziers head (figures 39–40), comes from a known context. Just when this statue took its place in that imperial group is difficult to ascertain, since this assemblage took form over a number of years rather than being planned as a single, coherent commission; the majority of the statues appear to date from the time of Tiberius, but the portraits of Augustus and Agrippa must already have stood in the forum considerably earlier. The rationale for the addition of Livia's image, however, may have been the same as for her representation on coins of A.D. 22–23: the celebration of the lineage of Drusus II, whose likeness also appeared in the Béziers group, possibly accompanied by that of his young son Tiberius Gemellus. Livia's "adoption type" was to undergo a series of permutations in the following years, becoming increasingly goddess-like. Later versions of Livia's portrait coiffure with the middle part have sometimes been identified as her "Ceres type," but this is a misnomer, since all of her known portrait types, including those with the *nodus* coiffure could appear with the attributes of Ceres.[146]

On cameo gems and in some works of sculpture, Winkes has identified another variant on this type for Livia, when she appears in the specific context of priestess of the cult of Augustus. He originally considered this "priestess portrait" to follow a separate prototype from her sculptural portraits, but now groups all versions of her middle-part coiffure as variants on a common type. In these gems, unlike in the Kiel portrait and the related marbles, she wears long, loosely waved shoulder-locks, and a soft queue that hangs down the nape of the neck, rather than a tight bun.[147] In a pictorial composition, Julia Augusta's two roles, as priestess to the dead emperor, and Ceres Augusta, the divine mother of the living emperor, could both be more fully expressed, as is the case in at least one and possibly two such cameo gems. Here Julia Augusta appears as a priestess holding the object of worship, a small bust of the deified Augustus, while she herself wears the distinctive costume of, in one case, Cybele, and in the other, Venus Genetrix.[148] (Figures 41 and 42). Privately

---

[146] Fittschen-Zanker 3, 3–5 no. 4. On p. 4, n. 9, Zanker lists 16 replicas of the "Ceres type."

[147] Winkes, "Bildnistypen," 1988, 558–560; Winkes, 1995, 49–50.

[148] A) Vienna, Kunsthistorisches Museum inv. IX a 95, Matthias inv. 2189.

owned luxury objects like these were restrained by far fewer taboos
against the open deification of living persons than were public sculptures: the Vienna gem presents her not as Latin Ceres but Asiatic
Cybele, the Magna Mater Deum with her turret crown, tympanum
and lion-familiar, implying a role both as potential ancestress of a
dynasty and as protectress of the Roman state. (Figure 41). Although
the head is veiled, the bulge at the back of the neck under the thin
fabric indicates that Livia must wear the hanging queue rather than
the small chignon, while the softly waved shoulder lock flows forward from under the veil and is prominently visible. Unlike the
Boston turquoise (figure 42), however, the Vienna gem combines the
trappings of divinity with an unmistakably contemporary garment,
the *stola*, with its braided shoulder straps. This article of clothing
reminds us of Julia Augusta's continued social role in the world of
the living, and suggests a date during her lifetime.

Here, as in the three issues of *dupondii* in A.D. 22–23, (figure 34)
she legitimizes the claims to power of her male relatives of three succeeding generations, at least five and possibly seven of whom were
still alive at the time of this gem's manufacture. Livia's grandsons Germanicus and Drusus II died in A.D.19 and A.D. 23 respectively, before Livia's own death in A.D. 29, but their sons, her great-grandsons
Nero I, Drusus III, Caligula, and Tiberius Gemellus, outlived her by
several years, and all were plausible candidates for succession to imperial power.

The interpretation of the Boston turquoise (figure 42) is slightly
more problematic, due in part to the damage that has broken away
the lower part of the composition, making it impossible to determine
with certainty whether the smaller male figure is a bust of Augustus
or a "rejuvenated" portrait of Tiberius as a young boy.[149] The distinction is of some significance, since in the former case, the Augusta
would still be the worshipful subordinate of her divine husband,
although he appears at one remove, as a portrait within a portrait,
while in the latter, the scale of her figure as mother-goddess would

Winkes, 1995, 189 no. 113; Oberleitner, 1985, 47–48; Megow, 1987, 254 no. B 15,
pl. 9, figs. 1–3, with full literature.

  B) Boston, Museum of Fine Arts inv. 99.109, turquoise cameo. Winkes, 1995,
98, no. 21; Winkes, 1982, 131–138; Megow, 1987, 256–257, no. B 19, pl. 10.5 with
full literature.

  [149] Winkes, 1982, p. 137, argues for an identification as Augustus, Megow, 1987,
256–57, for the more widely held identification as Tiberius.

virtually overpower that of the reigning emperor, who has been reduced to the status of a dependant child. In any case, however, the similarity of the figure to the Venus Genetrix and to the polysemous allegorical figure of the Ara Pacis (figure 31) is unmistakable, as is the less restrained style of the gem-cutting. Since this stone, unlike the Vienna cameo (figure 41), is not a layered sardonyx, the relief can be deeper and more rounded, and the figures are able to turn somewhat outward from the background, appearing in 3/4 view rather than strict profile.

In public and monumental sculpture, the earliest transformation of Livia's adoption type into an explicitly divine image is a colossal statue from Leptis Magna, the cult image of a small temple to "Ceres Augusta." (Figure 43). This temple and, by inference, the statue, were erected after Livia's death, but predate her deification by six or seven years.[150] This temple was a small shrine, consisting simply of a shallow cella with two columns *in antis* and a portico of four columns in front of it, in the center of the top of the theater cavea.[151] The colossal image within the cella must have been easily visible to the people passing by on the walkway at the top of the cavea. The inscription informs us that the proconsul C. Rubellius Blandus, who held that office in the year A.D. 35–36, dedicated the shrine, along with a woman named Suphunibal, possibly a priestess of the cult, whom the inscription hails as "the adorner of her city." (CERERI AUGUSTAE SACRUM C. RUBELLIUS. BLANDUS. COS. PONT. PRO. COS. DEDIC. SUPHUNIBAL. ORNATRIX. PA[TRIAE] ANNOBALIS RUSONIS [F.D] S.P.F.C).[152] Despite the fact that the ruling emperor, Tiberius, was as stingy with honors to his mother after her death as he had been during her lifetime, the Roman official Rubellius Blandus and Suphunibal, obviously a wealthy woman

[150] Tripolis Museum inv. no. 26, h. 310 cm., from Leptis Magna. Winkes, 1995, 184–185 no. 107; Mikocki, 1995, 156 no. 37, pl. 14; Kreikenbom, 1992, 180–81, no. III 39, pl. 11c; Fittschen-Zanker 3, 4 n. 9, n (under no. 3); Caputo and Traversari, 1976, 76–79, no. 58, pls. 54, 55; Bartels, 1963, 55–56; Sande, 1985, 154–58, fig. 2. Sande points out that the inscription of the temple does not necessarily fix the date of the statue, since Rubellius Blandus could simply have rebuilt or renovated an earlier shrine in the older theater, while the statue of Livia as Ceres Augusta could have been added later. These possibilities are speculative, however; the strongest evidence for the date both of the temple and of the statue is the inscription of Rubellius Blandus.
[151] Hanson, 1959, 59–60 figs. 21–22.
[152] Bartels, 1963, 55; Mikocki, 1995, 151 no. 2.

of a local elite family, saw fit to honor Livia with a local cult, in a particularly visible location where the public would see her shrine and image on a regular basis.

The statue stands 3.10 meters tall, more than half again over life size, and represents the Augusta in a draped figure based on a Classical prototype often known as the "Kore of Praxiteles," although it could evidently be used to represent Demeter as well.[153] Like so many images of the chthonian goddesses, the characteristics of this prototype are modest dignity: the figure stands in a sturdy contrapposto, the weight firmly planted on the left foot, and wears heavy, enveloping drapery: a chiton, a heavier, sleeveless peplos over it, and a mantle draped diagonally around her body, under the right arm and over the left shoulder. Incongruously, the navel shows through the heavy drapery, but this may well be a characteristic of the original, or a deliberate embellishment by the copyist, rather than a mistake. The caryatids of the Erechtheion, works of unchallengable prestige and quality, show the same sort of physically impossible transparency, revealing the nipples and navels of the figures through two layers of heavy woolen fabric. In its effort to reconcile respectable modesty with sensuality, then, the statue of Livia from the theater of Leptis belongs to a venerable tradition. The gestures of the arms, the outward-pointing right toe, and the strong turn and lift of the head add some animation to the quiet stance of the figure, and interrupt its contours. The attributes on her head enlarge the significance of the image with polysemic references, since she wears not only the poppy and corn-ear crown of Demeter and Kore but the turret-crown of Cybele, often conflated with Ceres, an attribute also of Tyche-Fortuna. The Augusta thus appears very clearly as not only a bringer of prosperity but a protector and benefactor of cities, and presumably in particular of the city of Leptis Magna.

The breakage of the statue, unfortunately, obscures some details of the coiffure, but the hair at the nape of the neck does seem to have taken the form of a hanging queue, as in the cameo portraits of her lifetime that portrayed her as a goddess-like priestess, and here too there were evidently hanging elements on each side of the neck, although they may have been ribbons cascading from her garland rather than loose locks of hair. Another feature that this statue

---

[153] Rose, 1997, 75, 125, 148, 167, pls. 134, 192, 204; Caputo and Traversari, 1976, 78–79.

shares with the gems, and which is more dramatically visible in this large work, is that the hair around her face does not simply flow down to the ears in regular waves, but is drawn back from the face, in a busy pattern of waves that overlap eachother in a seemingly spontaneous pattern. Compare for example the head from the Béziers group (figures 39–40), which probably belongs to the Augusta's lifetime, with this statue of her as Ceres Augusta. Here the hair not only frames the face but radiates out from it in a sort of aureole. The sculptor has torn into the marble with deep and emphatic drill channels, a technical device perhaps dictated, again, by the colossal scale of the work and the need for bold treatment to make details of the face legible, but one that also lends a distinctly flamboyant quality to the representation, very different from the cool and modest portraits of her lifetime. The "Hellenistic" pose of the head, strongly turning to the left and tilting upward, contributes to the same effect.

The Leptis statue is a striking, but not a unique, work. At least one more statue of Livia—if its current reconstruction is accurate—combines a head with the "Priestess type" treatment of the hair and the corn-ear garland with a body of the "Kore of Praxiteles" type. This is a statue now in the Louvre that stands a little over life size, at 1.99 meters in height, although unlike the north African statue, it is not a colossus.[154] (Figure 44). Observers disagree on whether or not the head and the body belong together, but the marble surfaces of the neck and head seem to make an exact join.[155] Despite some damage and restoration to the head, Livia clearly parts her hair in the middle, draws it back across the ears in soft waves to a hanging queue at the nape, and has long, flowing shoulder locks. The back of the head and most of the shoulder-locks, where they hang free from the neck, are modern restorations, but the queue survives intact above the break through the neck, while the stumps of marble behind the ears prove that the shoulder locks belong to the coiffure. Enough of the neck survives to indicate that the strong twist and upward

---

[154] Paris, Musée du Louvre inv. MA 1245. Winkes, 1995, 150–151 no. 75; De Kersauson, *Louvre* 1, 1986, 100–101, no. 44; Fittschen-Zanker 3, 4 n. 9f; Winkes, "Bildnistypen" 1988, 560, fig. 7; Mikocki, 1995, 155 no. 32 pl. 3.

[155] Winkes, 1995, 150 no. 75, and 1988, "Bildnistypen," 560, argues that the head belongs to the statue, but De Kersauson, *Louvre* 1, 1986, 100, states that "La tête n'appartient pas à la statue." My own autopsy of the statue leads me to agree with Winkes: the entire extant neck is of marble and the join of the broken surfaces appears to be exact.

turn of the head are authentic characteristics of the original composition, and that the shoulder locks very probably hung away from
the neck, rather than adhering to it, just as they appear in the object
in its present state. Both of these characteristics belong also to the
statue from the theater at Leptis Magna. (Figure 43).

Although the original location of the Paris statue is unknown, it
came to the Louvre from the Borghese collection, an origin that
strongly suggests an Italian provenance.[156] The sculptor has taken a
slightly more conservative stylistic approach than his north-African
counterpart, using the chisel rather than the drill to articulate the
waves of hair, but they still form a busy pattern that radiates out
around the face, while the floral crown adds another busy texture
in which deep channels between the corn-ears and poppies create
an intricate play of light and shadow. The carving of the shoulder-
locks away from the neck was a virtuoso exercise in stone-carving,
requiring the sculptor to cut away the marble between the neck and
the relatively slender locks of hair. The play of solids and voids that
this treatment produced around the face would have rewarded this
rather expensive effort, and thus have appealed to a patron who
desired a flamboyant presentation. Whether this statue belongs to
the period after Livia's consecration or earlier is impossible to determine, but the very similar work from Leptis offers at least one precedent for such a statue still datable to the principate of Tiberius.

Portraits from the Principate of Gaius ("Caligula")

The accession of Caligula gave patrons who wished to honor the
living emperor an added incentive to honor his great-grandmother
as well, since she represented the glorious ancestry of Germanicus.
Caligula, like Tiberius, refrained from bestowing official divine honors
on Livia, an honor, ironically, in which her great-granddaughter Drusilla preceded her, but his situation vis-à-vis Livia was significantly different from that of his predecessor, simply because she had already died
at the time of his accession. She could thus be represented with the
extravagant honors suitable to an ancestor that, as Tiberius feared,
would have seemed inappropriate to a living member of the imperial

---

[156] De Kersauson, *Louvre* 1, 1986, 100.

family. It is possible that, had Drusilla's untimely death not forced a rearrangement of priorities, Caligula would have deified both Livia and his mother Agrippina I, probably in that order.

At least two, and probably three, extant portraits of Livia come from statuary groups securely datable to the principate of Caligula.[157] Of these, the group from the basilica of Velleia demonstrates with greatest clarity her significance in the propaganda of the third Julio-Claudian emperor.[158] (Figures 45–46). Although Livia had not yet formally been consecrated, her statue at Velleia was larger in scale than that of any other imperial woman in the group, and wore a crescent diadem, an attribute hitherto reserved for goddesses.[159] The body does not copy any known Classical prototype, although she does wear the Greek costume of chiton and himation, rather than the Roman *stola*: the honor of explicit identification with a goddess appears here to have been reserved only for Drusilla.[160] The appearance of Livia's statue, however, could discreetly hint at goddess-like status. Her coiffure is of the more classicizing "adoption type," rather than the *nodus*. The waves of hair are still drawn down smoothly around her face, rather than swept back from the hairline, and the cascading shoulder locks are absent, but here as in the colossal Leptis Magna statue (figure 43), deep drill channels separate the strands. As Rose has rightly observed, the statue from Velleia strongly assimilates Livia's appearance to that of Caligula and his siblings, making her face somewhat longer than usual and giving her eyebrows a slight flare toward the temples. The sculptors here may have preferred

---

[157] Rose, 1997, 60; 121–123, cat. no. 50, the group from Velleia, and 152–153, cat. 85, the group from Gortyn. Since both of these groups included portraits of Caligula, who would surely not have been represented after his death, the dates are secure. Rose also dates to the principate of Caligula a group from Paestum (Rose, 1997, 98, no. 26), but since this group includes only Tiberius and Livia, the dating is somewhat less secure. The god-like format of Tiberius's statue does seem to imply a date after his death, probably during the principate of his immediate successor.

[158] On the Velleia group: Saletti, 1968, passim. Goethert, 1972, 235–247, Jucker, 1977, 204–240. Rose, 1997, 121–26, cat. no. 5. Statue of Livia: Parma, Museo Civico inv. 1870 no. 146, 1952 no. 828, marble, h. 224.5 cm., of head 36.7 cm. Saletti, 1968, 33–37, no. 4, 106–110, pls. 11–12; Winkes, 1995, 152–153 no. 76.

[159] Saletti, 1968, 33–37, cat. no. 4, and 106–110, identifies this statue as Diva Drusilla, but concedes its resemblance in facial features and "*Salus* coiffure" to the images of Livia. In my opinion, the arguments of Goethert, 1972, 236–238, in favor of the identification as Livia are far more convincing; my autopsy of the statue confirms my opinion that it can only be Livia.

[160] Rose, 1997, 125.

the "adoption type" hairstyle not only for its goddess-like qualities but because of its resemblance to the coiffures favored by Agrippina II and Drusilla, with their middle parts and stiffly crimped waves around the face.[161] The sculptor of this statue has added one distinctively idiosyncratic touch: the soft fringe of locks that escape from the hair-line to hang softly down on the forehead.[162] This detail usually appears only on works of Eastern manufacture on portraits that wear the *nodus* coiffure. How the copyist at Velleia came to know of this orna-mental device must remain the subject of speculation, since we know nothing of his ethnic origin, but the locks here have two effects. As in eastern sculptures, they make the coiffure a little softer and more decorative. And they provide an element similar to, although not identical with, the little spit-curls along the hairline that appeared in the portraits of Drusilla, thus further strengthening the assimilation of the appearances of these two women. Although the statue of Drusilla at Velleia has lost its head, the portrait type must have been the same one that survives in a statue from Caere and in at least five other replicas, in which this fringe of curls is a consistent feature (figures 111–117).[163]

The assimilation of Livia's appearance to that of her great-grand-son and his sisters is also clearly evident in the portrait head from Gortyn, although here, the wisps of hair along the forehead do not appear.[164] Here again, however, her lower face is long, like that of Caligula, her eyebrows flare slightly toward the temples, as do his, and her hair has rather stiff and regular waves. Since only the heads of this group survive, we do not know the nature of the statues that belonged to them, but the Gortyn Livia, unlike the Velleia statue, does not wear a crescent diadem or any other quasi-divine attributes. The style of the Gortyn head is also more restrained, lacking the deep drill-channels of the work from Velleia. That statue, however,

---

[161] Rose, 1997, 123.

[162] Saletti, 1968, 109, cites this detail in arguing against the identification of the Velleia statue as Livia. Parallels however can be found in many portraits of Livia from Greece and Asia Minor: Inan and Rosenbaum 1966, 60–61, no. 11, pl. 7, 3–4; Inan and Rosenbaum, 1979, 61–62, nos. 5–6, pls. 4.2, 5.

[163] On the iconography of Drusilla, see Wood, 1995, 457–482. To the five repli-cas of the type that I identify in that article, Rose has added another, from Luna in Etruria: Rose, 1997, 94, no. 20, pl. 85, with earlier literature; Saletti, 1973, 37–46, fig. 2.

[164] Heraklion Archaeological Museum, marble head, h. 40 cm. Winkes, 1995, 108 no. 35 with earlier literature; Rose, 1997, 152–153, no. 85, pls. 194, 196.

despite its rather clumsy and provincial quality, anticipates things to
come. Use of the drill became increasingly popular during the principate of Caligula, particularly in the portraits of his mother Agrippina I, whose unruly curls offered sculptors an opportunity for displays
of virtuosity, and such drill work can be seen in some replicas of
Caligula's own portraits as well, despite the fact that, at his time,
men still wore their hair rather short. The extravagant tastes of the
emperor, the more flamboyant presentation of himself and his family, could have encouraged sculptors to explore the effects that they
could achieve with these devices more boldly than in preceding years.
As usual, however, the tastes of one individual are simply not sufficient
to explain a stylistic trend. The final decisions about the appearance
of these statues rested with the sculptors and patrons of the cities in
which they stood, and these people were clearly seeking a way to
honor the emperor's great-grandmother appropriately, in a manner
that would suggest divine status. As two prominent citizens in Leptis
Magna had already discovered late in the principate of Tiberius, a
richly ornamental reinterpretation of her most classicizing hairstyle
offered a means to this end.

Portraits from the Principate of Claudius

During the principate of Claudius, Livia finally achieved in the official
state religion the divine status that so many of her likenesses in statuary and, especially, in the more private medium of cameos had
already granted to her. Since a vocabulary of form already existed
for approximating her likeness to those of Ceres, Cybele, Venus Genetrix, and a variety of other goddesses and personifications, the task
of artists required to represent the new *diva* was not especially difficult.
The creation of a new cult required some impressively new visual
expression—in particular, the creation of cult images—but patrons
and sculptors could give such statues the appropriately divine appearance simply by using existing visual devices with increased flamboyance. No new portrait types appear to have come into existence at this
late date: the "adoption type" with its visual evocations of the goddess
Ceres, already existed, but during the principate of Claudius, this
existing type finds more dramatic interpretations. A device that had
already made its way into some portraits of Livia as early as the
principate of Tiberius now enjoyed its greatest popularity: the waves

of hair around the face flow outward rather than being combed smoothly downward. When deep drill channels, or deeply cut chiseled incisions, articulate these strands, the effect is striking: the strands radiate outward around her face like an aureole. If the hair was gilded, as it may in many instances have been, the resemblance to a sunburst would have been unmistakable.[165]

A statue of Livia that illustrates well the transition from her Caligulan to her Claudian images belongs to a group from Rusellae in Etruria (of which unfortunately no photographs are yet available), found in an apsidal building that seems to have been a shrine of the imperial family. Here, as at Velleia, we are dealing with a dedication in central Italy, within easy traveling distance of the capital city, and in such towns we can expect to see somewhat more faithful reproduction of official images than in some of the farther-flung provinces. The group included statues of Britannicus and Octavia, the children of Claudius, and of Claudius himself, but that portrait appears, like Claudius's statue at Velleia, to have been recut from an image of Caligula after the assassination and *damnatio memoriae* of the latter. The statues, therefore, must belong to at least two phases, of the principates of Caligula and of Claudius.[166] Dominating this group were huge enthroned figures of Augustus, in the guise of Jupiter, with drapery across his lap but a nude upper torso, and the Augusta, wearing a large crescent diadem.[167] Here, as at Velleia, she wore Classical drapery, a peplos over a chiton, and a heavy mantle draped over her head, around her shoulders, and across her lap. The drapery conceals the nature of her coiffure in back, but since there are no shoulder locks, this statue, like the slightly earlier standing figure at Velleia, seems to conform to the relatively conservative portraits of the time soon after her adoption, rather than to the more flamboyant representations of her in works like the Louvre and Leptis Magna statues. As at Velleia, however, the sculptor has used

---

[165] Rose, 1997, 73, 118.

[166] Winkes, 1995, 108 no. 33a; Kreikenbom, 1992, 82–83; Rose, 1997, 116–118, cat. no. 45.

[167] Statue of Augustus: Grosseto Museum inv. 97 737, from Rusellae. H. 210 cm.; head not preserved. The identity of Augustus can be inferred from context. The group has not yet received full publication. See Kreikenbom, 1992, 168 no. III 22, with list of references that mention the object. Statue of Livia: Grosseto Museum inv. 97 738 (torso) and 97 772 (head), h. 200 cm. Kreikenbom, 1992, 182–83 no. III 42; Fittschen-Zanker 3, 4 n. 9 L under no. 3. Discussion of the group as a whole: Rose, 1997, 116–118, no. 45.

the drill liberally to articulate the strands of hair, and this time, we see the modification of the coiffure, described above, in which the strands flow outward rather than downward.

Whether this statue belongs to the Caligulan or to the Claudian phase of this sculptural assemblage is impossible to establish beyond doubt, but Rose has recently made a convincing case for the latter, suggesting that the Rusellae statue may be a direct copy of the cult image that Claudius placed in the Temple of the Deified Augustus in Rome.[168] Regardless of the specific date, however, the statue displays stylistic similarities to the Velleia statue (as one would naturally expect in two works that cannot be more than about ten years apart), but also represents an advance in the presentation of the Diva Augusta. Both the body type and the interpretation of the hair and face cross the line from the almost-goddess like image at Velleia to an unambiguously divine one.

Some similar representations of the Deified Augusta include a head in the Capitoline Museum that wears a large, high diadem adorned with corn ears and poppies (figure 47), and an over-life-size statue in Copenhagen that likewise combines the attributes of Ceres with a crescent diadem, as well as, in this case, the attributes of Fortuna-Tyche (figures 48–49).[169] The latter work demonstrates a particularly skillful use of deep drill channels to articulate the strands of hair around the face. It is not uncommon for female portraits of this phase of the Julio-Claudian era to be misdated to the Antonine period; Gross made a very plausible case, for example, for dating the Copenhagen statue to some imperial group of the time of Marcus Aurelius or Commodus in which she might have accompanied the deified Augustus, forming a parallel, perhaps, to the more recent imperial couple of Antoninus and Faustina the Elder. The theory would be appealing were it not for the subsequent discovery of a statuary group in a nymphaeum at Baia, which Gross could not of course have predicted in 1962, that provides such close technical

---

[168] Rose, 1997, 60, 118. Rose points out the parallel between this statue and the image on Claudian *dupondii* of an enthroned female figure identified by the inscription DIVA AUGUSTA, probably a representation of that cult image.

[169] Rome, Museo Capitolino, Stanza degli Imperatori 9, inv. 144, marble head set on bust to which it does not belong. Winkes, 1995, 157 no. 82; Fittschen-Zanker 3, 3–5, no. 3, pl. 2.3, with full literature.

Copenhagen, Ny Carlsberg Glyptotek, cat. 531, I.N. 1643, marble statue, h. 215 cm., of head 29.5 cm. Winkes, 1995, 119 no. 43; Poulsen, *Portraits* 1, 73–74, no. 38, pls. 60–63; Andreae in *Baia*, 54, 63, fig. 131. Gross, 1962, 118–119. Johansen, 1994, 102–3 no. 39.

and formal parallels to the Copenhagen statue as to suggest that the statue of the Diva Augusta may even have belonged to the Baia group. (See figures 64–66, 69–71). Evidence for such an attribution is admittedly very tenuous, but whether or not the statues stood in the same original setting, there is good reason to attribute them to the same approximate date, and the same Naples-area atelier. The Copenhagen statue was found at Pozzuoli, near the site of the submerged nymphaeum. That image of the Diva Augusta wears an openwork lotus-palmette diadem similar to the one worn by Antonia Minor in the Baia group (figures 64–66), and shares with the statue of the child Claudia Octavia (figures 69–71) a virtuoso use of drill-channels in the hair.[170] The presence of the daughter of Claudius in the Baia nymphaeum confirms the dating of that sculptural assemblage to the principate of Claudius, and strongly supports a similar date for the Copenhagen statue of Livia.

Why do the statues and busts of deceased women of the Julio-Claudian family insist on frustrating our orderly art-historical schemata of technical developments in Roman sculpture, displaying flamboyant drill-work in their coiffures a century and a half before sculptors are supposed to be able to do this? Kleiner has demonstrated in his reconstruction of the lost arch of Nero that Julio-Claudian architects were capable of far more baroque design than we might imagine from surviving structures, and in sculpture as well, extant material offers us a picture that is far from complete.[171] In the case of sculpture, such devices appear to have been used sparingly precisely because of their power. Full, burgeoning and unruly hair has an emotional impact reflected in the customs and mores of many human societies: hair is the part of the body that can most obviously be seen to grow and increase, it suggests the life-force, is often regarded as a sign of fertility, and in a woman, therefore, alludes to her procreative powers. Full curls provide a source of visual fascination for the onlooker and an excuse for virtuoso displays of texture and pattern by a painter or sculptor. From the time of Alexander the Great onward, long,

---

[170] Gross, 1962, 119, arguing for an Antonine date, stated "Die geringen Spuren, nach denen das Diadem ergänzt ist, machen es wahrscheinlich, daß es von Anfang an ähnlich durchbrochen angelegt war. Auch dafür gibt es in claudischer Zeit keine Parallele . . ." The Baia statue of Antonia, however, does supply the missing parallel. See Rose, 1997, 82–83 no. 4, pls. 60–61; Andreae in *Baia*, 63. On the statue of Octavia in the Baia group, see Amedick, 1991, 378–380, and Rose, 1997, 72, 82–83, pls. 62–63.

[171] F. Kleiner, 1985, passim.

full and curly hair became part of the visual stereotype of the charismatic young ruler, a detail often combined incongruously with the
realistically aged faces of Hellenistic and Roman republican men.[172]
The slick, tightly controlled hair of women in the restrained style of
Augustus's lifetime expressed their chastity and allegedly circumscribed
political role (the facts, of course, were quite different from the desired
political message). By the time of Claudius, when Livia had become
Diva Augusta, the deified ancestress of the Claudian branch of the
Julio-Claudian family, the mother, great-grandmother and grandmother of the last three emperors, a Medusa-like aureole of twining,
deeply drilled locks of hair undulating outward from her face had
become a far more appropriate coiffure than the prim *nodus*.

The Baia building included niches for eight statues of which only
four were found *in situ*, implying that the others had been removed
in antiquity.[173] The geological process that caused the submersion
was evidently slow, and would have allowed for salvage operations,
but since moving heavy statues in swampy terrain is obviously difficult,
the salvagers would naturally have concentrated their efforts on the
members of the group still of political importance: the first emperor,
still a potent figure in political imagery, and his deified wife. Andreae
argues against this hypothesis that the Copenhagen statue is much
larger than those found in the nymphaeum, more than half a meter
taller than the life-sized Antonia, but the Rusellae group offers a
parallel for a composition in which a colossal image of the deified
Augusta appeared with life-sized images of other members of her
family, both living and dead—and it is worth noting that the Rusellae
group, too, included an image of Claudia Octavia as a child.[174]
Whether or not the Copenhagen statue and the Baia sculptures originally appeared together, however, they are works of comparable
quality and style that offer instructive contrasts in the ways that artists
could represent a living person, a dead but not deified ancestress,
and a diva.

---

[172] L'Orange, 1947, 30–38, 39–44, 49–53.

[173] F. Zevi in *Baia*, 12–13. The statues could have been removed at any time
between the end of the Julio-Claudian dynasty, when the composition of the group
would have ceased to have great political significance, and the seismic action that
caused the nymphaeum to be submerged under several feet of water, which probably did not occur before the 6th century A.D.

[174] Andreae in *Baia* 63. On the Claudia Octavia in the Rusellae group, Rose,
1997, 116, 118 no. 45.

The Baia Antonia (figures 64–66) shares with the Copenhagen Livia (figures 48–49) not only the openwork diadem but also the overt identification with a goddess, this time Venus, with allusions also to Kore. Antonia's hair, like Livia's, is parted in the middle and drawn back from the hairline in irregular waves, but unlike Livia's, the channels between the locks are not drilled, the volume is less full, and the effect more modest and controlled. The emperor's revered mother was important, but not *as* divinely powerful as the first Diva Augusta. Claudia Octavia (figures 69–71) shares with her grandmother the filmy chiton slipping from one shoulder that would probably remind viewers of Venus Genetrix, but her image includes as well an allusion to another deity, one associated with Venus, in the elaborate piece of jewelry that she wears in her hair along the top of her head. This attribute usually identifies Eros, and is most commonly borrowed for portraits of little boys rather than girls: her brother Britannicus invariably wears it in his childhood portraits, but this is the only replica of Octavia's childhood type in which the hair ornament appears.[175] Britannicus probably also appeared in the Baia family group; although the head of his statue does not survive, a number of fragments found in or near the third niche of the east wall appear to belong to a nude statue of a boy-Eros holding Psyche in the form of a butterfly over a *thymaterion*. In view of the discovery of these fragments among a gallery of imperial portraits, it is most likely that this Eros bore the portrait face of Britannicus.[176] Both imperial children, then, had visual associations with Venus and Eros. Claudia Octavia is not explicitly identified with any one divine being, but her potential for future fertility (that was, unfortunately for her dynasty, to prove false) is unmistakably suggested. She wears her hair in an arrangement typical for young girls: short in front, forming bangs, longer over the ears, and shoulder-length in back. The hair on the top of her head is smooth, but it breaks into rich, deeply drilled curls below the ears, curls that in a little girl do not yet need to be tightly controlled in a coiffure.[177] In the hierarchical order of the dynasty, however, both she and Antonia are subordinate to the image of Livia; only the senior Diva Augusta can be

---

[175] Amedick, 1991, 373–378 and 380–386 on the portrait of Britannicus, 378–380 on the Baia portrait of Octavia and its extant replicas.

[176] Andreae in *Baia*, 58–60.

[177] Amedick, 1991, 378–380.

presented with the Medusa-like mane of hair around a beautiful, idealized young face.

The differences in characterization of Livia and of Antonia in the Copenhagen and Baia sculptures can perhaps shed light on the identity and iconography of two more works of Claudian date in which the apotheosis of an imperial woman is so complete that her personal features almost vanish. One of these is the magnificent colossal head known as the Juno Ludovisi (figures 50–51), and the other, a fragmentary relief in Ravenna (figure 52) that represents the deified Augustus with members of his family.[178] Both the "Juno" and the female figure who stands immediately to the right of Augustus on the Ravenna relief have been identified by some observers as Livia, and by others as Antonia Minor. The two works differ in scale, degree of idealization, and, of course, medium, since one is a sculpture in the round and the other a relief, but they share with eachother a feature that appears also both on the Copenhagen Livia and the Baia Antonia: a crescent diadem decorated in relief with floral patterns. Both also represent a coiffure of thick, soft waves, parted in the middle, drawn back softly so as to conceal the tops of the ears, and looped into a queue that hangs down the back of the neck. They differ in that the "Juno" (figures 50–51) has long corkscrew curls that hang to the shoulders on each side, intertwined with the beaded strands that hang from each side of the *infula*, while the Ravenna figure (figure 52) has no shoulder locks. The Ravenna relief also shows some traces of individuality: a low, broad forehead, tapering chin, softly modeled nasolabial folds, and creases at the corners of the mouth that discreetly suggest maturity without too harshly interrupting the smooth and softly modeled surfaces of the face. If,

---

[178] Juno Ludovisi: Rome, Museo Nazionale Romano, Palazzo Altemps, inv. 8631, marble head and neck unit made for insertion into statue or bust, h. 116 cm. Published: Winkes, 1995, 163 no. 86; Kreikenbom, 1992, 92–93, recent refs. n. 730; Giuliano, ed., 1992, 122–127 no. 10 (Alessandra Costantini); *MNR Sculture* Vol. 1 part 5 (Rome, 1983) 133–137 no. 58 (Lucilla de Lachenal); Felletti-Maj, 1953, 69–70 no. 118; Kokkinos, 1992, 119–120 fig. 79; Erhart, 1978, 199–200, fig. 7, p. 210 no. 7; Tölle-Kastenbein, 1974, 241–253, pls. 91, 95 fig. 2, 96 fig. 2; Helbig⁴ 3, 263–264, no. 2341 (H. von Heintze); von Heintze, 1961, 3–16; Rumpf, 1941, 3–36 pl. 1. On the controversy re identity of the head, see Laubscher, 1976, 83 n. 62; Freyer-Schauenburg, 1983, 37–38.

Ravenna relief: Museo Nazionale, Ravenna, marble, h. 140 cm. Winkes, 1995, 198 no. 136 (as "Benennung als Livia unsicher"); Rose, 1997, 100–102 no. 30 with full literature; Kokkinos, 1992, 114–115; Pollini, 1981, 117–140. On the portrait figure in the guise of Venus, *LIMC* 8, 222 no. 330, s.v. "Venus" (Evamaria Schmidt).

on the other hand, the "Juno" (figures 50–51) represented any historical woman, that identity would have had to be conveyed to the
viewer by the inscription rather than the face. The sculpture was
accepted for years as a purely ideal head of a goddess before Rumpf
argued on the basis of its attributes and coiffure that it must represent a woman of the imperial family. The "Juno" has the calm, evenly
proportioned features of the Classical period of Greek sculpture: the
level eyebrows, the perfectly straight line in profile from forehead to
nose, without an indentation; the full lips, round, prominent chin,
and regular curve from chin to throat, without any trace of fleshiness
under the chin. The coiffure, however, has closer parallels in portraits
of Julio-Claudian women than in any known Classical representations
of goddesses, and is encircled by an attribute that also points to mortal identity: around the base of the diadem, she wears a beaded *infula*
with hanging fillets on each side that intertwine with the hanging
corkscrew curls. This last item, which Rumpf identifies specifically as
the badge of a priestess of the imperial cult, convinces him that the
subject must be a mortal woman, and one who held the office of
priestess of a deified emperor.[179]

The possible candidates from the Julio-Claudian dynasty would be
Livia, Antonia, or Agrippina II, who became the priestess of Claudius
after his death; Rumpf believed Antonia's coin portraits to provide
the closest match for the coiffure of the "Juno." Winkes has more
recently argued, however, that the coiffure most closely matches that
of Livia's portraits with the middle part, which could also represent
a queue of hair hanging down the nape of the neck rather than a
chignon. In favor of his identification is not only the form of the
coiffure, but its stylistic execution. The portraits of Antonia will be
discussed more fully in the next chapter, but the example of the
Baia statue, which shows her securely recognizable type in one of
its most goddess-like presentations, still shows the hair pulled back
tightly from the face so as to expose the ears completely. (Figures
65–66. The shadows in figure 66 partly obscure the ear, but the
hair loops above the upper rim of the ear rather than across it).
There is no use of the drill in the hair, and not for lack of will or
ability on the part of the sculptor, who did use that tool to articulate the lotus-and-palmette diadem. The "Juno," on the other hand,

---

[179] Rumpf, 1941, 21–31.

shows the waves swelling out more fully around the face, partly covering the ears, and separated by deeply carved channels, an arrangement well attested in representations of the deified Augusta. The *infula* that prominently appears in front of her diadem and intertwined (in a virtuoso display of carving) into the locks on the side of her head may identify her here not only as a priestess but as a deified woman. This ornament, as noted above, did not have just one restricted meaning, but conveyed sanctity to various types of figures and objects. Drusilla, the first Roman woman to be deified, wears this ornament on five of her extant portraits, and four of them clearly seem to have been recut to add the *infula*, suggesting that those portraits were made during her lifetime and then altered to show her new status after she became a *diva*. By the time of Livia's consecration, this meaning of the beaded strand would have been well established and understood, allowing the sculptor of the Ludovisi head to incorporate it with more elegance and confidence into that majestic and imposing work.

The figure to which it belonged might have been a cult image of the deified Livia, or the type of colossal votive statue that could be set up in the temple of a major deity, like the statue of Drusilla in the temple of Venus Genetrix that equalled the size of the cult statue. Another colossal statue more securely identified as Livia offers a close, if not exact parallel, for the headgear: an enthroned figure from Leptis Magna that once appeared in a group with the deified Augustus, Tiberius, Claudius, and Messalina.[180] The group must then be Claudian, datable to the time shortly after Livia's deification, and like the Juno Ludovisi, it wears a high diadem (this time without floral decorations in relief) and a beaded band that encircles its base. She wears the middle-part coiffure, which this time is a little more conservatively rendered, without flamboyant drill-work. The hanging ends of the *infula* do not hang down the sides of the neck here as they do in the Juno Ludovisi, but nonetheless, the similarities between the headgear of the "Juno" and of the Leptis statue are compelling. No securely identified image of Antonia Minor presents as close a parallel.

---

[180] Tripolis Museum, marble statue, h. 209 cm., of head, from chin to top of diadem, 32.5 cm. Winkes, 1995, 182 no. 106; Rose, 1997, 184–185 no. 126 pls. 231–232; Kreikenbom, 1992, 185 no. III 45, pl. 11d.

The archaeological provenance and original setting of the Juno are unknown, but the woman of the Ravenna relief appears in the context of an imperial family group. Unfortunately, however, that composition is incomplete, and can allow for endless speculation as to what other figures may have been present. It is difficult, therefore, to infer the identity of the surviving figures from context. The female in question stands next to Augustus, an appropriate position either for Livia, as his wife, or for Antonia, as the woman who succeeded her as priestess of his cult. Her identification with Venus suggests that she is a mother of future emperors, just as Venus was the *genetrix* of the Julian line—an appropriate identification, again, for either Livia or Antonia. To her right are a young man in partial nudity who appears to have worn a star of apotheosis on his forehead, a mature man in the armor and *paludamentum* (long cape) of a general, and the fragmentary figure of a seated, draped woman.

Most observers agree that the young man is Germanicus, who was never officially deified, but whose beloved memory was immensely useful to his children and living relatives. The identity of the man in armor is more problematic: some hypotheses include Claudius, the brother of Germanicus; Drusus I, his father, or Domitius Ahenobarbus, the biological father of Nero. As these diverse theories would suggest, none of the heads on the relief conform closely to established portrait types, a phenomenon common in relief sculpture, where, as noted above in relation to the Ara Pacis, sculptors tend to be making freehand rather than measured copies of prototypes. Most observers today do at least agree, however, that the work is no earlier than the principate of Claudius, and possibly as late as that of Nero— that it must, in other words, postdate both the deification of Livia and the death of Antonia Minor. The statue of Antonia from Baia, which explicitly identifies her with Venus, offers some support for the latter identification, since the Baia statue shares with the figure on this relief not only a floral diadem but a little figure of Amor perched on the left shoulder. If the semi-nude young man is Germanicus, then his close juxtaposition to the figure of his mother would be most appropriate. On the other hand, the woman's face, with its low, broad forehead and short, tapering lower face bears somewhat more resemblance to the portraits of Livia than to those of Antonia, who tends to have a higher forehead and longer, thinner face, although the liberties that sculptors were obviously willing to take with physical appearance should caution us against basing

an identification on physiognomy alone. More to the point, therefore, we see here as in the Juno Ludovisi a full and soft treatment
of the coiffure (although this time without elaborate drill work) that
partly conceals the ears. The identity of this figure, and the interpretation of the entire Ravenna relief, is a problem that cannot be
solved to everyone's satisfaction until and unless more evidence should
come to light; suffice it for now to observe that the arguments in
favor of the identification of the standing woman as Livia seem
slightly more convincing than those for Antonia.

Augustus and the woman are explicitly identified with major
Olympian gods—Jupiter and Venus respectively, while the young
man appears god-like, but lacks a specific association with a particular deity, and the man in armor appears to be portrayed in an
honorific but strictly mortal guise. The poses, the swing of the drapery and the graceful repetitions of rhythm from one figure to the
next such as the bend of the woman's leg that mirror-images that of
the young man, suggest a logical progression in the hierarchy of the
dynasty, from the officially deified founding couple, Augustus and
Livia, to Germanicus who is honored almost as a *divus* although that
status has not been officially established, to a mortal figure, who
either receives his earthly authority from these glorious predecessors
or is part of the genealogical progression that passes it on to the
ruling emperor.

One more work of problematic interpretation, but one on which
Livia's portrait at least can be recognized beyond serious doubt is
the huge sardonyx cameo known as the "Grande Camée de France,"
or sometimes the "Gemma Tiberiana," although the portraits of
Claudius and Agrippina II in the central register demonstrate that
the work must be no earlier than the principate of Claudius (figure
145).[181] The complex imagery of this gem has provoked numerous
interpretations and controversies that can most appropriately be discussed in a later chapter, but all scholars agree at least on the fact
that the figures enthroned at the center are Tiberius and his mother
Livia. The occasion represented, which involves the acknowledgment

---

[181] Paris, Bibliothèque Nationale, Cabinet des Médailles inv. 264, sardonyx cameo,
h. 31 cm., w. 26.5 cm. Winkes, 1995, 49, 145 no. 71; Megow, 1987, 202–207 no.
A 85, with full literature, pls. 32.5–10, 33. Mikocki, 1995, 21, 157–58, pl. 8, for a
discussion of the portrait of Livia. See chapter 6 for a discussion of the program
of the gem.

either of Germanicus or of the son of Germanicus as the legitimate heir to the empire, must have taken place decades before the creation of the gem, when both Tiberius and Livia were alive, but by the time the cameo was carved, Livia's deification had taken place, a point that someone eager to flatter Claudius would have had good reason to emphasize. Claudius had displayed his *pietas* toward his grandmother by giving her the long-deferred honor of deification, and could now claim direct descent from a *diva*, in addition to his far more tenuous connection to the deified Augustus.

Livia, therefore, holds the corn-ears and poppies of Ceres, and appears very close to the center of the composition. Although the enthroned Tiberius occupies the exact center, her figure, to his left and the viewer's right, appears in the foreground, overlapping that of her somewhat embarrassing and unpopular son. It is he who has the authority to transmit power to his chosen successors, and so he wears some of the divine attributes of Jupiter as well as holding emblems of earthly authority like the *lituus* in his outstretched right hand, but it is Livia, with the attributes of the bountiful and maternal Ceres, whom the Claudians prefer to remember as their ancestor. Tiberius derives his authority from Augustus, whose deified figure in the upper register of the gem hovers above him, but Tiberius, as any viewer of this gem would know, owed his adoption and succession to power to his mother's marriage to Augustus. The use of the portrait type with the middle part and the looped queue down the nape of her neck (although not, in this case, the shoulder locks), helps to emphasize that connection, since this is a portrait type that commonly appears on cameo gems in connection with the Augusta's priestly role. On the Grande Camée de France, the coiffure has an additional resonance: her great-granddaughter Agrippina II, who sits behind her on a lower but still impressively ornate throne, likewise wears a looped queue down the back of her neck. The status of Agrippina II as the wife of the emperor and mother of his stepson and prospective heir bears obvious similarities to that of Livia; the maker of the gem may well have hoped to flatter Agrippina II and Claudius with the reflected glory that the first Augusta could shed on the living holder of that title.

Portraits of Livia with the *nodus* coiffure, of course, continued to appear even at this late date, just as they had appeared alongside the newer type with the middle part during the principate of Tiberius. Patrons of the time of Caligula, on the evidence of the datable

states, strongly preferred the "adoption type," but a newer type
could never entirely supplant one that had been in use for a long
period and was still visible in many existing monuments. A slightly
unorthodox variant on the *nodus* coiffure, however, now enjoyed
renewed popularity, perhaps precisely because it allowed sculptors a
certain freedom in reinterpreting her well-known and highly recognizable image. This is the coiffure that first appeared on provincial
coins of the lifetime of Augustus, in which two narrow braids encircle the crown of the head, instead of running directly back along
the crown (figure 21).[182] An especially appealing representation of the
Augusta with this hairstyle is a marble bust which, to judge from the
representation of the shoulders and upper chest, must be no earlier
than the time of Claudius, and must therefore belong to the period
after her deification.[183] (Figures 28–29). Here, the Augusta has long
and thick escaping locks that cascade to the shoulders, while the hair
both of the nodus and of the waves around her head have loose,
irregularly undulating strands that suggest that the hair is about to
escape its confinement. Both of these elements produce effects comparable to those of the variations noted above on the coiffure of her
"adoption type" in its later copies. The format of the sculpture, on
the other hand, which was definitely a bust rather than a statue,
suggests private ownership. This may have been an object like the
little bronze from the lararium of Atespatus in Gaul (figures 32–33)
that would have expressed the loyalty of a wealthy citizen to the
imperial family, not a work for public display.

One other portrait with this coiffure, that of the Munich Residenz,
likewise shows long, thick locks escaping at the nape of the neck,
although they are not long enough to reach the shoulders, unlike
those of the Copenhagen example. In the other three examples, these
shoulder-locks are absent.[184] Another however, in the Ankara Museum

---

[182] Gross, 1962, 35–36, pls. 4, 6–8, coins from Pergamon.
[183] On Copenhagen 616, supra n. 79. On the Claudian date, see Inan and
Rosenbaum, 1979, 62 no. 7, and Gross, 1962, p. 103. Winkes, 1995, 35–37, 115,
no. 40, seems undecided whether the date is Augustan or Claudian, giving the date
as "augusteisch" on pp. 35 and 115 but stating on p. 37 that "Der Scheitelzopf
fehlt bei der claudischen Replik Kat. 40 . . ." The bust-form of the Copenhagen
marble shows a broad area of the chest, including the shoulder caps, a form too
late to be Augustan or Tiberian.
[184] Winkes, 1995, 35–37; Gross, 1962, 104, on the head from Butrinto and the
overlifesized head in Vienna, a work apparently of Balkan origin. Fittschen-Zanker
3, 2, no. 1, note 4, nos. 4c–e.

in Asia Minor, shares with the Copenhagen bust a very loose and soft aureole of hair around the face, as well as a softly modeled and highly idealized treatment of Livia's features that almost approximate a Classical oval.[185] She also has a long, elegant swan-neck that turns gracefully upward. The Munich head, in contrast, shows sharp-edged, emphatically modeled features that give the Augusta an expression both more energetic and more dour than her standard likenesses, with eyebrows that flare sharply toward the temples and pursed lips. The slightly over-life-size scale may have required the sculptor to resort to a bolder and less subtle treatment of her features than was customary, but assimilation to the appearance of one of her descendants may also have influenced the form of this face. The flaring eyebrows and in particular the pursed lips, with creases at the corners, empha- size her a resemblance to a number of the Julio-Claudian men.[186]

Summation

At every phase of her life and "Nachleben," there is nothing acci- dental or casual about the associations conjured up by Livia's images or the impact that these images were designed to have on the viewer. During the lifetime of her husband, when her power and her public role in some realms such as religious observance was acknowledged, it was important to emphasize that her importance was strictly that of a prominent mortal woman; a dignified *stolata* and the wife of the "first citizen," but one whose image must be scrupulously differentiated from those of divine and semi-divine beings. The special exceptions to this rule are the relief of the Ara Pacis and the privately owned and provincial works that enjoyed some independence from official dogma. During her widowhood and after her death, however, Livia's images become truly polysemous, balancing the mortal nature of the woman who was still alive or who had recently lived with the visual allusions to Ceres, Fortuna, and Venus Genetrix. In posthumous por- traits she sometimes wears purely Greek Classicizing costume, but the coiffures that enframe her face never deviate too far from those she could have worn in life. Within the strictures of historical accu-

---

[185] Ankara bust: Winkes, 1995, 35, 81 no. 2; Inan and Rosenbaum, 1966, 59–60 no. 10, pl. 7.1–2; Fittschen-Zanker 3, 2 n. 1 no. 4b.
[186] Winkes, 1995, 138–139, no. 62, with full literature; Poulsen, 1968, 12–14, 22.

racy, however, sculptors had the option of interpreting those coiffures in any manner from cold restraint to flamboyant virtuosity.

Livia's portraits also demonstrate perhaps more clearly than those of any other imperial woman, thanks to their great number and rich variety, that an individual's "public image" was not, and could not be, something entirely determined by an official line of propaganda. Naturally both the reigning emperor and the subject of a portrait would attempt to maintain some control over the iconography of her likenesses, by patronizing portrait artists whose style suited their tastes, and by disseminating the prototypes that those artists created. It was, however, impossible to prevent the patrons who commissioned copies of those prototypes from demanding certain variations on them or the sculptors from interpreting and adapting them as they chose. On occasion, if an emperor knew of a donor's intentions, he could have some say in the nature of the dedication, requesting, for example, that the honors be less extravagant than those that the donor had proposed.[187] The statue and temple of Livia as Ceres Augusta from Leptis Magna proves, on the other hand, that there was no way to prevent local cults from coming into being even before an individual had received official consecration. Livia's personality, her benefactions to provincial cities, and her relationship to every one of the Julio-Claudian emperors made her important not only to the official propaganda of the imperial family but to communities and individuals throughout the empire. Her image was potent, her memory, after her death, obviously revered. Whatever the reality of her character may have been, the enormous physical evidence of her representations in art suggest that it is no exaggeration to call her a beloved figure.

---

[187] Rose, 1997, 142–144, no. 74, on an inscription from Gythaeum that records a dedication of three imperial portraits, and a response from Tiberius that requests appropriately human, rather than divine, honors to living members of the imperial family.

CHAPTER THREE

ANTONIA MINOR

Antonia Minor, like Livia, was a woman whose lifetime spanned more than two principates and whose image continued to be a potent dynastic symbol after her death. Her images, therefore, defy categorization in one principate or another; her earliest appearance on a public monument dates to the time of Augustus, on the Ara Pacis (figures 53–54), and her only securely identified portrait type must, to judge from the hairstyle that it wears, have been created during the principate of Tiberius, but the identification of that portrait rests on coins minted well after her death, when her son Claudius was emperor, and many of the extant sculptural replicas of her portrait must also be posthumous. Some can be securely dated by context; others, perhaps, by the attributes of the Priestess of the Deified Augustus, a title that she held for only a very brief period before her death, but which later became a very useful source of political and spiritual prestige for her son. Portraits that explicitly emphasize her priestly role, therefore, are most probably posthumous images.

Biographical Information

The younger daughter of Marc Antony and Octavia Minor, the wife of Livia's son Drusus I, and the mother of Germanicus, Claudius and Livilla I, Antonia Minor was a prominent member of the Julian family who figured in the dynastic plans of both Augustus and Tiberius. (See Appendix, Chart no. 4). Unlike Livia, she never enjoyed the status of the living wife or mother of a ruling emperor, but both her husband Drusus I and her son Germanicus were able and popular men regarded as worthy successors to power before their untimely deaths. One of her sons, Claudius, eventually did succeed to power, four years after Antonia's death, at which time her public images achieved their greatest importance in imperial propaganda, and her images and coins at this time very deliberately draw parallels between her and Livia. As the daughter of Antony, however, Antonia also represented a "wild card" in the imperial succession, since through her, descendants of the defeated enemy of Augustus could, and eventually did, come to power. Born in 36 B.C., Antonia could not have known her father, and was raised in Rome by the formidable Octavia, who was always unshakably loyal to her brother and his policies. Antonia undoubtedly learned from her the same loyalty to the Julians and to the ruling emperor, as well as her mother's standards of proper female conduct. Like Octavia, Antonia was never the subject of any sexual scandal, and her portraits, as we will see, conform well to her reputation for chaste modesty.

In one respect, Antonia perhaps exceeded the expectations of Augustus for monogamous behavior, in that she refused to remarry after the death of Drusus I in 9 B.C., although she was still a young woman with many potential childbearing years ahead of her. Augustus's social legislation, through the *Lex Iulia de maritandis ordinibus*, encouraged fertile widows to remarry. According to the same law, on the other hand, Antonia, having already produced three children, enjoyed the legal rights of freedom from *tutela*, or guardianship, and consequent control over her own property, that *ius liberorum* conferred.[1] She could thus perhaps exercise some independence in decisions about marriage that the *princeps* would ordinarily control. By choosing to remain faithful to her dead husband, Antonia enjoyed the status of a *univira*, wife of only one husband, that Roman society revered. Such women enjoyed special religious status in that only they were sufficiently pure to participate in some rites or to touch certain ritual objects. Although her decision not to remarry did not conform to Augustus's policies, it later won Antonia praise from the Senate, in its decree recording the condemnation of Cn. Piso for the murder of Germanicus. The decree specifically mentions that Antonia has had only one marriage, and is worthy in the sanctity of her ways of her membership in the family of the deified Augustus.[2]

---

[1] Antonia's refusal to remarry: Josephus, *AJ* 18.180; Val. Max. 4.3.3; Kokkinos, 1992, 15–16. On the *Lex Iulia de maritandis ordinibus*: Suet. *Aug.* 34.1; Gardner, 1991, 20, 54; Balsdon, 1962, 76–77.

[2] *S.C. de Cn. Pisone Patre*, lines 140–142: "itemq(ue) Antoniae Germanici Caesaris matris, quae unum matrimonium Drusi Germ(anici) patris experta sanctitate morum dignam se divo Aug(usto) tam art a propinquitate exhibuerit . . ." Eck, Caballos and Fernández, 1996, 48–49, 244.

Status of *univirae*: Dion. Hal. *Ant.Rom.* 8.56.4; Gardner, 1991, 50–51; Flory, 1984, 318. Only newly married women and *univirae* could worship the goddess Fortuna Muliebris, and no woman married more than once could touch the cult statue or crown it with garlands.

Antonia's daughter Livilla I married Drusus II, the son of Tiberius, and gave birth to his twin sons, an event that Tiberius celebrated extravagantly and commemorated on coinage.[3] Antonia thus had two claims to prominence during the principate of Tiberius, as the mother of his adopted son, and as the mother-in-law of his own son. Her relationship to Germanicus, however, must sometimes have made relations with the ruling emperor difficult, and occasional caused her, whether deliberately or not, to pursue an agenda somewhat different from that of Tiberius.

Since the memory of Germanicus, as the intended heir of Augustus and as political martyr, figured prominently in the claims to power of all three of the Julio-Claudian emperors after Tiberus, and since his mother consequently demonstrated an important bloodline, it is appropriate here to briefly consider that young man's truncated career. Germanicus, through his father Drusus I, was the grandson of Livia as well as the great-nephew of Augustus. His demonstrated military ability, as well as his connection to the bloodline of the Julian family undoubtedly recommended him to Augustus as an eventual heir to imperial power. He was also a charismatic and popular leader, who enjoyed the intense—and occasionally excessive—loyalty of his troops. During a mutiny shortly after the death of Augustus in A.D. 14, the troops in Germany acclaimed Germanicus as emperor, an election which he, at risk of his life, refused.[4] Despite his demonstrated loyalty, this incident undoubtedly caused Tiberius to perceive his nephew as a potential rival, as well as an obstacle to the succession of his own son Drusus II. The suggestion, therefore, that Germanicus was sent to the eastern frontiers of the empire in A.D. 18 in order to separate him from his legions in Germany, seems entirely plausible, although whether or not Tiberius harbored more sinister plans at that time or any later time is unprovable.[5]

Germanicus further aroused the suspicions of Tiberius by making an unauthorized and illegal tour of Egypt, the personal province of the emperor. Tacitus describes this as an entirely innocent venture

---

[3] *RE* 13 (1927), 924–927 (Lotte Ollendorff). Tac. *Ann.* 2.84, on the birth of the twins. Coins in honor of the birth: *RIC* 1² 97, no. 42, pl. 11; *BMCRE* 1, 133 nos. 95–97, pl. 24, fig. 6.

[4] Tac. *Ann.* 1.33–35; Suet. *Calig.* 1.1; Dio 57.5–6. For a review of the career of Germanicus, see Barrett, 1996, 22–32. Barrett, p. 26, expresses skepticism about the efforts to acclaim Germanicus emperor.

[5] Tac. *Ann.* 2.5, 2.69–75.

during which Germanicus, unaware that his travels were forbidden and motivated solely by antiquarian curiosity, visited the historical sites of Pharaonic Egypt. Tiberius, however, had reason to suspect an agenda more serious than sightseeing, and an interest on the part of Germanicus in far more recent historical events.[6] Kokkinos has recently raised the remarkable and provocative suggestion that Germanicus, the grandson through his mother Antonia of Marc Antony, was deliberately making a sort of pilgrimage through regions that Antony had once controlled, territories where some local people could still have felt resentment about the outcome of the civil war between Antony and Octavian, and held lingering loyalty toward the family of Antony. Earlier in his travels through the Greek and Eastern provinces, Germanicus visited Actium, where he inspected both the spoils dedicated by Octavian and the site of Antony's camp. Whether or not he intended any disloyalty to Tiberius, that visit along with the subsequent trip to Egypt could easily have aroused the suspicions of the notoriously paranoid emperor. Some inscriptions from cities along the route of his journey specifically honor his mother Antonia, which might suggest that she accompanied him at least part of the way, in which case not only Germanicus and his children but the entire Antonian branch of the family, including Antony's own daughter, would have been with him as he visited these regions.[7] The evidence for Antonia's presence on this journey is circumstantial—a member of the imperial family need not visit a city in order to be its benefactor, and to be honored with statues and inscriptions—but even if Antonia was not there in person, the inscriptions in her honor make it clear that her public image, money, political prestige, and highly significant name were very much present along with her son.

The situation of Germanicus in the east was made difficult by a bitter personal rivalry with Gn. Calpurnius Piso, the governor of Syria. When Germanicus suddenly fell ill in the fall of A.D. 19, therefore, both he and his wife Agrippina I were convinced that he was the victim of poison at the hands of Piso and Piso's wife Plancina. This rumor, according to Tacitus, quickly spread to Rome even before the death of the popular general.[8] Allegations of poisoning are of

---

[6] Tac. *Ann.* 2.60–61; Kokkinos, 1992, 17–22.
[7] Kokkinos, 1992, 17, 20–21, 43–45, 70–83.
[8] Tac. *Ann.* 2.82.

course always unprovable, but if Tacitus's account is accurate, Germanicus was unquestionably the victim of malicious harrassment by someone, since curse tablets, human body parts and various magical objects were discovered in the floor and walls of his house. The Senatus Consultum condeming Piso, however, makes no mention of witchcraft.[9] Even if the information about the magical objects is accurate, moreover, their presence does not prove poisoning. If Germanicus had fallen ill of natural causes, some personal enemy might simply have taken advantage of the situation, attempting to insure by magical means that his illness would be fatal. It has even been suggested that friends of Germanicus, convinced that Piso was to blame for his condition, planted the objects themselves in order to strengthen the case against the governor.[10] Whatever the cause of the illness, Germanicus died convinced that Piso and Plancina were responsible, and urging his friends to avenge him against them.

The trial of Piso was inconclusive, ending abortively with his apparent suicide, but the Senate condemned him posthumously for *maiestas*, treason, on several charges including the death of Germanicus.[11] Tiberius broadcast the information of this sentence to the provinces by official decree, several copies of which have survived. This document also records his decision to display clemency toward Piso's widow Plancina, at Livia's request.[12] The pardon of Plancina, as discussed in the previous chapter, probably sufficed to convince Germanicus's supporters, notable among them his widow Agrippina I, that Piso and Plancina had acted on direct orders from Livia and Tiberius, and that Plancina's pardon was the final, cynical payoff of the conspiracy. Suetonius repeats these suspicions in so many words, while Tacitus and Dio, without directly accusing Tiberius, emphasize the fact that Tiberius found the death of Germanicus very convenient.[13] Suetonius also reports a rumor which he does not credit, that Drusus I, the husband of Antonia and father of Germanicus,

---

[9] Tac. *Ann.* 2.69.3; *S.C. de Cn. Pisone Patre* 28; Eck, Caballos and Fernández, 1996, 154–155.

[10] Eck, Caballos and Fernández, 1996, 154 n. 402; Flower, 1997.

[11] The fullest surviving accounts of the death of Germanicus and trial of Piso are Tac. *Ann.* 2.69–71 and 3.12–16; *S.C. de Cn. Pisone Patre.* Reconstructed text of decree published in Eck, Caballos and Fernández, 1996, 38–51.

[12] Tac. *Ann.* 2.43, 2.82, 3.15, 3.17; *S.C. de Cn. Pisone Patre* lines 109–120, Eck, Caballos and Fernández, 1996, 46–47, commentary 222–228; Eck, 1993, 199.

[13] Suet. *Calig.* 2.1; Tac. *Ann.* 3.2; Dio 57.18.6–10.

had fallen victim to a similar plot by a ruling emperor because of the admiration of Drusus I for the republican system of government and his determination to restore it if he should come to power. Tacitus mentions the same rumor without either explicitly endorsing or dismissing it, reporting in indirect discourse the speculation that the motives for the deaths of both men were the same, since Germanicus, like his father, had intended to restore the republic. Since the emperor at the time when Drusus I died was the revered Augustus rather than the hated Tiberius, Suetonius rightly dismisses the story as incredible.[14] The fact that such a notion existed at all, however, is evidence of the degree of paranoia and rumor-mongering that must have taken place at the time of the death of Germanicus.

Unlike Agrippina I, Antonia appears to have remained on good terms with the emperor Tiberius after the death of Germanicus, though the conspiracy theorists were convinced that Tiberius and Livia had forcibly prohibited her from attending his funeral. Tacitus grudgingly concedes that her ill health, rather than a sinister plot, might have kept her at home, but also mentions that there is no written record of her participation in any events in the events related to her son's death. The newly discovered text of the *Senatus consultum* condemning Piso gives the lie to that claim, since that decree does mention her by name, along with other members of the imperial family, implying her presence at the deliberations.[15]

Several ancient authors inform us that, a few years later, Antonia was instrumental in bringing about the fall of Sejanus, and thus freeing members of the imperial family from the rivalry of a powerful outsider who may or may not have been guilty of the conspiracy charges against him.[16] Some modern historians are skeptical of the true extent of Antonia's true role in these events, suspecting that the story that Antonia saved Tiberius from a treasonable conspiracy was invented after the fact to glorify the mother of Claudius and grandmother of Caligula.[17] Whether or not Antonia was the sole agent of Sejanus's downfall, however, there are clear and corroborating accounts

---

[14] Tac. *Ann.* 2.82; Suet. *Claud.* 1.4.

[15] Tac. *Ann.* 3.3.2; *S.C. de Cn. Pisone Patre* 140–142, Eck, Caballos and Fernández, 1996, 48–49, 242–244; Flower, 1996, 250–252, and 1997.

[16] Dio, 58.11.6–7 and 65.14.1–2; Josephus, *AJ* 18.181–182; Boddington, 1963, 7–8, 12; Kokkinos, 1992, 25–27.

[17] Nicols, 1975, 48–58. For a defense of the traditional view of her role, see Kokkinos, 1992, 25–27, 42.

in the works of two ancient authors that it was she who first alerted
Tiberius to the existence of a plot against him, writing a letter to
him at his retreat in Capri to warn him of Sejanus's activities. Antonia
may have had self-interested as well as honorable motives for her
action, since Sejanus endangered the succession to power of her own
grandsons, but in any case, her own family did not escape unscathed
from the ensuing political upheaval. The frantic hunt for political
enemies after the fall of Sejanus led to the death of her own daughter Livilla I on charges of complicity in the murder of Drusus II.
According to some accounts, Antonia herself carried out the sentence of death. The Senate later voted a condemnation of memory
against Livilla I and ordered the destruction of all her images, public and private.[18]

Caligula's public display of *pietas* when he succeeded to power
included great honors for his paternal grandmother, to whom he
offered the title of Augusta (which she may, however, have refused)
and the privileges of an honorary Vestal virgin. She also became
the priestess of the Deified Augustus, thus inheriting the religious
status of Livia.[19] This priestly office had evidently been vacant for
several years since Livia's death in A.D. 29, but Antonia did not
acquire the office until Caligula appointed her to it in A.D. 37, as
both Dio and Suetonius clearly indicate. Had Antonia lived longer,
her role in public imagery might have matched that of Caligula's
sisters, with whom she shared honorary status as a Vestal, but her
death only a few months after Caligula's accession removed her from
significance in Caligula's public propaganda, which focused on honors specifically to his parents and on his lineage, through his maternal line, from Augustus. (See Appendix, chart no. 7). During Caligula's
principate, Antonia does not appear on any issue of Roman coinage,
and aside from observances of her birthday by the Arval brothers,
she seems not to have been honored with public ceremonies comparable to those for Agrippina I.[20] No statues of her can be dated
with certainty to the principate of Caligula, but her name does appear
in Caligulan inscriptions.[21]

---

[18] Tac. *Ann.* 4.7–8 on the death of Drusus II; Dio 58.11.6–7 on Livilla I's involvement in the death of Drusus II and her execution; Pekáry, 1985, 137 and Tac.
Ann. 6.2 on the destruction of her portraits.
[19] Dio, 59.3.3–4; Suet. *Calig.* 15.2; Suet. *Claud.* 11.2.
[20] Observance by the Arvals: Barrett, 1990, 62; Kokkinos, 1992, 36.
[21] Rose, 1997, 65–66 and 116–118, no. 45. Inscription in honor of Antonia at
Corinth (not connected with a statue): 139, no. 69.

Antonia's memory, however, was less valuable to Caligula that of Agrippina I or Drusilla, and was in one respect an embarrassment: she was the grandmother not only of Caligula but of his cousin Tiberius Gemellus, a potentially dangerous rival for power whom Caligula executed on charges of treason in A.D. 38.[22] His lack of attention to the memory of his grandmother may have prompted the reports that his contemptuous treatment of her drove her to suicide, but as Barrett has observed, this allegation, like so many against Caligula, lacks credibility. Antonia died in May of A.D. 37, only a few months after Caligula's accession to power, during most of which time he was absent from Rome, leaving very little time for Caligula to mistreat his grandmother. The only evidence of this mistreatment that Suetonius and Dio can produce is that Caligula denied her the privilege of a private interview, speaking to her in the presence of his Praetorian prefect and mentor Macro. Caligula certainly could not have desired her death, since he obviously had plans for her participation in the public worship of Augustus.[23]

When Claudius succeeded to power, he, like Caligula before him, would have needed both to distance himself from the memory of a hated predecessor and to elevate his mother's memory to its rightful dignity. Although Antonia did not require rehabilitation, as Agrippina I did, the posthumous honors her son granted her bear a distinct resemblance to those Caligula had earlier granted to Agrippina I: a *carpentum* that carried her image around the circus in the ceremonies before public games, and representation on coins struck in her own name rather than that of the emperor.[24] (Figures 55–56). These coins, to be discussed below, are also the first from the mint of Rome to confer on the portrait of a mortal woman the attributes of a major goddess, the corn-ear crown of Ceres. This identification, like the titles "Augusta" and "priestess of the deified Augustus," drew the attention of the public to the parallels between Antonia and Livia, whom Claudius had recently deified. Die-cutters of the imperial mint clearly wished to indicate that Antonia, although not a *diva*, was second in prestige only to the deified wife of the first emperor.

In reality, of course, Antonia's role in the imperial family differed from that of Livia in significant ways. Livia enjoyed a long period

---

[22] Barrett, 1990, 37–39, 69, 74–76; Dio 59.8.1–2; Suet. *Calig.* 23.3.
[23] Suet. *Calig.* 23.2; Dio 59.3.6; Barrett, 1990, 62.
[24] Suet. *Claud.* 11.2.

of direct access first to her husband and later to her son, during all
of which time her consultations with Augustus, her patronage of individuals and of provincial clients were a matter of public record. After
the death of Augustus, she was the priestess of his cult for the almost
15 years of her widowhood. Antonia, on the other hand, had only
a brief tenure in this priestly role, and fewer opportunities for direct
access to and influence of a ruling emperor. Those opportunities
resulted from her role in uncovering the plot of Sejanus: her loyalty
on that occasion gave Tiberius a much greater respect for her advice,
and on at least one occasion she used that influence to persuade the
reclusive Tiberius to hold a hearing on a matter concerning the Jewish
prince Agrippa. After Tiberius, as a result of that hearing, imprisoned Agrippa for an ill-considered remark, Antonia intervened with
the Praetorian prefect Macro to ensure that the conditions of Agrippa's
custody were humane, and later, after the death of Tiberius, she
advised Caligula to oversee the release of Agrippa in an appropriately discreet manner.[25] This episode allows us to infer others that
have not been reported; Antonia, like Livia, had personal friends
and clients among provincial royalty and aristocracy, and used her
influence for their benefit.[26]

Her period of influence with Tiberius came rather late in her life,
but long before then, she had already possessed power of another
sort, through her great personal wealth and extensive land-holdings
in Egypt, some of which she had inherited from her father Marc
Antony.[27] As both Livia and her mother Octavia had done, she used
some of this wealth for philanthropic purposes, both to individuals
and to cities, and accordingly received the honor of statues and
inscriptions that call her "euergetis" in at least two cities of the
Greek-speaking east.[28] The rights granted to a mother of three children would have given her control over that property without the
intervention of a *tutela*, or guardian. Like Livia, then, she was able
both to present herself as a public example of the chaste, loyal wife
and widow, and at the same time to act in very public ways with
a considerable degree of independence, a situation that no one seems
to have considered paradoxical.

---

[25] Josephus, *AJ* 18.179–186, 202–204, 236.
[26] Joseph. *AJ* 18.143 mentions Antonia's friendships with both Berenice and Agrippa.
[27] Kokkinos, 1992, 68–83.
[28] Kokkinos, 1992, 43–45. She lent a large sum of money to the Jewish prince
Agrippa: Josephus, *AJ* 18.164–65.

Antonia Minor: The Portraits

The first public monument on which Antonia is known to appear is the Ara Pacis Augustae (figures 53–54), on which she and her husband Drusus I appear on the south frieze, turning to one another in a charming, intimate gesture, with their baby son Germanicus between them.[29] The graceful composition succintly communicates the successful union between the Julian and Claudian branches of the family. Like the Livia on the same frieze, however, her face here is so idealized that it cannot be described as a portrait in any meaningful sense. The context, not the features of her face, establish her identity. She wears her hair parted in the middle and drawn back in soft, natural waves, partly covering the ears, to a small bun formed of tightly wound braids low on the back of the neck. This coiffure resembles but is not identical to the one later represented on her coin profiles during the reign of Claudius, and on her sculptural portraits, all of which images probably follow a later prototype from the time of Tiberius. She also wears a laurel crown, an attribute with which she does not, to my knowledge, appear again. The relief portrait of the Ara Pacis is useful for establishing Antonia's prominence in the imperial family, the importance of her marriage and children in Augustus's dynastic plans, but is of little value for the identification of her portraits in other media. This portrait has occasionally been invoked as a parallel justifying the identification with Antonia of problematic works like the Juno Ludovisi and the woman beside Augustus on the Ravenna relief, both of which show soft coiffures that partly cover the ears, but those works, as discussed in the previous chapter, show much closer affinities to the official sculptural portrait types of the deified Livia, whom I believe them to represent.[30]

During the principate of Tiberius, Antonia enjoyed the status of

---

[29] Erhart, 1978, 196–197; Simon, 1967, 19, pl. 15.

[30] Erhart, 1978, 196–202, makes the Ara Pacis relief the keystone of her "youthful, idealized type" of Antonia. It is questionable, however, whether any portraits on the Ara Pacis, especially those of the women, conform to any established type. Kokkinos, 1992, 113–115, compares the Ara Pacis and Ravenna relief, and prints side-by-side details of the faces of Antonia on the former and the problematic woman on the latter. The comparison reveals some differences in the coiffures, however, in that the hair of the Ara Pacis figure is drawn back from the hairline while that of the Ravenna figure flows down from the part in waves around the face, and then is drawn back below the temples. Both faces are too idealized to be of much value in fixing an identity.

mother of the prospective heir and merited appropriate ceremonial honors. Her likeness appeared in at least one public statuary group securely datable this time (figure 59), in the Old Forum of Leptis Magna, where an inscription in Neo-Punic allows a fairly detailed reconstruction of the group's appearance. The two heirs, Germanicus and Drusus II, appeared in chariots, accompanied by standing figures of their mothers, Antonia Minor and Vipsania Agrippina, and their wives, Agrippina I and Livilla I, respectively.[31] The Neo-Punic and Latin inscriptions indicate that the people of Leptis probably erected this monument in the year A.D. 23 or soon afterward, shortly after the death of Drusus II, and certainly before A.D. 32, the year of the *damnatio memoriae* of his wife Livilla I, who appeared prominently in the group. This information allows a fairly precise dating of all the sculptures that belonged to the monument.[32] Antonia's representation in a provincial city like Leptis Magna allows us to infer that her image appeared in public statuary groups throughout the empire.

After Antonia's death early in the principate of Caligula, her memory was of less than compelling importance to the new emperor. During the principate of her son Claudius, on the other hand, Antonia suddenly became a key figure in the family tree. It was through her that Claudius could trace his lineage to the family of the deified Augustus—to Octavia, if not to Augustus himself—while the fact that she was the mother of Germanicus gave Claudius another way to emphasize his brother's beloved memory and to enjoy the reflected glory of his military achievements.

From the first year of his reign, Claudius honored both his parents with coins in all three metals. In every case, one issue in each denomination devoted to his father Drusus I has a parallel and pendant in an issue honoring Antonia. The issues of *aurei* and *denarii* that honor Antonia are devoted entirely to her, in obverse and in reverse type, another example of the increasing acceptability of such honors to women.[33] (Figures 55–56). When the Roman mint under Caligula

---

[31] Statue of Antonia:Tripolis Museum, fragmentary marble statue, h. of head 30 cm. Rose, 1997, 182–84, no. 125, pl. 225; Trillmich, 1988, 59 n. 24; Erhart, 1978, 210, no. 10 and 211, no. 14; Aurigemma, 1940, 74–75, figs. 51–52, 76–77.

[32] Trillmich, 1988, 51–60; Aurigemma 1940, 20–26; Levi della Vida, 1935, 15–27.

[33] *RIC* 1² 124, nos. 65, 66, pl. 15 (*aurei* and *denarii* with reverse of "*Constantiae Augusti*") and 124, nos. 67–68 ("*Sacerdos Divi Augusti*"), pl. 15, reverse; *BMCRE* 1, 180, nos. 109–111, pl. 33, figs. 19, 20 (*aurei* and *denarii* with reverse of "*Constantiae Augustae*"); 180, nos. 112–114, pl. 33, figs. 21, 22 (*aurei* and *denarii* with "Sacerdos Divi Augusti" reverse); Trillmich, 1978, 69–77 (Constantia and Sacerdos issues).

issued coins devoted entirely to Agrippina I, they were bronze *sestertii*, the least valuable metal. Bronze was, of course, the coinage issued under the nominal authority of the Senate, and the presence of Agrippina's image together with the initials "S.C.", "Senatus Consultum," made a powerful statement to the public about the legitimacy of Caligula's claim to authority through his glorious descent, which the Senate thus publicly honored.[34] On gold and silver issues, nonetheless, the coins issued by direct authority of the emperor, the elder Agrippina's image appeared on the reverse, subordinated in importance to the image of the living emperor on the obverse. When Claudius, on the other hand, appears on coins with his mother, his figure on the obverse is a tiny full-length figure, holding priestly emblems, while her likeness on the reverse takes the form of a large portrait bust.[35] In all three metals, Antonia's face appears with the simple but eloquent inscription "ANTONIA AUGUSTA." Antonia shared the highly honorific title of "Augusta" with only one other imperial figure, Livia, whom Claudius had recently deified.

The bronze *dupondii* that honor Antonia (figure 57) associate her with Claudius in his capacity as Pontifex Maximus, while the parallel issue with the reverse portrait of his father Drusus I (figure 58) portrays Claudius in his two other capacities, as first citizen and as military commander.[36] The little full-length figure of Claudius on the obverses of the latter sits on a *sella curulis*, or curule chair, the official seat of civil political authority, while holding in his outstretched right hand the laurel branch emblematic of victory. Armor and weapons, presumably the spoils of his successful campaign in Britain, are strewn under the chair. The two issues, between them, summarize the three aspects of an emperor's authority—religious, political and military— while associating the corresponding virtues of *pietas*, *iustitia* and *virtus* with his mother in the first case and his father in the latter two.

---

[34] I am indebted for this observation to Professor John Pollini of the University of Southern California.

[35] *RIC* 1² 127, no. 92, pl. 16 and 129, no. 104; *BMCRE* 1, 188, nos. 166–171, pl. 35, figs. 8–9; Trillmich, 1978, 20–24, 63, 64–69, pls. 7–9. Note that there is some dispute which face of these coins is the obverse, and which the reverse: Mattingly, Sutherland et al. refer to the side with the portrait face of Antonia as the obverse, but Trillmich argues that the side with the inscriptions of the ruling emperor is the obverse, and the side with the portrait of Antonia the reverse.

[36] Sestertii in name of Drusus I: *RIC* 1² 127, no. 93, pls. 16 and 129, no. 109; *BMCRE* 1, 186–187, nos. 157–159, pl. 35, fig. 7; Trillmich, 1978, 64, pl. 11, figs. 16, 17.

Both Antonia and Drusus I in the bronze issues are bareheaded, presented in an honorific but fully human guise. On gold and silver coinage, however, (figures 55–56), Antonia wears the corn-ear crown of Ceres. The maternal goddess who presides over fertility of all sorts, the protector of children and the mythological mother both of "Wealth" (Ploutos) and of Kore, the bringer of renewed life in the spring, is an obvious figure with whom to identify the mother of an emperor. We have seen that Livia was called "Ceres Augusta" in inscriptions and apparently portrayed as such possibly even during her lifetime; some provincial coinages of the Greek east likewise represented Agrippina I as an enthroned Demeter during the reign of her son Caligula (figure 84), while coins from Smyrna and some works of sculpture identified the elder Agrippina's daughter Drusilla with Kore both during her lifetime and after her deification.[37] The coins in honor of Antonia are the first from the official mint, however, to make such an identification explicit, or to associate openly divine attributes with a woman's recognizable portrait face and an unambiguous identifying inscription. As such, they mark another milestone in the institutionalization of such honors to imperial women.

This obverse type of Antonia as Ceres appears with two separate reverses; the two issues might have been concurrent, or one might have succeeded the other, but without datable information such as imperial titles, their chronology must remain undetermined. It is, however, certain, that they present Antonia in two distinct aspects: a specific, earthly title which she held, and a more general virtue with which Claudius wished to associate both her and himself. In the former case, the reverse bears the legend SACERDOS DIVI AUGUSTI, priestess of the Deified Augustus.[38] (Figure 55). Antonia received this priestly office, so important for the ideology and dynastic propaganda of the descendants of Augustus, after Livia's death, and held it only briefly before her own, but this distinction, like the title Augusta, reminds the viewer that in the Julio-Claudian family tree she is second in honor only to the deified Livia and, for Claudius, represents another crucial link to the deified Augustus. By the time the mint of Rome issued these coins, overt identifications of Livia

---

[37] On the provincial coins in honor of Agrippina I and Drusilla, see Chapter 5, and Wood, 1995, 462–463.

[38] *RIC* 1² 124, 67–68, pl. 15, reverse; *BMCRE* 1, 180, nos. 112–113 (*aurei*) and 114 (*denarius*); Trillmich, 1978, 19–20, 70, 72–77, pl. 6, lower half of page, under "Sacerdos Serie."

in visual and in verbal form as "Ceres Augusta" had become common-place, and thus the representation of Antonia with the corn-ear crown of Ceres identifies her both with the archetypal good mother of mythology and with a more recent figure to whom she bore strik-ing parallels, most notably the fact that her son became emperor. The reverse type portrays two torches (usually ornate affairs consist-ing of several cone-shaped tiers, but occasionally simplified) bound together by a beaded string that probably represents an *infula*. This beaded fillet with hanging strands on each side can adorn either a person or a sacred object such as an altar. The *infula* does not belong exclusively to the cult of deified emperors, as it has sometimes been interpreted, but does appear in the context of the imperial cult and forms the headgear of the priestesses. On some, though not all, of the obverses of this issue, the hanging ends of Antonia's crown take the same form, represented as rows of dots rather than as a con-tinuous line; at least some of the die cutters evidently wished to emphasize that she wore an *infula* along with the corn-ear crown of Ceres.[39]

This same combination of attributes appears both in at least one sculptural portrait of Livia (figure 38) and in a statue of a woman found in the *macellum* of Pompeii, apparently a private citizen and priestess of some local importance.[40] The coiffure of the Pompeii statue, with its mass of curls around the face, suggests a Claudian or Neronian date. Whether the statue predates or postdates the similar public pre-sentation of the mother of Claudius, it seems clear that here as in so many other cases, public honors to an imperial family member could follow a form that was acceptable for private citizens, but give those honors greater impact simply by virtue of the wider and more pub-lic dissemination of the images of the imperial figures.

The other issue of gold and silver coins associates her not with a specific earthly honor, but with a more general virtue: CONSTAN-TIAE AUGUSTI, "The Constancy of the Emperor."[41] (Figure 56).

---

[39] Trillmich, 1978, 74, and 1971, 197, fig. 7. Trillmich's enlarged photo unmis-takably shows the form of the beaded *infula*.

[40] Statue of Livia: Louvre, inv. MA 1242. Winkes, 1995, 148–150, no. 74 with full references; De Kersauson, *Louvre* 1, 102–103, no. 45. Statue of priestess from the macellum of Pompeii: Naples, Museo Nazionale Archeologico inv. 6041. Rumpf, 1941, 22, no. 2, pl. 2c.

[41] *RIC* 1² 124, nos. 65–66, pl. 15; *BMCRE* 1, 180, nos. 109–111; Trillmich, 1978, 17–19; 69–70, 72–77, pl. 6.

The portraits of Antonia on the obverses of these coins recognizably follow the same type as those of the "Sacerdos" issue, albeit with the inevitable stylistic variations that occur when various die-cutters replicate an image over a long period of time. Trillmich has suggested that the more simplified and linear treatment of Antonia's face on this series suggests a later date.[42] In this issue, as in the other, however, she wears the corn-ear crown of Ceres, and this time the crown is invariably fastened with a beaded *infula*; the die-cutters of this series seem to have felt that if her priestly office was not explicitly mentioned on the reverse, it was all the more important to preserve that mark of her status in the obverse image.[43] On the reverses, Constantia appears as a female personification, holding a cornucopiae in her left arm and a torch in her right. Some issues of gold and silver in Claudius's own name have the same reverse inscription, but a somewhat different reverse image, since in those coins Constantia takes the form of an enthroned figure. The connection of the personification of this virtue with the emperor's mother clearly conveys the message that he has inherited from her this quality, that she had most dramatically demonstrated when she foiled the plot of Sejanus, and for which she was rightly admired.

In all of these portrait profiles, Antonia's features consistently follow the same pattern, but her hair shows two slight variations. In all coins, she appears as a woman in early middle age, with slight suggestions of maturity like a fleshy chin-line, and with non-ideal features like a large, slightly arched nose and retreating lower lip, but with the flatteringly elegant style typical of most Julio-Claudian portraiture. She appears as she would have looked in her prime, not at the end of her long life. It is probably safe to assume, then, that an official portrait type was created for her during the principate of Augustus or early in that of Tiberius, when she enjoyed the status of mother of the official heir, Germanicus. At the time of Tiberius's accession to power, she would have been about forty nine years old. Her hair is of a fashion clearly out of date by Claudius's own time, and probably already old-fashioned at the time of her death early in the reign of Caligula: she wears it parted in the middle, drawn back severely to the nape of the neck, allowing only a few very shallow waves on each side of the face, and fastened in a queue that

---

[42] Trillmich, 1971, 199.
[43] Trillmich 1971, 197.

hangs down her nape. In some bronze coins, however, and some *aurei* and *denarii* of the "Sacerdos" series, Antonia has a few little escaping curls in front of the ear that alleviate the severity of the style. In some of the larger portraits on the *dupondii*, these curls can be seen to continue along the hairline to the top of the forehead, forming a little decorative fringe around the face. Trillmich has concluded on the basis of several numismatic considerations that the dupondii that represent this coiffure are earlier, and that the type is gradually supplanted by the simpler style, without the decorative locks. The latter style, ironically, would be even more dated-looking than the style with the ringlet fringe. The severity of the fashion however also allows a clear differentiation of her status, both from the deified Livia, whose hair in her late posthumous statues is fuller and more dramatic, and from the living women of the family, with their pretty but somewhat more ornate and frivolous coiffures. The middle part and simple waves around the face give her more similarity to the former than to the latter, and place her in the company of the heroized dead ancestors of the dynasty.

A number of extant marble portraits closely resemble the profiles of these coins, in physical features and in treatment of the coiffure. Two distinct types that exist in multiple replicas (figures 59–66, 68 and figures 74–77) have been identified as her portraits, but only one of these can be considered secure on the basis of the evidence of coins; there are several more problematic and controversial identifications of her as well, in unique objects that might or might not be variants on her standard types. Let us first, however, examine the works that do recognizably replicate common prototypes. The marble sculptures that most closely resemble Antonia's coin profiles include the eponymous replica of Antonia's "Wilton House" type, a work now in the Harvard Art Museums (figures 60–61). The head does not belong to the bust, but is otherwise well preserved and of high quality. At least 12 other examples have survived, including two complete statues, one in the Louvre (figures 62–63), another recently discovered in a Claudian family group in a nymphaeum at Punta Epitaffio near Baia (figures 64–66).[44] A more fragmentary

---

[44] Small, 1990, 221, lists ten replicas of the type; to these may be added the Baia statue (see below) and two marble heads from an imperial group at Velia, both recognizable replicas of the Wilton House type; Rose, 1997, 120–121, no. 49, pls. 129, 130, 131.

statue that conforms to the Wilton House type came to light in the excavations of the Old Forum of Leptis Magna (figure 59), but because of its mediocre quality, the excavators did not initially recognize it as Antonia. Aurigemma mistakenly called it a portrait of Livia, leaving the way open for the erroneous identification of another and very different head from the same site as the Antonia of the chariot group (figures 74–75).[45]

Complete or incomplete, all these replicas of the Wilton House type share one attribute: a headband visible just above the forehead that runs horizontally across the part, then vanishes under the waves of hair that are swept back from the sides of the face. In some cases, like the Harvard (figures 60–61) and Alberta heads (figure 68) and the Baia statue (figures 64–66), the band appears to be a thick, twisted cylindrical cord; in others, like the Louvre statue (figures 62–63), it is beaded, similar to an *infula*. This headband is usually taken to signify Antonia's role as the priestess of the deified Augustus, but in that case, all examples would have to date from near the end of her life at the earliest.[46] The statue from Leptis (figure 59), which also wears this attribute, probably dates to A.D. 23 and can be no later than A.D. 32, proving that the Wilton House type of Antonia was already well established fourteen years prior to her death, and that she was wearing this attribute long before she became any kind of priestess.

The likeliest explanation of the headband is personal adornment, nothing more or less than a hair-ribbon that Antonia happened to wear when she sat for her official portrait. No other imperial portrait type shows exactly the same attribute, which appears unique to

Harvard Art Museums inv. 1972.306, formerly in the Wilton House collection, marble head set on bust to which it does not belong. Life-size, h. of bust in present condition 53.4 cm., of head and neck, 28 cm., of head from chin to back of head, 23 cm. Erhart, 1978, 193–212 with earlier literature; Polaschek, *Antonia*, 1973, 19, pl. 2, fig. 1, 4, fig. 1, 6, fig. 1.

Paris, Musée du Louvre, Ma 1228, marble statue, h. 203 cm. De Kersauson, *Louvre* 1, 170–171, no. 79 with earlier literature; Bieber, 1977, 164, fig. 726; Polaschek, *Antonia*, 1973, 29–30, pl. 7, fig. 2, pl. 12, fig. 1, pl. 13, fig. 1, pl. 15, fig. 1.

Statue from Baia group in provisional deposit at Castello Aragonese, Baia, marble, h. 155 cm. Rose, 1997, 82–83, no. 4, pls. 60–61; Kokkinos, 1992, 116–118, fig. 77 and frontispiece; Andreae in *Baia*, 54–56, figs. 122–130; Andreae, 1982, 202–207.

[45] Aurigemma, 1940, 74–77, figs. 51–52, and 88–90, figs. 65–66; Kokkinos, 109–113 on the identification of the "Leptis-Malta" type.

[46] See Small, 1990, 224–228.

Antonia. Conceivably, the simpler version of the ornament, the twisted fabric cord, could be a *vitta*, the identifying mark of a married woman, although the *vitta* that appear in private funerary reliefs appears to be a wider swatch of fabric worn over the head like a scarf.[47] The form of the *vitta* could perhaps have changed with time and fashion to a narrower ribbon by the imperial period. The replicas of Antonia's portrait that substitute a beaded band, on the other hand, are probably posthumous, and show an adaptation of the type to represent her new status in the year A.D. 37, as honorary Vestal and as priestess of the deified Augustus. Possibly in these latter cases we should call this attribute a *tutulus*, rather than *infula*, since it does not simply encircle the head like a diadem, as portraits of Livia, Agrippina I, and Drusilla wear the *infula*, (cf. figures 38, 50–51, 93–94, 111–117), but emerges from and disappears under the waves of hair on the sides of the face.

Festus defines the *tutulus*, when worn as the mark of the *flamenicae* (the wives of the priests known as *flamines*), as a purple band *woven into* the hair. Furthermore, not a single extant example of Antonia's Wilton House portraits in marble shows the hanging ends of this band, which must therefore be somehow bound up in the hair out of sight. One of the characteristic features of an *infula* is its hanging ends; it is described as an emblem worn "bound around the head like a diadem, from which fillets hang down on each side."[48] Antonia's coin profiles show the ends of a beaded band emerging from a knot at the back of her head, suggesting that in these contexts she does indeed wear the *infula*, but the ends do not appear in sculpture, even though they could have been represented along the sides of the neck, as they were in Drusilla's portraits (see chapter 5 and figures 111–117). Without the paint, unfortunately, we have no way of knowing whether Antonia's headband in these busts and statues of the Wilton House type was purple, the color of the *tutulus*, or white, the color of the *infula*, but if the emblem had a ritual significance, the color of the attribute in its original state would have made its meaning self-evident to most Roman viewers.[49]

---

[47] Kockel, 1993, 52. An especially clear example is Palazzo dei Conservatori inv. 2231, Kockel's no. F1, 119–120, pl. 31a, detail fig. 33a.

[48] ". . . in modo diadematis a quo vittae ab utraque parte pendent." Isid. *Orig.* 19.30.4, quoted by Sensi, 1980–81, 70.

[49] Festus p. 355 defines *tutulus* as *vitta purpurea innexa crinibus*. See Rumpf, 1941, 30–31 n. 5.

One possible portrait of this group that does not show the headband is a marble bust from Tralles, a work of good technical quality but nonetheless a product of an atelier far from the origin of the
prototype.[50] The subject of this bust wears the *stola* of a Roman
matron, and the same simple coiffure as Antonia, with the middle
part and the shallow, natural waves pulled back severely to a queue
at the nape, leaving the ears are fully exposed. Though the face displays undeniable similarities to the profiles of Antonia on coins, however, the frontal view betrays equally striking differences from the
many well-established replicas of the Wilton House type: the lower
face is wider, the jaw squarer, and the eyebrows flare more sharply
toward the temples. Poulsen first identified this bust as Antonia, and
has been followed in that opinion by a number of scholars including Trillmich, who argues that given the tendency of replicas of prototypes to display stylistic shifts over time, the fact that this work
has no exact replicas should not militate against its acceptance as a
portrait of Antonia. Such variations on an official type, both over
time and in geographically far flung locations, are an undeniable
fact, as the portraits of Livia abundantly demonstrate, but there
Antonia's portraits differ from Livia's in that they were never as
widespread, and therefore not as subject to the variations that can
enter a replica series through copying, recopying, and deliberate
alteration. The 124 securely identified portraits of Livia that Winkes
has catalogued in his recent study of her portraiture, and the sub-
categories that he has assembled within each of her major portrait
types, clearly demonstrate the process by which local copyists could
transform one official type in several different directions. There are,
on the other hand, only 13 securely identified copies in existence of
Antonia's "Wilton House" portrait type. Anomalous works like the
bust from Tralles do not emerge from any coherent context, as do the
variants on Livia's types, but appear isolated. Polaschek was probably correct, therefore, to reject that work as a portrait of Antonia.

Another anomalous work sometimes claimed as a variant on
Antonia's "mature-realistic" portrait type is a head from the Augustan-

---

[50] Ny Carlsberg Glyptotek cat. 607, I.N. 743, marble bust, h. 43 cm. Poulsen,
1946, 30–31, figs. 21–23; Poulsen, *Portraits* 1, 77–79, no. 42, pls. 70–71; Trillmich,
1971, 204–206, figs. 13–17; Polaschek, *Antonia*, 1973, 42–44. Furnée van Zwet,
1956, fig. 32, p. 20, mentions the bust but apparently does not accept the identification
as Antonia.

to-Tiberian group at Béziers.[51] (Figure 67). Here too, the headband is absent. Despite some physical resemblance to Antonia's features, however, such as the long, thin nose with an arched bridge and the characteristic Julio-Claudian overbite, this head deviates significantly from her established likenesses. The Béziers head shows two twisted segments of hair on each side of the middle part that run backward along the top of her head, in a manner comparable to the "melon coiffures" fashionable in Hellenistic times, and still occasionally visible in Augustan portraits. This portrait head, as I have argued elsewhere, is probably not an imperial woman at all but a wealthy local citizen whose portrait happened to appear in the same building (although probably not the same group) as those of imperial figures. The subject's rather old-fashioned coiffure might be explained by her provincial origins.[52] As noted in the first chapter, the statues of Eumachia from Pompeii and of the Balbus family at Herculaneum demonstrate that local patrons of public building projects could and did decorate those buildings with statues of themselves and their families.[53] The porticus of Eumachia consciously emulated that of Livia in Rome, and the statue of the Augusta may well have stood in the apse of that structure, flanked by personifications of Concordia and Pietas, while that of Eumachia herself had a more humbly concealed location in the cryptoporticus behind the apse—not visible at the same time as the portrait of Livia, but quite deliberately aligned with it.[54]

If we set aside the problematic Tralles and Béziers portraits, the remaining replicas of the Wilton House type form a highly coherent group. Their profiles so closely match those on Claudian coins that a seventeenth-century owner of the portrait now in the Sackler

---

[51] Toulouse, Musée Saint-Raymond inv. 30 005. Fragmentary marble head, h. 25 cm. Rose, 1997, 128, pl. 165; Balty, 1996, 205, no. 144; Balty and Cazes, 1995, no. 9, 104–111, figs. 25, 98–99, 102, 105–106; Poulsen, 1946, 9, fig. 8, 10, 24–32; Clavel, 1970, 472, 493, figs. 58–60.

[52] Wood, 1996–97, 7–9.

[53] On the Balbus group: Deiss, 1985, 158–66; Barker, 1908, 155–57, figs. 12, 14. On the female statues and the dating of their hairstyles: Polaschek, 1972, 162–164; Bieber, 1977, 150, pl. 116, figs. 683–687.

On the statue and building of Eumachia at Pompeii: Kleiner and Matheson, 1996, 33–34; Dobbins, 1994, 647–661; Richardson, 1988, 194–98, fig. 31; MacDonald, 1986, 165, fig. 149; Mau, 1902, 110–118, figs. 45–50, statue of Eumachia, p. 112, 445–46, fig. 255. On the statue of Eumachia, see Hanfmann, 1975, 83–84, no. 52, with earlier literature. The statue is more ideal than portrait-like, but the inscription establishes its intended identity.

[54] Kleiner and Matheson, 1996, 33; Dobbins, 1994, 652; Richardson, 1988, 197.

Museum at Harvard had already correctly identified the subject, inscribing the name of Antonia on the shoulder of the restored bust.[55] The severe coiffure, smoothly drawn back to a hanging queue at the nape, the fairly high, straight forehead, thin lips, retreating lower jaw, firm, rounded chin and fleshy chin line in every replica of this type faithfully match the coins, while the nose, when it is completely or almost completely preserved, is long, narrow and straight with a slightly pendulous tip. Polaschek has pointed out some variations within the portraits of this group: some, like the statue in the Louvre, treat the coiffure in a slightly more decorative manner, introducing a few little curls into the waves along the hairline between the temples and the ears.[56]

A bust now in the University of Alberta (Figure 68) and another example in the Villa Borghese have long, loosely waved locks that emerge from the queue at the nape of the neck and hang down to the shoulders.[57] The Villa Borghese sculpture suffered distorting alterations in modern times when it was incorporated into a sculptural pastiche of Leda and the Swan, and the Alberta sculpture may have undergone some less drastic alterations, but despite the recutting in both cases, the shoulder-locks appear to have been authentic parts of the ancient works of sculpture. We have seen in the case of Livia that long, full shoulder-locks, added to a contemporary coiffure, give a recognizable individual a point of similarity with divine images; in the case of Drusilla, we will see that the shoulder locks distinguish portraits of the chosen heir during her lifetime, and the *diva* after her death and deification, from her sister Agrippina II, whose coiffure is otherwise identical. The Alberta and Villa Borghese replicas of Antonia's portrait may then have originally presented her in some particularly goddess-like, honorific context.

Polaschek has attempted to divide these sculptures into two different replica series, the "smooth type" and the "temple-ringlet" type, a distinction that Small and Erhart, among others, have rejected as too minute.[58] The inclusion or omission of a few small curls, they believe, falls within the normal range of variations that one can

---

[55] Erhart, 1978, 195.

[56] Polaschek, *Antonia*, 1973, 25–30.

[57] Small, 1990, 220.

[58] Polaschek, *Antonia*, 1973, 19–24 on the replicas of the Harvard (formerly Wilton House) type and 25–30 on what she describes as the "Schläfenlockchentypus;" Erhart, 1978, 206–209, 211 ("Mature, individualized type"), Small, 1990, 218–221.

expect in reproductions of a single type by copyists of different workshops and regions. In my opinion, however, the issue is semantic. The addition or omission of clusters of curls in front of the ears may not be a variation large enough to justify the use of the term "type," but the varying treatments of Antonia's coiffure do give the replicas distinctly different characters, in some cases, slightly more pretty and decorative, in the others, more austere. One of these versions, I believe, was created later than the other one, at a specific time and place, and for a specific reason. To that extent, Polaschek's distinction between the two groups of replicas is valid.

Which of these versions, the simple or the more ornate, belonged to Antonia's first prototype, and which was the alteration? In coins, Trillmich has observed a clear chronological distinction. The bronze dupondii that show these curls apparently belong to the earliest phase of the series. Those that can be dated to the year 50/51 or later by the appearance of the title PP (*Pater Patriae*) in Claudius's inscriptions, on the other hand, portray Antonia almost exclusively with the simpler type of coiffure.[59] In the gold and silver issues, the problem is somewhat more complicated; in an earlier article, Trillmich confidently asserted that Antonia's coin profiles demonstrate a coherent development from a more detailed and richly modeled likeness to a simplified, linear version in which both the volumes and line of the face and the pattern of the hair are reduced to the most essential forms possible, but by 1978 he was less certain of the evidence for these datings.[60] The evidence of the *dupondii* suggests, however, that die cutters tended to move from more detailed to more simplified interpretations of Antonia's portrait.

Sculpture, on the other hand, appears to tell the opposite story. The only replica of Antonia's portrait that is securely datable to her lifetime, the statue from Leptis Magna (figure 59), omits these curls, suggesting that they were a later embellishment, designed to enhance the beauty of Antonia in her posthumous likenesses. The most securely datable of her posthumous portraits, the statue from Baia (figures 64–66), does include them. Antonia appears in the Leptis Magna

---

[59] Trillmich, 1978, 65–66.

[60] Trillmich, 1971, 198–200, and 1978, 75–76. In the later publication, Trillmich demonstrates that one can make an equally plausible case for the earlier dating of the Constantiae series, on which the type with ringlets appears, or for its later dating on the grounds of its similarities to the portraits of Agrippina II on coins datable, of course, after Agrippina's marriage to Claudius.

statue as a respectable, and strictly mortal-looking matron, wearing
the Roman *stola* that marks her social status, and the more austere
version of the coiffure accords well with the overall character of the
work, whereas the Baia statue, with the attributes and costume of
Venus and Kore, is the most overtly goddess-like portrayal of her
in existence. These sculptures would seem to suggest that the version of Antonia's portrait with curls is the later one. The evidence
of the coins and the sculptures, however, need not contradict each
other if we remember that all of Antonia's coins date to the principate of Claudius, whereas the sculptural type must have been
created earlier. The sculptural type probably did not originally include
the curls at the temples, but the new honors that Claudius granted
his mother after his accession required artists in all media to find
ways to enhance and glamorize her image, without of course sacrificing
its modest character, or infringing on the prerogatives of Livia, who
unlike Antonia had been formally deified. The clusters of curls in
front of the ears would have been the solution to that problem, and
the die-cutters who produced her earliest coin likenesses would have
dutifully included it. As years passed, however, and entropy took its
inevitable toll, die-cutters would have reverted to the earlier, simpler
version of her type. In sculpture, however, the embellishment remained
popular, and the majority of sculptural replicas include it.

Even after the accession of Claudius, however, the presentation of
Antonia could vary considerably depending on the setting and intended
audience, as the two statues datable after her death attest. The Paris
statue (figures 62–63), which represents her with the beaded headband of a priestess and which therefore cannot be earlier than 37
B.C., represents Antonia bareheaded except for her *tutulus*, in a quiet
stance, modestly swathed in heavy masses of drapery. Her costume
resembles, but does not directly copy, those of Hellenistic muses. She
stands in a stable *contrapposto*, the weight on the right leg, emphasized by the vertical folds of her rather heavy undergarment, her
left foot trailing out to one side. Whether she is wearing a *peplos*,
chiton or *stola* is difficult to determine, since a heavy mantle wraps
around her entire torso, from shoulders to thighs, concealing the
shoulders and almost completely covering both arms. Only the hands
emerge from the mantle: the right hand lightly fingers the drapery
on the chest, while the left hand, hanging at her side, gathers up
some folds of the mantle, creating some movement and play of folds
in the fabric of the mantle near its lower hem where it angles up

above the knee of the relaxed leg. The pose is staid and modest, the body compact, the limbs held close in to the mass of the torso, but the severity softened by a few enlivening gestures and decorative details. This body belongs to a well-established statuary type that survives in at least thirty replicas, many of which depict imperial women, including Marciana, Matidia, Sabina, and Julia Domna.[61] From at least A.D. 100 onward, many replicas also hold the attributes of the goddess Ceres: the corn ears and poppies in the lowered left hand and occasionally the torch in the upraised right, although this latter attribute rarely survives. Bieber suggests that all women depicted in this guise were priestesses of Ceres, and that such a priestesshood may have been a special prerogative of imperial women. More probably, however, the statues identify the women with Ceres herself, particularly those, like the Sabina from Ostia, that must postdate the death and deification of the subject.[62] Most of these women, after all, were either the mothers of emperors or the potential mothers of heirs to power. Ceres, the solemn, dignified maternal goddess who bestows prosperity on the earth makes a highly appropriate parallel for them. Whether the sculptural type had this meaning and association as early as the time of Antonia is not certain, but as Bieber rightly observes, it appears more than once in her representations. The relief figure of Antonia on the Ara Pacis (figures 53–54) has virtually the same drapery, except that the gesture of her left hand, which holds the hand of her little son, differs from the statuary type.[63]

The statue from the nymphaeum at Punta Epitaffio (figures 64–66), on the other hand, is both more flamboyant and more blatantly goddess-like. The body is a free but recognizable replica of the Kore Albani type, a Greek model that had already been used for at least one statue of Drusilla, the replica from Caere (figure 111). The "Kore Albani" wears a light *chiton* that covers the torso but reveals the contours of the breasts and abdomen quite clearly with its delicate, crinkly folds, and a heavier *himation* that is swept over the left shoulder, across the back, and looped well below the waist, where an overfold forms a triangular "apron" that hangs to the left knee. The

---

[61] Bieber, 1977, 163–167, figs. 728–733, 738–740.
[62] Bieber, 1977, 165, figs. 732–33; Calza, 1964, 79–80, no. 127, pls. 75–76, and 1977, 50–51, no. 63, pls. 49–50.
[63] Bieber, 1977, 164, figs. 726, 727.

pattern of drapery is more complex, with more contrasts of heavier and lighter folds, than that of the Paris statue, and in its slightly more revealing character suggests a youthful, girlish figure appropriate for Kore, the original subject of the statue. Antonia also wears an ornate crescent diadem decorated with open-work lotuses and palmettes, and carries in the crook of her left arm a miniature figure of an adolescent *Amor* that transformed her into a syncretic goddess with features both of Kore (appropriate to a deceased mortal) and of Venus Genetrix, the emblem of the descent of the Julian dynasty. The assimilation of Kore to Aphrodite had ancient precedents, especially on Italian soil, since both were life-giving goddess of fertility.[64] In front of the diadem, Antonia's characteristic headband recognizably appears, emerging as usual from the waves of hair on each side of her face, and the features faithfully follow those of the Wilton House type. There is just one rather surprising departure from the type in the treatment of the hair at the back of the head, which forms a small chignon above the nape, rather than a queue hanging down. But since the rear of the head was clearly never intended to be seen when this statue stood in its original niche, this variant on the prototype is relatively unimportant, and does not undermine the security of the identification, which both the context and the many other physical features of the face establish beyond serious doubt.

The Baia statue is that rare and fortunate object, a work from a secure archaeological context. It was one of a group of Julio-Claudian statues set into the niches of a nymphaeum of an imperial villa at that fashionable seaside resort.[65] The room in which it appeared was an extraordinary and extravagant visual fantasy, a vaulted, apsidal chamber to which guests apparently had to be transported by boat, and where they would be entertained at banquets on a raised central platform, surrounded by water and by statuary in the niches of the room, over which the light reflected off the water would play and shimmer. The large apse at the end of the room contained a dramatic, multi-figured group representing the well-known episode from Homer's *Odyssey* in which the hero and his companions blind the Cyclops, a

---

[64] Zuntz, 1971, 164–68, 177–78. There has been some debate whether this statuary type originally represented Kore or Aphrodite; see Wood, 1995, 480–481, for a summary of the dispute; *LIMC* 2, 24, no. 149, s.v. "Aphrodite" (R. Fleischer).

[65] For the nature of the building, G. Tocco Sciarelli in *Baia*, 19–21. For the mythological figures excavated in the nymphaeum, and a reconstruction of the entire sculptural complex: Andreae in *Baia*, 49–53 and 68–71; Andreae, 1982, 200–220.

popular subject for statuary groups in private sculptural "theme parks" like this one. The fanciful aquatic dining hall is unusual but not entirely unprecedented; a comparable triclinium at Sperlonga, fashioned in that case out of a natural grotto, graced a private villa of the late Republic that later passed into the possession of the emperor Tiberius, and it too housed a group of Odysseus and the Cyclops.[66] The figures along the side walls of the Baia triclinium, however, were not parts of mythological groups but single figures, of which two represented Dionysus, whose presence in a dining hall requires no explanation. The remainder were imperial portraits. Two of these survive relatively intact, the Antonia and a charming portrait of a little girl who must be her granddaughter, Claudia Octavia (figures 69–71), while a headless torso of a male statue and a few fragments of a statue of a little boy indicate the presence of male family members. There were a total of eight side-niches in the room; the two statues of Dionysus and those of the two children account for the sculptural program along one side wall, while portraits of adult family members evidently faced them from the other side. Andreae postulates the presence of two couples: Augustus and Livia, the deified founders of the Julio-Claudian dynasty, and Drusus I and Antonia, the parents of the living emperor, through whom he could trace his ancestry back to the families of both *divi*.

Although no statue of Livia was found *in situ* at Baiae, the hypothesis has been advanced that the statue of Livia-Fortuna (figures 48–49) in Copenhagen could conceivably be none other than the missing Livia from the imperial nymphaeum. As noted in the previous chapter, this remains strictly an hypothesis; the only evidence in its favor is the provenance of the Livia-Fortuna at Pozzuoli, not far from Baia, and its close technical and stylistic similarities to the Baia sculptures, most notably its very distinctive and fairly rare treatment of the diadem as a lacy, openwork design of lotuses and palmettes outlined by drill channels.[67] If the Livia did belong to the Punta Epitaffio group, however, it (and, presumably, its pendant statue of Augustus) would have dramatically dominated the assemblage by its sheer size: at 2.15 meters, the statue of Livia is well over-life-size, while the

---

[66] For a recent discussion of the date of the Sperlonga complex, see Higginbotham, 1991, 304.

[67] On the Copenhagen statue: Winkes, 1995, 119–120, no. 43 with complete literature; Poulsen, *Portraits* 1, 73–74, no. 38, pls. 60–63; B. Andreae in *Baia*, 63.

statue of Antonia is life-size for a petite woman, and the statue of
the little Claudia Octavia of course even smaller than the statue of
Antonia. Andreae, indeed, rejects the membership of the Copenhagen
statue in the Baia group on this basis. Yet the headless male statue
found at Baia must have been of similar stature, approximately 2.10
meters. Andreae postulates that the two male statues flanked the two
female ones, so that each couple would appear together with the larger
figures on the outside, just as the two Dionysi on the opposite wall
flanked the smaller children, but it is just as possible that the larger
Augustus and Livia stood in the outer niches, protectively surrounding
and framing the smaller Drusus I and Antonia, in such a way that the
two women appeared together as a pair, and likewise the two men.

Unless and until stronger and more compelling evidence about the
precise provenance of the Copenhagen Livia should come to light,
its attribution to the Baia group remains unproven. We are on firmer
ground however, as noted in the last chapter, in assigning the Copenhagen and Baia statues to the same Naples-area sculptural atelier,
and in assuming that any statue of Livia that once stood in the Baia
group would have shared many of its iconographic and stylistic qualities. Andreae argues that the hair of the Copenhagen Livia shows
rich drillwork in contrast to the severely simple hair of the Antonia.
As we have seen in the previous chapter, however, any statue of the
deified Augusta from the time of Claudius that stood in such a group
would probably have shared with the the Copenhagen statue the
latest and most dramatic permutation of her middle-part coiffure,
and would have been very likely to show similar drill-work, while
the smoother and simpler coiffure of Antonia set her quite deliberately apart from the woman who held the title of Augusta before her.
In the groups at Velleia (figures 45–46), and at Rusellae, sculptors
scrupulously distinguished the rank and hierarchical order among
the generations of the imperial family by means of scale and presence or absence of divine attributes.[68] A group that identified Antonia
with both Kore and Aphrodite would necessarily have heroized the
deified Livia even more. Unlike the Antonia, the portrait statue of
Claudia Octavia does show rich drill-work, demonstrating that the
sculptors of this group were fully capable of using such devices if
they chose. (Figures 69–71). Claudia Octavia, being a young child,

---

[68] Rose, 1997, 116–118, nos. 45 and 121–126, no. 50.

wears her hair loose except for an elaborate, beaded ornament that
runs along the crown from front to back, a decoration found also
in portraits of her brother Britannicus and probably borrowed from
images of *Amor*.[69] Sculptors have used the running drill to form deep
channels between wavy strands, and drill holes for the centers of the
curls at the termination of each strand. Because her hair is unre-
strained, it forms a different pattern than those of Livia's later portraits, tumbling down around the face instead of being swept outward
to form an aureole around the head, but in both cases the rich locks
suggest burgeoning life, a notion reinforced in the statue of the child
by the similarity of her drapery, which slips from one shoulder, to
that of Venus Genetrix.[70] Although still a preadolescent child, she
represents the hope for Julio-Claudian children in the future, and
her potential fertility must therefore already be celebrated at this
early age.

Any statue of Livia at Baia would probably have given her attributes of Ceres such as corn ears and poppies. "Ceres Augusta" was
by that time the oldest and most popular of identifications for the
deified Augusta. Antonia's statue followed images of Kore, the daughter of Ceres-Demeter. Kore always appears younger and smaller than
her mother, but the pair of goddesses together form a powerful diad:
they are the Eleusinian deities who preside over fertility and rebirth.
Antonia simultaneously resembles Venus, however, while Claudia
Octavia, her living grandchild, has elements of the iconography both
of Venus and of Amor, the child of Venus. The child Britannicus
was undoubtedly also present in the group, although all that remains
of his figure is a hand holding a butterfly, a fragment sufficient to
demonstrate that this statue too followed a well-established type for
Amor holding the emblem of "Psyche," the butterfly, over a burning
altar.[71] The divine imagery of the descent of the Julians thus per-
vaded the entire group in a complex series of syncretic associations.
Such a complex of statues was never intended for the eyes of the

---

[69] Baia, Castello Aragonese, marble statue, h. 120 cm. Rose, 1997, 82–83, no. 4,
pls. 62, 63; Andreae in *Baia*, 56–58, figs. 156–157. Iconography of Claudia Octavia
and Britannicus, and significance of attributes: Amedick, 1991, 373–395, pls. 95–104.
Portrait of Britannicus with similar hair ornament: Palermo, Museo Nazionale inv.
697, from Tindari, fragmentary head, h. 20.5 cm. Published: Bonacasa, 1964, 44,
no. 50, pl. 23, figs. 1–2; Amedick, 1991, 373–378, pl. 95, fig. 1.
[70] Andreae in *Baia*, 57.
[71] Andreae in *Baia*, 58–60.

general public, however. Members of the imperial family and their privileged guests, high-ranking members of the court and the emperor's inner circle, would have seen the sculptural decoration of this room, but persons admitted to such a place could presumably be trusted already to sympathize with the dynastic politics of the reigning emperor. As is typical in works intended for a small and private audience, therefore, the portrait statues can present their subjects in an unrestrainedly divine guise.

One more major work of sculpture, finally, has met with wide acceptance as a posthumous image of Antonia Minor, although Winkes more plausibly ascribes it to Livia: the colossal marble head known as the Juno Ludovisi (figures 50–51).[72] This head wears both a high diadem with lotus-palmette reliefs and a beaded *infula*. The latter item, which Rumpf identified specifically as the badge of a priestess of the imperial cult, convinced him that the subject must be a mortal woman who held the office of priestess of a deified emperor.[73] The colossal scale and lotus-palmette diadem would have indicated imperial status. The possible candidates from the Julio-Claudian dynasty would, according to this interpretation of the *infula*, be Livia, Antonia, or Agrippina II, who became the priestess of Claudius after his death; of these three, the coin profiles of Antonia represent a coiffure that most closely approximates that of the "Juno." Even the coiffure, however, does not make a perfect match with Antonia's coin profiles or "realistic-mature" portraits: the hair is far less severely confined, the waves fuller, articulated with drill channels to suggest a soft, rich texture, the waves partly conceal the ears, and the queue is not as tight or narrow and does not hang as far down the back of the neck.[74] Two of the replicas of Antonia's "mature, realistic" type do show shoulder locks, but they are not a common feature of her portraiture, in sculpture or on coins, and when they do appear in the Alberta (figure 68) and Villa Borghese replicas, they seem to be a variant introduced by the copyist. Neither of these works show the ends of the *infula* intertwined with the locks of hair, as the Juno Ludovisi does. Finally, the headband that appears consistently in the

---

[72] Juno Ludovisi: See Chapter 2, note 178, for references. On the controversy re identity of the head, see Laubscher, 1976, 83 n. 62; Freyer-Schauenburg, 1983, 37-38.

[73] Rumpf, 1941, 21–31.

[74] Tölle-Kastenbein, 1974, 247, pl. 95, figs. 1 and 2.

replicas of the mature, realistic type is not worn in the same manner as the beaded band here, which encircles the head and is visible for its entire length: the headband on the better-established portraits is partly concealed under the waves of hair on the side, emerging into view only at the top of the head. The difference in arrangement probably merits the use of different terms to describe these objects: the colossal "Juno Ludovisi" wears an *infula*, the portraits of Antonia a *vitta* or a beaded *tutulus*.

Erhart has pointed out that there is at least one precedent for a highly idealized representation of Antonia, and one, moreover, that dates from relatively early in her life: the figure on the Ara Pacis discussed above (figures 53–54). On the basis of this relief, Erhart postulates the existence of a third group of portraits for Antonia, in addition to the "youthful-realistic" and "mature-realistic" series: a group of portraits, including the Juno Ludovisi, which she designates the "youthful, idealized" portrait type. Examples of this type would include a sardonyx intaglio and two life-sized marble heads, one in the art market at the time of the publication of Erhart's article, the other, mounted on a statue to which it does not belong, in the Museo Nazionale of Catania.[75] As Erhart herself freely admits, however, these objects, while sharing certain features in common, are not exact enough replicas of a common model to constitute a portrait type. Indeed, her own photographic comparison of the profile of the Juno Ludovisi and the Catania sculpture reveals the far more portrait-like quality of the latter, with its thinner lips and slightly retreating chin. Erhart's hypothesis rests primarily on the relief of the Ara Pacis, a work that proves beyond doubt that Antonia could be represented in a highly idealized manner, with non-portrait like features, but in assessing the evidence of the Ara Pacis, we must not forget that it is a relief. Relief portraits, unlike those in the round, were necessarily worked with the slab in a vertical position, and could not be precisely measured with the methods of triangulation that a marble carver could use for a statue or bust.[76] Almost inevitably, then, reliefs demonstrate a far greater deviation from standard portrait types than do freestanding sculptures.

---

[75] Erhart, 1978, 196–202. For Catania statue, see also Bonacasa, 1964, 63, no. 77, pls. 36.1–2, 90.3.

[76] Pfanner, 1989, 197, for diagram reconstructing measuring method for sculpture in the round, and 217–218 on relief portraits.

We must ask ourselves, furthermore, in what context such a colossal portrait could originally have appeared. Kokkinos suggests that
it was the cult image of a temple to the deified Antonia. Antonia,
however, was never officially deified.[77] Private citizens and provincial cities could and did sometime establish cults to imperial figures,
whether they had been consecrated or not, but would such a private cult in the capital city have had the funds to patronize a cult
image of this scale and quality? The literary evidence for the existence of a temple of Antonia in Rome is, furthermore, very sketchy
and unreliable. The "Juno" is in my opinion far likelier to represent a woman who did receive official consecration. Drusilla was the
first such *diva*, but even her beautiful posthumous portrait in Munich
(figures 116–117) retains the washboard-stiff crimped waves around
the face and decorative spit-curls along the forehead of her lifetime
coiffure.[78] Several securely identified portraits of Livia, on the other
hand, offer closer parallels for the coiffure of the Juno; these include
the statue of Ceres Augusta from the theater at Leptis Magna (figure
43), where the inscription established her identity; the statue in the
Louvre (figure 44) that has more recognizably portrait features; and
cameo gems like the Marlborough turquoise (figure 42), all of which
share the middle part, hanging queue at the nape, and long shoulder-locks. Another colossal statue of Livia from Leptis Magna, moreover, displays a nearly identical arrangement of the *infula* encircling
a high diadem.[79]

There is, finally, a group of portraits for which a mistaken identification as Antonia has proven extraordinarily persistent. This is the
so-called "Leptis-Malta" type (figures 74–77) that survives in at least
ten examples, one of which, as the provisional name implies, came
from the imperial group at Leptis Magna.[80] Since the Neo-Punic
inscription attested Antonia's presence there, and since every other

---

[77] Kokkinos, 1992, 119–120, 161–162.

[78] Portrait of the deified Drusilla in Munich: Munich Glyptothek, inv. 316, marble
head and neck, life-size. Wood, 1995, 476–77, figs. 24–26, with earlier references.
See Chapter 5 for fuller discussion.

[79] See previous chapter for fuller discussion of these works and complete references.
Winkes, 1995, 184, no. 107 (statue from theater of Leptis Magna), 150, no. 75
(Louvre statue); 98, no. 21 (Marlborough cameo, now in Boston); 182–183, no. 106
(colossal seated statue from Leptis Magna).

[80] See the next chapter for a fuller discussion. On the Leptis-Malta type: Rose,
1997, 68–69; Kokkinos, 1992, 109–113; Erhart, 1978, 202–206, 210–211; Polaschek,
Antonia, 1973, 39–45.

imperial woman known to have appeared in the same group seemed
to be accounted for by other sculptures, the Leptis head received
the name of Antonia by default.[81] As noted above, however, there
was a fragmentary statue of Antonia in her Wilton House type (figure
59) that the excavators found nearby but failed to recognize. The
following chapter will discuss in more detail the "Leptis-Malta" portraits and their possible identifications, but suffice it here to observe
that the physical features differ too strongly and too consistently from
Antonia's Wilton House type to be representations of the same
woman. The Leptis-Malta type (figures 74–77) shows a short, broad
face, a nose with a thick bridge, and a jutting profile line entirely
different from that of the Wilton House portraits of Antonia. These
are elements of bone-structure that could not change with age.
Another difference is the coiffure: again, the hair is pulled back
severely in shallow waves, exposing the ear, but this time there is a
row of spit-curls carefully arranged across the forehead, an element
for which the first datable parallels in sculpture appear on the portraits of Caligula's sisters.[82] It is most unlikely, therefore, that the
prototype could be earlier than the Wilton House type of Antonia.
The large number of replicas does indicate that the subject must
have been an important member of the imperial family, but she cannot be Antonia. The two most plausible current hypotheses are Livilla
I, the daughter of Antonia, or Livilla II, the youngest sister of Caligula.

What conclusions, then, can we draw about the presentation of
Antonia in public sculpture? Antonia's secure portrait type is austere and modest, characterized by chaste, smooth surfaces, closed
contours, and a severely controlled coiffure that is even less decorative than the *nodus* coiffure, with its fuller waves around the face,
that was fashionable at the time of Augustus. At the time, most
probably, of the accession of Claudius, this type acquires a slightly
more decorative variation, in which the curls in front of the ears
alleviate the severity of the coiffure, and the drill holes that form
their centers introduce a little play of light and shadow. The original

---

[81] Aurigemma, 1940, 88–90, figs. 65–66. Although Aurigemma mistakenly identified
the statue of Antonia as Livia (pp. 76–77), he did not identify the other head as
Antonia, describing it instead as a "ritratto di ignota." Later authors, however,
assumed by process of elimination that the portrait of the young woman with curls
along the hairline must be Antonia: see Kokkinos, 1992, 109–110, and Erhart,
1978, 203.
[82] Polaschek, 1972, 200–210; Trillmich, 1983, 21–37; Wood, 1995, 464–482.

prototype of these portraits must be no later than A.D. 32, the latest possible date of the group at Leptis Magna in which one of its replicas appeared (figure 59), and is probably considerably earlier. Antonia's age at the time of its creation is impossible to estimate, since some replicas show subtle signs of maturity (figures 60–61) while others do not (figures 64–66). The latter could be idealizing interpretations, but the former could just as easily be the work of copyists skillful enough to revise the prototype slightly so as to demonstrate Antonia's seniority within a family group. She was however, in any case, neither the wife nor the mother of a ruling emperor at the time of its creation, and her status accordingly subordinate to that of Livia. Like the latter, she appears attractive but modest; unlike Livia, however, her features are not so strongly assimilated to those of Augustus or Tiberius, and her coiffure with the middle part is never allowed the same rich, burgeoning treatment, but always appears primly confined.

Most of the replicas of this type, on the other hand, probably belong to the years after her death: Rose has securely documented the presence of Antonia's image in 11 imperial portrait groups, of which one (the Ara Pacis Augustae) is definitely Augustan, three Tiberian, two possibly either Caligulan or Claudian, and five definitely Claudian.[83] The conclusion that this data suggests is hardly surprising: the bulk of Antonia's extant portraits probably date to the principate of her son. These posthumous likenesses of Antonia would have presented the viewers of imperial family groups with a striking contrast to the portraits of living women, who by then were sporting artificially crimped waves and spit-curls around the face. The natural, rather than crimped, waves of Antonia's hair, and the simplicity of her coiffure, drawn simply back to the nape, would have given her elements of similarity to many Classical types of goddesses, in particular the virgin goddesses Athena and Artemis, whose hair

---

[83] Rose, 1997, 82–83, no. 4; 92, no. 16; 95–96, no. 23; 100–102, no. 30; 103–104, no. 32; 108–110, no. 37; 113–115, no. 42; 116–118, no. 45; 120–121, no. 49; 126–128, no. 52; 182–184, no. 125; 185–188, no. 128, and concordance pp. 191–197. Rose lists Antonia as appearing in thirteen such groups, but of these the relief at Ravenna (100–102, no. 30), is somewhat speculative, since he identifies Antonia with the seated female at the viewer's left whose face has broken away. As noted above in the text, I dispute the identification of the head in the Béziers group (126–128, no. 52), as Antonia. The remaining 11 appearances of Antonia's portrait are however securely documented, either by inscriptions or by sculptures that recognizably follow the Wilton House type.

is drawn back, not in a looped queue but in a plait down the back in a number of Classical types, including the Athena of Velletri type, the Athena of Piraeus, and the very popular, widely replicated Artemis of Dresden type.[84] This last work particularly resembles Antonia's portraits in frontal view, thanks to the severity with which her hair is drawn back, completely exposing both ears. Sculptors of Antonia's portraits probably intended no explicit assimilation with youthful and virgin deities, since her claim to importance in every public group would have been as a wife and mother of imperial princes. Claudian copyists, however, could exploit the classicizing possibilites of her coiffure to set Antonia apart both from the living women of her family, by her nobly simple treatment, and from the more dramatically goddess-like portraits of Livia that they were producing at the same time. The Baia group explicitly endows Antonia (figures 64–66) with the attributes of Venus Genetrix, and also suggests that she could sometimes play Kore to Livia's Ceres/Demeter.

Unlike her predecessor as Augusta and Priestess of the Deified Augustus, however, Antonia's portraits are both fewer in number and less richly varied. Only thirteen securely identified portraits of Antonia survive, as opposed to well over one hundred for Livia, and Rose, as note above, has documented her presence in only eleven portrait groups, while inscriptions and extant sculptures attest Livia's in at least fifty nine.[85] The replicas of the Wilton House type follow a prototype faithfully, with just one significant but subtle alteration probably at the time of Claudius's accession, and only an occasional addition of some other detail like hanging shoulder locks. Stylistically, their interpretations are less adventurous and flamboyant that those of any of Livia's types.

Claudius, although he honored his mother highly, never deified her and probably never intended to; his thirteen-year principate would have given him ample time to do so, but he seems to have concluded that the honors he initially granted her would suffice.

---

[84] Athena of Velletri: *LIMC* 2, "Athena," 980, no. 247 (Pierre Demargne). *LIMC* II, "Athena/Minerva," 1085, nos. 146–146b (Fulvio Canciani).

Athena of Piraeus: *LIMC* 2, "Athena," 980–981, no. 254.

Dresden Artemis: *LIMC* 2, "Artemis," 637, no. 137 (Lilly Kahil and Noëlle Icard), and "Artemis/Diana," 799–800, no. 9a–l (for complete list of replicas); Bieber, 1961, 21, fig. 40; Blümel, 1938, 26–27, no. K 242, for discussion of type and its attribution to Praxiteles.

[85] Rose, 1997, concordance, pp. 191–197.

Having deified his grandmother Livia, thus giving the Claudian branch of the family a deified ancestor to whom they could trace their lineage directly rather than through marriages and adoptions, Claudius probably decided that any more consecrations of women of his family tree would appear overly egotistical. Worse, they could remind the public of the excesses of Caligula, whose deification of Drusilla may already have become the subject of open mockery.[86] Antonia's secondary importance in relation to the senior *diva* must be scrupulously established, but so must her seniority over the wives and living relatives of the emperor.

---

[86] Drusilla's deification was certainly no longer taken seriously by the early years of Nero's principate: see Sen. *Apocol.* 1.

CHAPTER FOUR

VIPSANIA AGRIPPINA AND LIVILLA I,
THE WOMEN OF THE FAMILY OF TIBERIUS

Historical Information

When Tiberius came to power in 14 A.D., he was an unmarried man without close female relatives of his own blood. There were, however, four women of his family who played key roles in his plans for succession and whose images consequently had a place in the public art of his principate. One of these, Antonia, was the mother of his adopted heir Germanicus, and therefore figured in some public sculptural groups of his time, as we have seen in the previous chapter. The other three were his former wife Vipsania Agrippina, and his daughters-in-law Livilla I and Agrippina I. Tiberius attempted to suggest his dynastic plans subtly and discreetly to the Senate and public, as his treatment of his own mother has indicated: he was willing to make use of her image on the coins of A.D. 22, for example, but not to institutionalize her role with official titles and privileges. None of the younger women of his family, therefore, appeared on coins at all during his principate, and we consequently lack the most useful form of evidence for their identifications in other media.[1] Antonia and Agrippina I have been identified with certainty in existing sculpture only because those women received the honor of representation on coins at a later date, after the death of Tiberius. There is, however, some circumstantial evidence for the recognition of sculptural portrait types of the other two.

Vipsania Agrippina, although Tiberius had been forced to divorce her before his assumption of the principate, was the mother of his only surviving son. (See Appendix, chart no. 5). [Claudia] Livia Julia, better known by her family nickname of Livilla, was the niece and daughter-in-law of Tiberius, wife of Drusus II and mother of the

---

[1] The coins of A.D. 22 with reverses of PIETAS and IUSTITIA are almost certainly not portraits, despite efforts to identify them with various women of the imperial family. See Chapter 2, n. 119.

emperor's twin grandsons (see Appendix, chart no. 6), while Agrippina I was the wife of his adopted son Germanicus and mother of three more potential male heirs to the principate (see Appendix, chart no. 7). Gaius "Caligula" Caesar, the youngest son of Agrippina I and Germanicus did in fact eventually succeed Tiberius, and this historical turn of events guaranteed the survival of Agrippina I's images in many replicas, which sculptors continued to copy long after her death, and which appeared on coins of her son's principate. In fact, the great majority of her extant images date after her death, and for that reason will be more appropriately discussed in the following chapter. The one universally accepted portrait type of this woman, however, was first created to honor her as the living daughter-in-law of Tiberius, since at least one example comes from the group at Leptis Magna, which must date to 23 A.D. or soon afterward (figure 86). The inscriptions from that same group prove furthermore that Vipsania Agrippina and Livilla I, the mother and wife of Drusus II, were also honored with public portraits.[2]

Vipsania Agrippina was the daughter of Agrippa by his first marriage, and thus a member of a family to which Augustus wished to bind his own as closely as possible. Agrippa was a brilliant general, the true architect of Augustus's military victories at Actium and Naulochos, and for that reason was at one time the clear intended successor of the first *princeps*, a man of experience and proven ability whom Augustus trusted to assume the reins of power in the event of his own death. Augustus therefore married his daughter Julia to Agrippa, probably with the intention that if Agrippa was to be his immediate heir, then his own grandsons would eventually come to power, and he arranged the marriage of his stepson Tiberius to Agrippa's daughter. At this period, Tiberius was relatively far from the line of intended succession, although Augustus was aware that his stepsons might one day become his successors. Nonetheless, there was little compelling reason to represent Tiberius and his wife in Augustan public groups.

The marriage of Tiberius and Vipsania Agrippina was a very happy and successful one, yet it ended in divorce, not due to the wish of either party but because after Agrippa's death, Augustus forced Tiberius to divorce Vipsania Agrippina so as to marry Julia.

---

[2] Rose, 1997, 182–184 no. 125; Aurigemma, 1940, 10; Levi della Vida, 1935, 15–27.

The alliance was necessary to secure the position of Tiberius as the intended heir to power, but Tiberius openly resented the callous order and continued to display his sorrow after both he and Vipsania Agrippina had remarried.[3] He bore a bitter grudge against Vipsania's second husband C. Asinius Gallus which continued even after the death of Vipsania in A.D. 20, and which culminated in the conviction of Gallus for treason, his exile, and his eventual murder or suicide in A.D. 30.[4] When Augustus finally adopted Tiberius as his heir, furthermore, he once again forced his stepson to put aside personal feelings toward his own immediate family, requiring Tiberius to adopt his nephew Germanicus. Tiberius would undoubtedly have preferred for the imperial power to pass directly to his own son, Drusus II, the child of his beloved first wife, but he again complied with the orders of Augustus. During his principate, he made a show of treating the two young men with scrupulous equality, a policy that the material evidence of sculptural groups bears out: they frequently appeared together as a pair, equal in scale and honorific attributes. The very fact that Augustus's choice for the succession enjoyed no more obvious public favor that Tiberius's own son, however, suggests a discreet effort on the part of Tiberius to shift the terms established by the will of the first princeps, and to present both men as equally worthy. The death of Germanicus left the way open for Drusus II, and at that point Tiberius abandoned all pretence of reticence in the promotion of his son's public image. Whether or not Tiberius was responsible for the death of Germanicus, the event was undoubtedly convenient for the emperor's own plans.[5]

During Vipsania's marriage to Gallus, while her husband was still a prominent political figure, public references to her earlier marriage to Tiberius and its unhappy conclusion would have been somewhat embarrassing. As the mother of Drusus II, however, she could appropriately appear in some family groups, although such appearances are rare. Her image is most likely to have occurred in such contexts after her death, when she could appropriately take her place not as a living member of the family but as a distinguished ancestress who

---

[3] Suet. *Aug.* 63, *Tib.* 7.2–3.

[4] Dio 57.2.7 and 58.3.1–7 on Tiberius's persecution of Gallus, motivated at least partly by jealousy of Gallus's marriage to Vipsania Agrippina; *RE* 2 (1896) 1585–1587 no. 15, s.v. "C. Asinius C.f. Gallus", and *PIR* 1² (1933) 245–249 no. 1229, s.v. "C. Asinius Gallus," *PIR* 3 (1898) 443 no. 462, s.v. "Vipsania Agrippina."

[5] Tac. *Ann.* 4.1.

represented the blood-line of Drusus II and his sons. The neo-Punic
inscription from the Old Forum of Leptis Magna proves that her
image did appear in an imperial family group that honored the two
princes Germanicus and Drusus II. The epigraphic evidence also indicates that this group must date no earlier than A.D. 23, after the death
of Drusus II, and thus at least three years after the death of his mother.[6]

Livilla I's presence in public statuary groups, unlike those of
Vipsania Agrippina, presented no difficulties until her disastrous fall
from grace and death in A.D. 31. Before then, however, she enjoyed
a long period of public prominence, as a daughter of distinguished
parents, as the wife of an imperial heir, and finally as his widow
and the mother of his surviving children, that allowed time for widespread replication and distribution of her portraits. Livilla's father
was Drusus I, the son of Livia and brother of Tiberius, who had
died in A.D. 9, and her mother was Antonia Minor. Livilla I thus
belonged to both the Julian and the Claudian families, and was the
great-niece of the Deified Augustus. (See Appendix, chart no. 6). At
an early age she had been betrothed to the first emperor's eldest
grandson and heir Gaius Caesar, but the untimely death of Gaius prevented the fulfillment of the engagement.[7] Considering the importance of Gaius and Lucius Caesar in the dynastic plans of Augustus,
the fact that she was chosen for such an honor dramatically illustrates
the importance of the bloodlines that she carried. Her first and only
marriage was to her cousin Drusus II, the son of her father's brother
Tiberius, by whom she had several children including twin sons,
whose birth Tiberius publicly celebrated. About two years after their
birth, when it seemed that both children would survive infancy, the
Senatorial mint honored the boys on coins that represented them
emerging from a pair of cornucopiae, thus presenting them as the
hope for the happiness and prosperity of the Roman state.[8] This
issue of A.D. 22–23 formed part of the same program of dynastic
messages as the three issues of *sestertii* with the reverses of *Salus
Augusta*, *Iustitia*, and *Pietas*, discussed in Chapter 2, that drew attention
to the relationships of Tiberius, his mother, and his son Drusus II
to the deified Augustus.[9] The twins were born in A.D. 19, not long

[6] Trillmich, 1988, 51–60.
[7] *RE* 13[1] (1926) 923, s.v. "Livia Iulia" (Lotte Ollendorf).
[8] Tac. *Ann.* II.84; *RIC* 1[2], 97 no. 42, pl. 11; *BMCRE* 1, 133 nos. 95–97, pl. 24.6;
Banti-Simonetti, *CNR* 11, 4–12 nos. 2–7/2.
[9] Winkler, 1995, 49.

after the death of Germanicus, while the public was still in mourning for the popular young general, and the partisans of Germanicus (to judge from the sarcastic tone of Tacitus) considered the emperor's delight about the birth to be rather distasteful. His reasons for political as well as personal joy were understandable, however, if less than diplomatic, since the death of Germanicus had left his own son Drusus II as the likeliest heir to power. The births of two male heirs must have made the security of his own line seem even more firmly assured. Because of Livilla's descent from Octavia, the sister of Augustus, any child of hers would have been closely enough related to the line of the Deified Augustus to enjoy a strong claim to succession. One of the twins died at the age of about four, but the other, Tiberius Gemellus, remained healthy, allowing Livilla I still to enjoy the status of the mother of a potential heir.[10]

A few years after the birth of her sons, however, in A.D. 23, the chain of events began that led to her downfall. In that year, Drusus II died under circumstances that seemed to arouse no suspicion at the time.[11] Eight years later, however, the arrest and execution of Sejanus for plotting a *coup d'état* wracked the goverment of Tiberius, and led to an inquisitorial search for other traitors. At that time, Sejanus's widow Apicata committed suicide, leaving a letter to Tiberius in which she alleged that Sejanus and Livilla I had been lovers and had together murdered Drusus II by administering slow poison. Two of the accomplices that she accused of involvement, a physician named Eudemus who had supposedly supplied the poison, and Lygdus, a eunuch who had helped to administer it, confirmed Apicata's accusations in confessions under torture.[12] Livilla I met with her own death in short order, although Dio appears uncertain whether Tiberius executed her or whether her stern mother Antonia Minor carried out the sentence privately. In either case, the Senate and public evidently considered her guilt a matter of record, since the Senate decreed a *damnatio memoriae* the following year, and ordered the destruction of her images.[13]

By the standards of Roman history, particularly in regard to assassination plots, a letter of accusation from a party likely to know of

[10] Tac. *Ann.* 2.84, 4.15.
[11] Suet. *Tib.* 62.1: "Quem cum morbo et intemperantia perisse existimaret..."
[12] Tac. *Ann.* 4.11; Dio 58.11.6–7.
[13] Tac. *Ann.* 6.2.

the conspiracy, and two confessions from accomplices is very powerful evidence. It is not unreasonable for Tacitus to narrate the accusations of Apicata as fact in his account of the death of Drusus II,
especially since he reviews with appropriate caution and skepticism
some of the more outlandish rumors that circulated about the death
of Drusus II in later years, after the disgrace and death of Sejanus
and Livilla I.[14] Tacitus, however, admits bewilderment at Livilla's
motives: why should the wife of the heir apparent to the empire,
and the mother of his sons, trade her status and security for very
uncertain prospects as the wife of a man of a lower order who hoped
to seize power by force? He can only explain her behavior by the
argument that a woman capable of adultery is capable of anything.[15]

Still, although there is no evidence against the version of the death
of Drusus II as Tacitus accepts it, Suetonius describes an atmosphere
of paranoid hysteria surrounding the investigation of the alleged
murder that should encourage some skepticism.[16] According to Suetonius, Tiberius tortured and executed many people including at least
one man from Rhodes who had no connection to the affair, whom
he interrogated by mistake. A contemporary reader who recalls 20th
century events like the red-baiting of Senator Joseph McCarthy and
the witch-hunts for child abusers of the 1980's and early 1990's
might well suspect that Livilla I was the victim of false accusations
during a frantic search for any surviving accomplices of Sejanus. The
testimony of Lygdus and Eudemus is hardly unimpeachable, since
confessions extracted under torture are notoriously unreliable, while
Apicata had ample reason for malice toward Livilla I no matter what
the behavior of the latter. After the death of Drusus II, Sejanus had
requested permission to marry the widowed Livilla I, and although
Tiberius denied the request, Apicata would naturally have been jeal-
ous of the higher-ranked woman with whom her husband wanted
to replace her.[17] If Dio's account of Livilla's death is reliable, however, the evidence against her was damning enough to convince her
own mother, who had been instrumental in exposing Sejanus's plot.

The facts of Livilla's guilt or innocence are as irrelevant today as
they are undeterminable. Of far more interest to us is the way in

---

[14] Tac. *Ann.* 4.7–8, on death of Drusus Minor; 4.11 on the nature of the evidence and the more unbelievable of the rumors.
[15] Tac. *Ann.* 4.3: "neque femina amissa pudicitia alia abnuerit."
[16] Suet. *Tib.* 62.1.
[17] Tac. *Ann.* 4.39–41.

which Tacitus characterizes her, and contrasts her with Agrippina I, the woman whose status in the imperial family most closely mirrored hers. Both were daughters-in-law of Tiberius, both had sons whose rights to succession they naturally defended, especially after the deaths of their respective husbands, and both were women of personal wealth and influence, with large households of slaves and freedmen of their own.[18] Given the society that had produced them and the dynastic system that had taught them that women must fight for the succession of their own sons at all costs, a rivalry between the two was more or less inevitable. Tacitus is by no means an unqualified admirer of Agrippina I, whom he describes with the very pejorative term "atrox" on at least one occasion, and accuses of overstepping the proper role of a woman.[19] He clearly sympathizes with the supporters of Germanicus, however, quoting with evident agreement the rumors that circulated when the first reports of Germanicus' illness reached Rome. Tiberius, according to these anonymous accounts, had ordered his adoptive son to a remote province and placed him at the mercy of Piso because Germanicus had intended to restore the republic.[20] Tacitus therefore treats Agrippina I, despite her unfeminine traits of character, with at least grudging respect for her valiant efforts to bring the murderers of Germanicus to justice, and to champion the rights of his sons. Once again citing popular opinion, he bestows on her, although admittedly in an indirect quote, extraordinarily high praise: "The glory of her country, they called her—the only true descendant of Augustus, the unmatched model of traditional behavior."[21]

Her conduct, moreover, can here serve as a foil to that of two villainesses: Tacitus emphasizes, when quoting the rumors about the malice of Tiberius toward Germanicus, that Livia and her personal friend Plancina, the wife of Piso, had been complicit in the alleged plot against Germanicus from its very inception, and that they had

---

[18] *RE* 13[1] 925, s.v. "Livia Iulia" (L. Ollendorff).

[19] See Kaplan, 1979, 410–411. Kaplan points out that "atrox" is a term normally used to describe male behavior in battle.

[20] Tac. *Ann.* 2.82: "ideo nimirum in extremas terras relegatum, ideo Pisoni permissam provinciam; hoc egisse secretos Augustae cum Plancina sermones. Vera prorsus de Druso seniores locutos: displicere regnantibus civilia filiorum ingenia, neque ob aliud interceptos quam quia populum Romanum aequo iure complecti reddita libertate agitaverint." See also Barrett, 1996, 23.

[21] Tac. *Ann.* 3.4: "Nihil tamen Tiberium magis penetravit quam studia hominum accensa in Agrippinam, cum decus patriae, solum Augusti sanguinem, unicum antiquitatis specimen appellarent..." Translation quoted in text: Grant, 1971, 121.

encouraged Tiberius to send him into danger by their behind-the-scenes plotting and scheming, a form of behavior quite different from the very public, if impolitic, accusations of Agrippina I against her husband's alleged assassins.[22] Likewise, when describing how Sejanus plotted to eliminate rivals for his own bid for imperial power, Tacitus implicitly contrasts the behavior of Livilla I, whom Sejanus seduced and corrupted while her husband was still alive, with that of Agrippina I, whose chastity was untouchable even during her widowhood.[23] When Sejanus requested permission to marry Livilla I in A.D. 25, he gave as one of his reasons the need for an ally against the elder Agrippina's attacks on him.[24] In this situation, then, Tacitus presents Agrippina I as the paradigm of good female behavior, in contrast to that of Livilla I.

During the years after the death of Germanicus, the elder Agrippina's relations with both Tiberius and Sejanus became increasingly bitter and hostile. At the instigation of Sejanus, she and her oldest son were finally sent into exile, where both died, while her second son was imprisoned and killed in Rome. Until her banishment, however, Tiberius was obliged to treat her with public honor. She figured prominently in monuments that honored the memory of Germanicus after his death: most notably, an arch in Rome on which a statue of Germanicus appeared in a triumphal chariot, accompanied by statues of Agrippina I and all of their many children.[25] Similar monuments undoubtedly stood in other cities of the empire as well, in emulation of the Roman arch, one notable example being the Leptis Magna group.[26] This later monument, which post-dates the death of Drusus II, honored both princes in a manner modeled on the earlier monuments in honor of Germanicus alone, with the result that statues of Agrippina I and Livilla I appeared as pendants on each side of the chariot group. Since by far the most numerous surviving portraits of Agrippina I are posthumous, postdating her rehabilitation by her son Caligula, the discussion of her image in official propaganda belongs most appropriately to the next chapter of this study. Although scantier and somewhat more difficult to identify, the sculptural portraits of Vipsania Agrippina and Livilla I now merit our attention.

---

[22] Tac. *Ann.* 2.82. See note 20.

[23] Tac. *Ann.* 4.12.

[24] Tac. *Ann.* 4.39: "satis aestimare firmari domum adversum iniquas Agrippinae offensiones . . ."

[25] Gonzalez, 1984, 55–100, text of inscription 58–59; Rose, 1997, 108–110 no. 37.

[26] Trillmich, 1988, 55–56; Rose 183.

Vipsania Agrippina: The Portraits

Vipsania Agrippina never appeared on Roman or provincial coinage, but as mentioned above, the inscriptions from Leptis Magna offer indisputable evidence that after her death, at least, she did appear in sculptural groups. The Leptis Magna inscription has led in turn to the identification of a work of sculpture from the site for which the circumstantial evidence is fairly strong. (Figures 72–73). This is a handsome marble head, made for insertion into a statue, that represents a woman who matches no known portrait type for any of the other women that the inscription names. By process of elimination, therefore, Aurigemma identified this head as Vipsania Agrippina.[27] Bianchi-Bandinelli preferred to identify it as a private citizen, and Trillmich has recently raised the objection that its marble is of a different type than that of the rest of the Julio-Claudian statues, arguing therefore that it cannot belong to the same group.[28] In view of the fact that the head was carved separately from the body for which it was intended, however, a very common procedure in the production of Roman portrait statues, it is not unlikely that the portrait specialist might happen to use one or two pieces of marble from a separate quarry or lot from the material used for the rest of the group. Since the discoveries at Leptis, at least one and possibly two replicas of this same portrait have been identified, one from Rusellae, the other from Pozzuoli.[29] The existence of more than one replica, from such far-flung locations, would indicate that the woman was of empire-wide importance, and therefore an imperial figure. The replica from Rusellae is so badly weathered that the features are almost obliterated, but it recognizably shares with the Leptis head its coiffure and general facial shape. The other, from Pozzuoli, appears in the only photograph yet published to be somewhat softer and more idealized than the other two, with more decorative, wavy hair. Its coiffure does conform in general to that of the Leptis-Rusellae type, but until the work is more thoroughly published and available for study, the question of whether or not it is a true replica of the Leptis and

---

[27] Aurigemma, 1940, 66–70, 72–73, figs. 45–46; Boschung, *JRA* 1993, 58–59 no. M.

[28] Bianchi-Bandinelli, 1964, 87, pl. 97; Trillmich, 1988, 53, 59 n. 26.

[29] Boschung, *JRA* 1993, 58–59 no. M. The Rusellae group is unpublished, but I am greatly indebted to Dssa. Celuzza, director of the Museo Nazionale Archeologico di Grossetto for permitting me to examine this head. Pozzuoli replica: Pozzi, 1983, 382, pl. 17, fig. 1.

Rusellae heads must remain unproven. This head, unlike the others, survives with its body, a somewhat over-life-size draped figure. The scale of the statue and its discovery in a public place, however, do not necessarily prove the imperial status of the subject.

The Leptis and Rusellae heads represent an attractive woman, but one with subtle signs of maturity like the "Venus rings" of her throat and the slight fleshy folds at the corners of her mouth. Her hair is parted in the middle, according to fashions of the later first century B.C. and early first century A.D., swept upward from the forehead and pulled back very severely, leaving the ears completely exposed. At the base of the skull, her hair is bound into a small, tight chignon. The drapery that veils the heads of the Rusellae and Pozzuoli replicas obscures this detail, but the Leptis head shows it. No curls or wisps escape from the coiffure around the face, although a lock of hair may hang down the back of the neck of the Leptis head, and the strands incised into the marble have no undulation whatsoever. The woman's hair is not curly or even wavy but stick-straight. The strands of the Rusellae head, unfortunately partly erased by weathering, do not appear quite so severe, and those of the Pozzuoli marble have a soft, full undulation, suggesting some freedom in the interpretation of a prototype by various copyists. In all cases, however, the coiffure has one distinct feature: where the hair is swept up and away from the forehead, it forms two crest-like puffs, one on each side of the central part.

The woman's distinctive physical characteristics include a high forehead which her coiffure helps to emphasize; a rather heavy bone structure as evidenced by the thickness of the bridge of her nose; hooded eyes, wide cheekbones, and a broad, fleshy mouth with a full, generously curved lower lip. All of these physical traits she shares with the portraits of Agrippa, which are securely identified, although of course her features have a somewhat more feminine delicacy.[30] If the portraits do represent Agrippa's daughter, whose marriage to Tiberius was such an important alliance for the Julio-Claudian family, then one would naturally expect portraitists to emphasize her family resemblance to her father. When Vipsania appears after her death

---

[30] Boschung, *JRA* 1993, 50, Fa, fig. 19. An especially good example of Agrippa's portrait type is a head from Gabii in Paris, Musée du Louvre, MA 1208, marble, h. 46 cm. De Kersauson, *Louvre* 1, 1986, 54–55 no. 22 with earlier literature; Kleiner, *Sculpture*, 1992, 75, fig. 52.

as a revered ancestress, this resemblance would take on added meaning, demonstrating the blood-lines of Drusus II and his children back to the great general Agrippa. The Leptis portrait securely belongs to a time after Vipsania Agrippina's death and that of her son Drusus II, but a time when Tiberius Gemellus was still alive and still a serious contender for succession. The portrait of Drusus II that appeared in the Leptis group also demonstrates family resemblances to the woman in the portraits in question, most notably in his high forehead, his thick nose-bridge, the shape of his eyebrows and his slightly hooded eyes.[31] His mouth is thinner-lipped than hers, and has a more pronounced overbite—a Claudian characteristic that establishes his resemblance to Tiberius—but the resemblance to the woman is also noticeable.

The precise location of the discovery of the Rusellae head unfortunately is not known, although it probably came to light either in or near the Casa degli Augustali, where a number of other Julio-Claudian statues were found. These included some securely identifiable portraits ranging in date from the principate of Tiberius to that of Claudius. Here again, it is likely that she stood near a likeness of her son Drusus II whose resemblance to her the viewers of the group could easily have observed.

I have suggested in the first chapter that another portrait type, commonly accepted either as Julia f. Augusti or as Octavia, may in fact represent Vipsania Agrippina wearing the more old-fashioned coiffure that was fashionable at the time of her marriage to Tiberius. (Figures 18–19). This identification, initially proposed by Bartels, again rests on circumstantial evidence, and lacks the corroboration of inscriptions that we possess for the Leptis-Rusellae type. It is perhaps prudent therefore not to draw many conclusions from the style and form of the Béziers-Copenhagen type about the public presentation of the first wife of Tiberius. It shares, however, a number of physical features with the Leptis-Rusellae type. It too appeared in a group with a portrait of Agrippa, the father of Vipsania Agrippina, and displays strong physical resemblances to him: the heavy bone structure, hooded eyes, and broad, full lips to name a few. Had the portrait represented the sister or daughter of Augustus, one would expect to see a stronger emphasis on their family resemblance to

---

[31] Aurigemma, 1940, 60–62 figs. 39–40.

him, since Julia's greatest political value to her father was as the
bearer of his bloodlines, and the mother of his only male heirs,
whom he had legally adopted as his own sons. Roman portraitists
are sometimes known to assimilate the appearance of a wife to her
husband, and Balty has suggested that this head from Béziers represents Julia as the wife of Agrippa, which would account for the
stylistic similarity of the two, but it is far likelier that the resemblance
is not stylistic but physical.[32] This portrait shows close technical and
stylistic affinities to another work in the same group, however: the
portrait of Livia (figures 39–40). That portrait, which conforms to
the type on Livia's "Salus" coins of 22–23, must date to the principate of Tiberius. The Livia and the portrait of the woman with the
nodus are probably the work of the same atelier, and therefore probably entered the group contemporaneously, in the years after the
death of Augustus and succession of Tiberius. After the disgrace and
exile of Julia, any new public portrait of her would have been unthinkable. It is likelier, then, that the Béziers portrait and its replicas follow another portrait type for Vipsania Agrippina, probably earlier
than the one represented at Leptis Magna.

    In none of these portraits is there any trace of heroization of the
subject, or of association with divine beings. No portrait type of
Vipsania Agrippina would originally have been intended for widespread public display: during her marriage to Tiberius, she and her
family were too far from the intended line of dynastic succession,
while after her marriage to Gallus she was once again a private, if
aristocratic, citizen. She could well have sat for portraits during both
those marriages, but only later would the sculptors of the first century
A.D. have used them as prototypes for copies distributed to places
like Leptis Magna. Nonetheless, the austerity of these images suited
well the tone that Tiberius seemed to prefer in the public images of
his family: the earlier type with the *nodus* coiffure conforms well to
the standard image of modest matrons of the Augustan era, and the
later one, with its middle part and exposed ears bears comparison
with the portraits of Antonia Minor. Antonia's "Wilton House" type
(figures 60–66, 68) differs from the portraits of Vipsania in the presence of the hair ribbon across the crown, and her hair is not swept
up from the hairline like that of the Leptis Magna head, but the

---

[32] Balty, 1996, 199 no. 138; Balty and Cazes, 1995, 58.

coiffures of the two women are sufficiently alike to identify them as members of the same generation, and as women who share the virtues of chaste respectability. The similarity of Antonia's images to Vipsania Agrippina's would have been especially striking when they appeared together in a symmetrically arranged group, as they did at Leptis, in their capacity as the mothers of the adoptive and the biological sons of the emperor.

As mentioned in the previous chapter, only one portrait-type of Antonia, the so-called "Wilton House" type, can be securely recognized.[33] A statue that conforms to this type did come to light at Leptis Magna (figure 59), and we may reasonably assume that this is the same statue that the Neo-Punic inscription attests as standing near the chariot-group of her son Germanicus.[34] Early publications of the Leptis Magna finds, however, misidentified this statue as Livia, an understandable error in view of the rather mediocre quality of the portrait head. The lower face is fuller and shorter than in the better replicas of the Wilton House type, for example, and the features blander, as often happens in provincial replicas that have been copied from copies of copies and have lost the subtleties of character of the prototype. Erhart, the first scholar to identify the statue correctly, admitted uncertainty about whether to include it among Antonia's "youthful and idealized" or "mature and individualized" portraits. The coiffure, however, conforms exactly to the rest of the replicas of the Wilton House group (Erhart's "mature and individualized type") in details including the hair-ribbon across the crown and the fully exposed ears, which never occur in Livia's portraits. This statue of a veiled Roman matron clad in the *stola* that identifies her status was therefore most probably the pendant to the portrait of Vipsania Agrippina in the chariot group.

The early misidentification of this statue left the way open for the mistaken identification of another work of sculpture found in the Old Forum of Leptis as Antonia Minor, and this misnomer has proved remarkably persistent in scholarly literature, despite persuasive

---

[33] Lists of extant replicas of type: Small, 1990, 221; Polaschek, *Antonia*, 1973, 19–24, 25–30. For more detailed discussion, see previous chapter.

[34] Aurigemma, 1940, 76–77, figs. 51–52. Aurigemma identifies this statue as Livia and postulates its presence in a second Julio-Claudian group, separate from the great chariot-group. Erhart and Trillmich have both recognized it as Antonia, however: see Erhart, 1978, 210–211, Group 1, no. 10, and Group 3 no. 14, and Trillmich, 1988, 53, 59 n. 24 with earlier references.

arguments by Polaschek and a number of other scholars that the woman this type represents cannot be Antonia. Let us next consider that problematic group of replicas.

Livilla I: The Problem of her Sculptural Portraits

Livilla I, like Vipsania Agrippina, never appeared in portrait likenesses on coins of the Roman mint. Thus, the only available means for the identification of her likenesses is the more tenuous matter of historical probability, wherever portraits appear in contexts that permit historical inferences. The Leptis Magna head of a young woman comes from such a context. (Figures 74–75). In his first comprehensive publication of the Leptis Magna sculptures, Aurigemma cautiously identified the handsome head of a pretty young woman as a "*ritratto di ignota*," portrait of an unknown person.[35] She must beyond doubt, however, have been an imperial woman, and one who enjoyed a long period of public prominence, because at least seven more replicas of this type exist, including examples from locations as diverse as Rome (figures 76–77), Rusellae, Sicily, Malta, Athens, and the Greek islands.[36] The subject of this type wears her hair parted simply in the middle, drawn severely back behind the ears in shallow, reg-

---

[35] Head from Leptis Magna, Old Forum: marble head, h. 22.5 cm., made for insertion into statue, part of nose and lips on right broken away, piece missing from forehead to right of part, near hairline. Published: Rose, 182–184 no. 125, pl. 230; Kokkinos, 109–110; Erhart, 1978, 202–203 figs. 12–13; Polaschek, *Antonia* 39–46; Aurigemma, 1940, 88–90, figs. 65–66.

[36] A) Museo Nazionale Romano delle Terme inv. 620, marble head made for insertion into statue or bust, h. 32 cm. Right-hand side of nose and both earlobes missing. Published: *MNR Sculture*, Vol. 1 part 1, 338–340 no. 202, with recent bibliography (Virginia Picciotti Giornetti); Felletti-Maj, 1953, 54–55 no. 85.

B) Vatican Museums, ingresso, ambulacro, inv. 103. Marble bust, h. 66 cm., of head and neck, 32 cm. Bust may not belong to head, drapery extensively recut. Published: Erhart, 1978, 202; Lippold, *Vatican* 3², 4–5, no. 5, pl. 4 no. 5.

C) Statue from Rusellae: Rose, 1997, 68–69, 117–118. Otherwise unpublished. Museo Nazionale di Archeologia, Grosseto.

D) Tindari head: Palermo, Museo Nazionale inv. 705, large-grained white marble, head and neck unit made for insertion, h. 38 cm. Head split horizontally through top; a triangular section of the middle of the forehead and parts of the hair on each side restored in plaster. Queue of hair at nape of neck broken away. End of nose restored in plaster. Published: Bonacasa, 1964, 60–61 no. 74 pl. 34, figs. 3–4.

E) Malta: Marble bust or herm, face well preserved, front of neck and of bust broken away. Discovered in the excavation of a Roman villa at Rabat, Malta.

ular waves and fastened into a small chignon at the base of the skull, above the nape of the neck. In frontal view, the coiffure is not unlike that of Antonia's Wilton House type (figures 59–66, 68), but differs from that group of sculptures in the neatly arranged fringe of little ringlets along the hairline that frame the forehead. These curls are clearly an intentional part of the coiffure, not "accidental" escaping locks like the small cluster of ringlets that appear in front of the ears of Antonia's Claudian-era portraits. Some of Antonia's coins from the Roman mint appear to show just such a row of curls, although it is not a standard element, and provincial coins from Alexandria definitely show the feature with far greater clarity.[37] Erhart classifies this group of sculptures as Antonia's "youthful, individualized type," as opposed to the "mature and individualized type" represented by the Wilton House group. Polaschek prefers to designate it the "Leptis-Malta" type, after two replicas from known provenances.[38]

A woman of Antonia's importance and longevity could well have had more than one official portrait type, one of which might date to her youth, representing her at the time of her marriage to Drusus I as the attractive wife of a prince of the imperial family, and the mother of children of Julian blood. According to the most commonly accepted identification, the Leptis-Malta type is that early portrait, which occasionally still appeared on coins minted after her death. There is, however, one serious obstacle to this identification: certain key physical features differ significantly from those both of the Wilton House sculptural type and of the coin profiles. Although the woman of the Leptis-Malta type, as we should for now cautiously designate it, shares with Antonia the typically Julian flaring eyebrows, thin lips, overbite, and triangular lower face, she also has a wide, short nose with flaring nostrils in frontal view and a straight bridge with a sharply jutting tip in profile. The profile line is crucial to identification

---

Published: Kokkinos, 1992, 111–112, fig. 73; Erhart, 1978, 202; Polaschek, *Antonia* 1973, 39–45, pl. 19, figs. 1–2, 20 fig. 2.

F) Athens: Agora Museum, inv. S 220, marble, h. 21 cm. Published: Erhart, 1978, 202; Harrison, 1953, 24, no. 12, pl. 8.

G) Berlin head: Staatliche Museen zu Berlin, Antikensammlung, inv. 1802, white marble head h. 27.5 cm., from one of the Greek islands. Erhart, 1978, 202; Blümel, 1933, 11, no. R23, pl. 16; *MNR Sculture* 1¹, 339 (V.P. Giornetti).

[37] For an example of a Roman dupondius that shows the fringe of ringlets, see Trillmich, 1978, 21 no. 3, pl. 7, fig. 3 (Glasgow I 102 no. 72). Alexandrian coin: Erhart, 1978, 200, figs. 11, and 205; Bernoulli, 2¹, 1882–1886, pl. 33.12.

[38] Polaschek, *Antonia*, 1973, 39–45.

of Roman portraits, because it is one of the elements that could be most faithfully reproduced by the methods of measuring used in Roman sculptural ateliers.[39] The shape of a nose is not a physical feature that could change naturally with age, nor is it a feature that Roman sculptors would be likely to vary at will. The same is true of the jaw, which is smaller and shorter than Antonia's, and of the overall shape of the face, which is short and round.

When dealing with any portrait representation made by means other than a mechanical form of reproduction such as photography or a cast taken directly from the subject's face, we must of course always bear in mind that we are dealing with a man-made artifact, to which we cannot apply the same criteria of physical resemblance that might, for example, be used by a pathologist or forensic expert to determine identity. Some elements of proportion and facial structure will inevitably be dictated by artistic convention rather than by the subject's actual appearance, even in the most seemingly realistic works. In Roman sculpture, however, the typical practice throughout the first and second centuries of our era is to retain the same basic facial structure in all portrait types of the same individual, while varying details of hair when a new official type is created. This holds true even for the very diverse portraits of Livia; although the portraits of her Fayum type (figures 22–23) give the face a broader form than her earlier Marbury Hall (figures 26–27) and Albani-Bonn (figures 24–25) types, the facial structure remains recognizably the same. Even signs of age seem to remain constant, or at best to be modified with very superficial details. Kleiner has documented in case after case how the appearance of an emperor is "frozen" at the age at which he assumed imperial power, whether he was young, middle aged, or elderly, and remains constant in subsequent types.[40] It would be an extraordinary break with precedent and with contemporary sculptural practice, then, for the creators of Antonia's mature portrait type not only to add signs of age like the consider-

---

[39] Pfanner, 1989, 204–208.

[40] Kleiner, *Sculpture*, 1992, 208–212, discusses this phenomenon in particular in relation to Trajan; Fittschen has observed a similar phenomenon in the coin portraits of Faustina the Younger, who was honored with a new portrait type on the occasion of the birth of each of her many children but whose facial structure remains basically unaltered. Fittschen, 1982, 126, 38–43 on coin portraits, 44–65 on sculptural portraits, 66–68 on basic consistency of facial type despite changes in coiffure. See also Pfanner, 1989, 213–217.

ably slacker chin-line, but to alter the shape of her face and jaw, and the length, width, and profile line of her nose.

This more youthful type, then, probably represents another woman of the imperial family. Polaschek has made the very plausible suggestion of Livilla I, the daughter of Antonia Minor, whom she would of course have resembled.[41] The coiffure of these portraits, with their simple middle part and shallow waves, appears to be of a type fashionable during the reign of Tiberius, although the ornamental curls along the forehead point toward a trend that became most popular at the time of Caligula. On the other hand, many of the extant replicas show no signs of the deliberate vandalism one might expect in the portraits of a woman who suffered a *damnatio memoriae*.[42] There is of course no way to know how many more replicas once existed that have been destroyed, but the damage to most extant examples is of the sort one would expect from accidental falls rather than intentional vandalism. Only one, the replica from Tindari now in the Palermo museum, shows a horizontal split through the cranium that could be the result of a chisel-blow.

There are other candidates for identification with this type that must also be considered. Sande proposes that this is the earliest likeness of Agrippina II, from the time of Tiberius, when the children of Germanicus are known to have appeared in public statuary groups.[43] Sande correctly points out similarities in the facial type with later likenesses of Agrippina II, but here, as so often happens in Julio-Claudian iconography, genetics and stylistic assimilation both complicate the issue. Livilla I would probably have had some family resemblance to her niece, the daughter of her brother Germanicus. Against the identification is the soft and rounded shape of the jaw, which in all the younger Agrippina's other portraits is very square, and the large number of replicas; why should a portrait of Agrippina II from her adolescence continue to be replicated for a long period after she was a grown woman, and mature portrait types of her were available?

The only complete statue of this portrait type, the example from the Casa degli Augustali at Rusellae, suggests to at least one observer yet another possible identity. Rose has pointed out that this work combines the face with a very girlish, immature-looking figure, although

---

[41] Polaschek, *Antonia*, 1973, 44–45.
[42] Tac. *Ann.* 6.2.
[43] Sande, 1985, 178–183.

the *stola* that she wears over her tunic identifies her as a married
woman. A larger statue of Germanicus appeared in the same statuary
group, suggesting that this woman is younger and lower in status
than he, and could be one of his daughters. Agrippina II, as Sande
has proposed, would be one possibility. The only known type for
Drusilla, the second daughter of Germanicus, has in my opinion,
been satisfactorily identified in a different portrait type, one that shows
both a different coiffure and a longer face than the Leptis-Malta
type. The Rusellae statue could, however, represent the youngest sister, Julia Livilla (hereafter, Livilla II).[44] The coiffure of this type is
somewhat different, and more old-fashioned, than that of the earliest
secure portraits of Agrippina II and of Drusilla, who wore their hair
stiffly crimped into broad, flat waves with slightly indented crests.
(Figures 107–110 and 111–117). It does share with them, however,
the carefully arranged row of ringlets along the hairline. Against the
identification as Livilla I, Rose points out the relatively good condition of the statue and its discovery with other imperial statues, suggesting that it remained on view with them and suffered no vandalism.
Rusellae was not far from Rome, and the people there must have
heard of the Senatorial decree ordering the removal and destruction
of the elder Livilla's portraits. This young woman, then, would be
someone who never received a *damnatio memoriae*.

On the other hand, the large number of surviving replicas suggest that this woman was of greater importance to the ruling emperor's
dynastic plans than Livilla II, who never had children, and whose
importance, unlike that of her sister Agrippina II, ended with her
exile in A.D. 39. Although her uncle Claudius recalled her to Rome
after the death of Caligula, she soon fell afoul of Messalina, who
ordered her into exile again and allegedly had her murdered.[45] It is
possible that local patrons could have honored her with statues during the period of her recall, but unlikely that there could have been
many of them. The Leptis Magna replica, moreover, comes from a
context in which there is no evidence for the presence of the children of Germanicus, but in which the inscription clearly documents
the presence of the two princes' wives. The head could conceivably
belong to a later Caligulan addition to the sculptures of the Old

---

[44] Rose, 1997, 68–69; 117–118.
[45] Suet. *Claud.* 29.1; Tac. *Ann.* 14.63; Dio 59.22.6–9; *RE* 10, 938–39 (Fitzler);
Levick, 1990, 56.

Forum, perhaps consisting of the emperor and his siblings, who carried such great dynastic importance in his official imagery, but that site has yielded no other evidence of a dedication during Caligula's principate. Livilla I, the wife of Drusus II and mother of his twin sons remains, after all, the likeliest candidate. The relatively small scale of the figure in the Rusellae group could plausibly express the status of Livilla I in relation to her husband if this group, like the Leptis assemblage, postdated the deaths of both the young princes. Local sculptors might then logically have heroized the deceased men with larger-scale figures, while representing their living widows in life-size images. The elder Livilla's presence as the mother of the living child Tiberius Gemellus would however have been vitally important in such a group, despite the modesty of her presentation. As for the relatively pristine condition of the statue, the fact that the Senate decreed a *damnatio memoriae* did not always guarantee that the destruction of such images would actually be carried out. Well-preserved portraits of many emperors who suffered condemnation of memory nonetheless survive at sites in Italy, in contexts that suggest that they even remained on display. The statue of the emperor Nero as a child at Velleia, for example, shows no signs of vandalism, and was found with the other statues of the group. That group had been modified earlier to remove the name and image of Caligula; the fact that Nero's portrait later escaped a similar fate illustrates the erratic and incomplete nature of such condemnations.[46] The fact remains, however, that Rose has raised legitimate questions about the identification of this type with Livilla I, and in favor of that as Livilla II. Its identification with either of those two women must as yet remain hypothesis rather than an accepted theory. Despite the presence of this type in several imperial groups, none unfortunately demonstrate her relationship to the other figures with complete clarity. In another medium, however, that of cameo gems, images of a young woman do appear in contexts that support far more strongly an identification as Livilla I. These images follow a different prototype from the Leptis-Malta sculptural replicas; whether they could represent the same individual remains to be discussed.

---

[46] Nero in Velleia group: Rose, 1997, 122–123 no. 50, pls. 133, 150, 151, full earlier bibliography pp. 125–26. Portrait of the emperor Nero from the Palatine Hill: Museo Nazionale Romano, inv. 618, marble, h. 31 cm. Kleiner, *Sculpture*, 1992, 138–139, fig. 112; *MNR Sculture* 1¹ 272–73, no. 168 (E. Talamo); Felletti-Maj, 1953, 73 no. 123; Helbig⁴ 3, 219, no. 2302.

Livilla I: The Glyptic Images

Two cameo gems, one in Berlin and the other in Paris, represent a young woman with the corn-ear and poppy crown of Ceres, holding two tiny male babies in the fold of her mantle, which she gathers into a sort of sling with her upraised right hand. (Figures 78–79).[47] These cameos differ in minor details—the Berlin example (figure 79) wears a necklace with a *bulla*-like pendant, while the one Paris (figure 78) wears a string of beads around her neck—but the pose, gesture and format are so similar that they must follow a common original. These works have a strong claim to represent Livilla I on the occasion of the birth of her twins in A.D. 19, or perhaps on one of their subsequent birthdays, before the death of one of the boys in A.D. 23. In the Berlin cameo (figure 79), the babies, tiny as they are, still have recognizably divine attributes: one holds a cornucopiae, and the other a more enigmatic object. Some observers have recognized it as a serpent, suggesting an identification of this child with the infant Hercules, and of his twin brother with Harpokrates, but Greifenhagen suggests that both children were carrying cornucopiae, and that the attribute in the hand of the baby on the viewer's left was either poorly executed or damaged in later times.[48] If both boys carried this attribute, the gem would show an iconography closely comparable to that of the Roman *sestertii* issued a few years after their births, in which the twins emerged from crossed cornucopiae.[49] The association of both children with bountiful fertility would accord well with the attributes of Ceres that their mother wears. In either case, the imagery establishes that these children must have great dynastic importance.

Several more gems approximate the composition of the Berlin and Paris examples in varying degrees, although no others represent the two babies, and in these cases the identification as Livilla II is more

---

[47] A) Berlin, Schloß Charlottenburg, Staatliche Museen inv. 11096, sardonyx cameo, h. 7.6 cm., w. 6.0 cm. Mikocki, 1995, 34–35, 174 no. 161 pl. 4, with full literature; Megow, 1987, 29–31, 295–96 no. D22, pl. 12.7; Möbius, 1975, 46; Vollenweider, 1966, 73 n. 59, pl. 84.2. Greifenhagen, 1964, 32–36, fig. 4.

B) Paris, Bibliothèque Nationale, Cabinet des Médailles, inv. 243, Mikocki, 1995, 174 no. 162, with full literature, pl. 4; Megow, 1987, 29–31, 296 no. D23, pl. 12,6; Möbius, 1975, 46; Greifenhagen, 1964, 33–36, fig. 6.

[48] Vollenweider, 1966, 73–74 n. 59; Megow, 1987, 295 no. D22; Greifenhagen, 1964, 34.

[49] Supra n. 8.

tenuous, resting on the parallels of those gems to the examples that do represent the children.[50] Of these objects, another cameo in the Bibliothèque Nationale de Paris is the best preserved and presents the closest parallel to the other two, representing the same coiffure and a nearly identical profile. The face here however is a little less idealized than that of the cameos that show the woman with her children: this example displays a heavy, square jaw and rather thin, pinched mouth, whereas the other two show a more gracefully rounded jawline and full, sensuous lips.[51] The identification as Livilla I with her sons is not, of course, secure beyond doubt, since there were other imperial women such as Julia I, the daughter of Augustus, who had two or more male children, but the form of the woman's coiffure points to a Tiberian date, making Livilla I by far the likeliest candidate. The woman on these cameos parts her hair simply in the middle, draws it back from her face in soft but shallow waves that leave the ears fully exposed, and fastens it into a small chignon—not a hanging queue of the sort that Antonia Minor and Agrippina I wore, but definitely a bun, worn low on the base of the skull but above the nape of the neck. The Paris gem (figure 78) shows an escaping lock behind the ear and another at the nape, but the Berlin cameo (figure 79) does not. Reliably dated comparanda include Antonia Minor's "Wilton House" portrait type (figures 59–66, 68), which shares the shallow, natural waves, middle part and exposed ears: these features were fashionable at the time of Tiberius.[52] The bun, rather than a hanging queue, is somewhat rarer, but does have parallels on portraits datable by other criteria to the principates of Tiberius and Caligula.[53] Megow argues, furthermore, that the style and technique of cameo carving point to a date close to A.D. 19.[54]

All these features establish a date too late for a representation of Julia I, the daughter of Augustus, while the fact that both the babies are naked, and therefore probably male, rules out Messalina, who had one son and one daughter. Agrippina I had three sons, but these cameos bear no resemblance to her only securely established

[50] Mikocki, 1995, 174–75, nos. 163–164, pl. 4, fig. 163; Megow, 1987, 296 nos. D24, pl. 12, 5, 296–297 no. D25, pl. 12, 3, and 297, no. D26, 12,9.

[51] Paris, Bibliothèque Nationale, Cabinet des Médailles no. 242, sardonyx cameo, h. 3.5 cm., w. 2.5 cm. Megow, 1987, 296 no. D24, pl. 12.5, with earlier literature.

[52] Polaschek, 1972, 164–166, fig. 8 nos. 1–3.

[53] Polaschek, 1972, 171, fig. 9 nos. 5 and 8.

[54] Megow, 1987, 30–31.

portrait type, either in coiffure or in physiognomy. (See figures 80 and 85–96). And finally, both the Paris and the Berlin cameos represent the two babies on exactly the same scale, implying that they are of the same age. Their similarities to the standard coin images of Romulus and Remus suckled by the she-wolf would also seem to emphasize and celebrate the fact that these children were twins.[55] Only one of the possible candidates, Livilla I, was the mother of twin sons.[56]

Do these gems confirm or undermine the identification of the Leptis-Malta type with Livilla I? Unfortunately, the objects do not yield an unambiguous answer. The coiffure of the woman in the Berlin cameo, (figure 79), of Paris 242 and of Paris 243 (figure 78), resembles that of the Leptis-Magna sculptural portrait type, but with a few important differences. The waves of hair in the cameos flow back from the hairline around the face in natural-looking waves, while those of the sculptural portraits (figures 74–77) are shallow but regular, as though crimped with a curling iron, and flow down around the face from the central part. The fringe of little curls along the forehead does not appear in the cameos, and the chignon appears to be softly looped up from the nape of the neck, without any visible fastening. The chignon of the sculptural portraits also takes the form of a small, soft loop of hair, but a braid or twisted cloth cord around its base clearly secures it in place. All these adjustments are not unthinkable in a highly idealized image that openly identifies its subject with Ceres: they would make the coiffure more like that of a Classical goddess, while retaining the same basic form and shape as the actual fashion worn by its subject. In the life-size sculptural replicas of the Leptis-Malta type, (figures 74–77), the curls along the forehead are very small, shallowly carved, and discreetly indicated, while the precise form of the bun, usually obscured by setting in a niche or against a wall, would not concern most viewers unduly so long as its shape was recognizable.

Comparisons of physiognomy yield similarly inconclusive results. The profiles in the cameos (figures 78, 79) bear some resemblance to those of the group of sculptures (figures 75, 77): a low, straight forehead, low eyebrows that dip toward the nose and flair upward toward the temples, large round eyes with hooded upper lids, a jut-

---

[55] Möbius, 1975, 46.
[56] Vollenweider, 1966, 74 n. 59; Möbius, 1975, 46.

ting nose with a straight bridge, a distinct overbite and retreating lower lip, but a firm, rounded chin. Although the cameos show their subject in profile, she appears to have the same sort of chubby-cheeked, round face as the subject of the Leptis-Malta sculptures.

Again, however, the parallels are not perfect. The Paris gem no. 243 (figure 78) appears to give the nose a slightly pendulous tip; on the Berlin gem (figure 79) a chip at the tip of the nose obscures this detail, but the surviving part seems to indicate that the shape was the same here as in the Paris gem. The sculptural replicas in which the nose survives intact, on the other hand, such as the Leptis Magna head (figures 74–75) or nearly intact, like the example in the Museo Nazionale Romano, do not show a pendulous tip. The Leptis head also shows a much deeper indentation between the forehead and the bridge of the nose than is evident on these cameos, although most other replicas, including the replica from Rome illustrated here (figures 76–77), show a shallower and gentler indentation at the root of the nose. The two gems that represent the woman with her children, fur-thermore, depict fuller and more sensual lips than those of the sculp-tures, although Paris 242, as noted above, does show a rather thin and pursed mouth.

None of these deviations, however, rule out the possibility that the Berlin and Paris gems represent the same woman as the Leptis-Malta replica series, in a more strongly idealized manner. Although the face, with its typically Julio-Claudian eyebrows and overbite, is unmis-takably portrait-like, the gem-cutters of the two largest and most detailed cameos, the ones that show her with the two babies, man-aged also to give her features a style reminiscent of ideal Greek sculpture of the fifth century B.C. The nearly straight, continuous lines of forehead and nose and the rounded line of the jaw and chin are both typical of the Classical style. Indeed, earlier publications of these gems displayed some doubt whether a portrait or a purely ideal image of "Ceres Kourotrophos" or "Pax Augusta" was intended.[57] If these gems all follow a common prototype, as seems very likely from their similarity of pose and composition, that prototype could have been an unusually idealized version of Livilla's standard por-trait, created on some special occasion between A.D. 19 and 23. If that prototype was a work of glyptic art, it would then have been

---

[57] Greifenhagen, 1964, 35–36 for a review of earlier interpretations.

perpetuated by replicas in that medium, while the less goddess-like
Leptis-Malta type remained current for sculptural representations.
Although the parallels between the gems and the sculptures are
imperfect, these cameos resemble the Leptis-Malta type in coiffure
and in physiognomy more closely than they do any other established
portrait of an imperial woman of the appropriate period. Comparison
of the sculptural and glyptic works does not confirm the identity of
either group of objects, but the identifications of both as Livilla I
are not mutually exclusive.

Let us then accept the working hypothesis that these cameos and
the Leptis-Malta group of portrait sculptures represent Livilla I, the
wife of Drusus II. How, then, do they present her? One of the most
striking aspects of all replicas, both glyptic and sculptural, is the
apparent youthfulness of the face, with its round-cheeked, girlish
form. The only complete statue, at Rusellae, treats the body in a similar manner, with the slender proportions of a teen-aged girl, although
the stola identifies her as a married woman. If her youth and feminine features suggest fertility, the woman's hairdo implies respectable
chastity, with its smooth and tightly controlled strands. Even the decorative fringe of curls in the sculptural replicas that help to emphasize
the roundness of the face by lowering the apparent height of the
forehead are neat and orderly, while in the cameos this decorative
detail does not appear at all. The portrait thus presents a striking
contrast to that of Agrippina I, with whom Livilla I would often
have appeared in public statuary groups like the one at Leptis.[58]
(Figure 86). A comparison of the Leptis portraits of these two women
(figures 74–75 and 86) is instructive: both wear their hair parted in
the middle, drawn back behind the ears and fastened at the nape
of the neck, but the similarities end there. Agrippina I, who probably had the sort of naturally curly hair that defies confinement, has
masses of escaping ringlets in the waves on each side of her face.
The creator of the prototype, and most copyists, have been at some
pains to give these curls a seemingly random pattern, although later
copyists and glyptic artists became increasingly lazy about preserving this spontanous appearance, and tended to line up the curls into
neat ranks and files. Two full, wavy locks also escape from the

[58] Statue of Agrippina I from Leptis: Tripolis Museum, marble, life-size. Rose,
1997, 182–184 no. 125, pl. 224; Aurigemma, 1940, 79, figs. 56–57. See next chapter
for fuller discussion.

coiffure behind her ears and hang to the shoulders, a feature clearly
visible in the Leptis portrait despite the veil that covers the back of
her head. Livilla I has no such shoulder-locks in any of the sculptural
replicas of her portrait. Only in the Paris 243 cameo (figure 78) does
a loosely waved lock of hair escape behind the ear, and it ends well
above the shoulder; the individual cameo-cutter appears to have
added this embellishment on his own.

When images of the two princesses appeared in close juxtaposition,
Agrippina I would have looked flamboyant and somewhat goddess-
like in her presentation, Livilla I more modest, but for that very reason reflecting the virtues of a good Roman wife. The differences in
coiffure also dictated stylistic differences: Livilla I's portraits would
be virtually free of drill work, thus lacking the strong contrasts of
highlight and shadow that the drill produces, while Agrippina I's
curly hair necessitated extensive use of deep channels to articulate
the curls and emphasize their centers. Here, the copyist could exercise
some personal discretion: the hair of the Leptis Magna statue of
Agrippina I is richly drilled, but that of a head from the Domus dei
Mosaici at Rusellae uses the drill only for the centers of curls.[59] The
Rusellae head comes from a context that also yielded portraits of
Tiberius and Drusus II, evidence that would imply a date during
the principate of Tiberius and the lifetime of Agrippina I. The evidence is not conclusive, since the Agrippina I is of finer marble and
much better workmanship than the two male portraits, and could
have been added at a different time. There is no evidence from the
Domus dei Mosaici, however, to indicate a date later than the principate of Tiberius, and so it is probably safe to assume that the Rusellae
replica belongs to the elder Agrippina's lifetime. The relatively restrained workmanship would be understandable as an interpretation
of this portrait by a copyist of the time of Tiberius, when Germanicus
and Agrippina I were engaged in a none-too-subtle power struggle
with Tiberius. The flamboyance of the elder Agrippina's image, in
particular, may say much about the ambitions of this woman and
of her husband; people of their personal wealth and prominence in
the imperial family presumably had considerable say over the appearance of their own images, and may not have cooperated with the

---

[59] Michelucci, 1985, 115, 32 (identified by the author as Livia). Portraits found
in same context: pls. 30–31 (Tiberius), and 33 (Drusus Minor).

desires of the emperor in this regard. Both Agrippina I and Germanicus were known on many celebrated occasions to act directly against imperial orders. Their conflict with Tiberius, and its reflections in art and propaganda, are best addressed however in the following chapter.

CHAPTER FIVE

AGRIPPINA I AND HER DAUGHTERS:
THE FAMILY OF GERMANICUS

During the principate of Tiberius, the second most prominent women in the imagery of the imperial family after Livia were the wives of his two heirs, Livilla I, whose problematic images were discussed in the previous chapter, and Agrippina I, the wife of Germanicus and mother of nine children, including three boys who survived infancy. The terms of Augustus's will had required Tiberius to adopt Germanicus, and therefore, whatever the second emperor's personal feelings may have been, celebration of the role of Germanicus was a necessary aspect of his propaganda, stressing as it did his own legitimate role in the planned line of succession that Augustus had established. This emphasis on Germanicus as the next successor in turn required emphasis on the children of Germanicus, and the hope that they represented for the future of the dynasty—and consequently also on the woman whose remarkable fertility had provided three more potential heirs to the principate. An inscription discovered in Spain records a Senatorial decree shortly after Germanicus's death in A.D. 18 that mandated the construction of a triumphal arch in his honor in the Circus Flaminius at Rome. The decree specifies that the statuary group crowning the arch is to include Agrippina I and all the couple's children.[1] Although this arch and its sculptural program are lost, the slightly later Leptis group, which honored both Germanicus and Drusus II, attest to the fact that patrons of provinces throughout the empire closely emulated this extravagant monument.[2]

Ironically, however, although the elder Agrippina's lifetime portrait type was an officially commissioned and displayed creation, it often served the propaganda purposes of dissidents and opponents

[1] González, 1984, 55–100. Text of inscription 58–61. Rose, 1997, 25–27, 108–110 no. 37.
[2] Rose, 1997, 183 and pls. 217 A and B for a reconstruction of the group; Trillmich, 1988, passim, for its relationship to the arch of Germanicus in Rome. On the Neo-Punic inscription: Reynolds and Ward-Perkins, 1952, 12, no. 28; 101. On the statue of Agrippina I: Trillmich, 1984, 137–138; Aurigemma, 1940, 79–80.

of the emperor during Tiberius's reign. The replicas of this portrait
played their most important role after the deaths of both Agrippina
I and Tiberius, during the principate of her son Gaius "Caligula,"
whose extravagant honors to the memory of his mother served not
only to glorify his own immediate family but to implicitly rebuke
the cruelty of his hated predecessor. Her portraits also had a prominent place in imperial family groups during the reign of Claudius.
In order to understand why her memory was so important to the
imperial propaganda of Caligula and Claudius, it is necessary to
understand the circumstances of her dramatic and eventful life, during
much of which she, her husband, and her children were the objects
of love and loyalty for a large faction of the Roman aristocracy, and
thus a source of a divisive feud within the imperial family.[3]

Agrippina I was the granddaughter of Augustus, one of the children born to his daughter Julia I and his brilliant general Agrippa.
(See Appendix, chart no. 7). The *Senatus Consultum* condemning Cn.
Piso praises Agrippina I for the high respect in which Augustus held
her (*"q[u]oi erat probatissuma . . ."*), a phrase that is probably more than
just boilerplate flattery, since the marriage that Augustus arranged
for her, and the line of succession that his will put in place, virtually guaranteed that the imperium would pass through her to her
sons. She, unlike her sister Julia II, whose exile for adultery had
embarrassed the imperial family, appeared to be a worthy candidate
for such an honor. As with so many women of Augustus's family,
her marriage to a cousin of the Claudian branch was designed to
unite the Julian and Claudian houses more closely, but the marriage
appears to have been a personal as well as dynastic success, and the
Senatus Consultum praises her as well for the fidelity and concord (*"unica
concordia"*) of the match.[4] Agrippina I accompanied her husband on
campaigns even at times of great personal danger, often pregnant,
and with small children in tow. During the mutiny of A.D. 14, her
presence and that of the children proved enormously useful, since
Germanicus was able to shame his rebellious troops into submission
by threatening to send Agrippina I and the children from the camp,
implying that the Roman soldiers could no longer be trusted with

---

[3] Tac. *Ann.* 2.43.
[4] *S.C. de Cn. Pisone Patre* 137–39; Eck, Caballos, and Fernández, 1996, 48–49,
242. On Julia II: Suet. *Aug.* 64.1–2, 65.1, 72.3, 101.3–4; Augustus not only exiled
his granddaughter, but razed her luxurious villa and forbade her burial in the imperial mausoleum.

their safety.[5] Agrippina I, according to Tacitus, initially resisted Germanicus's decision to send her from the camp, but eventually cooperated, perhaps recognizing the value of her symbolic role as a Roman woman who required the protection of Roman men.

On another occasion, her intervention during an emergency was both more active and more unconventional. While Germanicus was pursuing the German chieftain Arminius in territory beyond the Rhine, a rumor reached the camp that the Roman army had been cut off and that the Germans were approaching. Panicked soldiers attempted to demolish the bridge, a move that would almost certainly have meant disaster to Germanicus and the troops stranded on the other side of the river, but Agrippina I personally prevented them from doing so, and attempted to maintain the sagging morale of the troops by providing food and clothing. When Germanicus's troops returned, she personally greeted and thanked them at the bridge, the route to safety that her own efforts had preserved for them.[6] Tacitus's feelings about her conduct on this occasion are very mixed; on the one hand, she had quite probably saved her husband's life, for which Tacitus rewards her with the description "a woman of great spirit," "*femina ingens animi . . . ,*" but on the other, she had displayed herself publicly and by assuming command of the troops, had performed a task that no woman should do: ". . . *munia ducis per eos dies induit.*" Providing food and medical care to the soldiers in the camp might accord well with the acceptable roles of a woman as nurturer; these actions were a sort of military version of the philanthropy that Octavia and Livia practiced in the civilian sector, but publicly greeting and congratulating soldiers was another matter. Tacitus, having grudgingly praised her conduct, follows that account almost immediately with criticisms, placed in the mouth of Tiberius, who takes Agrippina's actions not as a demonstration of her own bravery but as a commentary on the unmanliness of his generals, if a mere woman could prove more effective than they at controlling the mutiny. Later in the *Annals*, a speaker of somewhat greater moral authority criticizes the presence of any woman on military campaign, reiterating Tiberius's claim that they feminize and sap the valor of the men, while expressing horror that a woman

---

[5] Tac. *Ann.* 1.40–45; Barrett, 1996, 26–27.
[6] Tac. *Ann.* 1.69.

could even preside at military exercises.[7] The latter criticism could,
by the time of this Senatorial debate, have applied not only to
Agrippina I but to her archenemy Plancina, who had been impli-
cated in the alleged murder of Germanicus. There is, Tacitus implies,
a principle involved in banning women from all military matters:
the elder Agrippina's presence in Germany might have proved
beneficial, but the activities of a woman in such a realm had a far
greater potential for harm.

Agrippina I also, of course, accompanied Germanicus on his journey to the eastern provinces of the empire, although once again, she
was pregnant. She gave birth to her youngest daughter, Livilla II,
on the island of Lesbos, where inscriptions duly celebrated her fertility.[8] The possible implications of Germanicus's travels in those
regions, his conflicts with Piso, and the sudden illness and death of
Germanicus at Antioch have been discussed above in Chapter 3.
Suffice it here to add that Tacitus makes a point of mentioning the
elder Agrippina's presence at her husband's death bed, and narrat-
ing Germanicus's last words, which consisted of a plea to his friends
to avenge him, but a warning to Agrippina I to remember her own
relative weakness and to avoid provoking Tiberius. In the same passage, Tacitus takes a characteristic jab at women, quoting Germanicus
as lamenting the "typically feminine deviousness" of his death by
poisoning—this despite the fact that he suspected both Plancina and
her husband Piso of culpability. He contrasts once again the masculine virtue of open aggression on the battlefield with the feminine
scheming behind the scenes that Tacitus regards as embodying the
worst aspects of dynastic rule.[9] In Agrippina's case, however, Germanicus obviously fears too much frank and open aggression on her
part. As Tacitus characterizes this couple, Germanicus understood
his wife well enough to know that she preferred the active role she
had played in the crisis at the Rhine bridge to that of the passive
and helpless female that she had been forced to assume during the
mutiny of A.D. 14.

---

[7] Tac. *Ann.* 3.33. For a discussion of Tacitus's account of the Senatorial debate,
and its implications, see Santoro L'Hoir, 1994, 5–25, and Barrett, 1996, 27. Barrett
suggests that Aulus Caecina, who shared the command in Germany with Germanicus,
had personal reasons for humiliation at Agrippina's success and his own failures
during the crisis of A.D. 15.

[8] Rose, 1997, 25, n. 55.

[9] Tac. *Ann.* 2.71–72. "... inlacrimabunt quondam florentem et tot bellorum super-
stitem muliebri fraude cecidisse."

After Germanicus's death, Agrippina I returned to Rome with the ashes of her husband, determined to bring the suspected murderers to justice. Once again, her journey to Brundisium and from there through Italy demonstrated the elder Agrippina's talent for political theater, and her ability to turn her presence into an event that could manipulate public opinion, just as she had done during both crises in the German provinces.[10] The unsatisfactory end of Piso's trial, however, and the pardon of Plancina, served to convince Agrippina I as well as many others of the complicity of Tiberius in the death of her husband.

The career of Germanicus and his possible, unfulfilled political agenda, have been discussed in Chapter 3. As his staunchest ally, Agrippina I was instrumental in fostering his after-life as a political symbol and martyr. Like John F. Kennedy, he was a young man whose assassination had prevented the fulfillment of his potential, and his career therefore provided a blank slate upon which his followers could write any utopian dream that they pleased: just as Kennedy might have ended the Vietnam war by fiat, Germanicus might have been a better emperor than Tiberius; he might even have restored the republic. Agrippina I, as her behavior during her husband's lifetime had demonstrated, was an intelligent, ambitious and occasionally reckless woman. She was not, therefore, prepared to retire quietly to private life after the condemnation of Piso. Her open feuds with Tiberius and his Praetorian prefect Sejanus put her in danger of arrest for treason, but the much-maligned Livia, while she was alive, seems to have restrained Tiberius from taking action against her. Immediately after the Augusta's death, Tiberius (now living in retirement in Campania) sent a letter to the Senate denouncing Agrippina I and her son Nero I, and a few years later succeeded in banishing her and her two older sons.[11] Agrippina and Nero I died in exile; Drusus III, in prison at Rome.

The account of Tiberius's first accusation of Agrippina I provides an intriguing footnote on the importance of portraits as political symbols, since the supporters of Agrippina's family are described as crowding around the Senate house with "effigies" of Agrippina I and Nero I.[12] These "effigies" must, obviously, have been light and portable

---

[10] Tac. *Ann.* 2.75; Barrett, 1996, 30–31.
[11] Tac. *Ann.* 5.3–5.
[12] Tac. *Ann.* 5.4.

objects, such as panel paintings on wood, small bronze busts of the sort known to have belonged to private owners (like the Neuilly-le-Real busts of Augustus and Livia, figures 32–33, discussed above), and cameos, many of which survive with portraits of imperial family members and most of which were small enough to be worn as jewelry. As we have already seen, privately owned portraits of public figures enjoyed a certain freedom from the officially established prototypes. This anecdote makes clear their occasional function as instruments of dissent quite different from what the original patrons of their prototypes might have intended.

Since Drusus II, the son of Tiberius, had died in A.D. 23, Tiberius was succeeded by Agrippina I's youngest son Caligula, whose first official act after the funeral of his predecessor was to rehabilitate the memory of his mother and brothers. He personally brought their ashes back to Rome, where he buried them with great pomp in the mausoleum of Augustus, a ceremony deliberately modeled on his mother's earlier journey back to Rome with the ashes of Germanicus. Caligula severely punished persons who had earlier insulted Agrippina I; he instituted games and sacrifices in honor of his mother; he had her image carried around the Circus Maximus in a *carpentum* during the opening ceremonies of the games, and he issued coins in all three metals honoring both his parents.[13] These include the first issue of Roman coins ever to bear the portrait likeness of a woman, with an identifying inscription, on the obverse, and to be devoted entirely to her in both its obverse and its reverse types. The *sestertii* struck in honor of Agrippina I specifically commemorate the honors paid to her at the official games, portraying the *carpentum* that carried her image, with the inscription "MEMORIAE AGRIPPINAE," "To the Memory of Agrippina."[14] (Figure 80).

Even in the small format of these coins, the car appears to be an ornate and eye-catching contraption. Its star-studded, curved canopy was supported at its four corners by little caryatid statues, each rep-

---

[13] Suet. *Calig.* 15.1–2; Dio 59.10.4 (on Caligula's humiliation and execution of a man who had insulted Agrippina I); Barrett, 1990, 59, 60–61.

Aurei and *denarii* with reverse portraits of Germanicus: *RIC* 1² 108 nos. 11–12, pl. 13, fig. 12; 109 nos. 17–18, 25–26; *BMCRE* 1, 147, nos. 11–13, pl. 27, figs. 9–10; 148, nos. 18–20, pl. 27, figs. 15–16; 149, nos. 26–27, pl. 27, fig. 22.

Aurei and *denarii* with reverse portraits of Agrippina I: *RIC* 1² 108 nos. 7–8, pl. 13, fig. 7; 109 nos. 13–14, 21–22, pl. 13, fig. 13; *BMCRE* 1, 147 nos. 7–9, pl. 27, figs. 6–7; 148 nos. 14–15, pl. 27, figs. 11–12; 149 nos. 22–23, pl. 27, figs. 18–19.

[14] *RIC* 1², 112, no. 55 pl. 14, *BMCRE* 1, 159, nos. 81–87, pl. 30, figs. 4–6.

resenting one of the four seasons, and its sides were decorated with paintings or reliefs. The walls were subdivided into panels decorated with an undulating serpent, dancing satyrs, and stars of apotheosis.[15] The entire program made elaborate reference to the religious honor paid to the dead, and hinted at deification, though Agrippina I had not officially been consecrated. Conceivably, although this must remain in the realm of conjecture, Caligula had been planning to deify both his parents as soon as possible, although the unexpected death of his sister Drusilla forced a change in those plans, causing her to receive this honor ahead of both Agrippina I and Livia. The carpentum on these sestertii is perhaps meant to resemble a small temple on wheels, but also stresses the earthly political status of Agrippina I. Wheeled vehicles for personal transportation had been strictly forbidden in Rome from the time of Julius Caesar except to the Vestal Virgins. Livia may also have been granted this privilege in A.D. 22/23, along with the right to sit with the Vestals at the theater, but other women, even those of aristocratic status, traveled either on foot or by sedan-chair.[16] The conferral of such a posthumous honor on Agrippina I elevated the emperor's mother to a rank comparable to the Vestals, the highest civil and religious status that a woman could obtain.[17]

Another issue of bronze coins, probably contemporaneous with the *sestertii* in honor of Agrippina I, commemorate Caligula's father Germanicus (figure 81). The design of these *dupondii* resemble those of Agrippina's *sestertii* closely enough to suggest that the two issues were designed to complement one another. The *dupondius* portrays, on its obverse, Germanicus in his triumphal quadriga, with the inscription GERMANICUS CAESAR to the right in the field, and on its reverse, Germanicus standing, with the inscription SIGNIS RECEPT DE VICTIS GERM.[18] ("Standards recaptured from the conquered Germans"). The differences in choice of subject material on the respective bronze issues are significant: the *sestertius* of Agrippina I emphasizes the emperor's piety toward his mother after her death, while the coins of Germanicus celebrate his father's military achievements in life, thus implying that Gaius has inherited his father's

---

[15] Jucker, 1980, 211–212, pl. 40, fig. 2; Kent, 1974, pls. 46–47, fig. 164. For the funerary significance of the serpent, Verg. *Aen.* 5.84–96.

[16] Winkler, 1995, 53.

[17] Jucker, 1980, 208–209.

[18] *RIC* 1², 112 no. 57, pl. 14; *BMCRE* 1, 160–1, nos. 93–101, pl. 30, figs. 9–10.

military brilliance. The designs of Germanicus's chariot and Agrippina's *carpentum*, on the other hand, bear close comparison, in their over-all design, the mirror-image movement of the respective vehicles and the placement of the legend in relation to them.[19] The choice of the higher denomination, with a larger flan, for the emperor's mother, may be significant; it was through her, not through Germanicus, that he could trace his ancestry to the deified Augustus.

Caligula also accorded great and unprecedented honors to his three living sisters: they too were granted the same rights and priv-ileges as Vestal Virgins, including that of transportation within the city by *carpentum*, they were included with Gaius in public oaths of allegiance, and at state banquets they took turns sitting in the place of honor below the couches of the emperor and his wife.[20] Agrip-pina II, Drusilla I and Livilla II also share with their mother Agrip-pina I the distinction of being the first women to appear on Roman coins with an inscription that identifies them by name. (Figure 82). Even Livia was not so honored until the accession of Claudius four years later. This issue of bronze *sestertii*, unlike the *sestertius* in honor of his mother, combines an obverse portrait of the emperor himself with the reverse type honoring his sisters; they are represented as little full-length figures with faces far too small to be recognizable portraits, but the inscription leaves us in no doubt of who they are.[21] Their attributes identify them with divine personifications: *Securitas*, leaning on a strong pillar; *Concordia*, holding a patera, and *Fortuna*, holding a rudder. All three hold cornucopiae, which suggest the pros-perity brought to the empire by good government under the favor of the gods. This association of living women with deified abstrac-tions may have some precedent in coins from the lifetime of Livia, such as the *dupondii* with the reverse of Livia as *Salus Augusta* (figure 34). In the Caligulan *sestertius*, however, the inscription dispenses with subtlety and ambiguity. And just as the *sestertius* of Agrippina I formed a pendant to the *dupondius* of Germanicus, this coin is one of a pair honoring the siblings of the emperor, whose dead brothers were rep-resented on a *dupondius*.[22] (Figure 83).

---

[19] Jucker, 1980, 206. I arrived independently at similar conclusions about the similarity of the types.

[20] Suet. *Calig.* 15.2 and 24.1.

[21] *RIC* 1² 110 no. 33, pl. 13. *BMCRE* 1, 152, nos. 36–37, pl. 28, fig. 4.

[22] Jucker, 1980, 206–7. *RIC* 1², 110 no. 34; *BMCRE* 1, 154 no. 44, pl. 29, fig. 1.

Like the three living sisters, Nero I and Drusus III were represented not by portrait faces but by miniature full-length figures: they
appeared on horseback, charging from left to right across the flan.
Though they were given no overtly divine attributes, a Roman viewer
could hardly have missed their resemblance to the Dioscuri, who
often appeared on Roman coins as a pair of horsemen. Thus, again,
visual association assimilated the emperor's relatives to gods, and
specifically to patrons and protectors of Rome, the gods who had
miraculously intervened in the battle of Lake Regillus in 496 B.C.
to secure victory for the Roman side.[23] Caligula incorporated into
his own palace the temple in the Roman forum that commemorated
this miracle, and reportedly "stood between" the statues of Castor
and Pollux in the temple; whether this means that Caligula himself
might have presented himself in the temple on certain occasions or
whether Suetonius is referring to a statue of the emperor set up in
the temple is difficult to ascertain, but in either case, it is clear that
Caligula wished to associate himself particularly closely with these
two young gods, and with their role in folklore as saviors of the
Roman state.[24] A pair of young men of his own family, his two older
brothers, would make a particularly appropriate parallel for them.

The *dupondius* in honor of Nero I and Drusus III is unlikely to
have shocked many Romans of Caligula's time. It is easier to understand why the *sestertius* in honor of his sisters, on the other hand,
with its frank near-deification not of dead but of living members of
Caligula's family could have offended some senators, who still could
not tolerate behavior that was too overtly regal. The extravagant
honors Caligula paid to his sisters inspired malicious, and probably
false, gossip about the nature of his relations with them, a type of
calumny that appears in the biography of virtually every emperor
who came to a bad end, and is such an obvious *topos* that it should
be treated with automatic skepticism.[25] Caligula, like rulers both
before and after, left himself open to such charges by striking a prud-
ish stance in public, banishing the *spintriae*, the erotic entertainers
whose performances Tiberius had supposedly enjoyed, and taking

---

[23] Miraculous appearance of Castor and Pollux at Lake Regillus: *LIMC* 3 (1986),
sv. "Dioskouroi/Castores" (F. Gury), 608–9 on the legend and 622 nos. 106–8 on
the iconography of the Dioscuri as galloping horsemen. Ancient sources for the legend: Dion. Hal. *Ant.Rom.* 6, 13; Cic. *Nat.D.* 2,2,6; Val. Max. 1,8,1.
[24] Barrett, 1990, 147; Dio 59.28.5 and 60.6.8; Suet. *Calig.* 22.2.
[25] Barrett, 1990, 85; Balsdon, 1962, 116.

legal action against public obscenities.[26] Any effort to legislate sexual morality virtually asks for retaliatory charges of hypocrisy; Domitian
later was to suffer the same consequences for taking the office of
censor perpetuus, censor for life, and conducting purges of the college
of Vestals.[27] Caligula's actual motive for honoring his sisters as he
did was undoubtedly to present them as the potential mothers of
heirs to imperial power, and to celebrate the piety and harmony
within what was left of the family of Germanicus and Agrippina I.[28]

That harmonious unity was soon to be shattered. Caligula had
arranged a marriage between his sister Drusilla and his best friend
M. Aemilius Lepidus and had named Drusilla the heir to his empire
during his serious illness in A.D. 37, intending, no doubt that in the
event of his death her husband would exercise the powers of empire,
but that the succession would pass through Drusilla to a male heir
of the Julian family.[29] Why Drusilla should thus have been honored
over the other sisters remains controversial; the ancient historians of
course attribute it all to the emperor's irrational and incestuous
attachment to her, but it is possible that Drusilla, not Agrippina II,
was the eldest of the three, and so enjoyed seniority.[30] Whatever the
reasons for Caligula's choice, local patrons throughout the empire
quickly understood her role as the intended mother of heirs; some
coins of Greek cities called her "θέα," goddess, and several inscriptions named her specifically "νεὰ Ἀφροδίτη," "new Aphrodite," honors normally reserved for a woman of the imperial family who had
already given birth.[31]

---

[26] Suet. *Tib.* 43.1; *Calig.* 16.1; Barrett, 1990, 44.
[27] Vinson, 1989, 433–438.
[28] Barrett, 1990, 63.
[29] On Drusilla's first marriage to Lucius Cassius Longinus, and her divorce from
him and remarriage to Lepidus, see Suet. *Calig.* 24.1 and Dio 59.11.1. Suetonius
reports that Caligula took her from her first husband in order to live with her himself, and Dio that her second husband Lepidus was the homosexual lover of Caligula,
but both these claims are such commonplace *topoi* in the biographies of unpopular
emperors that they should be dismissed out of hand. It is far likelier that Caligula
dissolved Drusilla's first marriage in order to arrange a second match for her that
he considered more politically desirable. Barrett, 1990, 81–82 and 1996, 58, argues
that Lepidus must have been the actual heir to the imperium, and that the ancient
historians must be mistaken when they describe Drusilla as heir, but as I have
argued elsewhere (Wood, 1995, 459), his decision, while unorthodox, does make
sense as a way of ensuring that the succession would pass to her children.
[30] See Barrett, 1996, 230–232 on the problem of the birth-dates of Agrippina II
and Drusilla.
[31] Inscriptions: Mikocki, 1995, 43, 184–85 nos. 228–233, *IG* XII 2 no. 172b =

The premature celebration of her fertility by all parties involved, unfortunately, proved to be unwise. Drusilla's untimely death only a year later left Caligula not only grief-stricken but politically embarrassed: Drusilla had no children, and he himself was both childless and divorced. Making the best of a bad situation, he made her a goddess, built a temple to her in Rome, placed a colossal statue of her in the temple of Venus Genetrix, and took all oaths from then onward by the "*numen Drusillae*," the "godhead of Drusilla." If Drusilla could be of no practical use in perpetuating the Julian family, she could at least become a protective patron goddess associated with the family's origins and destiny. Thus, a young and, in real terms, relatively unimportant person became the first Roman woman to be deified, since Livia did not achieve this status until the principate of Claudius.[32] Although Roman writers like Seneca later ridiculed this consecration, Greek imperial coins indicated that her status as the heir of Caligula and, later, her cult met with favor in the cities of the old Hellenistic world, where the concepts of divine kingship and worship of royal figures of both sexes were traditions of long standing. Coins from Smyrna datable to her lifetime portray her with the attributes of Kore.[33] Another issue from Apamea in Bithynia that must postdate her death and deification represents a group busts of the three sisters in which Drusilla forms part of a close-knit triad but enjoys a special status indicated by the star over her head and by her central, frontal placement. (Figure 84).[34] Unlike an issue from another provincial city of uncertain identity, which is clearly copied from coins of the Roman mint that portray the three sisters, this Apamean issue has no models in official numismatic design, and could well have been inspired by a monumental sculptural group of the sort known to have stood in cities all over the empire.[35]

The prominence of the other two sisters after Drusilla's death was short lived; both were exiled in A.D. 39 on charges of adultery with

---

IGR IV, no. 78; *IGR* IV no. 145. On the significance of the epithet "θέα" and of identifications with Aphrodite, see Rose, 1997, 13 and 25.

[32] Suet. *Calig.* 24.2–3; Sen. *Apocol.* 1; Dio, 59.11.

[33] *BMC Ionia* 269 nos. 272–276, pl. 28.9, Klose, 1987, 15, 217–28, nos. 1–36, pl. 20 r. 1–36. *RPC* 2472, p. 419.

[34] Banti-Simonetti, *CNR* 13, 169–171, figs. 1–3; Trillmich, 1978, 108–109, pl. 13.11; Cohen, 1880, 248–249, "Drusille, Julie & Agrippine," no. 1. *RPC* 2012, pp. 341, 343.

[35] Banti-Simonetti, *CNR* 12, 185; Trillmich, 1978, 110–111, pl. 13.12 for the coin copied from the Roman issue of *sestertii* with the three full-length figures as *Securitas*, *Concordia*, and *Fortuna*. *RPC* 2014, pp. 341, 343.

Lepidus, the widowed husband of Drusilla, and conspiracy with him to overthrow Caligula.[36] At least part of these accusations was probably true: Lepidus, having once come close to inheriting the empire during Caligula's illness, only to lose his principle connection with the imperial family when Drusilla died, would have been understandably anxious to marry one of the surviving sisters. They, in turn would have been equally eager to inherit Drusilla's role as the consort of the chosen heir. The temptation for Agrippina II, in particular, to initiate a relationship with Lepidus without the formality of waiting for the death of her gravely ill husband would have been strong, but whether her intrigues extended to a plot against Caligula himself can never be known.[37] The trial of Lepidus, Agrippina II and Livilla II, evidently took place outside Rome, in Gaul or Germany, since Caligula had Lepidus summarily executed and then sent his sister Agrippina II back to Rome with the ashes of her alleged lover, a cruel and humiliating parody of her mother's and namesake's far more honorable journey with the ashes of Germanicus, and her brother's own similar act of piety toward her mother.[38] Caligula's grotesque parody of a ceremony that he had once used with good effect to celebrate the bonds of devotion within the family of Germanicus is typical of his ineptitude in handling public opinion, and his inability to understand how his actions would be perceived.

Agrippina II and Livilla II both outlived their brother, and the former enjoyed renewed prominence in the following principate as the fourth and last wife of her uncle Claudius. Livilla II also returned from exile at the invitation of Claudius, but soon fell from favor due to a rivalry with his third wife Messalina, who had her exiled again and later murdered.[39] Caligula's behavior toward his sisters was typical of his arrogant and autocratic treatment of everyone with whom he came in contact, including the Senate, which he crudely insulted, and the Praetorian guard, a miscalculation that eventually cost him his life.[40] Whether or not Caligula was mentally ill as the term is

---

[36] Suet. *Calig.* 24.3, 29.1–2; Dio, 59.22.5–9; Barrett, 1990, 106–110 and 1996, 63–67.

[37] Balsdon, 1962, 117; Barrett, 1990, 109–110.

[38] Barrett, 1990, 106; Griffin, 1984, 26–27.

[39] Suet. *Claud.* 29.1; Tac. *Ann.* 14.63; Dio 60.4.1–2, 60.8.4–6; *RE* 10, 938–39 (Fitzler); Levick, 1990, 56.

[40] Suet. *Calig.* 22–60, details Gaius's career as a "monster." For his mistreatment of Senators, see in particular 26.2–3; on the Praetorian plot, 56, 1–2.

understood today is impossible to determine, but he was beyond doubt far too young and inexperienced for the office into which he was suddenly advanced, and his ineptitude betrays itself in every surviving aspect of his policy, including his public presentation of the imperial family. Suetonius informs us that Caligula's costume in his public appearances did not conform to established Roman practice, but that he affected the embroidered cloaks and jewelry more appropriate to the image of a god, and that he sometimes wore an artificial gold beard and carried a divine attribute such as a thunderbolt or trident, thus making his self-identification with the major Olympian gods explicit.[41] Such details of costume are ephemeral, except as they are preserved in works of portraiture, and we have to trust the written record for the fact of their existence. More durable works like coins and sculpture illustrate that Caligula was willing to borrow from divine imagery for representations of his brothers and sisters, in a manner that had some precedents in Roman custom but in which, as usual, Caligula went farther than his predecessors. Although Caligula himself does not appear in explicitly divine guise on his coins, the more private medium of "performance art," so to speak, in banquets and audiences, would have given him ample opportunity to do so. In this instance, therefore, we have every reason to trust the basic accuracy of Suetonius's account. As Barrett has recently argued, Caligula's self-identification with gods, and the types of public worship accorded him were based on established precedents in Greek and Roman religion, and are certainly not evidence of an irrational state of mind. However, the tactless and egotistical manner in which Caligula demanded to be worshipped—his transformation of the worship of the *genius* of the emperor, for example, from a private observance within the homes of citizens to a public cult—demonstrate his clumsiness in manipulating public symbols.[42]

The extravagant exaltation of women of Caligula's family did not extend to his wives, of whom far less is known.[43] It would seem that Caligula was reserving high public honors specifically for the family of Germanicus. His marriages to Livia Orestilla and Lollia Paulina were brief, presumably unhappy and certainly dynastically unsuccessful,

---

[41] Suet. *Calig.* 52.
[42] Barrett, 1990, 147–153.
[43] On Caligula's marriages, Suet. *Calig.* 12.1 and 25, Dio 59.3.3. See also Giacosa, 1974, 30.

but the last wife, Milonia Caesonia, did produce a female child, and
thus enjoyed public ceremonial honors approaching those he had
earlier granted his sisters. Caesonia's fertility was the primary, and
possibly only reason for her prominence, since Suetonius describes
her as neither young nor beautiful. She and Caligula conceived their
daughter out of wedlock, but were hastily married so that the expected
child could be Caligula's legitimate heir. Caligula named the baby
for his deified sister, and proudly displayed both Caesonia and the
baby Drusilla II in public, presenting his wife dressed in military
armor before the troops.[44] Given Caligula's flair for costume and
pageantry based on the images of gods, it is possible that this costume likened Caesonia to Minerva, whom he invoked as the special
patron goddess of their daughter. Soon after the birth, he had presented the baby to all the goddesses who had temples in Rome, a
ceremony culminating at the Capitoline temple, where he placed the
little Drusilla II in the lap of Minerva and entrusted the child's education to her.[45] Since the virgin goddess Minerva would have made
at best an imperfect parallel for the mother of an heir, however,
Caesonia could have been presented instead in the guise of the
amazon-like Dea Roma. Had Caesonia and Caligula lived longer,
her image might have become as prominent in coinage and public
sculpture as the other women of his family, but both Caesonia and
her child perished with Caligula in the Praetorian coup of A.D. 41.[46]

The images of two women of Caligula's family, however, outlived
his fall, those of the elder and younger Agrippinae. In A.D. 49, after
the disastrous end of the marriage of Claudius and Messalina, and
the acute embarrassment that Messalina's execution for adultery and
treason caused to the emperor, Claudius married Agrippina II. In
order to do so, he had to change Roman incest laws, which had
prohibited the marriage of an uncle and niece, but evidently felt
that the political advantage outweighed the scandal. This marriage
not only linked him more closely to the memory of the beloved
Germanicus, but supplied him with a highly capable political ally.[47]
For the remainder of his reign, Agrippina II figured prominently in

---

[44] Suet. *Calig.* 25.3 on Caesonia and her marriage to Caligula.
[45] Dio 59.28.7; Suet. *Calig.* 25.4. Dio states that Caligula placed the child in the
lap of the statue of Jupiter, rather than Minerva, but both authors agree that he
invoked Minerva as the patron of the child Drusilla II.
[46] Dio, 59.29.7.
[47] See Barrett, 1996, 95–96.

sculptural groups of the imperial family, during which time at least two new portrait types were created for her, and Agrippina I, as the mother of the emperor's wife, once again enjoyed a conspicuous place in coinage and sculpture. Her bust appears on the obverse of Claudian *sestertii* in a composition almost identical to that of the obverse of the Caligulan "*Memoriae Agrippinae*" issue, except that for obvious reasons, the die-cutters have prudently shifted the formula of the inscription to identify her as the wife of Germanicus rather than the mother of Gaius.[48] The reverse now takes the form of an inscription with Claudius's names and titles, rather than the image of the *carpentum*, since the emphasis no longer is on a specific act of piety in her memory, but on her enduring position in the imperial family's genealogy. (Figure 85).

Given the prominence of Agrippina I on the coinage of Claudius, it is likely that she, like his mother Antonia Minor, also appeared in statuary groups and other such public representations of the imperial family. At least one inscription, from Gabii, attests her presence in a group of Claudian date, specifically identifying her as the grandmother of Nero, who by then had emerged as the chosen heir of Claudius, while a portrait head of Agrippina I from Tenos came to light in a small temple along with a statue of Claudius and other fragmentary statues.[49] Sculptural replicas of the lifetime portrait of Agrippina I, therefore, presumably span the period from the principate of Tiberius at least through that of Claudius, undergoing a series of stylistic transformations depending on the political agenda of the imperial family.

The Portraits of Agrippina I, Part 1: The Securely Identified Type

Only one portrait type appears to have been created for the elder Agrippina during her lifetime, but like those of Livia (although, perhaps, not to the same degree), it underwent a wealth of variations and adaptations in its various copies, despite their recognizable dependence on a common original. I have argued elsewhere that a second, posthumous type was created for Agrippina I during the

---

[48] *RIC* 1², 128 no. 102 pl. 16; *BMCRE* 1, 194, nos. 219–223, pl. 37, fig. 1.

[49] Rose, 1997, 90, no. 13 and 158, no. 94. On the head of Agrippina I from Tenos, with photographs, see Queyrel, 1985, 609–620, figs. 1a–d.

reign of Claudius, as part of the political agenda of Claudius and his last wife Agrippina II, a time when coinage and public sculptural groups laid heavy emphasis on the connections of Claudius to the family of Germanicus, both through his own genealogy and through his marriage. This identification, to be discussed below, remains controversial, but if any posthumous type existed it must in any case have been derived from the elder Agrippina's lifetime portrait type. Let us, therefore, first examine those works, whose identification is established beyond serious dispute.

The essential features of Agrippina I's portrait type, which repeat themselves in all replicas, are the physical features—high forehead, long, rectangular jaw, a long, slightly arched nose, eyebrows that flair toward the temples, and a small but full-lipped mouth—and the coiffure. Unlike many women of her family, she does not have an overbite, a characteristic of the Claudians but not of Agrippina I, who had no Claudian blood. (Figures 86–94). The fine-boned and delicate features give her some resemblance to the Julians; the long face and high forehead, to her father Agrippa. Her hair is invariably parted in the middle, drawn back over the ears so as to conceal all but the earlobes, and braided into a looped queue that hangs down the nape of the neck. Two long, softly undulating shoulder locks and many small ringlets around the face "escape" from the waves on each side of her head. Within this basic formula, however, numerous variations are possible, particularly in the treatment of the hair on the sides and back of the head. The little loose curls around the face, for example, follow an exact pattern near the front that unmistakably derives from the prototype. Particularly distinctive are the two curls over the right temple that diverge from one another in a horizontal Y-shape, one curl twisting upward and the other downward, that are clearly reproduced even in miniature replicas like the portrait on the Gemma Claudia (figure 95, right, rear profile).[50] As is common in replicas, however, the feature can be mirror-reversed, sometimes appearing on the left instead of the right temple, as on the Gemma Claudia, where Agrippina's left profile turns toward the viewer. Further back from the face, the curls can be arranged in virtually any pattern that the copyist chooses. In some replicas, the hair behind the ears, where it is pulled back toward the queue, is

---

[50] Fuchs, 1936, 227–230.

braided, in others twisted, and in others, simply drawn back in soft waves.[51] Two replicas, in the Capitoline Museum (figures 91–92) and in Dresden, also show vertical corkscrew curls above the braids, toward the back, on the proper right-hand side of the head. An over-life-size portrait from Coimbra that must certainly date long after Agrippina I's lifetime, and probably to the principate of Claudius, shows a remarkable variation on this theme: a series of vertical corkscrew curls behind the ears, descending to the hairline on the nape of the neck.[52] How a hairdresser could realize such a coiffure in an actual woman's hair is difficult to imagine, and the detail looks suspiciously like an artistic convention used to fill space on large portrait heads. The remaining examples (that is, those in which the back of the head is not concealed with a veil) do not show any such vertical twists, in front of or behind the ears. The little curls around the face can be deeply and intricately articulated with drill channels, or more subtly represented with the chisel (although the centers of each curl, at least, are invariably formed by drilled holes).

---

[51] Replicas with braids at sides of head:

A) Rome, Museo Capitolino, inv. 421. Marble bust, h. of ancient part 31 cm., of head from chin to crown, 24 cm. Recent references: Tansini, 1995, 25–26, 69, figs. 9–12; Fittschen-Zanker 3, 5–6, no. 4, pls. 4–5, with full earlier literature.

B) Istanbul, Archaeological Museum inv. 2164. White marble head and neck, h. 37.5 cm., w. 20.5. Recomposed of three fragments: upper part of head; lower lip and chin: neck. Piece of back of head, worked separately, now missing. Holes on right side of head suggest some later attachment, possibly a diadem. Tansini, 1995, 35, 59, figs. 39–40; Inan and Rosenbaum, 1966, 63, no. 16, pl. 11, 1–2, with earlier literature; Hafner, 1954, 54–55, NK 14, pl. 23.

C) Venice, Museo Archeologico inv. 183, marble head, h. 41 cm., of face 26 cm. Tansini, 1995, 26–27, 79, figs. 21–22; Traversari, 1969, 38–39, no. 18. In this and the following example, the "braid" has become a somewhat confused form, resembling a braid that has started to unravel.

D) Dresden Albertinum Inv. 2 V 2342, cat. 351. Tansini, 1995, 26, 58, figs. 13–14; Trillmich, 1984, 142–143; Fittschen-Zanker 3, 6 under no. 4, n. 3 r, Beil. 2.

Replicas with twisted coils at sides of head:

E) Paris, Musée du Louvre, MA 1271, marble head from the Palatine in Rome, h. 36 cm. Nose restored, surface cleaned. Tansini, 1995, 49, 65, figs. 37–38; De Kersauson, *Louvre* 1, 1986, 134–5, no. 61, with earlier references; Fittschen-Zanker 3, 5, no. 4, n. 3 b, Beil. 1a–b; Queyrel, 1985, 615–16, 618.

Replicas with no braid or coil, only loose waves:

F) Paris, Musée du Louvre, MA 3133, marble head from Athens, h. 44 cm. Lower half of the nose and left half of the chin missing, shoulder locks partly broken away, surface chipped and weathered. Tansini, 1995, 26, 66, figs. 17–18; De Kersauson, *Louvre* 1, 1986, 132–3, no. 60; Fittschen-Zanker 3, 6, no. 4, n. 3 q, Beil. 1c–d.

[52] Tansini, 1995, 31, 56, figs. 29–30 with earlier literature.

In general, it appears—predictably—that the coiffure tends to be more complex in the earlier examples and more simplified in the replicas farther in time or place, or both, from the creation of the original. The Leptis Magna statue (figure 86), datable on external evidence to her lifetime and specifically to A.D. 23, shows deep, serpentine drill channels separating strands, drill-holes at the centers of each curl, and a painstaking duplication of the intricate pattern around the face.[53] Sculptors could exercise some personal discretion in their stylistic approaches, since the recently discovered head from Rusellae shows very little drill-work in the hair, causing the excavators to mistake the portrait for Livia, but Agrippina I's characteristic curls were nonetheless very painstakingly worked with the chisel.[54] Although the evidence for the date of this head is less strong than that of the Leptis Magna group, the Agrippina I does appear to have belonged to a group with portraits of Tiberius and Drusus II, and therefore to date to her lifetime.[55] In her recent corpus of the extant portraits of Agrippina I, Tansini has noted that these lifetime portraits also share a firm and compact treatment of the volumes of the face, and a serious, almost slightly dour, facial expression: Agrippina I is represented as a handsome woman with a far more decorative coiffure than that of her counterpart Livilla I, but is not yet being treated with the idealization and slightly sentimental emotion of the posthumous replicas.[56]

Another portrait datable to her lifetime, however, shows a more dramatic interpretation of the type.[57] (Figures 89–90). The discovery of this head in the same context as a portrait of Tiberius confirms

---

[53] Tripolis, Archaeological Museum, marble statue, precise measurements unavailable. Rose, 1997, 182–184 no. 125, pl. 224, with recent literature; Tansini, 78, fig. 34; Aurigemma, 1940, 79, figs. 56–57.

[54] Head from Rusellae: Marble, h. 34.5 cm., w. 25.5, d. 21 cm. Michelucci, 1985, 71, no. 641, pl. 32, fig. 41; *Roselle*, 1990, 81–82 no. 14, pls. 33–34; Tansini, 1995, 34, 74. For the associated heads of Tiberius and Drusus II, see Michelucci, 1985, 154–55, pls. 30–31, and 157, pl. 33; and *Roselle*, 1990, 80–81, 83–85, nos. 13 and 15, pls. 32, 35, 36.

[55] See *Roselle*, 1990, 84–85. In this publication, however, Michelucci suggests that the portrait of Agrippina I may belong to the time of Caligula. The sculptural finds from Rusellae are still not completely published. In an earlier article (Wood, 1988, 411), I mistakenly associated this head from the Domus dei Mosaici with a Claudian group also from Rusellae, but this latter assemblage comes from the Casa degli Augustali; see Tansini, 1995, 34. I am greatly indebted to Dssa. Celuzza of the Museo Nazionale di Grosseto for permitting me to study this group.

[56] Tansini, 1995, 49–50. See also Queyrel, 1985, 615–616.

[57] Istanbul Archaeological Museum inv. 2164, references supra n. 51.

its date to his principate, and therefore presumably to the time before the elder Agrippina's disgrace and exile. The work was excavated at Pergamon on the terrace of the temple of Demeter, apparently part of an imperial family group like the one at Leptis. The Pergamon portrait faithfully reproduces the coiffure, and since this, unlike the Rusellae and Leptis versions, does not wear a veil, we can see that the sculptor has carefully represented the braid behind the proper left ear, although the plait on the right received somewhat more summary treatment. The corkscrew curls on the side of the head that appear in the Capitoline (figures 91–92) and Dresden heads are absent; since those two replicas are probably datable to the time of Caligula, it is uncertain whether those curls were part of the original prototype or a later embellishment. (In the Rusellae and Leptis portraits, unfortunately, the veil conceals this part of the head). This work interprets the type with a distinctively Pergamene flamboyance in the use of the drill, which forms dramatically deep channels between thick, ropy strands of hair, and softens the angular bone-structure of Agrippina I's face so as to give her an idealized beauty. The face appears to gaze outward and slightly upward, however, rather than to show the subtly melancholy, downcast gaze of many posthumous interpretations.

After the elder Agrippina's rehabilitation in A.D. 37, her portraits from Rome, and from sites near enough to the capital for access to good prototypes, still represent the coiffure in painstaking detail, even in works of otherwise mediocre quality like the statue in the Caligulan group at Velleia (figures 87–88).[58] Compared with the lifetime portraits from Leptis (figure 86) or Pergamon (figures 89–90), however, the sculptor Velleia statue punctuates the flowing waves of the curly hair around her face with far more snail-curls, the centers formed by single perforations, whereas running channels dominated the texture of the hair in the earlier replicas. Perhaps the finest surviving replica, the bust in the Capitoline Museum in Rome, (figures 91–92) shares this feature. The Capitoline bust comes from an unknown archaeological context but was probably found in or near Rome, and is generally agreed to date to the principate of Caligula. The

---

[58] Parma, Museo Archeologico inv. 1952, no. 829, marble statue, h. 208 cm. Rose, 1997, 121–123, 125, no. 50, pls. 133, 141, 142; Tansini, 1995, 25, 68, figs. 5–8; Saletti, 1968, 30–33, 103–106, no. 3, pls. 7–10; Goethert, 1972, 236–37; Jucker, 1977, 204–11.

emphasis in this work on Agrippina I's physical resemblance to her son, its technical similarity to many of his portraits, and the subtle melancholy suggested by the expertly nuanced modeling of the face that evokes her new status as political martyr, all support such a date.[59] This work shows both the most complete and detailed representation of Agrippina I's intricate coiffure, with the braids and corkscrew-curls on the side of the head, and the most virtuoso drillwork of the surviving replicas, a treatment consistent with its production in Rome, where direct access to the original prototype can be inferred. Quite far from Rome, another replica of the time of Caligula from Asia Minor, a fragmentary head from Trebizond, likewise shows extensive drillwork, and a painstaking replication of the braid behind the left ear.[60]

A portrait in the Louvre that is known to have come from Athens, on the other hand, shows a looser and softer interpretation of the coiffure, without braids or corkscrew-curls.[61] The drill has been used very discreetly, to form the center of a few ringlets, but the coiffure is executed predominantly with the chisel. This head is probably also datable to the time of Caligula, therefore some time after Agrippina I's death, at a time when simple inertia might tend to make even the best marble carvers less conscientious about reproducing every detail of a complex hairstyle, particularly for a statue or bust destined to stand in a niche or against a wall where these details would be difficult to see. The Athens head is certainly the product of an atelier based in the heart of the Greek world, where Classicizing traditions in sculpture were still a powerful force. We see here, perhaps, a distinctively Athenian and Classical interpretation of Agrippina I's portrait that can contrast with the Hellenistic flamboyance of the Pergamene version from her lifetime; Pergamon was a city

---

[59] For more detailed discussions of the chronology of this bust, see Tansini, 1995, 25–28, and Wood, 1988, 411, in which I elaborate on the technical parallels between the Capitoline Agrippina and a marble head of Caligula in the Worcester Art Museum, inv. 1914.23, h. 48 cm., published Milkovich, 1961, 26–27, no. 9.

[60] Istanbul Archaeological Museum inv. 4503, marble head from Trabzon (Trebizond), h. 29.0 cm., of head from chin to crown, 23 cm., w. 21.5 cm. Broken diagonally through neck, back of head broken off, shoulder locks and piece of hair above forehead broken away. Surface chipped, weathered, and encrusted. Tansini, 1995, 60, figs. 15–16; Inan and Rosenbaum, 1966, 63–64, no. 17, pl. 11, 3–4. Tansini states that "I capelli dietro le orecchie non sono intrecciati," but Inan and Rosenbaum's photograph of the left profile clearly shows this detail, although Tansini's figure 16 shows with equal clarity that the braid does not appear on the right.

[61] Musée du Louvre, inv. Ma 3133. References supra n. 51 F.

where the "baroque" qualities of the original are likely to have met a more friendly reception.

Smaller scale replicas of the type, on coin dies and cameos, tend to simplify the coiffure because of the pressures of reduced scale: her earliest coin representations, under Caligula, tend to regularize the curls around the face into neat rows, and to represent the shoulder locks as tightly coiled corkscrew curls rather than as loose waves.[62] (Figure 96) Such a regularization of the coiffure appears also in two life-size marble portraits: a head made for insertion, from Luna, and a more fragmentary but recognizable head, set on a statue to which it may not belong, from Tindari (figures 93–94).[63] The Luna head still has the distinctive lyre-shaped pair of locks over the left temple, but the Tindari head obscures even this typical feature, lining up the pairs of curls into neatly parallel rows, with the result that some observers do not accept the identification as Agrippina I. Trillmich, for example, tentatively prefers an identification as Agrippina II, but Tansini rightly points out that the shape of the high forehead is that of the elder Agrippina.[64] The small, full-lipped mouth without an overbite, and the distinctive profile line of this head also point to an identification as the mother rather than the daughter.

Both these representations wear crescent diadems and so probably date to well after her lifetime. The Luna head comes from the same site, although not the same immediate vicinity as, portraits of Caligula and Drusilla, with which it shares some stylistic features, notably a tendency to simplify the forms of the prototype.[65] The Drusilla from Luna omits the small curls along the forehead that appear in every other extant portrait of her (see figures 111–117), and represents the waves around the face as single waves of equal width rather than the more complex broad waves with indented

---

[62] Trillmich, 1971, 181–96. Example of a cameo portrait: British Museum cat. 3593, sardonyx with profile of Agrippina I, laureate, to right, 4.9 × 2.9 cm., ex collection Marlborough. Walters, 1926, 338, no. 3593, pl. 40; Trillmich, 1984, 140 pl. 28a.

[63] Luna head: Rose, 1997, 94; Tansini, 1995, 30–31, 61, with complete literature; Fittschen-Zanker 3, 5, no. 4, n. 3 f; Frova, 1973, 538 pl. 128, 1–4; Trillmich, 1984, 139–140.

Tindari portrait: Palermo, Museo Nazionale di Archeologia, inv. 698, marble statue, h. 210 cm., of head and neck, 37 cm. Tansini 32, 64; Bonacasa, 1964, 58, no. 70, pl. 32, 3–4; Trillmich, 1984, 139 n. 20.

[64] Trillmich, 1984, 139 n. 20; Tansini, 1995, 32.

[65] Rose, 1997, 94 no. 20, pls. 84–85.

crests that appear in the more faithful replicas (figures 111–115), just as the portrait of her mother regularizes the curls around the face. All the portraits from Luna, then, were probably works of the same atelier, and very likely to have been made at approximately the same time, during the principate of Caligula. Whether or not they all originally formed part of the same group, public works of sculpture in the same town would have presented both the emperor's mother and his sister to the public in images that shared two significant attributes: not only the crescent diadem, but the *infula*.

Both the Tindari and the Luna portraits of Agrippina I show a thick, beaded fillet, worn in front of the diadem and encircling the crown of the head. We have seen that this ornament, variously described by different authors as a *vitta*, a *tutulus* or an *infula*, appears also on some likenesses of Livia and of Antonia Minor, and has often been interpreted to be the distinctive mark of a priestess of an imperial cult.[66] As noted above, however, this interpretation is probably too narrow. Similar beaded fillets appear in Roman art of the late Republic, Augustan period, and Julio-Claudian dynasty draped over the horns of sacrificial beasts, over the skulls of sacrificed animals, and over altars; they seem to correspond to the object designated by the Roman word *infula*, which confers a general aura of sanctity rather than having just one ritual meaning.[67] In the cases

---

[66] For a recent discussion of this ornament and its significance, see Small, 1990, 225. Rosenbaum, 1960, 43, no. 16, discussing a different portrait from Cyrene, argues that the Cyrene portrait cannot represent Agrippina I (as I agree that it does not) because it wears such a beaded fillet, which Agrippina I would not have been entitled to wear. The Tindari and Luna portraits, however, bear a far closer resemblance to the standard lifetime type of Agrippina I, despite their variations in the treatment of the coiffure, and cannot be so easily dismissed.

Definition of "infula:" Isid. *Orig.* 19,30,4. On the meanings of the various possible terms for this ornament, see Sensi, 1980–81, 60–64, 70–71, 73, and Wood, 1995, 478–479.

[67] Examples of sacrificial animals or skulls of sacrificed animals wearing the *infula*:

Republican suovetarilium relief in the Louvre, so-called "altar of Domitius Ahenobarbus." Recent publication: Kleiner, *Sculpture*, 1992, 49–51, fig. 31.

Silver cup B from Boscoreale, now destroyed. Recent publication: F. Kleiner, 1983, 287–302. Pl. 5 fig. 3 clearly shows the beaded *infula* draped over the horns of the bull in the sacrificial procession.

Fragments in the garden facade of the Villa Medici, reconstructed in plaster casts in the Museo della Civltà Romana. Published: Strong, 1962, 27–28, 92–93, pl. 49; Kleiner, *Sculpture*, 1992, 142–145, fig. 119, with full recent literature p. 164.

Metope from the Porticus of Gaius and Lucius. Zanker, 1990,117, fig. 95

Frieze from Porticus Octaviae or nearby structure: Zanker, 1990, 123–125, fig. 102a, pp. 126–7.

of Livia and of Drusilla, the ornament probably also calls attention to the deified status of these women.

Since Agrippina I neither held a priesthood during her lifetime nor achieved official consecration after her death, the presence of the *infula* in these portraits could refer to her posthumous status as an honorary vestal. Her statue in the Velleia group lacks the *infula* but portrays her holding a small box of incense in one hand, a fairly clear reference to a sacrificial rite and to the virtue of *pietas*. Whatever the significance of the extravagant attributes, however, the Tindari and Luna sculptures unmistakably reproduce Agrippina I's characteristic facial structure, and both are close enough in the treatment of the coiffure to allow the identifications to be accepted without serious doubt, despite their regularization of the pattern of curls.

Some other replicas that Tansini dates, probably correctly, to the time of Claudius, show another deviation from the prototype: a tendency to transform the soft and loose shoulder-locks into tight corkscrew curls that lie smoothly along the neck, a detail surely easier to carve, and one already long since adopted in coin and gem representations. The head from Coimbra and a head from Samos that is now lost both display this characteristic.[68]

Regardless of individual interpretation, and degree of classicism or "baroque" flamboyance in the style of execution, all these replicas share unmistakable points of similarity to well-known Classical works of statuary. The arrangement of hair drawn back over the ears and long shoulder locks appears in statues of both male and female deities, including Apollo: "*Alterius crines umero iactentur utroque:/Talis es adsumpta, Phoebe canore, lyra*" ("Another girl throws her locks over each shoulder; so do you appear, musical Phoebus, when you take up the lyre"), the caryatids of the Erechtheion (figure 97), the Demeter of Knidos, (figure 98) and the Eirene (figure 99) attributed to Kephisodotos.[69]

---

[68] Tansini, 1995, 31–32, 75, figs. 29–31. Photographic reproductions of the lost head from Samos: Trillmich, 1984, pl. 29, figs. c–d; Tölle-Kastenbein, *Samos* 1974, 174, fig. 335.

[69] Ov. *ArsAm.* 3, 141–142. A fairly characteristic Apollo with shoulder locks and hair drawn back over the ears is the "Tiber Apollo," Rome, Museo Nazionale Romano 608. This statue represents a nude Apollo possibly once holding the laurel branch and bow, rather than a "Kitharoedos," but like the type Ovid describes, has a coiffure that resembles that worn by females both in Classical Greek and in Roman statuary. Recent publications: *LIMC* 2 (1984), s.v. "Apollon" (W. Lamrinudakis), 258 no. 600, and "Apollon/Apollo" (E. Simon) 373–4, no. 38, with literature. Simon believes the Tiber Apollo to be an Antonine copy of an Augustan original, but Lamrunidakis argues that the relationship to the Riace bronzes confirms an early

226   CHAPTER FIVE

The Erechtheion maidens and the Demeter of Knidos, being original works of the fifth and fourth centuries respectively rather than
Roman copies, confirm that this coiffure has precedents of the Classical
period, while the Eirene, surviving as it does in more than one copy
of Augustan or Julio-Claudian date, would presumably have been
an available source of inspiration for Roman sculptors whether or
not they had access to the original work in Athens.[70] Copies of the
caryatids of the Erechtheion also existed in Augustan Rome, in the
figures of the upper colonnades in the Forum Augustum, and would
have been not only well known to the sculptors whose ateliers had
produced these copies but a familiar visual reference to the general
public in the city of Rome, many of whom would frequently have
seen these replicas in a major public space that had special significance
for the Julio-Claudian dynasty and its claims to glorious descent.[71]
These figures, as it happens, wear the coiffures most closely resembling that of Agrippina I, since their hair, except for the corkscrew
curls over each shoulder, is plaited into intricate queues down the
backs of their necks, while the Demeter and the Eirene seem to wear
their hair loose below the fillets that encircle their heads. The arrangement of hair in these two works as seen from the principal frontal
view, however, shares the features of soft waves over the ears and
long shoulder-locks. Those two works, the Eirene in particular, appear
to have been influenced by the caryatids, and the resemblance of
the faces of the two late-Classical works to eachother is not coincidental. The Demeter and Eirene both represent maternal beings: the
Demeter was undoubtedly once accompanied by her daughter
Persephone, toward whom she may have turned her head, while the
Eirene holds a baby—not her own child, but Ploutos, the son of
Demeter, for whom she performs the role of *kourotrophos*. Peace, both

---

Classical date. *MNR Sculture* 1¹, 208–213, no. 130 (E. Paribeni); Ridgway, 1970, 71
no. 2.
    Caryatids of the Erechtheion, discussion specifically of their costume and sculp-
tural type: Ridgway, 1981, 105–108; Bieber, 1977, 29–30.
    Demeter of Knidos: British Museum 1300. *LIMC* 4 (1988), 859 no. 138, s.v.
"Demeter" (L. Beschi); Robertson, 1975, 462–3, n. 39, pl. 143c, 144a, with full
earlier references.
    Eirene and Ploutos: most complete replica in Munich Glyptothek 219. De
Grummond, 1990, 667, fig. 6; *LIMC* 3 (1986), 702–703, s.v. "Eirene" (E. Simon);
Vierneisel-Schlörb, 1979, 255–273 no. 25; Bieber, 1977, 30 n. 19; Robertson, 1975,
384, pl. 125a.
[70] On the date of replicas, Vierneisel-Schlörb, 1979, 256.
[71] Zanker, 1972, 12–14, figs. 25, 26.

literally and metaphorically, supports and nurtures the god of Wealth who is born out of the earth.[72] It is for this reason that her iconography is assimilated to that of Demeter, the mother of Ploutos.

The similarity to the Eirene of Kephisodotos in particular would have been compelling in some statues of Agrippina I, if she was ever represented carrying a baby in her arms. No such examples survive, but the inscription describing the statuary group on the arch of Germanicus, in which Agrippina I appeared with her entire large family, suggests that it is not only possible but likely that Agrippina I was sometimes represented in such a composition, as were later imperial women in surviving statues and coin types. (Messalina and the child Britannicus appear in such a statue, found in Rome and now in the Louvre: figures 123–125).[73] The visual association of the wife of a warlike general with Eirene, or Pax, so that the couple can represent the two happy sides of "Peace through victory," and the resulting good fortune of the Roman people, has ample precedents on the Ara Pacis Augustae, in which the parallels between the Livia and Pax on the one hand and Augustus and Aeneas on the other have already been remarked. The Ara Pacis must undoubtedly have been an influential monument in Rome during the reign of Tiberius, when the public images of Germanicus and Agrippina I were created, and the female deity on the east facade of the Ara Pacis shares her middle part and long, tumbling shoulder locks not only with the figure of Livia on the same monument but with the portraits of Agrippina I that were created some years later.

Although the soft waves drawn back over the ears and the shoulder locks have parallels in statues and statuary types of Classical goddesses, the loose ringlets around the face generally do not. In this respect, the sculptor who created Agrippina I's lifetime type seems to agree with Ovid that "Even 'neglected' hair becomes many women: you would often think that woman who just combed her hair had

---

[72] On the presence of Persephone in the Knidos group, see *LIMC* 4 (1988), 859 no. 138, s.v. "Demeter" (Luigi Beschi). On Eirene as *kourotrophos* for the child of Demeter, *LIMC* 3 (1986), 702–703, no. 8, s.v. "Eirene" (Erika Simon); Vierniesel-Schlörb, 1979, 258–260.

[73] Arch of Germanicus: Rose, 1997, 108–110, no. 37, with full earlier literature; Gonzalez, 1984, 62–69.

Statue of Messalina with the child Britannicus: Paris, Musée du Louvre, MA 1224, marble statue, h. 195 cm. Recent publications: De Kersauson, *Louvre* 1, 1986, 200–201, no. 94; Mikocki, 1995, 44, 185–86 no. 239, pl. 25; Wood, 1992, 219–226, with earlier references.

slept on it yesterday night." (*Et neglecta decet multas coma; saepe iacere/ Hesternam credas; illa repexa modo est*).[74] No doubt the physical trait is genuine, but portraitists could, if they chose, have omitted this as they omitted other physical features (for example, signs of age) from the faces of so many of their subjects. If Agrippina I is shown with unruly, burgeoning curls, and if they have been converted into a decorative asset in their richly drilled patterns, there must be a reason for it: full, curly hair, as observed above in relation to Livia's late, deified portraits, suggest vitality and fertility. The latter was an area in which Agrippina I had amply demonstrated her outstanding qualifications by the time she was honored with public portraits. Loose curls are certainly associated with youthful beauty in both sexes, as attested by at least one statuary type of a male deity, the Kassel Apollo, which like Agrippina I wears most of his hair bound up and drawn back across his ears, but has long escaping locks on each side of the neck and numerous small ringlets escaping from the waves around his face. (Figure 100). This Apollo probably follows a bronze original of the fifth century, although scholars do not and probably never will agree on the identity of the sculptor.[75]

Whether or not the Kassel Apollo specifically could have served as a direct inspiration for the type of Agrippina I is less certain, since all extant copies appear to be of Hadrianic date or later. Ridgway proposes in fact that the hairstyle of this Apollo is a classicizing Roman creation. Surviving bronzes such as Riace Warrior A and the Delphi Charioteer, however, offer examples in fifth-century originals for separately cast curls that could be fastened to a bronze head to achieve a somewhat comparable decorative effect.[76]

---

[74] Ov. *ArsAm* 3.153–4.

[75] The commonest attribution is to Pheidias, but it has also been associated with the styles of Kresilas and Myron. *LIMC* 2 (1984) s.v. "Apollon," (W. Lambrinudakis), 219, no. 295, with list of extant replicas in Greece, and "Apollon/Apollo" (E. Simon) 374–5, no. 41. Robertson, 1975, 1, 337, n. 108 with full literature; Ridgway, 1970, 137, 140–141, and 1981, 184–5. In the earlier book, Ridgway accepts the Kassel Apollo as authentically early Classical in all aspects of its style including the curly hair, but states in the 1981 volume that the type may be either a Roman creation or a pastiche of Classical models in which the hairstyle is Roman.

[76] Boardman, 1985, 86, fig. 68. On the extant 5th century bronzes: Houser, 1987, 86, bibliography p. 119, on the Delphi Charioteer, and 169 on "General A" from Riace; Houser, 1983, 20–31 on charioteer and 116–127 on Riace Warrior A; Busignani, 1981–82, 90–91, figs. 24–25 on similarities of Riace Warrior A to Kassel Apollo, especially in treatment of hair. Arias, 1986, 45–49, also discusses this relationship. Ridgway, 1981, 237–239, considers the Riace bronzes to be late Hellenistic or Roman period works, but this is a minority opinion.

The fact, then, that no extant examples of the Kassel Apollo seem
to be of Julio-Claudian date does not mean that it, and works like
it, were not available as inspirations to artists of the early Julio-
Claudian period. The above-quoted couplet about Apollo's hairstyle
from Ovid's *Ars Amatoria* implies that a coiffure that enhances the
beauty of the young god could be used just as appropriately by an
attractive woman. The ideal proportions for the human face in
Classical sculpture seem to have been identical for young males and
young females, with the result that the sex of a beardless head preserved out of context can sometimes be quite difficult to determine.
Such is the case of the Bologna head now known to belong to a
Classical type of Athena, but identified by more than one observer
as a male.[77] Given the androgynous standard of Classical beauty,
then, it is not at all surprising to see that a certain arrangement of
hair could be appropriate to either sex. Images of Apollo could have
provided a source of inspiration for the creator of the elder Agrippina's
portrait type, and another level of divine associations for its viewers.
One can only wonder to what extent the visual invocation of a male
deity might have appealed to the strong-willed and independent-
minded subject of these portraits.

The contrast between Agrippina I's charismatic, goddess-like image
and the severely chaste portraits of Livia from the lifetime of Augustus
demonstrate a change of mentality on the part of at least some imperial patrons in just one generation: no longer is the living wife of
an imperial figure presented as an example of modesty and restraint,
a "role model" for respectable Roman women, but as a visible
embodiment of the imperial family's dynastic ambitions. Her image
contrasts, however, with that of the wife of the other heir to power,
Livilla I. The cameo profiles that securely represent Livilla I identify her with Ceres and give her a Classicizing coiffure, but one that

---

[77] Hartswick, 1983, 335–346, pls. 42–46; Protzmann, 1984, 7–22. In my opinion, the technical evidence presented by Protzmann proves conclusively that the
Dresden head of the "Athena Lemnia" type does belong to Athena torso in Dresden
with which it has been reconstructed, but Hartswick's comparisons of the Bologna
replica to male types, pp. 340–342, figs. 17–18, are striking, although his efforts to
date the creation of the head to the Hadrianic era prove only, in my opinion, that
the Roman copy in Bologna is Hadrianic. When I speak of "more than one observer"
who has mistaken this for a male head, I am referring to anecdotal information
from a former student of mine, Dr. James Glazier, who had a poster-sized reproduction of the Bologna head in his room at Harvard: Dr. Glazier observes that his
friends routinely mistook the Athena for an Apollo.

is still orderly and restrained into smooth waves bound neatly up in back. (Figures 78–79). The Leptis-Malta portrait type, if it does in fact represent Livilla I (a point on which we cannot be certain), likewise shows natural forms under strict control: the waves of the hair are drawn back severely, the only curls visible obviously artificial and marshalled into an orderly pattern. (Figures 74–77).

The "Olympia Type:" the Controversy

If my identification of a posthumous type for Agrippina I is correct, her images appear, ironically, to have become more contemporary-looking, rather than more goddess-like, many years after her death, a transformation for which I believe that there were good political reasons. Several later replicas of the securely identified portrait of Agrippina I show an unmistakable trend toward regularization of the coiffure into neat rows of curls on each side of the face, rather than the apparently spontaneous pattern of the prototype from her lifetime, and some of these later copies have corkscrew-curls rather than loosely waved strands escaping behind the ears and falling to the shoulders. The portraits of Agrippina I from Luna, Coimbra, Samos and Tindari (figures 93–94), all display this tendency.[78]

Some years ago, I suggested that this development in the interpretations of the prototype from the elder Agrippina's lifetime led eventually and logically to the creation of a new, posthumous type, one that no longer attempted to reproduce the precise coiffure of the Capitoline portrait type (figures 87–94), but that showed considerable similarity to its late interpretations. This later portrait type, according to my analysis, deliberately emphasizes the resemblance of Agrippina I to her daughter at the time of the younger Agrippina's marriage to Claudius. To this end, portraitists represented Agrippina I with a coiffure similar to that of her daughter, although still with her recognizably different physical traits, but gave her a new mark of honor with the addition of a crescent diadem. My proposal has been disputed by at least one recent study, but I think it appropriate to consider the evidence, or lack of it, for other proposed identifications of this group of marbles.[79]

---

[78] See Tansini, 1995, 30–32, for a recent discussion of the Claudian-era replicas of this type.

[79] Tansini, 1995, 44 no. 8.

At least three extant replicas reproduce this type: a head in the Museo Chiaramonti of the Vatican that was found, presumably, in Rome (figures 101–102), another from the Via Varese in Rome that is now in the Terme museum, and a third marble head found at Olympia (figures 103–104).[80] A possible fourth, a statue in Vienna is more problematic: the face and coiffure are similar, but it lacks the diadem and it may be a private portrait.[81] Zanker groups all four of these works with the replicas of Agrippina II's "Ancona type," but the facial structure of the three, which form a cohesive and typologically consistent group, is completely different from that of Agrippina II, lacking in particular her low forehead, which as Tansini rightly notes is always especially emphasized in the portraits that show her with a diadem.[82]

The Olympia head (figures 103–104), because of its known provenance, has figured prominently in every attempt to identify the type. Despite its discovery in a scientific excavation, this marble had left its original context and been used as building material in a Late Antique wall in the palaestra. It bears, however, close technical and stylistic relationships to a statue of Agrippina II that was found near (but not inside) the Metroon (figures 105–106), not only in style but in the grain and patina of the marble. The modeling of the area around the eyes bears especially close comparison. The latter work represents the wife of Claudius with the pose and gesture of a priestess, and has generally been associated with the statue of her deified

---

[80] Vatican, Museo Chiaramonti, inv. 1480, marble head, h. 48 cm. Wood, 1988, 419 n. 27 with earlier references; Fittschen-Zanker 3, 7, no. 4, n. 4 k, Beil. 5, a–d; Bol, 1986, 289, figs. 5–8; Amelung, *Vatican* 1, 625–626, no. 477, pl. 66.

Via Varese head: Museo Nazionale Romano inv. 12136, marble, h. 30 cm. *MNR Sculture* I⁹, 155–156 no. R111 (B. Di Leo); Wood, 1988, 419 n. 27 with earlier references; Fittschen-Zanker 3, 7 no. 5, n. 4 o under "Typus III Ancona;" Bol, 1986, 289, fig. 9. Di Leo accepts Bol's identification as Claudia Octavia; Zanker identifies the head as Agrippina II.

Olympia Museum inv. λ 147, h. 35.5 cm. Rose, 1997, 148–49; Tansini, 1995, 15–16, 44; Hitzl, 1991, 117–119; Wood, 1988, 419 n. 27 with earlier references; Bol, 1986, 289–307. Hitzl rejects Renate Bol's identification of this head as Claudia Octavia, and mentions my proposed identification but is noncommittal as to whether or not he accepts it, p. 32 n. 271.

[81] Vienna, Kunsthistorisches Museum I 1550, marble statue, exact measurements unavailable, life-size. Fittschen-Zanker 3, 7 no. 5, n. 4, "Typus III: Ancona" p, photo Beilage 5.e–g. In private correspondence to me, Trillmich has expressed the opinion that this is a private portrait.

[82] Tansini, 1995, 32; her remarks about the identity of the Palermo statue are equally applicable to the treatment of the forehead and hairline of this group.

husband found inside the Metroon, although Rose has recently pointed
out that the findspot of the statue of Agrippina II does not necessarily justify such a reconstruction.[83] The Agrippina II might instead
have stood outside the Heraion. In any case, there is good stylistic
evidence at the least to attribute that statue of Agrippina II and the
diademed head to the same time and the same local atelier, and it
is not unreasonable to speculate that they originally stood in close
proximity.

The Olympia, (figures 103–104), Vatican (figures 101–102) and
Via Varese heads have long been recognized as replicas of a common prototype, but in addition to my proposed identification as
Agrippina I, there are two other conflicting identifications in current literature. Tansini seems uncertain which to accept: she observes
that scholarly consensus gives these portraits to Agrippina II, but
adds that Bol's recent proposal that the Olympia (figures 103–104)
and Via Varese heads represent Claudia Octavia seems "valid." The
Olympia and Via Varese heads, however, constitute two out of a
group of three. If the consensus of scholars is decisive, then Bol's
hypothesis cannot be valid, and vice versa.[84] The uncertainty is understandable: the portraits surely cannot represent Agrippina II, since
they differ from her established likenesses in important physical features. The younger Agrippina's face is short and squarish, her lips
are thin, her lower lip retreats sharply and her small chin juts forward in a classic symptom of mandibular retrognathia. None of those
features are present in this type. But the hairstyle is almost identical to that of the younger Agrippina's "Ancona type," to which I
believe that the creators of this group intended a resemblance. Viewers
in antiquity would have seen such statues on inscribed bases that
would have prevented any confusion about a subject's identity, thus
allowing portrait sculptors to assimilate the appearance of one person to another quite freely, but modern spectators, unfortunately, do
not enjoy that convenience.

---

[83] On the findspots of the sculptures: Rose, 1997, 148; Treu, 1897, 255, 260, pl.
64.6; Bol, 1986, 289, 292–294; Hitzl, 1991, 117–119.
[84] Tansini, 1995, 44: "Le repliche di questo ritratto individuate dalla Wood sono
inoltre concordemente attribuite dagli studiose ad Agrippina Minore. Circa il rico-
noscimento della testa di Olimipia, appare valido quello proposto dal Bol e cioé
con Claudia Ottavia, sulla base del confronto con un ritratto conservato al Museo
Nazionale Romano." The head in the Museo Nazionale Romano that Bol cites, is
of course precisely one of those "concordemente attribuite dagli studiosi ad Agrippina
Minore." See Bol, 1986, 289, fig. 9.

Vagn Poulsen proposed to recognize this type as Claudia Octavia, the daughter of Claudius and first wife of the emperor Nero, a theory followed by Renate Bol.[85] The basis for this theory, however, bears re-examination. We have seen in the previous chapter that an identification of a portrait type as Antonia Minor, based on an error of interpretation of the Leptis Magna sculptures, has proved extraordinarily persistent despite the lack of valid evidence, and the same may be true of this identification of "Claudia Octavia."

Poulsen initially identified this group of portraits on the basis of just one argument: the Olympia head (figures 103–104) had been found on the same site, although not in the same place, as a portrait head of an adolescent whom he identified as the young emperor Nero at the time of his accession. There was, however, a problem with the identification as "Claudia Octavia" of which Poulsen was uneasily aware: the fact that the female portrait seems to represent a woman far more mature than the 19–year-old Claudia Octavia at the time of her divorce and exile, the latest possible age at which any portrait could have been created for her. Poulsen dismissed this problem on the grounds that "it is a well known fact that children mature quickly in the South," and that imperial portraits of adolescents tend to make their subjects look precociously mature. But the discrepancy between Claudia Octavia's age at the time of her exile and the apparent age of these portraits has troubled other observers as well.[86] Poulsen's only evidence in favor of the identification, the head of "Nero," is hardly conclusive, since most scholars today, including Bol, reject the identification of that head.[87] Without the head of "Nero" from Olympia, the identification as "Claudia Octavia" of the female head at Olympia (figures 103–104), rests on thin air, and so does that of its replicas.

Bol proposed two new arguments in favor of the identification. The first was its context in the group from the Metroon, which included securely identified likenesses of Claudius and Agrippina II. The only other female member of the family of Claudius and Agrippina II who could have appeared in such a group, she argues, was

---

[85] Poulsen, 1962, 109–111, and 1954, 300–301, and 1962, 110–111; Bol, 1986, 301–302.

[86] Poulsen 1962, 108; Sande, 1985, 218–19.

[87] Bol, 1986, 301: "Freilich gibt das dort als Pendant vorgestellte Bildnis sicher nicht den jungen Nero wieder..."

Claudia Octavia. Rose, as noted above, has questioned the accuracy of that reconstruction of the Metroon group, but there is still good reason to associate the statue of Agrippina II and the diademed head.[88] I disagree, however, with Bol's reasoning that there is only one possible identification for a woman who could appear in the younger Agrippina's company. Given the importance of Agrippina Augusta's mother in the coinage and public imagery of Claudius's principate, and the very common practice of representing long-dead members of the dynasty along with their living descendants in statue groups, there is at least one other very strong possible candidate. Bol's second argument is the existence of some provincial coins from Perinthus that represent a woman identified by inscription as Claudia Octavia who wears a coiffure and diadem similar to those in these portraits. Roman coins, however, never depict Claudia Octavia, and when dealing with provincial coins we must always ask ourselves what the prototype for the portraits could have been. It is not unknown for provincial die-cutters to attach a name to a purely ideal head, or to adapt the portrait type of an earlier woman of the same dynasty to represent a contemporary one. A clear case in point is an issue from a mint in the Balkans that directly copies the *carpentum-sestertius* of Agrippina I, both the obverse portrait and the reverse type, but with an inscription that identifies the woman as Agrippina II: AGRIPPINAE AUG GERMANICI F CAESARIS AUG (Agrippina Augusta, the daughter of Germanicus and wife of Caesar Augustus).[89] The coins of Perinthus that Bol illustrates are of good quality, with a carefully executed profile that looks extraordinarily similar to the coin profiles of the two Agrippinae on coins from the Roman mint, from which they could easily have been adapted. The Perinthus issue tells us only that Claudia Octavia is depicted wearing the coiffure that was fashionable at the time, and that in this provincial city, at least, it was considered appropriate to represent her with a divine attribute. It is also common for coins from cities of the Greek east to grant titles and epithets like "θέα," "goddess," to living women of the imperial family, and other honors to which they were not officially entitled.[90]

---

[88] Rose, 1997, 148.
[89] Banti-Simonetti, *CNR* 16, 45–46 no. 1; Von Kaenel, 1984, 141–144, pl. 24, figs. 25–31.
[90] Rose, 1997, 13; Trillmich, 1978, 125 n. 429; *IGRR* IV 206, in which Livilla I,

My own arguments in favor of the recognition of this type as Agrippina I are as follows:

First, these portraits share all the key physiognomic features of the Capitoline type: the high forehead, long face, deep-set eyes, square jaw, small but full-lipped mouth without any trace of an overbite, and firm chin.[91] One would, incidentally, expect portraits of the daughter of Claudius to display more obviously Claudian features, in particular the overbite that ran in that family. This feature can be observed in a portrait that I tentatively identify as the daughter of Claudius and Messalina as an adolescent (figures 128–129). The profile lines of all copies of the Olympia type, in contrast, are strikingly similar to those of the Capitoline type.

Second, although the coiffure does not match that of the Capitoline sculptural type (figures 86–94), it does conform to the coiffure that Agrippina I wears on coins from the Roman mint (figures 80 and 85), and on some gems: neatly arranged rows of curls around the face, and corkscrew curls behind the ears that hang to the shoulders. One cameo gem in the British Museum that scholars have universally recognized as Agrippina I since it reproduces her characteristic features in excellent detail, shows a treatment of the coiffure virtually identical to that of the Olympia portrait type (figure 96).[92] We have seen some of the late replicas of the Capitoline type also displaying the corkscrew curls—sometimes, as in the lost head from Samos, two corkscrew curls behind each ear—and the tendency to regularize the curls around the face (figures 93–94).

Third, the context of the Olympia head argues for a woman who belongs in a family group that included Agrippina II. The Gemma Claudia (figure 95) offers an example of such a grouping, in which the deceased and heroized couple, Germanicus and Agrippina I, face their daughter and Germanicus's brother. The crescent diadem of the Olympia head implies that she is someone who outranks Agrippina II, whose statue from the same site does not wear one.

---

the daughter of Antonia Minor, is identified as ΘΕΑ: "... ΚΑΙ ΛΕΙΒΙΑΣ ΘΕΑΣ ΑΦΡΟΔΕΙΤΗΣ ΑΝΧΕΙΣΙΑΔΟΣ ..." Since Livilla I died in disgrace, the inscription must date to her lifetime.

[91] Tansini, 1995, 44.

[92] British Museum 3593, inv. 99.7–22.3, sardonyx cameo, 4.5 × 3.5 cm. Megow, 1987, 292 no. D14 with earlier literature, pl. 18.6; Trillmich, 1984, 140 pl. 28a.

Fourth, this group of portraits bears stylistic resemblance to the latest replicas of the Capitoline type, such as the Luna and particularly, the Tindari replicas (figures 93–94). Comparing the Luna and Tindari heads with the Olympia, Terme and Vatican replicas (figures 101–104), one can in fact see them as members of the same stylistic continuum, except that in the portraits of the Olympia group, copyists have given up every pretence of reproducing the complicated pattern of hair of the Capitoline type.

And finally, there are precedents in the history of Roman art for just this sort of invention of a posthumous portrait on the basis of types from the subject's lifetime. The portraits of Livia discussed in chapter 2 display a rich array of variations on both her *nodus* coiffure and her middle-part coiffure in posthumous images, many of which develop almost into new types of their own. The handsome bust of Agrippina II from an *imago clipeata* in the Forum Traianum (figures 143–144) does not match any of the lifetime portrait types of that woman: the coiffure is an imaginative and very free re-interpretation of her "Ancona" type, in which the little snail-curls on the sides of her head become three tiers of corkscrew curls, while four smaller corkscrew curls hang down on her cheeks in front of each ear.[93] The hair on the back of her head is twisted into melon-like segments that run from front to back. The likeness of the face, however, is unmistakable. This head is a unique object of extraordinarily high quality, made for a special situation, whereas the Olympia type was designed for replication and distribution. But the Trajanic Agrippina II demonstrates that good Roman portraitists had the will and ability to invent such posthumous images, and were willing to depart freely from lifetime models so long as the subject's most recognizable features remained intact. In both cases, the motivation for the type is similar: the desire to pay new honors (in one case, through colossal scale, in the other, through the crescent diadem) to a long-dead person for the political gain of the current ruler.

The identification of the "Olympia Type" is, admittedly, a far from proven hypothesis, and I would not claim it as a secure identification. However, the identification as Agrippina II is untenable, while Poulsen built the identification as Claudia Octavia on one erroneous assumption about a portrait he believed to be Nero. This

---

[93] Fittschen-Zanker 3, 6–7 no. 5, pl. 6.

identification, which has very little supporting evidence, has survived since on the basis of little more than the *ipse dixit* of Poulsen. Claudius would have had good reason to emphasize the resemblance of his fourth wife to both her parents, who were beloved figures remembered as political martyrs, and this emphasis on resemblance could as easily be achieved by assimilating the image of the dead woman to that of her living daughter as vice versa. Agrippina II, a woman whose political ambition and determination to have her power officially acknowledged are amply documented, especially during the early years of her son's principate, is more than likely to have had some influence on Claudius, and later on Nero, in decisions about artistic patronage. It is at any rate unmistakably clear that immediately following her marriage to Claudius, the content of his coin types shifts to an almost exclusive emphasis on the family of his new wife, and the status of her son Nero. The *cui bono* of this new focus in official propaganda is obvious; it benefitted Claudius in shifting attention away from his disastrous marriage to Messalina, and asserting his new alliance with the daughter of the beloved Germanicus, but it obviously also promoted the ambitions of Agrippina II and her son. It is surely significant that an inscription that attests the presence of Agrippina I in a Claudian portrait group identifies her as the grandmother of Nero, and that her portrait appeared here on a gilded bronze shield, a format associated in particular with revered ancestors.[94]

The images of Agrippina I, then, begin even during her lifetime as flamboyantly goddess-like, rich in Classical associations, and are later transformed into more "contemporary" looking form. This is true of the securely identified late replicas of her Capitoline type (e.g. figures 14–15) as well as of the controversial "Olympia type." They seem, then, to have progressed in the opposite direction from the images of Livia, which developed in her later years and after her death into less severe and more goddess-like representations. The reasons for the alterations to the elder Agrippina's image, like those to Livia's, can of course be found in the political needs of her living relatives.

---

[94] Rose, 1997, 90, no. 13. On *imagines clipeatae*, Winkes, 1979, 481–484.

The Sisters of Caligula

The oldest of Caligula's three sisters, Agrippina II, enjoyed a long period of public prominence that spanned the principates of two emperors and part of a third. The other two sisters were more ephemeral figures: Drusilla's portraits, although widely distributed during Caligula's principate, lost their political significance with his fall, and would not have been replicated after his death. The youngest sister, Livilla II, would have been represented in public only a very brief period, between Caligula's accession to power in 37 and her own disgrace and exile following her alleged involvement in a plot agaist her brother in 39. Livilla II, like Agrippina II, outlived Caligula, but unlike her older sister never regained prominence; Claudius recalled her from exile, but Messalina soon had her exiled again and murdered.[95]

During the principate of Caligula, however, all three women unquestionably appeared in public sculptural groups, and replicas of at least two of those portrait types survive. Distinguishing the sisters from one another and correctly identifying them presents the usual difficulties: like all Julio-Claudian imperial portraits, their idealized images display close assimilation both to one another and to the reigning emperor. Subtle physical differences and distinguishing attributes, however, indicate that several very similar works must represent two separate individuals. The first of these groups consists of at least six life-sized replicas, including fine heads in the Museum of the Rhode Island School of Design (figures 107–108) and in Schloss Fasanerie bei Fulda (figures 109–110), as well as several cameos and miniature sculptures in semiprecious stone.[96] The second survives in

---

[95] Supra note 39.

[96] On the Providence-Schloss Fasanerie type: Rose, 1997, 70, pl. 54; Wood, 1995, 465–470; Trillmich, 1983, 21–37.

A) Providence, Rhode Island School of Design Museum inv. 56.097, white marble head, h. 30.5 cm., w. 22.2, d. 23.7, set on a bust of colored marble probably of the eighteenth century. Tip of nose restored, some minor chips, cracks and weathering. Published: Ridgway, 1972, 86–87, 201–204, no. 33, with earlier literature (identified as Agrippina II); Polaschek, 1972, 201–210, figs. 5, 8, 10; Trillmich, 1983, 27, no. 5 (as Agrippina II); Fuchs, 1990, 116–118 (as Drusilla); Wood, 1995, 465–470, figs. 5–7 (as Agrippina II).

B) Schloss Fasanerie Cat. no. 22, head and neck unit made for insertion into statue, yellowish-gray marble, h. 32.2 cm., of head 19.5 cm., of face 15 cm., w. 19.3 cm. Top of head, originally worked in a separate piece of marble, now missing. Most of queue at nape of neck broken away, tip of nose and hair behind ear

a full-length statue, now in the Vatican (figures 111–113), from in or near the ruins of the theater at Caere; in a head made for insertion into a statue that was excavated in the precinct of the temple of Kore at Cyrene; in a weathered but recognizable replica in the Von Hessen collection (figures 114–115); in a head from Spain now in the Hispanic Society of America; in a marble head from Luna in Etruria; and in a somewhat later, slightly simplified and idealized replica in the Munich Glyptothek (figures 116–117).[97]

Both types share a distinctive coiffure, which Polaschek identifies as typical of the time of Caligula: the hair around the face is crimped

---

on right side also missing. Published: Von Heintze, *Fulda*, 1968, 32, 100 (with earlier literature), no. 22, pls. 37, 38, 114b. Polaschek, 1972, 201–210, figs. 1, 6. Trillmich, 1983, 27 no. 1, fig. 1; Fuchs, 1990, 116–118; Wood, 1995, 465–470, figs. 8–10.

[97] Rose, 1997, 68; Wood, 1995, 470–482.

A) Caere statue: Vatican, Museo Gregoriano Profano 1050, h. 204 cm., of head, 25 cm. Forearms, nose, left ear, part of chin and upper lip, fragments of costume and hanging locks alongside neck missing, formerly restored in plaster, restorations now removed. Published: Rose, 1997, 83–86 no. 5, pls. 65–66; Tansini, 1995, 42–43 no. 3; Wood, 1995, 471–475, figs. 15–17; *Caere 2*, 3, 6–7, 76–79 no. 8, 120–121, figs. 4, 65–72, 132–135; Boschung, *JRA* 1993, 68–69 figs. 53–54, no. Ua; Vierniesel-Schlörb, 1979, 163–169 under no. 15; Bieber, 1977, 122 figs. 544–545; Polaschek, *Porträttypen*, 1973, 26–27, pls. 11.1, 14.1, 16.1; Helbig[4] 1, 1050 (H. von Heintze); Giuliano, 1957, 29, no. 32, with earlier literature, pls. 20–21. (On information about the group and the inscriptions, 22–23).

B) Cyrene head: Cyrene museum, acc. no. C 17030. Marble head and neck, found 1926 on sanctuary terrace in the ruins of the south wall of the temple of Kore, h. 39 cm., of face from chin to crown 26 cm.; w. 22.2 cm. Most of nose broken off, otherwise well preserved. Published: Tansini, 1995, 41–42 no. 2, figs. 48–49; Wood, 1995, 475, figs. 20–21; Rosenbaum, 1960, 43, no. 16, with earlier literature; pl. 16, 1–2.

C) Von Hessen private collection, listed with collection of Schloss Fasanerie bei Fulda cat. 23, marble head and neck made for insertion into statue, badly weathered, most of nose missing, h. 32.2 cm., of face 19.5 cm. Published: Mikocki, 1995, 181–82 no. 211, pl. 12 (as either Agrippina the Younger or Drusilla); Wood, 1995, figs. 18–19; Trillmich, 1983, 34–36; Polaschek, *Porträttypen*, 1973, 16–17, 23–24, pl. 2, fig. 2, 4, fig. 2, 6, fig. 2, 8, fig. 1; von Heintze, *Fulda*, 33–34 no. 23, pls. 40, 41, 113b.

D) Hispanic Society of America, New York City, inv. D203, marble head made for insertion, ht. 0.39 m. Lower third of nose broken away, rear of head unfinished. Wood, 1995, 475–476 n. 70, figs. 22–23, with full earlier literature; Polaschek, 1973, 30, pl. 12, fig. 2, 15 fig. 1, 18 fig. 1; Vermeule, 1980, 289 no. 246.

E) Luna head: Genoa-Pegli, Museum, marble head, h. 26.1 cm. Rose, 1997, 94 no. 20, pl. 85 with earlier literature; Saletti, 1973, 37–46, fig. 2; Polaschek, *Porträttypen*, 30–33, pls. 13, 15, fig. 2, 18 fig. 2.

F) Munich Glyptothek 316, marble head and neck, life-size, precise measurements unavailable. Fuchs, 1990, 118–120, figs. 10–13; Trillmich, 1983, 35; Polaschek, *Porträttypen*, 1973, 11–19, pl. 2, fig. 1, 3 fig. 1, 4 fig. 1, 6 fig. 1, 17 fig. 2; Wood, 1995, 476–477, figs. 24–26.

into broad, stiff waves, the crests of which are flattened and slightly indented. The hair is drawn back over the ears so as to leave all but the top of the ear exposed, and looped into a queue down the nape of the neck. A fringe of small ringlets along the hairline border the forehead and temples.[98] Provincial replicas like the head from Cyrene and Spain, or works of mediocre quality like the head from Luna, tend to simplify the coiffure somewhat, representing shallow waves of equal depth. The Luna head also omits the curls along the forehead. The conformity of its physical features to the Caere-Von Hessen type, however, its diadem and *infula*, and the context of its discovery along with a portrait of Caligula nonetheless support identification of the Luna head as one of the emperor's sisters.

The portrait type represented by the heads in Providence and Fulda (figures 107–110) has no shoulder-locks, but the Caere statue and Munich head have fragmentary traces where such locks apparently once existed, while sculptors obviously reworked corkscrew-curls to represent the hanging, beaded strands of the *infula* in the replicas from Luna, in the Hispanic Society of America, and in the Von Hessen collection (figures 114–115). The Cyrene head, which never underwent reworking, has well-preserved corkscrew curls along the neck. There are physical differences between the two types as well, despite an unmistakable family resemblance: the subject of the Providence-Schloss Fasanerie type has a thinner face and more angular profile, while the Caere type portrays a woman with fleshier cheeks and fuller lips. "Baby fat" is a feature that can change with age, but bone structure is not; the woman of the Providence-Schloss Fasanerie type has a distinctive profile line with a low forehead, short but slightly arched nose, thin lips, conspicuous overbite, and small chin that forms a sharp angle where it juts forward below the retreating lower lip. This same profile repeats itself very consistently in all the portrait types agreed to represent Agrippina II. The Caere type (figures 111–117) likewise represents a woman with an overbite, but a less severe one, and a larger, more rounded chin-point.[99] There is circumstantial, if not conclusive evidence that the second of those individuals was Drusilla, since inscriptions also found in the theater at Caere, along with the group of imperial statues, indicate the pres-

---

[98] Polaschek, 1972, 174–177 fig. 10, 200–210.
[99] Thanks to Dr. Diana Wolf Abbott, D.D.S., of Rochester, MI, for her kind assistance and information about the dental conditions represented in these portraits.

ence of statues of Agrippina I and of Diva Drusilla in that group.[100]
It is now generally agreed that the Caere statue cannot represent
Agrippina I.[101] The group of statues from Caere is heterogenous,
spanning several decades and principates, but the statue of Diva
Drusilla could have been dedicated only during the time of Caligula,
although it would probably have been allowed to remain on display
after his fall. The coiffure of the Caere statue (figures 111–113) and
its family resemblance to Caligula and Agrippina II would tend to
support a dating to the time of Caligula and to argue for its connection with the base inscribed with the name "Diva Drusilla."[102]

Evidence of coins like the Roman *sestertii* (figure 82) and Apamenean
bronze coins (figure 84) allow us to infer that replicas of these two
portrait types originally appeared together in statuary groups with
the third sister Livilla II, and that the bodies as well as the faces
were probably deliberately similar: the three figures on the Roman
sestertius all place the weight on the same leg and are draped in the
same way, apparently in Greek rather than Roman costume. Drusilla's
portraits, however, are the only ones among extant replicas to wear
attributes like the crescent diadem, as in the Luna, Von Hessen
(figures 114–115) and Hispanic Society replicas and in the later,
more idealized, head in Munich (figures 116–117). After her death
and deification, another attribute sets her apart from her sisters on
the coins from Apamea in Bithynia: the *infula* that appears, faint but
recognizable, along the neck of her frontal portrait bust. Conceivably
all three sisters might have been entitled, as honorary Vestals, to
wear the *infula*, but in marble sculpture, the *infula* and crescent diadem appear only in conjunction with the facial features of full lips
and a large, rounded chin—that is, on portraits of the Caere-Von
Hessen type. Polaschek has rightly disputed the assumption that the

---

[100] Rose, 1997, 84; Giuliano, 1957, 22–23, 29, no. 32; Helbig[4] 1, 1043, 1044,
1046 (Ekkehard Meinhard) and 1050 (H. von Heintze).

[101] Anti, 1928, 3–16, pls. 1–3. Tansini, 1995, 41–43, nos. 2–3, Rosenbaum, 1960,
43, no. 16, and Trillmich, 1984,137–138 dispute this identification. Anti's hypothesis that the Caere-Cyrene type dates to Agrippina I's lifetime and was later replaced
by the posthumous Capitoline type has been disproven by discovery of a replica of
the Capitoline type in the Leptis Magna group, which must date to A.D. 23: supra
n. 53.

[102] Polaschek, 1972, 172–174. Other proposed identifications include Messalina,
or Agrippina II recut from a likeness of Messalina; see Liverani in *Caere 2*, 121,
and Liverani, 1990–91, 165–167. I have addressed these hypotheses elsewhere: see
Wood, 1995, 472–3.

infula necessarily indicates deification, for the same reasons that I have disputed its interpretation specifically as the mark of a priestess of the imperial cult.[103] In this case, however, the emblem does seem to have distinguished the *diva* from her living sisters. In all but one of the portraits that show this attribute, moreover, the beaded band was a later addition: the Von Hessen, Hispanic Society, Luna, and Caere replicas all display signs of recutting for the purpose of adding the *infula*. In the first three, hanging locks of hair along the neck have been recut into beaded strands. The Von Hessen head (figures 114–115) shows a row of drill-holes across the crown, just in front of the diadem, where a beaded fillet could have been attached in plaster, while the heads from Luna and from Spain show the strand carved into, rather than in front of, the diadem. In the Caere statue (figures 111–113), the recutter seems to have begun by trying to transform hanging locks into beaded strands, but when the strands broke, he was forced to start again by carving the pattern in low relief against the throat, and removing some of the surface of the neck, with the result that the neck is now measurably wider in back than in front.[104] These four works, therefore, are probably lifetime portraits of Drusilla later modified after her deification. The Von Hessen, Luna, and Hispanic Society heads indicate that the diadem, on the other hand, was an attribute that belonged to this woman during her lifetime: perhaps as a way of setting apart Drusilla, the chosen heir, from her two sisters.

Since only one statue survives relatively intact, it is impossible to generalize about representations of the bodies in these groups, but the Caere statue (figure 111–113) follows a Classical model, the "Kore Albani" type, which represents a youthful, girlish goddess clad in a *chiton* and *himation*.[105] The former has an overfold falling to just above the waist and forming delicate, crinkly folds, while the heavier fab-

---

[103] Polaschek, *Porträttypen*, 1973, 15–16; Wood, 1995, 478–79. Supra n. 66–67.

[104] Liverani, *Caere 2*, 121.

[105] On the identification of Drusilla with Kore, Mikocki, 1995, 42–43, 184 nos. 223 (Smyrna coin) and 224 (Caere statue), pl. 27, nos. 223 and 224. Replicas of Kore Albani type:

A) Villa Albani inv. 749, marble statue, h. 185 cm. Left lower arm and parts of right hand restored. *LIMC* 2, 24 no. 149, s.v. "Aphrodite," (Robert Fleischer) with full earlier literature; Helbig⁴ 4, no. 3342 (Werner Fuchs); Bieber, 1977, 121–122, fig. 543.

B) Venice, Museo Archeologico, marble statuette of the 5th century B.C., probably a contemporary copy of the original, h. 106 cm. Both forearms were origi-

ric of the latter is looped over her left shoulder, across her back and
around the abdomen, below the waist, to form a triangular, apron-
like flap, the point of which hangs to the left knee. She rests her
weight on the left leg, turning her head and gesturing with her left
hand in the same direction, while her right arm, bent at the elbow
and lifted away from the body, held some attribute—probably, in
the original, at least, the torch of the Eleusinian mysteries. In all
replicas, both original hands have been broken away due to their
unprotected position, and the attributes they once held have been
lost with them. Fifth century Greek votive reliefs like the well-known
Eleusis relief of Demeter, Triptolemos and Kore, however, show
Kore with her distinctive torch, wearing identically arranged drapery and in almost the identical stance, except that the right rather
than the left leg supports the weight of the body.[106]

The evidence of these reliefs favors the traditional identification
of the Kore Albani type as the goddess of the Eleusinian mysteries,
although the statue of Antonia from Baia demonstrates that the type
could also appear with the attributes of Aphrodite (figures 64–66).
Either goddess, or a syncretic combination of both, would make
an appropriate parallel for Drusilla: both are goddesses of fertility,
which was Drusilla's primary responsibility as the heir to the empire.
The weight of the evidence indicates, however, that in the Caere
statue, Drusilla is assimilated to Kore, as she is in the bronze coins
of Smyrna which also date to her lifetime.[107] The Cyrene head was
found in the ruins of a temple of Kore, strong evidence that there,
too, Caligula's heir had an association with the chthonian goddess,
although the body type to which that head belonged has unfortunately been lost.

---

nally worked separately and are now lost. Restored: nose, top of head, part of left
shoulder. Published: Ridgway, 1981, 195–196; Traversari, 1973, 60–64, no. 24;
Anti, 1930, 38–41, no. 11.

C) Munich Glyptothek, cat. 208, headless marble torso, probably originally bearing a portrait head, h. 174.5 cm. Published: Vierneisel-Schlörb, 1979, 163–177, no.
15 with earlier literature.

D) Syon house, statue with a restored modern head of Livia. Vermeule, 1955,
147–148.

[106] Athens National Museum inv. 126. *LIMC* 4, 875 no. 375, s.v. "Demeter,"
(Luigi Beschi), with complete literature; Boardman, 1985, 182, fig. 144, refs. p. 246;
Ridgway, 1981, 138–141.

Relationship of the "Kore Albani" type to the Kore in the relief: Helbig[4] 4 no.
3342 (W. Fuchs); Vierneisel-Schlörb, 1979, 166; Bieber, 1977, 121.

[107] Supra n. 33.

Drusilla probably also appeared as Venus-Aphrodite in some of her public images—indeed, given the close association of her cult with that of Venus Genetrix, it would have been most surprising had she not. Her statue, on a scale equal to that of the cult image, stood in the temple of Venus Genetrix in Rome, identifying her closely with the lineage and destiny of the Julio-Claudian family.[108] Aside from its scale, we know nothing of the appearance of that image, but some statues of Drusilla could have followed the well-known Venus Genetrix type. None, unfortunately, survive intact, but a headless torso of the Venus Genetrix from the basilica at Otricoli, now wrongly restored as a portrait of Sabina, has good epigraphic evidence in its favor to support an identification as Drusilla.[109] Several inscriptions from Greece and Asia Minor call Drusilla "νεὰ Ἀφροδίτη," "new Aphrodite," and it is not unreasonable to assume that the statues that once stood on such statue bases translated that epithet into visual form.[110]

None of these divine associations, however, extend beyond the choice of type for the body of the statue. Drusilla's coiffure in every surviving replica is emphatically contemporary, with its stiff waves and regular, artificial ringlets, bearing no resemblance to Classical, Hellenistic, or even archaic Greek prototypes. The portraits of her mother Agrippina I, although she was never officially deified, are far more charismatic than those of her daughters. One posthumous replica of Drusilla's type, the handsome head in Munich (figures 116–117), displays a more flamboyant interpretation of the prototype, suitable for a *diva*. Drusilla's chubby face has been idealized to a nearly Classical oval, her neck has become slender and elongated, and her head has a graceful tilt and a subtly melancholy expression comparable to the sentimental treatment of her mother's posthumous likenesses from the time of Caligula. The shoulder-locks, instead of adhering to the neck, hung away from it, and are now broken away although the marble stumps are still visible. This is a difficult, virtuoso exercise of marble carving, but one that would have given the head a more elaborate contour and a more dramatic play of solids and voids than the efficiently compact lifetime portraits.

---

[108] Dio 59.11.2–3.
[109] Dareggi, 1982, 21–22 no. 5, figs. 32–33.
[110] Mikocki, 1995, 43, 184–85 nos. 228–233, *IG* XII 2 no. 172b = *IGR* IV, no. 78; *IGR* IV no. 145.

Drusilla, unlike her mother, was no political martyr, merely the victim of an untimely natural death, but in her posthumous images, as in those of Agrippina I, the better sculptors attempt to give visual expression to the spirit of mourning that moved Caligula to honor his dead sister so extravagantly. Her death, after all, was not only a personal but a dynastic blow: instead of producing Julio-Claudian sons, she had died childless. Compared with Caligulan portraits of her mother, however, the style of Drusilla's likeness even in the Munich head is less dramatic, and the coiffure remains strictly contemporary, without allusions to Classical sculpture.

Drusilla's deification receives no mention or representation on the coins of the Roman mint, only on the unofficial local coinages of the Greek provinces (figure 84). To have honored her on official issues of coins would have called attention to the fact that her mother, whose *carpentum sestertii* had only recently been issued and were probably still in abundant circulation, did not receive the ultimate posthumous honor, and would thus have reflected poorly on the *pietas* of the emperor. Caligula may have intended eventually to deify his parents; indeed, had not the unexpected event of Drusilla's death caused him to hastily change his plans, Agrippina I might have become either the first Roman *diva*, or the second, after Livia. We can, of course, never know for certain, but it is clear that Agrippina I retained her seniority in sculptural groups of the imperial family.

One such group from the basilica at Velleia demonstrates this hierarchy of living and dead family members in a context securely datable to Caligula's principate.[111] The most obvious distinctions among the statues of the group are of scale: Augustus and Livia, the founding couple, were the largest male and female statues respectively. Agrippina I's statue (figures 87–88) is smaller than Livia's (figures 45–46), but considerably larger in scale than that of Agrippina II (figures 118–119), which is probably a later addition to the group from the time of Claudius. A headless statue that probably represented Drusilla was also smaller in scale than either of the more senior women, despite the fact that her inscription indicates that she had already been deified.[112] Here, on the other hand, the

---

[111] Rose, 1997, 121–126 no. 50 with full earlier literature. The inscriptions found with the statues identify Drusilla, but not Livia, as "Diva," giving clear termini post and ante quem of 38 and 41. See Jucker, 1977, 207.

[112] On the various identifications proposed for the female statues from Velleia, see: Saletti, 1968, 33–37 no. 4; 103–119; Goethert, 1972, 238–244; Jucker, 1977,

statue followed a Classical prototype for Demeter or Kore, the so-
called "Kore of Praxiteles" type in which the mantle wraps diagonally around the body and is drawn up over the left breast and
shoulder. This was the same format in which Livia had already
appeared in at least one and probably two statues of Tiberian date
(figures 43–44). At Velleia, on the other hand, Livia and the other
women of the group wear drapery generally inspired by Classical
style, but do not assume the form of specific goddesses.[113]

Assuming that the head of Drusilla's statue at Velleia followed the
same type we have identified in the Caere statue and its replicas,
on the other hand, her appearance would have differed from that
of her mother and great-grandmother in another respect. Livia's
statue at Velleia followed the late portrait type with the hair parted
in the middle and drawn back in soft waves over the ears, its full-
ness and texture suggested by deep drill channels, while a little fringe
of escaping locks over the forehead (a rarity in replicas from the
Latin speaking west, but far more common in Greece and Asia
Minor) suggest additional spontaneity. The hair of Agrippina I visible
under her veil formed the usual spontaneous-looking mass of burgeoning curls, articulated here with deep, extensive drill-work, and
without the tendency toward regularization visible in some later replicas. Drusilla's hair would have shared with her great-grandmother's
portrait (figure 46) waves of hair flowing from a central part and
escaping strands along the forehead, although in Drusilla's case they
would have taken the form of neat curls rather than a soft, spontaneous fringe. With her mother (figure 88) she would have shared
small, tight curls with drilled centers around the face. But her coiffure
would have been stiffer and more controlled than either Livia's or
the elder Agrippina's, since the fashion that she and Agrippina II
wore during their brother's principate allowed sculptors very little
chance to suggest spontaneity.

The better preserved statue of her sister Agrippina II (figures
118–119), probably a later addition, likewise shows a primly controlled although ornate coiffure. In this rather rare type, preserved

205–207. I would agree with Goethert and Jucker that Saletti's no. 4, the tallest
female statue, matches Livia's Tiberian-period "adoption" type with the middle part,
that the identification of no. 3 as Agrippina I is uncontested, that no. 2 (Saletti pp.
26–30, 120–123) is Agrippina II, and that the headless statue must by process of
elimination be Drusilla.
[113] Rose, 1997, 75–76; 125. On the "Kore of Praxiteles" type in portrait statuary: Caputo and Traversari, 1976, 78–79.

in only two replicas, the younger Agrippina's hair forms waves that
have been plastered flat against her scalp into neatly scalloped rows.
Since the Naples replica betrays signs of recutting, portraitists may
have opted for this rather odd coiffure shortly after Agrippina II's
marriage to Claudius as a solution to the problem of recutting her
image from those of her disgraced predecessor Messalina.[114] In the
Velleia statue, the entire head has been replaced, again, probably,
on a body that originally belonged to a portrait of Messalina, but
the sculptor of the new head followed the prototype currently in
favor. Whatever the reason for the coiffure of this short-lived type,
it has the same pretty but neatly controlled quality as the hairstyle
that Agrippina II and her sisters wore a few years earlier. All of
these fashions are nonetheless ornate and complex, requiring the long
labors of at least a few ladies' maids with the curling iron. Agrippina II, Drusilla, and Livilla II evidently shared their brother's taste
for public ostentation and eye-catching dress; that is, at any rate,
how they appear in the sculptural types made under his patronage
and distributed during his principate.

The youngest of the sisters, Livilla II, must also have been represented, but the identification of her images remains problematic.
Rose identifies her in the Leptis-Malta portrait type discussed in the
previous chapter, but if this is true, then at least eight replicas of
her portraits survive—two more than those either of her deified sister Drusilla or of the Caligulan portrait type of Agrippina II. Accidents
of preservation could of course help to account for the survival of
so many portraits from a relatively short time, but as mentioned
above, the question remains open whether this represents Livilla II
or her older namesake, the wife of Drusus II.

Conclusions

During the reign of Caligula, both *princeps* and Senate abandoned
the last vestiges of pretense that imperial power derived its legitimacy

---

[114] Parma, Museo Nazionale di Antichità inv. 830, marble statue, h. 203 cm.
Rose, 1997, 122–124, no. 50, pls. 133, 148, 149; Fittschen-Zanker 3, 6, no. 5, n. 4,
"Typus I Neapel-Parma;" Saletti, 1968, 26–30; Jucker, 1977, 206.
   Naples, Museo Nazionale 6242. Published: Fittschen-Zanker 3, 6, no. 5 n. 4,
"Typus I: Neapel-Parma," a, with earlier literature; Saletti, 1968, 120; Ruesch,
1911, 18 no. 63. The Naples statue has oddly spaced drill holes in the hair that
are probably the remains of a coiffure with rows of ringlets around the face.

from anything but dynastic descent. Augustus had insisted that his
prospective heirs prove themselves in military and public service—a
requirement that in more than one case led to their untimely deaths
from injuries incurred in military service.[115] It was Augustus's policy, rather than any sinister scheming among his family, that accounts
for the high rate of casualties among his prospective heirs. But
Caligula, who had never held a public office or done military service, succeeded to power solely because his father was Germanicus,
and received immediately all the powers that Augustus had accu-
mulated over a lifetime. With the open acknowledgement of the
dynastic and hereditary nature of power came a new openness in
acknowledging the political role of women of the imperial family,
through whom one could trace descent and plan the dynasty's future.
Portrait types still observed a hierarchical distinction between living
women and deified or heroized ancestresses; the recutting of so many
portraits of Drusilla suggests a makeshift effort to transfer her from
the company of the former to that of the latter. Even after her death,
however, her portraits remained less dramatic than those either of
the deified Livia or of Agrippina I.

---

[115] See Pollini, 1987, 2.

CHAPTER SIX

MESSALINA, AGRIPPINA II, CLAUDIA OCTAVIA, POPPAEA: THE WIVES OF CLAUDIUS AND NERO

Historical Information

The two last Julio-Claudian emperors, Claudius and Nero, both came to power under circumstances that made them dependant upon the assistance of others. Claudius was physically handicapped, probably with cerebral palsy, although the exact nature of his disability is impossible to reconstruct from the descriptions of the ancient authors, and this problem had created the false impression that he was mentally disabled as well.[1] His intellectual pursuits in historical and linguistic research disprove the latter opinion, but because Claudius had never been taken seriously as an heir to power and had been treated as an embarrassment by the imperial family, he had never held public office. At the time of his unexpected elevation to power after the assassination of Caligula in A.D. 41, he had no military or political experience. Nero, the stepson of Claudius, ascended to power at the age of only seventeen, even younger than Caligula had been, and his need for older mentors during the early years of his reign was a generally acknowledged fact.[2] In both cases, the political inexperience of the *princeps* provided an opportunity to ambitious women to parlay their ceremonial and dynastic importance into political power, not only through the men of their family but in their own right, an effort in which Messalina failed disastrously but at which Agrippina II enjoyed a longer period of success before her final fall and assassination. The latter woman seems to have aspired not only to wield power but to have her position publicly recognized: *auctoritas*, as opposed to mere influence behind the scenes.[3]

During the early years of both principates, the emperor's ancestresses and his mother took pride of place in coinage and public

---

[1] Suet. *Claud.* 2–6; Levick, 1990, 13–16.
[2] Suet. *Nero* 8–9.
[3] Levick, 1990, 53.

ceremony as the most important of his female relatives, a tradition
that by then was well-established in the public presentation of the
imperial family. Almost immediately upon his accession to the principate, therefore, Claudius deified Livia, deliberately modeling her
cult on that of Augustus with honors such as the chariot drawn by
elephants that carried her image around the Circus at official games.
He thus elevated both members of the dynasty's founding couple to
nearly equal status, for the obvious reason that Livia was his own
paternal grandmother, whereas he could not trace his ancestry directly
back to Augustus. Livia's flamboyantly goddess-like images from this
period have already been discussed in the second chapter. Claudius
also, like Caligula before him, made a great show of *pietas* toward
his parents that stopped just short of deification, acknowledging a
seniority in which the founding couple of the dynasty outranked
more recently deceased persons, but according them all greater honors
than would be granted to a living person. His mother Antonia Minor
thus became the second most important woman in dynastic imagery
after the Deified Augusta, with whom she shared the latter title if
not the former: she had declined the title "Augusta" while still alive,
but Caligula and Claudius conferred it on her posthumously.[4]

In the early years of Nero's reign, on the other hand, the emperor's
mother, Agrippina II, was still alive, and determined to play a more
than symbolic role in government. Nero, like his predecessors, made
a few initial demonstrations of *pietas* toward his mother, but her
power struggles with her son and with his male advisers like Seneca
eventually led to an open rupture, her disappearance from public
imagery, and her eventual assassination. Before her fall, however,
the prominence of her portraits on coinage and in sculpture, and
the rich variety of their interpretations, accurately reflects her situation: she was the first wife of an emperor since Livia to survive her
husband and continue as a figure of power during the principate of
her son, the first woman since Livia to hold the title of Augusta during her lifetime, and the first woman ever to receive that title while
her husband was still alive. Like Livia before her, she is known to
have had provincial clients, most notably Ara Ubiorum (modern

---

[4] Suet. *Claud.* 11.2 for honors to Livia and to Antonia. Barrett, 1990, 62, points
out that the Arval records first identify Antonia with the title "Augusta" in 38, after
her death but before the accession of Claudius; contrary to Suetonius's assertion,
then, Claudius was not, then, the first to grant it to her.

Cologne), the city of her birth in Germany, for which she obtained the status of a Roman colony.[5] Also like Livia, she had personal friendships with members of the Jewish royal family, and may have used her influence with Claudius on their behalf on at least one recorded occasion; we may infer many others in which she represented the interest of provincial friends and clients.[6] Her presence at the surrender of Caractacus, seated on a dais alongside that of Claudius, implies a public acknowledgment and institutionalization of her role in foreign and provincial affairs.[7]

It is hardly surprising, therefore, that cities and private patrons throughout the empire honored her as their benefactor with public statues: Rose documents her presence in 11 groups of Claudian or Neronian date, ranging in location from Italy and Gaul to Greece and Asia Minor.[8] Her representation in groups is about equal, then, to that of Antonia Minor. Unlike Antonia's image, which faithfully follows the Wilton House type with only minor variations, Agrippina II's is more dynamic, demonstrating the creation of at least two new portrait types for her during the principate of Claudius and one more possibly from after the succession of Nero. The replicas of these types, moreover, display the sort of imaginative adaptation by copyists also documented in those of Livia, the woman whose position in the imperial family Agrippina II's most closely resembled. Livia's portraits of course survive in far greater numbers, but the circumstances of the two women's deaths easily explain the discrepancy. Livia's memory was held in honor, and her portraits continued to be replicated without interruption, whereas Agrippina II, officially at least, was declared a traitor and public enemy.[9] Not until

---

[5] Tac. *Ann.* 12.27.1–2; *Germ.* 28; Barrett, 1996, 114–115.

[6] Barrett, 1996, 125–26; Josephus, *AJ* 20.134–6; *BJ* 2.243. Josephus does not know as a matter of record that Agrippina II intervened on behalf of the Jews with Claudius, but speculates that she did so in response to a request by Agrippa II of the Jewish royal family.

[7] Tac. *Ann.* 12.37.5–6; Barrett, 1996, 123–24.

[8] Rose, 1997, 83–86 no. 5; 113–15, no. 42 pl. 116; 116–118 no. 45 (Agrippina II's presence here appears uncertain); 120–121 no. 49; 121–126 no. 50; 129 no. 54; 130–31, no. 57; 141 no. 72; 147–149 no. 80 (if Rose is correct, there were at least two portraits of Agrippina II at Olympia, one statue, now headless, found in the Metroon and another, with her Claudian-type portrait head, from outside the Heraion); 163–64 no. 103; 164–169 no. 105 (Agrippina II is represented twice on the Sebasteion reliefs, in a Claudian panel and another datable after Nero's accession).

[9] Tac. *Ann.* 14.12.

long after the death of the emperor Nero could she be rehabilitated and represented in a relatively few posthumous images.

Agrippina II, like Antonia Minor, was well represented in coin likenesses that allow in turn for secure identification of her sculptural portraits. Her predecessor Messalina, and the wives of Nero, in contrast, present far more problems. At least two sculptural portraits probably, in my opinion, represent Messalina, but this identification must remain only a working hypothesis; I am under no illusion that my arguments about the iconography of this woman will meet with any wider scholarly acceptance than other proposed identifications. The prominence of Agrippina II during the period of her marriage to Claudius in contrast to that of Messalina reflects Claudius's increasingly open acknowledgment of the power of the women of his family, although if my identification of Messalina's portraits is correct, these works illustrate that the honors to Agrippina II grew logically out of an existing trend. During Nero's reign, in contrast, the wives of the emperor vanish almost entirely from coinage with the exception of Poppaea, the mother of his only child, who appears only as a tiny full-length figure with that of the emperor (figure 146). The portrait types of Claudia Octavia as an adult and of Statilia Messalina have yet to be recognized with any certainty or even probability in monumental sculpture. Their relative invisibility reflects their relative lack of power, and perhaps the fact that both Claudia Octavia and Poppaea were more political liabilities than assets to their husband. Let us first, however, consider the roles and images of the women of the reign of Claudius.

Valeria Messalina

Two of Claudius's four marriages had ended before his elevation to the principate.[10] During those years, neither Claudius nor his children were taken seriously as potential heirs to power: it is therefore most unlikely that either of these two women, Plautia Urgulanilla or Aelia Paetina, enjoyed much public importance or would have been prominently represented in official art. Those early marriages produced a total of three children, but his son Drusus by Urgulanilla

---

[10] Suet. *Claud.* 26–27.

had died of a freak accident, prior to the ascension of Claudius to power, and he had disowned Claudia, who was born several months after his divorce from Urgulanilla. Only his daughter Antonia by Aelia Paetina was still a member of his family by the time he became emperor, and this daughter, for whom he arranged politically advantageous marriages, occasionally appears on provincial coinages.[11] (Figure 120). Her importance to Claudius was not great enough, however, to cause Antonia's mother to be represented in official art as part of the imperial family, although Suetonius and Tacitus report that after the fall of Messalina, Claudius considered a remarriage with Aelia Paetina.[12]

The picture is quite different for Messalina, who was married to Claudius when he became emperor, and for Agrippina II, who became his fourth wife after the disgrace and execution of Messalina. Valeria Messalina, descended through both parents from Augustus's sister Octavia Minor, (see appendix, chart no. 8), was a prominent member of the Julian family and the mother of Claudius's two children Britannicus and Claudia Octavia. The timing of her son's birth in A.D. 41 was a lucky accident for the imperial couple, coming soon after the accession of Claudius to power when the Senate and Roman public would have been delighted with evidence of a new beginning for the dynasty after the chaotic principate of Caligula. The Senate offered Messalina the title of Augusta on this occasion.[13] The date of Claudia Octavia's birth is more problematic; Suetonius implies that she was the elder child, in which case she would have been born before her father's accession to power. But if the information of Tacitus is correct that Claudia Octavia was in her twentieth year at the time of her exile in 62, then she must have been born after Britannicus, in late 42 or early 43.[14] Whatever the birthdate of

[11] Trillmich, 1978, 150–152; Banti-Simonetti, *CNR* 16 (1978) 35 nos. 1, 1/1; *BMCRE* 1, 199 no. 242 pl. 34, fig. 8, on which the obverse represents Messalina, while all three of Claudius's children appear on the reverse, and *BMC Cappadocia* 46 no. 13 pls. 8,9, on which Claudius appears on the obverse and his two daughters Claudia Antonia and Claudia Octavia appear on the reverse.

[12] Suet. *Claud.* 26.3; Tac. *Ann.* 12.2.

[13] Levick, 1990, 55–57; Suet. *Claud.* 26.2, 27.1–2; Dio 60.12.5; *RE* 15, ser. 2 (1955) 246–251 no. 403, s.v. "Valeria Messalina" (Gertrud Herzog-Hauser – Friedrich Wotke); *PIR* 3, 381, no. 161. For my own more extensive discussion of Messalina's historical role and presentation in art, see Wood, 1992, 219–234.

[14] Tac. *Ann* 14.64; Suet. *Claud.* 27.1; *RE* 3 pt. 2, 2894–2895, s.v. "Claudia Octavia" (Brassloff); *RE* 15, ser. 2 (1955) 246 no. 403, s.v. "Valeria Messalina" (Gertrug Herzog-Hauser – Friedrich Wotke).

Claudia Octavia, however, Messalina embodied both the past of the Julio-Claudian dynasty and Claudius's hope for its continuation. Her dynastic and symbolic importance, combined with Claudius's apparently genuine affection for her, gave her enormous influence with the emperor.[15] Claudius, however, appears to have believed that propriety demanded a clear subordination of her honors to those of his mother and grandmother: he did not allow her to accept the title of *Augusta* when the Senate offered it to her in A.D. 41.[16] He did, however, grant her the privileges of an honorary Vestal, just as Caligula had done for Antonia and for his sisters. She was permitted to ride within the city limits in a *carpentum*, an honor that she and Claudius very prominently displayed when she accompanied his triumphal procession in A.D. 44.[17]

Messalina was not, however, without competitors both for power and for the emperor's affections, and by the year 47 may have had good reason to fear for the security of her own position. Agrippina II and Livilla II, both condemned for adultery and for treasonable conspiracy against Caligula, had returned from exile to an enthusiastic public welcome. Not only were both of them daughters of Germanicus, still beloved despite the disastrous principate of his son, but both now shared with their parents the status of martyrs of a tyrannical regime. Furthermore, they were descended from Augustus himself, through their mother Agrippina I (see appendix, chart no. 7), whereas Messalina could trace her ancestry only to his sister Octavia Minor. Although Agrippina II and Livilla II were still legally barred from a marriage with the brother of their father Germanicus, it was not difficult to see that Claudius could persuade the Senate to change the incest laws to allow for such a match, as indeed he later did.[18] Messalina allegedly succeeded in getting rid of Livilla II again, first through exile on another charge of adultery and then by murder, and of disposing of several personal and political enemies by similar means, but Agrippina II was a more formidable rival.[19]

---

[15] Suet. *Claud.* 36.

[16] Dio 60.12.5.

[17] Suet. *Claud.* 17.3.

[18] Popularity of Agrippina and Nero: Tac. *Ann.* 11.12. Change of incest laws to permit marriage to the daughter of a brother: Tac. *Ann.* 12.5–6. See also Griffin, 1984, 27–29.

[19] On the exile and murder of Livilla II: Dio 60.8.4–5; Tac. *Ann.* 14.63.2; Suet. *Claud* 29.1; Sen. *Apocol.* 10.4. On Messalina's other alleged uses of trumped-up

As Levick has plausibly suggested, Messalina may have been driven by fears for herself and her son Britannicus when she entered into extramarital relationships with powerful men. Like Julia before her, she was certainly guilty of adultery, but probably also of more than that. She must surely have been acting on more than mere affection or lust when she took the extraordinary step of marrying her lover L. Silius in the presence of witnesses.[20] Bigamy, under Roman law, was impossible: a second marriage constituted a *de facto* divorce from the previous husband or wife. By marrying Silius, then, Messalina voluntarily sacrificed her legal position as the wife of the reigning emperor, yet according to Tacitus, she and Silius believed that such a step was in her interests, that "Messalina would have the same power, with added security, if they circumvented Claudius..."[21] Whether the couple planned to undertake an immediate *coup d'etat* or to keep their marriage secret until Claudius's natural death, at which time Silius could use his marriage to Messalina and adoption of Britannicus as a justification for taking power, must remain in the realm of speculation, because the couple's recklessness led to their prompt downfall.[22] Claudius's freedman Narcissus learned of the marriage, informed the emperor of it, and apparently managed to convince him that the couple expected to be supported by an uprising of the army and the people in an immediate bid for power.[23] Claudius, taking the threat seriously, ordered Messalina's arrest and summary execution.

Agrippina II

Messalina's fall was of course an acute embarrassment to Claudius, but left the way open for a marriage to Agrippina II in A.D. 49. Agrippina II supplied him not only with a much-needed ally, but

---

charges to eliminate other personal enemies: Tac. *Ann.* 11.1–3; Suet. *Claud.* 37.2; Dio 60.14.1–4; Barrett, 1996, 98–100; 104–105.

[20] Levick, 1990, 65–67; Suet. *Claud.* 26.2.

[21] Tac. *Ann.* 11.26: "mansuram eandem Messalinae potentiam, addita securitate, si praevenirent Claudium..."

[22] Griffin, 1984, 29 believes that the couple did intend to assassinate Claudius; Levick, 1990, 64–67, suggests that they had a more cautious plan of waiting until his natural death before making a bid for power.

[23] Tac. *Ann.* 11.30; Suet. *Claud.* 36.

with a ready-made heir, her son Lucius Domitius, who as the adopted
son of Claudius took the name of Nero.[24] Messalina's fall had inevitably
cast discredit on her children and raised doubts of their paternity.
Nero would make a more acceptable successor than Britannicus,
since there were precedents from the time of Augustus onward for
succession by an adopted heir who was not the emperor's own son
or even his closest male relative. Agrippina II's demonstrated fertility, meanwhile, offered the possibility of additional children, although
she and Claudius did not after all produce children of their own.[25]
Claudius appears to have presented this match to the public as a
new beginning, a line of propaganda that comes to dominate coinage
by 52–53 B.C.

The coin types that the Roman mint had issued since the accession of Claudius continued for a few years after his remarriage, but
were then replaced with a set of issues placing a consistent emphasis
on Agrippina II, her parents and her son Nero.[26] (Figures 85, 121–122).
Nero's marriage to Claudia Octavia in A.D. 53, the same year as
these issues of coins, secured his position not only as adoptive son
but as son-in-law of Claudius, and potentially as the father of Claudius's
grandchildren, an arrangement that might have helped reconcile
Claudius to passing over his own son in the succession.[27] If Tacitus
is correct about Claudia Octavia's age at the time of her exile, the
marriage must have taken place when she was only ten or eleven
years old, far younger than the Roman norm, but if she was in fact
Britannicus's older sister, born in A.D. 40 instead of 42, she would
have been a slightly more believable 13. Despite the efforts at an
alliance between Claudius's adopted son and his own children, a
power struggle between them was more or less inevitable, but Nero's
prominence on coins of the Roman mint (figure 122), contrasted
with the invisibility of Britannicus, leave little doubt as to who was
winning that contest in the final years of the emperor's life.

The succession of Nero may have been Agrippina II's single greatest political concern, but was far from her only one. Like Livia, she

---

[24] See Barrett, 1996, 95–99, on the political motives for the marriage of Agrippina
to Claudius.
[25] Tac. *Ann.* 12.6; in a speech in the Senate, Vitellius cited Agrippina's fertility
as a strong argument in favor of her marriage to Claudius.
[26] Trillmich, 1978, 55–63.
[27] Tac. *Ann.* 12.3–4; Suet. *Claud.* 27, *Nero* 7; *RE* 3, 2896, no. 428, s.v. "Claudia
Octavia" (Brassloff).

appears to have been her husband's partner in power; her activities on behalf of provincial clients has already been detailed above. She engaged as well in another activity unusual for women, that of writing her own version of history. At some point in her life, possibly during her first exile on Pontia, she composed a history of the Julio-Claudian family, copies of which survived her death long enough to provide source material for both Tacitus and Pliny the Elder.[28] The work was undoubtedly self-serving and propagandistic; the one specific reference to it in Tacitus occurs in the middle of a series of anecdotes all of which portray her mother Agrippina I as the wronged victim of Tiberius and Sejanus, in a manner that perhaps parallels her plight to that of Agrippina II during the latter's first exile or later period of estrangement from Nero. Agrippina II, perhaps even better than the males of her family, obviously understood the political importance of manipulating opinion by controlling perception of the past. Indeed, she was the only one of Germanicus's children to succeed in exploiting her beloved father's mystique, an advantage that Caligula had very quickly squandered, but that served Agrippina II well throughout her life. Even in the final crisis that led to her assassination, the Praetorian guard remained adamantly loyal to her. When Seneca asked Burrus whether the soldiers should be ordered to kill her as an enemy of the emperor, the latter responded that the Praetorians would not harm a child of Germanicus—this despite the fact that they had killed Caligula in A.D. 41.[29]

Agrippina II, like Messalina, is painted by Roman historians as a thoroughly unscrupulous woman who both used and abused her influence with Claudius to eliminate personal enemies and potential rivals. It is certainly not my intention here to attempt a revisionist defense of Agrippina II: the nature of court politics and of the constant struggle for succession in a monarchical system can indeed promote viciously self-interested actions. Both Barrett and Levick rightly

---

[28] Tac. *Ann.* 4.53; Pliny *NH* 7.46. At the time when she threatened to present Britannicus in the Praetorian camp, Tacitus appears to imply that she also threatened Nero with exposure of the entire history of the Julio-Claudian family: Tac. *Ann.* 13.14. For speculation on the date of composition, see Griffin, 1984, 23. Barrett, 1996, 5–6, notes that any elite woman would have been literate and educated, so that she could educate her own sons.

[29] Tac. *Ann.* 14.7: "ille praetorianos toti Caesarum domui obstrictos memoresque Germanici nihil adversus progeniem eius atrox ausuros respondit: perpetraret Anicetus promissa." See Barrett, 1996, 22–23, 118–120, 143–145, 189.

observe that modern readers would be wise to take descriptions of such behavior seriously.[30] Agrippina II was moreover the product of a society that encouraged women to act indirectly, through their familial and sexual roles, and therefore whether intentionally or not encouraged women to learn devious and manipulative forms of behavior. Griffin describes a similar phenomenon among slaves and freedmen: people born into a condition that puts their lives in the hands of others will, if they are intelligent, frequently learn to survive by telling their masters what the latter want to hear.[31] A ruler like Claudius who depended on the close advice and assistance of freedmen, therefore, was virtually asking for flattery and deception. Agrippina II, by the time of her marriage to Claudius, was the veteran of bitter political struggles within her immediate family that had cost the lives of her mother and two older brothers, caused her exile and that of her sister, and endangered her own life more than once. It would be surprising if such a past had not made her paranoid, and encouraged her to pursue her own interests by any means possible, regardless of ethics. Caligula was, for example, probably quite justified in sending her into exile for adultery with Lepidus, the widower of Drusilla. Agrippina II, like Julia the daughter of Augustus and Messalina, was probably prepared to use sexual liaisons when necessary to obtain powerful allies.

The fact that Agrippina II's devious ruthlessness was a product of her environment in no way exonerates her of responsibility for her own actions. Octavia Minor, the sister of Augustus, and Antonia Minor were products of the same society, the same dynasty and the same turbulent period of history, yet all available evidence indicates that those women conducted themselves toward others with integrity. Livia, whom Tacitus portrays with as much hostility as he does Agrippina II, seems to have pursued some goals beyond mere self-interest, in practicing philanthropy to enable families to raise children, financing their daughters' dowries to promote marriage, and founding or restoring temples and cults that encouraged desired moral reforms and social goals.[32] Some might see Livia as cynically positioning herself to represent "family values" and thus to enhance her own image as the ideal wife, but she did, in the contemporary ver-

---

[30] Barrett, 1996, xii–xiii, 107–8; Levick, 1990, 78–79.
[31] Griffin, 1984, 87–89.
[32] Flory, 1984, 319; Dio 58.2.2–3.

nacular, "put her money where her mouth was" to encourage marriage and child-rearing. Agrippina II may also have practiced philanthropy, since many provincial cities honor her with portraits and inscriptions, and exercised beneficial interventions on their behalf, but her only political goal throughout her life, the only ideology that seems to have mattered to her, was obtaining and then keeping the power of the principate for her own bloodline.

On the other hand, the tone of writers like Tacitus and Suetonius when describing Agrippina II should give us pause: the degree of hatred that these writers display must be understood in a larger context. All are writing from the perspective of hindsight: they know that Nero was a disastrously bad ruler who displayed defects of character from the earliest years of his principate despite an early period of apparent good government, and they were naturally inclined to blame such innate flaws on his parents.[33] All of them also understood that, although there were some precedents for her official role in that of Livia, Agrippina II had attempted more openly than any woman before her to encroach on traditionally male privileges. As noted above, for example, she had sat on a dais beside Claudius in front of the legionary standards when he received Caratacus and his family after granting clemency to them, a type of behavior that she later tried to repeat during Nero's principate when he received an Armenian delegation.[34] In the latter case, however, she attempted to go even farther, and to sit beside the emperor on his own dais, implying an equality of power. On this occasion, Agrippina II quickly learned the limits of tolerable behavior: Nero, on the advice of Seneca, descended from the dais to greet her, making a show of paying respects to his mother, but also preventing her from joining him.

Agrippina II was the first and only woman in Roman history to demand real, and official, power as opposed to influence, a behavior that arouses fear and hostility in some men, and as such provided a focal point for distrust of monarchical power. A woman who could wield power by virtue of her position as wife or mother embodied the unaccountable and therefore potentially unscrupulous nature of

---

[33] See Griffin, 1984, 50–66 and 83–99, and Barrett, 1996, 239, on the pattern described by the historians of a period of good government followed by a "turning point" toward tyranny at which Nero's true evil nature began to emerge.

[34] On the reception of Caratacus: Tac. *Ann.* 12.37. On the Armenian delegation to Nero: Dio 61.3.3–4. For discussion of the implications of these events, see Barrett, 1996, 123–24, 164–65.

such a regime, although in fact the imperial women owed their power
to their familial roles no more than did the men. Every emperor
from Tiberius onward had claimed power largely by virtue of his
parentage and ancestry; indeed, even Augustus had based his initial
claims to authority on his status as the adopted son of Julius Caesar.
But the representation of every unpopular prosecution or official
action as the work of someone acting behind the scenes for secret
motives could more easily arouse the anger and fear of the readers
to whom Tacitus was addressing his account of events, and such
actions could be portrayed as even more outrageous if they violated
societal norms for female conduct. Whether Tacitus himself was himself misogynistic in a pathological sense or merely making convenient use of prejudice and stereotype for rhetorical purposes can be
argued endlessly and is irrelevant: the fact remains that his portrayals
of all the Julio-Claudian women, but in particular of Livia and
Agrippina II, rely heavily on such negative stereotypes.[35] Early in his
account of her marriage to Claudius, Tacitus states his own opinion
that her ascension to power subjected the Roman state to a tyranny
that was "almost masculine." He later expresses a similar condemnation of her through the voice of another person, the freedman
Narcissus, who accuses her of "typically female lack of self-control,"
(*impotentiam muliebrem*) and "excessive ambition" (*nimiasque spes*).[36]

This latter statement appears in the context of an incident in
which Agrippina II was almost certainly in the right and Narcissus
in the wrong, as Tacitus narrates the facts. In A.D. 52, Claudius
twice attempted to inaugurate an ambitious public engineering project, a tunnel through the mountain between the Fucine Lake and
the river Liris. On both occasions, he planned grand ceremonial
events, involving staged battles and impressive public appearances
by the imperial couple in splendid regalia, but both times, the ceremony ended in embarrassment. The first time, the waterway proved

---

[35] See Barrett, 1996, 205–208 for a review of the scholarship on Tacitus's personal biases; Kaplan, 1979, 410–417 and Santoro L'Hoir, 1994, 5–25, for analy-
ses of the rhetorical patterns in his presentation of women who assume male roles
as dangerous and out of control.

[36] Tac. *Ann.* 12.7: "versa ex eo civitas et cuncta feminae oboediebant, non per
lasciviam, ut Messalina, rebus Romanis inludenti. Adductum et quasi virile servi-
tium . . ." and 12.57, on Narcissus' attack on Agrippina: "nec ille reticet, impotentiam muliebrem nimiasque spes eius arguens." See Barrett, 1996, 130; Santoro
L'Hoir, 1994, 17–25.

inoperable because it had not been sunk deep enough: it did not reach even halfway to the bottom of the lake. The second inauguration was an even worse fiasco: the unexpectedly powerful force of the water current swept away everything in the vicinity of the outlet, and nearly endangered the lives of the banqueters gathered to witness the opening. Narcissus, the freedman of Claudius, had been the direct supervisor of the project, and in the wake of this embarrassing debacle, Agrippina II accused Narcissus of graft and corruption that had resulted in unsatisfactory workmanship. Narcissus was a personal antagonist of Agrippina II's since the time of her marriage, but her charges regarding the Fucine Lake project probably had some basis. Clearly, Narcissus had been guilty at the least of incompetence, and probably also of graft: the failure of the project proved the shoddiness of the work. Narcissus seems to have made no effort to answer these charges on their merits, responding instead with the ad hominem, or ad feminam, statement quoted above. Yet Tacitus gives the rhetorical last word to Narcissus, ending his account of the debacle with his verbal attack on Agrippina II, rather than hers on him.[37]

The vilification of intelligent or powerful women throughout Western history, and particularly in Roman historiography, follows a form traceable later in Procopius's secret history of the reigns of Justinian and Theodora, and fully recognizable today in the character assassinations that anti-feminists routinely conduct against female public figures.[38] The elements of the stereotype are unbridled ambition, bloodthirstiness, sexual flagrancy, yet at the same time an ability to retain the loyalty of her husband with whom she smoothly collaborates in various crimes and conspiracies against mutual enemies. Attackers of such women routinely accuse them both of unfeminine frigidity and of promiscuity, loyalty to their husbands in the service of their ambitions and of adultery for the same reason. Tacitus, for example, claims that Agrippina II won over Claudius to marriage with her through her seductive wiles, exploiting her relationship to her uncle to visit him frequently, and implies that she began an affair with Claudius before their legal marriage. Unlike most purveyors of the stereotype, Tacitus is at least aware of its inherent

---

[37] On the Fucine Lake debacle: Tac. *Ann.* 12.56–57.
[38] Allen, 1992, 94–100. For a particularly egregious contemporary example, see Paglia, 1996.

contradictions and attempts to reconcile them, claiming that Agrippina II was chaste unless it suited her ambitions not to be, implying presumably that she maintained the devotion of Claudius through her fidelity to him. He later claims that the freedman Pallas was her lover as well as her political ally.[39]

Tacitus was one of the more scrupulous ancient historians in the factual accuracy of the information he reports, but was not and is not infallibly reliable. The recent discovery of inscriptions recording the condemnation of Cn. Piso vindicate the accuracy of some items that he reports, such as the intervention of Livia to obtain clemency for Plancina, but prove that in some others he either read his sources carelessly or willfully misrepresented information.[40] In matters of interpretation and analysis of character, his biases are frequently obvious, and his portrayals of both Agrippina II and Messalina merit critical scrutiny. Acknowledging that Agrippina II was most probably guilty of many of the offenses that historians charge does not necessarily require us to believe that she was guilty of all of them, and when crimes attributed to both women seem to follow the same *topos*, we may legitimately ask how valid either account is. An example is the woman's abuse of her power through the secret trial of a personal or political enemy.

Both women, according to Tacitus and later historians like Dio who presumably follow him, were the "éminences grises" behind prosecutions of a number of public figures, although in every case it was of course a man who brought the charges and conducted the prosecution. Charges against these various enemies could include political corruption, sexual misconduct, plotting against the emperor's life, or engaging in various forms of magic such as consultation of fortune tellers, but in every case, Tacitus claims to know of a hidden agenda: Messalina, for example, supposedly coveted the estate of Valerius Asiaticus; Agrippina II had charges brought against Statilius Taurus for almost identical motives of personal greed.[41] Yet in the former case, during the private trial of Asiaticus, the accused man's defense moved Messalina to tears and caused her to leave the

---

[39] Tac. *Ann.* 12.3 (on her seduction of Claudius); 12.7 on her calculating chastity: "nihil domi impudicum, nisi dominationi expediret," 12.25 on alleged affair with Pallas. Suet., *Claud.* 26.3, tells a similar story of her courtship of Claudius prior to their marriage.

[40] Flower, 1996, 250–252, and 1997.

[41] Tac. *Ann.* 11.1; 12.59.

room abruptly, an episode that must have been observed by several witnesses. Tacitus adds that in a private conversation immediately afterward, she urged Vitellius not to allow Asiaticus to escape punishment, but Tacitus or his source would have as evidence of this conversation only the unsupported word of Vitellius, who had every reason to disclaim as much responsibility as possible for the unpopular prosecution, and perhaps to blacken the reputation of Messalina after her own disgrace. After this private hearing, Asiaticus committed suicide, an action that inevitably leaves the outcome of a prosecution in doubt: in this case, Tacitus chooses to interpret it as evidence of pride in the face of unjust charges, although in other cases, like the suicide of the alleged murderer of Germanicus, he is happy to interpret suicide as proof of guilt.[42] Agrippina II supposedly engineered a similar prosecution of Statilius Taurus, who had allegedly committed various acts of extortion and magic during his recent term as provincial governor in Africa. She allegedly wanted to seize possession of his gardens, but his official accuser was his own lieutenant, Tarquitius Priscus, who might well have had good information of his superior's abuses of power. Priscus could also have had some personal grudge against Taurus that inspired him to bring malicious charges without the intervention of Agrippina II, but again, Tacitus claims to know the secret agenda, the conspiracy behind the scenes.[43]

The stereotype of the powerful woman, finally, is never complete without accusations of poisoning and of incest. Claudius, at the time of his death, was an old man who had long been in poor health, yet almost every ancient historian accepts it as a given that he died of poisoning at Agrippina II's hands, although Suetonius must concede that the stories are confused and contradictory.[44] Tacitus describes details about the administration of the poison that could only have been known to the persons directly involved in the alleged assassination, none of whom were ever prosecuted or apparently confessed.[45] Modern historians, including Griffin, who harbors no revisionist

---

[42] Suicide of Asiaticus: Tac. *Ann.* 11.3. Suicide of Piso: Tac. *Ann.* 3.15.

[43] Tac. *Ann.* 12.59. Barrett, 1996, 135–36, suggests that the charges against Taurus were warranted, but that Agrippina did indeed use his prosecution for gain, since the estate of Statilius Taurus was located near the Porta Maggiore, land that Claudius needed for the construction of aqueducts; had the land not been confiscated it, he would have had to pay for expropriation.

[44] Suet. *Claud.* 44.2–3. See Barrett, 1996, 140–142.

[45] Tac. *Ann.* 12.67.

sympathies for the emperor Nero or for Agrippina II, express doubts about these accounts, and suspect that perhaps Agrippina II's real offense consisted only of concealing Claudius's death until a convenient time, thus arousing suspicion of worse misconduct.[46] Charges of poisoning were of course unprovable in antiquity, before modern forensic methods existed for determining causes of death, a fact that modern readers of Roman history should bear in mind whenever such an accusation appears.[47]

Both Tacitus and Suetonius mention rumors that Agrippina II and Nero had an incestuous relationship. As in the case of similar accusations against Caligula and his sisters, however, we must regard with great skepticism this very common *topos* of political invective.[48] Tacitus has obviously heard several earlier accounts of this accusation: he quotes Cluvius as reporting that Agrippina II attempted to seduce Nero as a means of controlling him, implying that she failed in the attempt, but mentions also a conflicting account that Nero attempted to instigate the incestuous relationship. Here, however, as in every such case, we must remember the volatility of sexual gossip, and should ask how anyone besides the parties involved can really know for certain whether such a relationship exists. No one ever saw the couple engaged in sexual activity; Suetonius can only quote people who claimed that Nero's clothing was untidy and stained after riding in a sedan chair with Agrippina II. Experienced travelers are aware that clothes can become stained and rumpled for the most innocent of reasons during a journey. The logistics of having sexual intercourse in a moving sedan chair would, on the other hand, be extraordinarily difficult, especially when one of the two parties, Nero, was considerably overweight.

Whatever the truth concerning her character, Agrippina II does seem to have brought about her own political demise, in part at least, by a series of bad miscalculations about the acceptability of her public behavior. Coins and monuments of the early years of Nero's principate, to be discussed below, indicate that for a brief period, Agrippina II's power and the public acknowledgment of it

---

[46] Griffin, 1984, 32–33; Barrett, 1996, 142.
[47] Barrett, 1996, xiv–xv; Levick, 1990, 76–79 for a review of the circumstances surrounding the deaths of both Claudius and Britannicus, and the claims that both were murdered, which Levick is inclined to believe but considers unproven.
[48] Tac. *Ann.* 14.2; Suet. *Nero* 28.2.

were enormous, but her disappearance from coinage of the Roman mint after the second year of his principate may reflect an understanding that the presentation of a woman in such a role was doing more harm than good to the regime. Early in the principate of Nero, she possessed not only influence over the young princeps, but a network of allies that she had created within the Praetorian guard and the imperial freedmen.[49] She evidently intended also to act as the "regent" not only for her own son but for his stepbrother Britannicus, whom she at least once used as a pawn against Nero, threatening to present Britannicus to the Praetorians and to defend his rights as the son of Claudius.[50] The selection of Nero rather than the emperor's own son as heir had not been uncontroversial, and by playing the two rival princes off against one another, she probably thought that she could remain the most powerful member of the imperial family.[51] She was not content however to exercise power only behind the scenes but wanted some publicly recognized status. This demand to exercise her power visibly and openly may have been one of the factors, though surely not the only one, that provoked fatal opposition.

The incident at the reception of the Armenian delegation, which many observers must have witnessed, was a particularly visible manifestation of the power struggle that ensued in those years between Agrippina II, the mother of the teen-aged emperor, and his male, Senatorial advisors. It was Seneca, according to Tacitus, who advised Nero to prevent Agrippina from joining him on the imperial dais, and suggested the strategy of coming down to greet her.[52] By demanding official recognition of her authority, she not only overstepped the boundaries acceptable for a woman but violated Nero's own statement to the Senate upon his accession that he would keep the imperial house and the "republic" separate. This promise implied an end to the corrupt system under Claudius in which the emperor's wives and freedmen—people without official accountability—had enjoyed excessive power.[53]

---

[49] Griffin, 1984, 69; Barrett, 1996, 118–121, 127.
[50] Tac. *Ann.* 13.14.
[51] Josephus, *BJ* 2.249, suggests disapproval of Claudius's decision to pass over his own son in favor of Nero. He was of course writing after the death of Nero, with the knowledge that Nero's principate had been disastrous.
[52] Tac. *Ann.* 13.5.
[53] Tac. *Ann.* 13.4; Griffin, 1984, 69, 73, 87–88.

Agrippina II was acting more according to the expectations of her society, albeit illegally, when she listened to Senatorial deliberations from a hidden vantage-point behind a curtain, on the occasions when the Senate met at the Palatine.[54] Tacitus rightly describes this unauthorized eavesdropping as an abuse, but a society that expects women to exercise any sort of control indirectly and through others will inevitably teach intelligent women how to operate, literally and figuratively, from behind curtains. This was the social system that had shaped the younger Agrippina's character although she was obviously impatient with the limitations it placed on her.

The state religion of Rome did, however, afford women one highly prestigious means of public visibility, as priestesses of politically important cults. Agrippina II, as the priestess of the Deified Claudius, held a title and a ceremonial role that no imperial woman since Livia had enjoyed for any extended period. Antonia had held this title for only a few months before her death, when she was too feeble to make many public appearances in her priestly capacity. The prestige that her sacerdotal role conferred on Antonia had been largely posthumous, on the coins of the principate of Claudius that honored her (figure 55). Agrippina II, on the other hand, was young, vigorous, and had the potential to enjoy a long career in the public eye in a position that she was willing to exploit rhetorically. When she made her threat to present Britannicus in the Praetorian camp, Tacitus quotes her as invoking the shade of the Deified Claudius against her uncooperative son.[55] The speech must be his imaginative reconstruction of a private conversation, but the fact that Tacitus believes she would have said such a thing suggests that she was in the habit of invoking Divus Claudius when it suited her purposes. Small wonder then that it was she, not Nero, who was primarily responsible for the construction of the temple to the Deified Claudius that Nero eventually left unfinished. This large and ambitious project also included a public portico, perhaps deliberately modeled on those that Livia and Octavia Minor had patronized.[56] The Porticus Liviae in particular, which housed a small temple of Concordia, would have provided an obvious parallel to the later complex that

---

[54] Tac. *Ann.* 13.5.
[55] Tac. *Ann.* 13.14.
[56] Suet. *Vesp* 9; Seinby, 1993, 1, 277, s.v. "Claudius, Divus, Templum" (C. Buzzetti); Barrett, 1996, 148–50.

also celebrated the marital harmony of an imperial couple.[57]

The political situation during the year 54 may well have motivated Seneca's *Apocolocyntosis Claudii*, a bitter satire on the deification
of Claudius, which includes fulsome praise of the young Nero whom
he hails as ushering in a new and better era. Nero and his friends
must have had ambivalent feelings about the deification of Claudius,
which probably seemed politically necessary in A.D. 54 as a way of
demonstrating the *pietas* of the successor toward his adoptive father
and an official stamp of approval on the actions of Claudius, including his adoption of Nero.[58] Nonetheless, the consecration must also
have lent encouragement to the supporters of Britannicus, the son
of Claudius, who had at least as good a claim as Nero to succeed
his own father to power, and certainly enhanced the prestige of his
widow and priestess. A satire ridiculing the consecration therefore
undercut the positions of both Britannicus and Agrippina II.[59] Griffin
is skeptical of the extent to which the *Apocolocyntosis* had a specific
political agenda, pointing out that it does not mention Agrippina II's
suspected role in the death of Claudius nor the relationship of
Britannicus to the disgraced Messalina, which one would expect in
a work designed to undermine their positions. The satire, she argues,
was meant as little more than entertainment for a select audience
who had to pay public respect to the cult of Claudius but in private amused themselves by laughing at it.[60] In the very first year of
his principate, however, Nero's supporters could hardly call attention, even in private, to the fact that he had come to power as the
result of an assassination, if in fact this was true, which is far from
certain. During this delicate and unsettled early phase of his power,
criticism of his competitors for power, including his own mother,
had to be subtle and indirect. Even "preaching to the choir" has its
advantages in such situations, by encouraging a general attitude of
disrespect toward the deification of Claudius and, indirectly, toward
those who benefitted from it.

---

[57] On the Porticus Liviae: Flory, 1984, 309–330.

[58] Less than a century later, Antoninus Pius forced a reluctant Senate to deify
Hadrian on the grounds that failure to do so would constitute a vote of no-confidence
in his own adoption as successor: Dio, epitome of Book 70.1.2–3.

[59] Sen. *Apocol.* passim; Kraft, 1966, 120–121; Barrett, 1996, 165 and 202.

[60] Griffin, 1984, 97. Earlier, however, on page 40, she acknowledges that this
mockery of Claudius indicates "Agrippina's insecure grip on power."

Although the cult of Claudius remained in existence, it seems to
have received little attention after Agrippina II's murder in 59. When
the great fire of 64 damaged the unfinished Claudianum, Nero
modified it to become part of a nymphaeum of his Golden House,
rather than restoring the structure to its original purpose, and there
is no evidence that he intended to replace it with another temple
elsewhere.[61] A more concrete result of Agrippina II's threats and
intrigues was the apparent assassination of Britannicus, who died of
a seizure at the dinner table shortly after Agrippina II's threat to
defend his status as heir, and just before he was to come of age
legally. In this case, allegations of poisoning may very well be accurate, since the timing of the event seems too convenient for Nero's
purposes to be coincidental. Nonetheless, as with every alleged "poisoning" plot, there is no forensic evidence for murder, and possible natural causes for the death cannot be ruled out.[62] In any case, however,
the death of Britannicus demolished Agrippina II's hope to control
the two young princes by maintaining a balance of power between
them. Her horrified reaction to her stepson's death, which must have
been witnessed by many people at the dinner, made her personal
feelings clear.[63] She did not however give up her efforts to secure
allies against Nero within the imperial family, notably her surviving
stepchild Claudia Octavia, whom she now took as her protegé.[64]

As Nero's marriage to Claudia Octavia deteriorated, Agrippina II
became drawn into conflicts with her son that may have contributed
to her eventual fall, although they are unlikely to have been the only
cause. Since the marriage of Claudia Octavia and Nero had been
instrumental in establishing Nero as the heir and eventual successor
of Claudius, Agrippina II had an interest in preserving the union,
and therefore antagonized Nero by criticizing his extramarital affair
with a freedwoman named Acte. The effect of her interference was
to drive Nero away from her, and toward the guidance of Seneca,
who was not above pimping for the young emperor.[65] In A.D. 58,
Nero began a relationship with an aristocratic woman, Poppaea
Sabina that was not only embarrassing but dangerous to his union

---

[61] Seinby, 1993, 1, 277–278, s.v. "Claudius, Divus, Templum (Buzetti).
[62] Barrett, 1996, 171–72.
[63] Tac. *Ann.* 13.15–16 on murder of Britannicus; Griffin, 1984, 73–74.
[64] Tac. *Ann.* 13.18, 13.19.
[65] Tac. *Ann.* 13.12–13.

with Claudia Octavia, since Poppaea wanted marriage, something that he could reasonably contemplate with a woman of her rank.[66] The ancient authors allege that Agrippina II's antagonism toward this liaison convinced Nero that he must get rid of her, although as usual, Tacitus ascribes the final decision to the urging of a female agent behind the scenes, in this case Poppaea.[67] As Barrett has recently pointed out, however, the chronology of events does not support this explanation for the murder. Nero did not marry Poppaea until three years after Agrippina II's death.[68] It is far more likely that Nero could not accept Agrippina II's political power, and could find no other way of destroying it. Despite the silence of the ancient authors about her activities after the first two years of Nero's principate, there is good reason to believe that she continued to exercise power over her son's actions, just as Livia had done even during the last years of her life: ironically, the five good years of Nero's reign, the *"quinquennium Neronis"* that the emperor Trajan allegedly later praised may have been precisely those five years when Agrippina II was still alive.[69]

Historical accounts of the death of Agrippina II are lurid but remarkably consistent, indicating that in this case a political murder was so badly botched that the details became publicly known.[70] Nero had hoped to disguise the death as an accident: he invited his mother to Bauli, on the bay of Naples, where he entertained her at a lavish banquet and presented her with a luxurious yacht. After Agrippina II's party had set sail after dark, and was well away from shore, this yacht underwent some sort of prearranged accident, although here the accounts of the sources become more confused about the nature of the sabotage. However it was engineered, the simulated "shipwreck" went according to plan, but Agrippina II escaped and swam to safety. The next morning, she sent word to Nero of her survival, forcing Nero to deal in some other way with the woman who now not only opposed him but knew that he had attempted to kill her. His solution was to accuse her messenger of an attempt on his life and to have her summarily executed. Tacitus and Dio report

---

[66] Tac. *Ann.* 13.45–46.

[67] Tac. *Ann.* 14.1; *Octavia* 593–597.

[68] Barrett, 1996, 181–82.

[69] Barrett, 1996, 238–40; Aur. Vict. *Caes.* 5.

[70] Tac. *Ann.* 14.4–8; Suet. *Nero* 34.1–4; Dio 62.12–13; *Octavia* 593–645; Barrett, 1996, 181–195.

that she invited her killers to strike her through the womb that had given birth to her parricidal son, the sort of embellishment that may or may not be true but that no narrator of the event can resist repeating.

This powerful woman's great reversal of fortunes as the result of her own proud but flawed nature is the stuff of classic tragedy, and as such has appealed to playwrights like the unknown author of the *Octavia*, which survives with the writings of Seneca although it must have been written after his death, as well as to the composers Handel and Monteverdi as the raw material of opera. Even authors, including the writer of the *Octavia*, who had no sympathy for Agrippina II herself portray her murder as one of the greatest atrocities of Nero's infamous career.[71]

The Wives of Nero: Historical Information

In A.D. 62, Nero proceeded with his plans to divorce Claudia Octavia on the grounds of infertility and adultery. The former charge was at best premature, since a girl of nineteen (or twenty-one, if Tacitus has exaggerated her youth), whose marriage could not have been consummated very long ago, still had time to prove her ability to bear children. Nero inadvertently revealed the absurdity of the claim by later contradicting himself, when he accused her of having become pregnant by her lover and procured an abortion.[72] As for the charges of adultery, Roman writers seldom display sympathy to women accused of that offense, but in this case, the surviving accounts unanimously dismiss the charges against Claudia Octavia as transparent fraud. Tacitus approvingly relates that one of her slaves refused even under torture to incriminate her mistress, volunteering the opinion that Claudia Octavia's body was purer than her examiner's mouth.[73]

Despite the lack of evidence for his charges, Nero sent his wife into exile in Campania, only to discover that Claudia Octavia, as the daughter of the previous emperor, enjoyed greater public loyalty than he had expected. Her obviously unwarranted exile pro-

---

[71] *Octavia* 614–617: the ghost of Agrippina II appears to admit her own guilt in the deaths of Claudius and Britannicus; in lines 619–631, she predicts the coup that will cause Nero's downfall and death.

[72] Tac. *Ann.* 14.63.

[73] Tac. *Ann.* 14.60; Suet. *Nero* 35.1–2; Dio 62.13.1–2.

voked an outcry. It is unclear whether Nero actually did announce her recall or whether only false rumors to this effect circulated, but the belief that Claudia Octavia was about to return to Rome inspired a demonstration that became a riot, as her supporters stormed onto the Capitoline, tore down and vandalized Poppaea's images, decorated those of Claudia Octavia with flowers and carried them triumphantly on their shoulders through the forum and temples. The crowd reached the imperial residence on the Palatine before Nero resorted to military force to disperse the rioters.[74] This incident once again dramatizes the vital importance of portraits as political symbols and weapons, both in the service of the official line of propaganda and, on occasion, in opposition to it. It also, unfortunately, reminds us of the paucity of surviving evidence, since the images of Claudia Octavia that the crowd carried on their shoulders could not have been the heavy marble sculptures that form the bulk of our surviving evidence for the monumental portraits of all these women. A very large and excited crowd could possibly carry a hollow-cast bronze bust or statue, but the objects that figured in the riot of 62 were more probably painted panels or small works in lighter and more perishable materials.

The immediate effect of the riot on Nero, however, was to convince him that he must not only exile but kill Claudia Octavia, and to that end he finally obtained the "evidence" against her that he needed, by persuading Anicetus (his collaborator in the assassination of Agrippina II) to "confess" to adultery with Claudia Octavia. In his public statements, Nero, significantly, tried to depict this alleged relationship as an act of political treason: Claudia Octavia, he claimed, had seduced Anicetus in order to obtain power over his naval squadron. Knowing that the charges were fraudulent, he also understood that he must try to make them believable by ascribing to Claudia Octavia a plausible motive; using a sexual liaison as a means to gain power was behavior that the aristocracy of Rome in his time could understand. Anicetus, for his cooperation, received a comfortable exile in Sardinia, while Claudia Octavia was sent to the island of Pandateria and murdered only a few days later.[75] As with

---

[74] Tac. *Ann*, 14.61; *Octavia* 780–850; Pekáry, 1985, 141; *RE* 3 pt. 2 (1899), 2897 s.v. "Claudia Octavia" (Brassloff), *RE* 2nd ser. 22 (1953) 85–91, s.v. "Poppaea Sabina" (Hanslik).

[75] Tac. *Ann*. 14.62–63; *Octavia* 851–876, in which Nero claims that Octavia's

the assassination of Agrippina II, Nero's tactics for eliminating an
unwanted person were as incompetent as they were morally repug-
nant, and had the effect of turning public opinion against him, even
though a thoroughly cowed Senate and public cooperated with the
farce of public thanksgiving to the gods for deliverance from treason after Claudia Octavia's death.[76] The tragedy *Octavia* amounts to
a series of atrocity stories designed to justify the overthrow and death
of Nero, which must by the time of its composition have already
occurred, but which still needed political rationalization.

Nero's early accession to power for which he had neither train-
ing nor sufficient emotional maturity may have kept him somewhat
out of contact with political reality, but even he must have realized
the public outrage over his treatment of Claudia Octavia, and the
intense unpopularity of his marriage to Poppaea. For that reason,
perhaps, Poppaea's images are scarce and elusive. She, unlike Claudia
Octavia, did succeed in bearing a child to Nero, an event that Nero
celebrated with great public pomp, but since the baby died only a
few months later, many of the planned dedications of temples and
statues may never have taken place.[77] Nero, like Caligula before him,
salvaged a bad situation by deifying his baby daughter; if she could
never become the mother of imperial heirs, she, like Drusilla, could
at least become a symbolic protector of the Julio-Claudian line.
Poppaea became pregnant a second time but died before the child's
birth, the victim, according to both Suetonius and Tacitus, of Nero's
violent abuse. Nero's character gives us no reason to disbelieve this
account, although Claudia Octavia's supporters may have had reason
to circulate the story, as proof that her rival had come to a deservedly
bad end. In any case, Nero gave Poppaea an extravagant and unusual
funeral, embalming her body in the Ptolemaic manner rather than
cremating her, and eulogizing her as a great beauty and the mother
of a deified child. Tacitus acerbically observes that these were accidents of fate, rather than virtues, a remark that aptly summarizes
much of his hostility toward powerful women, who generally owed
their power to birth or marriage rather than merit.[78] In this regard,

---

ability to arouse public wrath (*populi furor*) constitutes treason and requires him to
put her to death.
[76] Tac. *Ann.* 14.63–64.
[77] Tac. *Ann.* 15.23.
[78] Suet. *Nero* 35.2; Tac. *Ann.* 16.6.

however, they were not very different from the males of the Julio-Claudian dynasty by the time of Nero, when accession to power depended almost entirely on descent rather than proven ability.

After Poppaea's death, Nero married once more, to a woman named Statilia Messalina.[79] This woman survived the coup that caused Nero's suicide, and apparently retained enough public honor to cause Otho, one of Nero's would-be successors in the civil wars of 68–69 to consider marriage with her.[80]

Of the wives of Claudius, only Agrippina II can be identified with any certainty in well-established portrait types. Messalina and her children present more difficulty, although there are a few extant objects that may cast some light on the public images of this woman and her daughter Claudia Octavia. Those of Agrippina II, however, are far more informative. Although Agrippina II's image in literature is uniformly negative, artistic monuments tell a somewhat different story: at least one portrait from long after her death strongly suggests that there were efforts to rehabilitate her, and that some remembered her with admiration, possibly even affection. Whatever the nature of Agrippina II's character, her prominence in Claudius's dynastic politics, and the ubiquity of her image, is undeniable. She, unlike her predecessor Messalina, does appear in clear portrait likenesses on coins of the Roman mint throughout the period of her marriage to Claudius, with the result that her portraits in monumental sculpture are securely identifiable. During that five-year period, not only were older portraits of her from the principate of Caligula recopied and distributed, but at least two and possibly three new official types were created, a remarkable flurry of artistic activity for such a brief period. We can infer that sculptors were attempting to meet a heavy demand for images of the Augusta for public statuary groups of the imperial family in cities throughout the empire. In the early years of the principate of Nero, both coins and public monuments document the continuing prominence of her likenesses. After her assassination, Nero apparently attempted something approximating a *damnatio memoriae* against his mother, although no such measure was ever legally passed: the tragedy *Octavia* describes his determination to destroy her images and erase her name from public

---

[79] *RE* 2nd ser. 3, 2209–2210, s.v. no. 45, "Statilia Messalina" (Nagl); Suet. *Ner.* 35.1. Tac. *Ann.* 15.68 mentions her as Nero's mistress prior to their marriage.
[80] Suet. *Otho* 10.2.

inscriptions.[81] The number of portraits and inscriptions that nonetheless survive demonstrate either that this information is not accurate
or that Nero's orders were very unevenly carried out.

Messalina, and her daughter certainly appeared in sculptural groups
as well; the two portraits of Claudia Octavia identifiable beyond
doubt are the portraits of her as a child from the Claudian groups
at Baia (figures 69–71) and Rusellae. As for the wives of Nero, no
coins of the Roman mint record their portrait profiles, although
Poppaea did appear as a tiny full-length figure on one issue.[82] (Figure
146). The incident described above, however, when a crowd stormed
the Capitoline, vandalized Poppaea's images and carried around those
of Claudia Octavia, proves beyond doubt that likenesses of both
women stood in a very prominent public place, even before Poppaea's
marriage to Nero became legal. Statilia Messalina's marriage to Nero
must have been very brief, since Nero could not have married her
before A.D. 66 at the earliest, only two years before his overthrow
and death. But some provinces had time to issue coins honoring the
emperor's new wife, and two years was sufficient time for the creation of at least a few public statues.[83] The evidence for their identification, however, simply does not survive.

Messalina and her Children: Portraits

The identification of Messalina's portraits will probably never be accomplished to the satisfaction of all scholars, for two reasons. First,
she was never represented on coins of the mint of Rome, and the
few provincial issues that do represent her are of questionable value
at best for establishing any more information than the nature of her
coiffure. (Figure 120). Second, because of her dramatic fall from grace
and execution, she suffered a *damnatio memoriae*, and many of her
public portraits would have been either vandalized or recut. Nonetheless, portraits of her must have existed in family groups: at least
two extant inscriptions, legible despite erasure after Messalina's condemnation, prove the original existence of her portrait statues, in

---

[81] *Octavia* 609–613.
[82] Mikocki, 1995, 47, 188 no. 255, pl. 13; Banti-Simonetti, *CNR* 16, 168–173
nos. 2–8; *RIC* 1² 153 nos. 56–57; *BMCRE* 1, 208, nos. 52–55, pl. 39, figs. 11–12.
[83] *RE* ser. 2 vol. 3, 2209–2210 no. 45, s.v. "Statilia Messalina" (Nagl).

Asia Minor and in north Africa.[84] Portraits in groups at such widely distant sites imply distribution of her image throughout the empire.

As usual, provincial coinages represent the emperor's wife even though the coins of Rome do not. Some, from Knossos in Crete, represent her in a purely ideal manner, wearing a small bun at the nape of the neck very different from the current fashions in Rome. These issues demonstrate a recognition of the significance of Messalina as the emperor's wife and mother of his children, but betray a lack of prototypes for the die-cutters to follow.[85] Several other provincial issues, however, represent her with a face and coiffure that are clearly intended to be portrait-like. Bronze coins from Cappadocia combine her portrait profile on the obverse with that of Antonia on the reverse, identifying the women respectively as MεCCAΛΛINA CEBACTOY (Messalina, wife of the Augustus) and ANTΩNIA CEBACTH (Antonia Augusta).[86] Her subordinate position in relation to the mother of her husband is emphasized by the difference in title; she is a wife of an Augustus, but does not hold the title in her own right as Antonia does, and the latter wears a corn-ear crown, as on Roman coins. On the other hand, Messalina's image parallels that of the Augusta. Her position as the successor of Antonia, and the next most important woman of the dynasty, is clear. Another issue of coins from Caesarea in Cappadocia, this time silver *didrachms* (two-drachma coins), represents her portrait profile on the obverse with little full-length figures of Claudius's three acknowledged living children: her own son and daughter Britannicus and Claudia Octavia, and Claudius's daughter by an earlier marriage, Claudia Antonia.[87] (Figure 120).

Another coin, possibly from Sinope in Paphlagonia, pairs her image with that of Claudius, while a medal from Nicaea, recorded by Cohen, represents her alone on the obverse with an architectural structure on the reverse.[88] All these coins, unfortunately, tend to be worn, and provincial coins are always unreliable at best as replicas

---

[84] Rose, 1997, 170–71, no. 108; 184–85 no. 126; Aurigemma, 1940, 34–35, fig. 19.

[85] Banti-Simonetti, *CNR* 16, 7–13, nos. 2–11. *RPC* 1001–02, p. 239.

[86] Trillmich, 1978, 148–150 with full references for existing specimens, pl. 15, figs. 8, 9. *RPC* 3657, p. 559.

[87] Mikocki, 1995, 45, 187, no. 245; Trillmich, 1978, 150–152; Banti-Simonetti, *CNR* 16, 35 nos. 1, 1/1; *BMCRE* 1, 199 no. 242 pl. 34, fig. 8 and *BMC Cappadocia* 46 no. 13 pls. 8,9. *RPC* 3627, p. 554.

[88] Coin from Sinope: Banti-Simonetti, *RPC* 2130, p. 358. *CNR* 16, 14 no. 13. Medal from Nicaea: Cohen, 1880, 1, 268.

of an official type: they could suggest the presence and availability
of such a type in sculpture or painting that die-cutters could duplicate, but on the other hand, the Messalina on the Sinope coin bears
such an obvious resemblance to those of Agrippina I on coins of
both Caligula and Claudius that local die-cutters probably borrowed
the image of one imperial woman to represent another. The Caesarea
coins show a different facial type, but one that betrays strong assimilation of Messalina's appearance to that of her husband, a feature
most noticeable in the heavy-lidded, hooded eyes and the long, thick
neck. On all these coins, Messalina wears a coiffure much like those
fashionable at the time of Caligula: her hair is drawn back to a long
queue down the nape of her neck, while two long corkscrew curls
escape just behind the ears to hang along her neck. The hair around
her face was somehow differentiated from the strands toward the
back of her head, and rose in higher relief, but unfortunately, because
such parts of a coin tend to suffer the most wear from handling, it
is difficult to ascertain on most of these coins whether this area of
hair took the form of artificially crimped waves, of ringlets, or of
some combination of the two.[89] Only the coin that may be from
Sinope is well enough preserved to suggest that this area consisted
of two rows of ringlets around the face, with narrow, artificially
crimped waves on the sides of the head behind the area of curls.

I have argued earlier that there are three marble portraits in existence, with a coiffure similar to this coin representation, that probably represent Messalina.[90] These works are a statue in the Louvre
of a veiled woman holding a male child in the crook of her left arm
(figures 123–125); a marble head in Dresden of a young woman
wearing a turret-crown and laurel wreath (figures 126–127); and a
badly battered and weathered head in the Museo Chiaramonti of
the Vatican that represents its subject wearing a turret crown, a laurel wreath, and a crested helmet decorated in low relief with a winged
horse and a griffin (figures 128–129).[91] This last work is probably

---

[89] Furnée-van Zwet, 1956, 2 figs. 33–34; Polaschek, 1972, 177–178.

[90] For a fully documented discussion of my identification of these portraits, see
Wood, 1992, 219–234.

[91] A) Paris, Musée du Louvre, MA 1224, marble statue, pieced together from
several large fragments, some restorations in body and drapery. Mikocki, 1995, 44,
185–86 no. 239 pl. 25, with full literature; Wood, 1992, 219–234, figs. 1–4; Fuchs,
1990, 120–122; De Kersauson, *Louvre* 1, 200–1, no. 94; Sande, 1985, 199–202,
figs. 13–14; Bernoulli, 1886, 1² 360–62, fig. 53.

not a replica of the same type as the first two, and I am no longer convinced that it represents the same woman, but the Louvre statue and Dresden head are true replicas of a common type. All three of these works have at various times received identifications as Messalina from other scholars besides myself, and a number of observers have recognized relationships among the group: Vagn Poulsen and Michaela Fuchs have recognized the Louvre and Dresden portraits as replicas; Sande rejects the association of these two works but argues that the Dresden and Vatican portraits represent the same woman, an opinion that Mikocki shares.[92] Since the appearance of my own earlier publication, I have concluded that Poulsen and Fuchs are probably correct. The close similarity of facial features among all three works, however, is no coincidence: there is strong, if not perhaps conclusive evidence that the Louvre and Dresden portraits represent Messalina, while the Vatican head may well portray her daughter Claudia Octavia. The latter would naturally display a family resemblance to her mother, although her hairstyle is of a recognizably later form.

The Louvre (figures 123–125) and Dresden (figures 126–127) portraits both represent a young woman with a short, round-cheeked face, a low forehead, wide-set, large eyes and a soft, full-lipped mouth that in both cases is represented as slightly parted, the lips separated by a deep drill channel. The woman has an overbite, giving her a retreating lower lip and chin. The chin point is fairly large and rounded, but definitely displays a receding form. The nose of the Louvre statue (figures 123–125) is remarkably well preserved, and is short and straight; that of the Dresden head (figures 126–127) is partly restored, but the surviving marble appears to show a shape consistent with the Louvre statue. In their present form, both heads display the following coiffure: the hair is parted in the middle and crimped into stiff, narrow waves with a curling iron. In the Louvre

B) Dresden, Albertinum, Skulpturensammlung cat. 358. Mikocki, 1995, 46, 187 no. 249, pl. 14 (as "Claudia Octavia"); Wood, 1992, 219–234, figs. 5–6; Fuchs, 1990, 120–122, figs. 14–17; De Kersauson, *Louvre* 1, 200; Wrede, 1981, 305, under no. 290; Sande 1985, 206–210 figs. 16–17; West, 1933, 218–19, pl. 59, fig. 259.

C) Vatican, Museo Chiaramonti no. 132 inv. 1814, marble, h. 0.29 m. Mikocki, 1995, 46, 187–88 no. 250, pl. 23 (as "Claudia Octavia"); Wood, 1992, 219–234, figs. 7, 8; Sande, 1985, 206–210, figs. 18–19; Wrede, 1981, 304–5 no. 290, pl. 36, figs. 2–5; West, 1933, 218; Amelung, *Vatican* 1, 396 no. 132, pl. 42.

[92] Poulsen, 1951, 133–34; Fuchs, 1990, 120–22; Sande, 1985, 206–210; Mikocki, 1995, 46, 187–88 nos. 249, 250.

statue (figures 123–125), the waves are tighter and the indentations
between them narrower and deeper than in the Dresden head, but
the pattern is essentially the same. Along the hairline is a fringe of
small, decorative curls that continue across the forehead without a
division at the middle part, and on each side of the central part, a
row of small ringlets runs back from the hairline toward the occiput.
The hair covers most of the ears on each side, and is fastened into
the looped queue typical of women's hairstyles from the time of
Tiberius onward. The Dresden head (figures 126–127) appears to
show escaping, softly waved locks of hair on each side of the queue,
but the veil of the Louvre statue conceals this detail. The coiffure,
then, closely resembles that of the Caligulan-era portraits of Agrippina II and Drusilla, but with two changes that may mark a shift
in fashion during the four intervening years. First, the waves are of
equal depth; the fashion for wide, flat waves with slightly indented
crests appears to have run its course and passed from popularity.
And second, the rows of curls running backward on each side of
the part add a new decorative element to the hair on the sides of
the head. We can see here the beginnings of the trend toward a
broad area of neatly coiffed ringlets around the face, like the one
that Agrippina II sported a few years later in her so-called "Ancona"
and "Milan" portrait types (figures 105–106, 134–137). A similar
fashion also appears on the coin portraits of Domitilla (the daughter of Vespasian who died before her father's accession to power,
but who was honored on coinage) and eventually developed into the
fanciful crests of curls popular in the Flavian era.[93] The subject of
the Louvre and Dresden portraits, however, belongs to the beginnings of that trend.

The Dresden portrait (figures 126–127) is unfortunately in rather
poor condition, having been split into three large fragments due to
some vertical blow to the head. The waves of hair on the proper
left of the head, and the accompanying section of turret crown and
laurel wreath, are modern restorations in marble. The part on the
proper right, however, is weathered but original. Sande has suggested that this head originally had a coiffure of the type that Agrippina II's Ancona portrait displays, with a broad area of ringlets
around the face, and that it has been incorrectly restored.[94] My own

---

[93] *BMCRE* 2, 246 nos. 136–38, pl. 47, figs. 11–13; p. 312 no. 68, pl. 61, fig. 11.
[94] Sande, 1985, 207.

autopsy, however, leads to a somewhat different conclusion: the crimped waves on the proper right are battered but original. Sande correctly observed rows of ringlets near the top of the head—despite the weathering, their deeply drilled centers are clearly visible—but I disagree with the assumption that this pattern of curls must have continued down each side of the face. The ringlets appear only in the two lines on each side of the part, as they do also in the Louvre statue (figures 123–125), and the Dresden head therefore bears a closer relationship to that work than it does to the Vatican head.

No identification of these portraits can be more than tentative, but several pieces of evidence argue in favor Messalina. First, the existence of two replicas, one of which has the explicitly divine attribute of the turret crown, argue for imperial status. The Louvre statue indicates that she was the mother of a male child; the coiffure, that she enjoyed her greatest status around the time of Caligula or the early years of the principate of Claudius. Agrippina II meets these criteria, as the mother of Nero, and the popular and respected niece of Claudius even before her marriage to him, but the facial structure of the Louvre and Dresden statues differs in many important details from that of Agrippina II, whose likenesses are well known. The latter, in every portrait type from Caligula's principate onward, has a square jaw, low eyebrows that flare toward the temples, and thin, rather pinched lips. Like the subject of these portraits, she had an overbite, but her small, sharp chin-point jutted forward below the retreating lower lip, forming a profile line quite different from that of this woman, who has a softer chin, a smaller and more rounded jaw, and whose eyebrows form relaxed arcs rather than the flaring shape so typical of the Claudian branch of the imperial family. Agrippina II's portraits, for obvious political reasons, emphasize her family resemblance to the beloved Germanicus, while the subject of the Louvre and Dresden portraits shows no such resemblance. Finally, although the face of the Louvre statue is remarkably well preserved, the torso was discovered in fragments, and the Dresden head was split into pieces by a heavy blow to the top of the head. In neither case can accidental damage be ruled out, but in both cases the damage could conceivably have resulted from a *damnatio memoriae* after Messalina's execution for adultery and treason.

If these portraits do represent Messalina, then, they characterize her as a very youthful and feminine woman. Her precise date of birth is difficult to determine, but is probably irrelevant: the most important personal attribute of this woman is her proven fertility, as the Louvre statue (figures 123–125) proudly demonstrates, and youthful women are more likely to be fertile—hence the tendency of portraitists to emphasize features like her childlike round face, small jaw, large eyes, and soft lips. Her coiffure, like that of Caligula's sisters, is complex and fashionable, but neatly controlled: Messalina's public images naturally had to project an image of respectability at the same time that they celebrated her reproductive role. Both extant replicas either directly quote or allude to images of Classical goddesses: the Louvre statue reproduces the pose, but not the drapery, of "Eirene and Ploutos" (Peace with the child Wealth) by Kephisodotos (figure 99), while the Dresden head endows her with the turretcrown of Cybele and of Fortuna-Tyche.[95] Both identifications are relatively rare, but not unprecedented. The Louvre statue may be the only surviving example of a Julio-Claudian woman holding a child in her arms, but it would be most surprising if other women before her, such as Agrippina I and Livilla I, had not appeared in a similar manner in some of the statuary groups, like the arch of Germanicus in Rome and the similar groups dedicated in honor of Drusus II a few years later. The *Senatus Consultum* prescribing the dedication of the former monument specified that its attic was to support images of Germanicus in a chariot, of Agrippina I, and of all their living children. Given the large number of children, at least six of whom were alive, and the limited space on the top of a triumphal arch, the statue of Agrippina I must have carried at least one of them. In other imperial groups from which inscribed bases survive, the arrangement of names on those bases strongly suggest that small children must have appeared in the arms of adults, both male and female.[96]

The turret crown of the other replica is relatively rare, but not unprecedented. Significantly, however, the only other imperial woman before Messalina to appear with such attributes was Livia. The cameo gem in Vienna, discussed in Chapter 2, probably belongs to the lifetime of the Augusta, since she holds a small bust of the deified Augustus in her hand, an attribute that distinguishes his divine sta-

---

[95] Mikocki, 1995, 44–45, 185–86 no. 239 and De Kersauson, *Louvre* 1, 200, on the Louvre statue; Mikocki, 1995, 46, 187, no. 249 for Dresden head with attributes of Tyche. See also Wood, 1992, 225–26 for an earlier discussion of the attributes of these portraits.

[96] Rose, 1997, 13, 108–110 no. 37; 149–151, no. 82.

tus from that of his living widow and priestess. On this cameo, Livia wears the turret-crown, holds corn-ears and poppies in her hand, and leans her left elbow on a tympanum decorated with a tiny lion.[97] For the eyes of the private owner of this gem, the identification of the ruling emperor's mother with the Great Mother of the Gods and the guarantor of the security of the Roman state seemed perfectly appropriate, but no such public uses of Cybele's attributes appear until after her death. The colossal statue at Leptis Magna, set up after her death although before her official deification, wears only the turret crown, and lacks the other attributes of Cybele.[98] The inscription of the small temple identifies her not as Cybele, but as "Ceres Augusta," a goddess with whom the Asiatic Cybele had been conflated at least since the fifth century B.C.[99] In this case, Livia-Ceres borrows the attribute of Cybele that identifies her specifically as a protector of cities.

The festival that Caligula established in honor of the deified Drusilla followed the form of the Megalesia in honor of Cybele, implying an identification of Drusilla with that goddess, although no representations of her with such attributes have survived.[100] And in private portraiture, there is a remarkable statue of an ageing woman enthroned with all the attributes of Cybele.[101] The Dresden portrait of Messalina (figures 126–127) thus is not unprecedented, but differs from all of these works in one striking respect: it probably was publicly displayed, not in a provincial city but in the capital itself, during the subject's lifetime. The circumstances of Messalina's fall guaranteed that she would not be so honored after her death, and the head is a life-sized work in marble from the city of Rome.

---

[97] Winkes, 1995, 189 no. 113; Mikocki, 1995, 26, 165 no. 101, pl. 21; Megow, 1987, 254 no. B15 with earlier literature, pl. 9, 1–3; Sande, 1985, 153–54 fig. 1; Oberleitner, 1985, 48 fig. 28.

[98] See Chapter 2, note 150.

[99] Euripides, *Helen*, 1301–1368, narrates the story of the rape of Persephone and Demeter's search for her daughter, but ends the story not with the return of Persephone to her mother but with the establishment of orgiastic rites of flute and drum music that comfort Demeter for her loss. Euripides is obviously conflating the Eleusinian goddess with Cybele in this passage, probably deliberately so and for poetic reasons too complex to analyze here, but the existence of this choral strophion indicates that such an identification of the Greek and the non-Greek goddesses would have long been familiar by the first century after Christ.

[100] Dio 59.11.3.

[101] Sande, 1985, 226–231 figs. 29–30; Wood, 1992, 226 n. 24; Frel, 1981, 42–43 no. 28; Bieber, 1968, passim.

Another divine figure who shared with Cybele the turret crown was Fortuna, and the Dresden portrait of Messalina may well intend a polysemous reference to both figures. As the mother of two imperial children, she could appropriately appear as the Magna Mater Deum, while her fertility had ensured the continuing good fortune of the ruling dynasty in particular and thus of the Roman state in general. As with the portraits of Caligula's sisters, however, it is the attributes rather than the stylistic treatment of the face and coiffure that convey associations with goddesses. Only the soft shoulder-locks that appear to escape from the queue of the Dresden head suggest a goddess-like element, and this by now had become a well-established element of actual fashion.

The importance of the three children of Claudius guaranteed that they too would appear in public sculpture throughout his principate. Although they, like Messalina, do not appear on coins of the Roman mint, die cutters in the provinces recognized their significance, as the issue of coins from Caesarea in Cappadocia indicates.[102] Already at the time of this issue, the potential existed for power struggles for succession within the imperial family, since the designer of the coin takes pains to identify Claudia Antonia with Concordia, holding a cornucopiae and clasping the hand of her half-brother Britannicus.[103] (Figure 120). Given the painstaking composition of this little group of figures, which has no exact precedents on Roman coins, the designer of the Caesarea reverse could well have drawn his inspiration from a public statuary group of the imperial family, although another possible source could be the Caligulan *sestertii* that represent the emperor's three sisters. In the latter case, the adaptation is a skillful and imaginative one, giving a new meaning to the figures through the introduction of the handclasp. The reverse of another issue from Patras honors all three children but emphasizes the special status of the only living male child, Britannicus, by representing his portrait as a frontal bust hovering between two crossed cornucopiae from which profile busts of his two sisters emerge.[104] This design probably owes its inspiration to the earlier Roman issue in honor of Tiberius's twin grandsons, but also displays similarities of design to the coin from Apamea in Bithynia with the reverse of

---

[102] Supra n. 87.
[103] Mikocki, 1995, 45, 187, no. 245.
[104] Banti-Simonetti, *CNR* 15, 271–73 nos. 1–4.

Caligula's three sisters (figure 84), in which a central figure, presented frontally, appears as part of a close-knit triad but at the same time is clearly superior in importance to the other two.[105] The Apamean coin is most unlikely to have found its way to Patras to influence the later issue in honor of Claudius and his children, but in both cases, die cutters of the Hellenistic east are adopting similar solutions of design to present a group of three siblings.

In sculpture, at least one portrait of Claudia Octavia survives for which external evidence allows a secure identification: the charming and artistically excellent statue from the Baia nymphaeum, in which Claudia Octavia wears a jeweled ornament along the crown of her head and a garment that slips from one shoulder in the manner of the "Venus Genetrix" type.[106] (Figures 69–71). This little statue is of course not a literal copy of the Classical Aphrodite that came to be associated with Venus Genetrix, the filmy and revealing drapery of which would have been inappropriate for a preadolescent child. But it does include more than one visual quotation of that famous original: not only the slipping shoulder strap, but the heavy, curtain-like mantle that falls in graceful catenary folds down the back. Despite her youth, Claudia Octavia already embodies the hopes for perpetuation of the Julio-Claudian line, and her assimilation to Venus resembles that of her grandmother Antonia in the same group, a woman whose fertility has already perpetuated the family and who appears as a syncretic Kore-Venus. The meaning of the hair ornament is more enigmatic, but may recall images of Eros with elaborate braids along the crown. Claudia Octavia, in this statue, is too young to wear her hair bound up in an elaborate coiffure. Instead, it falls loose in bangs over her forehead and curls on each side of her face in which the sculptor has displayed virtuoso drill work. The apparently spontaneous pattern is in fact highly calculated for decorative effect, as for example in the full, S-shaped swirls of hair across the forehead with tips that turn uniformly to the proper left. Such an arrangement of the hair across the forehead later appears in many

---

[105] On the Tiberian *sestertius*: *RIC* 1² 97, no. 42; *BMCRE* 1, 133 nos. 95–97, pl. 24, fig. 6; Banti-Simonetti, *CNR* 11. 4–12 nos. 2–7/2. Coin of Apamea in Bithynia: Wood, 1995, 463 fig. 4; Trillmich, 1978, 108–109, pl. 13, fig. 11; Banti-Simonetti, *CNR* 13, 169–71 nos. 1–2/2; Cohen, 1880, 1, 248–249.

[106] Rose, 1997, 82–83 no. 4, pls. 62–63; Amedick, 1991, 378–380 pl. 98; Andreae in *Baia*, 56–58, no. 8, figs. 156–62, 167, 169.

portraits of the adult Nero, but in a stiffly uniform pattern that reveals the artifice behind the effect of a sunburst around the face.

The same child-like arrangement of hair appears in the statue of a slightly older little girl, from the unpublished imperial group from the Casa degli Augustali of Rusellae, and on two more marble heads, in a private collection, and in Trieste.[107] Since the circumstances of the Rusellae find have not yet been fully documented, the evidence of the context is not as helpful as that of the Baia statue. But here again, the discovery of the statue in a Claudian-era group supports the identification as one of his two daughters, and the similarity to the Baia statue specifically as Claudia Octavia. Although the face is a little longer and less round-cheeked in these replicas, they may well follow the same prototype as the Baia statue, with suitable modifications to suggest a few additional years of age, since they too show the bangs in the same pattern of S-curves across the forehead. The pattern in these heads has already become somewhat more mechanical, however; they are technically good works, but not of the exceptional quality of the Baia statue. The use of the drill in the examples from Rusellae, Trieste and Spain is far more restrained than in that work, and the overall effect more sober and less flamboyant. Drill work is time-consuming, and therefore expensive—a costly work commissioned by the imperial family for private display would thus be more likely to show it than those commissioned by local and provincial patrons for public groups. Expense alone, however, cannot always explain the presence or absence of this technical feature, since works of modest quality like the portrait of Agrippina I from the Velleia group do show extensive use of drill channels. When the drill work is omitted in Claudia Octavia's statues therefore, we may suspect at least partly a stylistic choice on the part of artists and patrons. In the Rusellae statue, the drapery likewise is a modest contemporary costume rather than the goddess-like and provocative garment of the Baia statue, perhaps because the Rusellae statue was intended for the eyes of the general public, while the Baia group was available only to the favored few guests whom the imperial family entertained in that luxurious nymphaeum. Only in the Baia statue, furthermore, does she wear the hair ornament that was standard in the portrait type of her brother Britannicus.

---

[107] Rose, 1997, 116–118 no. 45; Amedick, 1991, 378–380 pls. 99, 100.

Several replicas of Britannicus's portrait type exist, and they, like those of Claudia Octavia, portray a child with a round-cheeked, appealing face, but also with a distinctively Claudian characteristic—the flaring eyebrows.[108] He, like she, has an ornamental pattern of long hair strands across the forehead, but the pattern differs from that of his sister: the strands flow outward from a central part and form a symmetrical pattern on the left and right, with the tips on both sides turned inward toward the center. No complete statues of this type now exist, but a likeness of Britannicus almost certainly did stand in the Baia group, probably in a figure modeled on Eros. Only a few fragments survive, but they are enough to prove the relationship of the statue to a well-known type of Eros holding a butterfly over an altar. If the head followed the same type as the Tindari, Munich and St. Petersburg replicas, the significance of the jewel ornament as an attribute of Eros might have been clearer than it is to us today in the surviving examples. Since Claudia Octavia appears to be no more than four or five, the Baia group probably predated Messalina's fall in A.D. 48; it is not inconceivable that the mother of the imperial children once accompanied them here, and was later replaced with one of the purely ideal figures of Bacchus. Although the images of some disgraced individuals appear to have remained on view after their fall, Messalina did suffer a *damnatio memoriae*, and her image could hardly have been allowed to remain on view in a group on the private property of the emperor who had ordered her execution for treason against him. If Messalina did appear here, then she, like Antonia Minor, would perhaps have been associated with Venus, and her children with Eros and a sort of composite Venus-female Eros respectively.

Claudia Octavia must certainly have been represented at a more mature age, as well, on the occasions of her betrothal and marriage to Nero. During the principate of Nero and before her divorce and exile, patrons of imperial groups must have continued to honor her

---

[108] Amedick, 1991, 373–378, 380–381. The replicas are:

A) Tindari, Museo Nazionale di Archeologia, Palermo, inv. 697, fragmentary marble head, h. 20.5 cm. Amedick, 1991, 373–378, ill. 1, pl. 95, fig. 1, 96 figs. 1–4; Bonacasa, 1964, 44 no. 50, pl. 23.1–2.

B) Marble bust in St. Petersburg, Hermitage Museum, Amedick, 1991, 374, n. 5 with earlier literature, pl. 95, figs. 2–4.

C) Munich, Residenz Museum, Amedick, 1991, 374, n. 6 with earlier literature, pl. 97.

with portraits along with her husband, since we know that the crowd of her partisans who stormed the Capitoline in A.D. 62 were able to carry such images about as they rioted. The most widely accepted candidates for portraits of Claudia Octavia as a young woman, however, present certain problems which I have addressed above in Chapter 5. These are the heads at Olympia, (figures 103–104) in the Museo Chiaramonti of the Vatican (101–102), and in the Museo Nazionale Romano that represent a woman with a long face, high forehead, curly coiffure very similar to that of Agrippina II, and a crescent diadem. The single strongest objection to the identification of this type is the apparent age of the subject: she looks well above Claudia Octavia's age of nineteen when the last images of her could have been made. Official prototypes of Claudia Octavia, moreover, are likely to have been created some time earlier, on a significant occasion such as the accession of her husband to imperial power, when she may have been only twelve. Assuming that Tacitus either made a mistake about her age or slightly exaggerated her youth for an effect of pathos, she was still no older than about fourteen or fifteen when Nero came to power and twenty-one or twenty-two at the time of her exile, and her portraits are likelier to show her at the former age than the latter.[109] Since she had no children, there were no such subsequent occasions to celebrate, while her estrangement from Nero makes it unlikely that he would have commissioned new official prototypes of her. My other reasons for disputing the identification have been addressed above. Another head in the Museo Chiaramonti, however, represents a much more youthful female, wearing attributes that strongly imply imperial rank, and this work has a much stronger claim to represent Claudia Octavia. (Figures 128–129). Although there are no extant replicas in sculpture, the same face may appear on two cameo gems that show a very young face with similar divine identifications.

The Museo Chiaramonti head has undergone severe damage of the sort that one might expect from deliberate vandalism. Given the circumstances of Claudia Octavia's fall, it is not unlikely that some supporters of Nero who either believed her guilt or found it convenient to claim that they did would have mutilated her images in this way: the entire nose, with a piece of the forehead and of the upper

---

[109] On the problems of establishing Octavia's birthdate, see supra, n. 14.

lip, is missing, as are most of the projecting parts of the headgear, while the weathering of the surface suggests immersion in water. Nonetheless, the woman's basic facial features are legible. She has a short, round face with a tapering jaw and rather weak, receding chin; large, round eyes, and eyebrows that form gracefully relaxed arcs. The profile has been badly damaged, but we can still recognize a straight, vertical forehead and a definite overbite. Stylistic conclusions are more difficult to draw, due to the damage, but the modeling appears to have been soft, allowing surfaces to flow into one another rather than to have been defined by hard angles, even before the damage exaggerated this effect. She wears an elaborate array of attributes: a helmet with a high central crest from which two plumes tumbled outward on either side, behind which a griffin and a winged horse appear in shallow relief; a turret crown, and a laurel wreath. These objects conceal most of her hair, but across the forehead the sculptor has gone to some trouble to indicate two rows of neatly aligned snail-curls. Behind the ears, the stumps of shoulder-locks appear from under the helmet.

This face bears a striking resemblance to that of the Louvre and Dresden sculptures provisionally accepted above as likenesses of Messalina (figures 123–127). There are, however, a few differences of physiognomy as well as coiffure: the forehead is slightly higher, the hairline more arched rather than horizontal, and the lower lip (the only part of the mouth to survive the damage) a little thinner. The high forehead and thin lips are features that Claudia Octavia, if that is who she is, could have inherited from Claudius, although the resemblance to her mother is far more striking. The coiffure, however, with at least two rows of large curls around the face, is of the type that appears to have come into fashion a little later, since it is the type that the Ancona and Milan portraits of Agrippina II wear. Claudia Octavia would logically have worn this fashion as well, by the time she was old enough for marriage, and the hairstyle would have helped to assimilate her appearance to that of her stepmother.

The attributes of this head are extraordinary, and probably convey a rather specific message for a unique situation. The turret crown could establish an identification either with Cybele or with Tyche-Fortuna, but it was also the attribute of place-personifications, specifically of city goddesses. The most familiar helmeted female in the art of the classical world was Athena-Minerva, one of the Capitoline triad of Rome, but another place personification, Dea Roma, appropriated this attribute. The helmet in conjunction with the turret crown and the military victor's laurel wreath could well associate this young girl with Rome itself. The helmet would also, however, conjure up almost unavoidable associations with Minerva. Despite her importance in the state religion of Rome, this goddess is a relatively rare choice for identification with imperial women during the Julio-Claudian era, for the obvious reason that she was a virgin goddess, and therefore inappropriate for assimilation with women whose dynastic role was to produce children. In certain special situations, however, such an identification could be desirable: for example, for an unmarried child, or a young woman who has just become engaged but not yet married, whose virginity the maker of the portrait might wish to emphasize. Caligula had earlier invoked the goddess Minerva as the special patron of his daughter Drusilla II, whom he ceremonially presented to all the goddesses that had temples in Rome, ending the ceremony at the Capitoline, where he placed the baby in the lap of Minerva's cult image. Caligula, like Claudius, undoubtedly intended that his daughter should eventually produce children, but her role in the meantime was to remain virginal until her father selected a dynastically suitable husband. Claudia Octavia, as the daughter of Messalina, undoubtedly suffered by association with her mother, whose sexual misconduct satirists gleefully and wildly exaggerated after her death. For that reason, special emphasis on the virginity of Claudia Octavia might have been a desirable element of propaganda.

The attributes of the Museo Chiaramonti head have polysemic associations with an entire array of divine beings—Fortuna, Cybele, Minerva, Dea Roma—but a cameo gem that may well also represent Claudia Octavia is far more direct. This object, in the Bibliothèque Nationale in Paris, represents a young girl wearing a crested helmet and the aegis of Minerva.[110] The helmet completely conceals the hair, making a comparison of the coiffure to that of the Vatican head impossible, but the facial features match in every detail: the straight forehead, large, round eyes, receding lower lip and round, retreating chin. The nose of the cameo takes a rather unusual form: short and slightly snubbed, which suggests that the subject is still very young. Another cameo, in a private collection, represents a

---

[110] Mikocki, 1995, 46, 188 no. 251 pl. 24 with earlier literature.

young woman with very similar features so far as they are preserved, since the profile has been mutilated by apparently deliberate vandalism, and she too wears an aegis, but this time drawn over her head like a veil.[111] Here too one can recognize a straight forehead, large, round eyes, and a chubby, child-like facial form, although the nose and chin have been hacked away. This time, however, the coiffure is visible, and takes the form of two large rows of snail-curls around the face. Mikocki tentatively identifies this cameo as a portrait of Poppaea, observing that its coiffure is of the type fashionable later in the principate of Claudius, and that since it clearly cannot be Agrippina II, it most probably represents one of Nero's wives. Poppaea is a possible candidate, but Claudia Octavia equally likely, and her images would have been just as vulnerable as Poppaea's to deliberate damage. The public farce of "thanksgiving" for the deliverance of the emperor from a treasonable enemy after her death could have prompted some nervous owners of cameos in her honor to destroy them, aware of the vindictiveness of Nero.

The scant evidence for the likenesses of Nero's other two wives can best be discussed later. In contrast to Messalina and Claudia Octavia, however, the images of Claudius's fourth and last wife, Agrippina II, offer voluminous material for study.

Agrippina II: The Numismatic Images

During the principate of her brother Caligula, Agrippina II, along with her two sisters, had become one of the first living women to be represented on coins of the Roman mint that identified them by name. As the wife of Claudius she achieved another "first:" to be represented both with an identifying inscription and with a recognizable portrait profile (figures 121–122). On the Caligulan coin (figure 82), her image had taken the form of a tiny full-length figure the face of which was almost completely illegible, and which appeared to wear an ideal rather than contemporary coiffure, but on the gold and silver issues of her husband's imperial mints at Rome and Lyons,

---

[111] Mikocki, 1995, 47, 188–89 no. 257, pl. 24; Megow, 1987, 260–61 no. B28, pl. 34, 14–16. Megow tentatively proposed the identification as Poppaea that Mikocki follows, but as Mikocki observes, the chronological evidence of the coiffure and historical probability could support an identification as either of the wives of Nero.

she appears in carefully detailed likenesses that emphasize her Claudian features like the square jaw, overbite, and small but sharply jutting chin. (Figures 121–122). That characteristic treatment of the mouth and chin area in all Agrippina II's portraits may have particular significance for the omen-conscious Roman people, since Agrippina II had a supernumerary canine tooth on the upper right jaw, a feature believed to portend good fortune.[112] An emperor as intrigued with religious lore as Claudius, and a woman as shrewd about manipulating public opinion as Agrippina II, could hardly have failed to publicize this happy information, and artists in all media who were aware of the trait would naturally have called attention to it.

These issues of coins also make Agrippina II the first living woman to wear the corn-ear crown of Ceres on the coins of the Roman mint, an honor previously bestowed only on Antonia Minor after her death.[113] Ceres is not only a goddess of fertility but the Roman equivalent of Demeter, the archetypal good mother who loyally and tirelessly searched for her missing daughter Proserpina until she obtained her release from the underworld, and there was a long tradition on Italian soil of images of "Demeter *Kourotrophos*," protector of youth, with a child in her lap.[114] Claudius, a scholar of religious history who had even contemplated transferring the Eleusinian rites to Rome itself, must have understood all these associations, as did the many Roman citizens who had undergone Eleusinian initiation.[115] The corn-ear crown was an easy and familiar way to conjure up all the associations of the beloved chthonian goddesses in connection with the new Augusta. Since Agrippina II's marriage to Claudius would have been illegal under the preexisting incest laws, the designers of these coins probably recognized her public image as a "hard sell," and accordingly invoked the most emotionally powerful allusions possible. The maternal nature of Ceres must have been par-

---

[112] Pliny, *NH* 7.71; Barrett, 1996, 41; Griffin, 1984, 23.

[113] Mikocki, 1995, 39, 179 nos. 192–193, pl. 5 no. 192; Trillmich, 1978, 55–56; Banti-Simonetti, *CNR* 16, 65–75 nos. 1–17, *RIC* 1² 125 no. 75, pl. 15, and 126 nos. 80–81, pl. 16 no. 81; *BMCRE* 1, 174–175, nos. 72–78, pl. 32, figs. 24–27, 33 figs. 1–3; 176 nos. 82–83, pl. 33, fig. 5.

[114] On the myth: *Hymn.Hom.Cer.*; Ovid, *Met.* 5.341–678; Ovid *Fasti* 4.417–620. The most familiar versions for Romans would have been those of Ovid. On Demeter *Kourotrophos*, see Zuntz, 1971, 110–114 pl. 14b; Langlotz, 1963, 54, 257, pl. 21 left; *LIMC* 4¹ 870 nos. 300–302, s.v. "Demeter" (Luigi Beschi).

[115] Mikocki, 1995, 39; Suet. *Claud.* 25.5; Clinton, 1989, 1513–1514.

ticularly evident to viewers of the coins in which Agrippina's son Nero appeared on the obverse (figure 122). Another association that would have come readily to mind for many viewers of the coins was with Antonia Minor, in whose honor Claudius had issued *aurei* and *denarii* on which her portrait wore the same attribute. (Figures 55–56). Agrippina II thus enjoyed the reflected glory of the emperor's mother, who had always been a respected and beloved figure, as well as Claudius's most direct familial connection to the divine Augustus. He, through Antonia, was descended from Augustus's sister Octavia Minor, but his marriage to Agrippina II established a new and closer link, since she was the great-granddaughter of the deified first emperor. The coins in honor of Antonia had most probably been issued in A.D. 43–44 and 45/46, and must have still been in circulation, since the oldest would have been only about six years old when Claudius and Agrippina II married in 49.[116]

Provincial mints had no trouble whatsoever understanding the gist of the imperial message. At Ephesus, for example, a coin appears probably in A.D. 50–51 that celebrates the imperial marriage with an obverse portrait of Claudius and an image of Agrippina II on the reverse.[117] At this point she wears no special attributes, but soon afterward, the imperial couple appear together on the obverses of coins in jugate portraits (figure 130). In these issues, Agrippina II wears the corn-ear crown and Claudius the military victor's laurel wreath, so that together the couple embodies victory and prosperity, the two sides of "peace through victory" that Livia and Augustus likewise represented on the Ara Pacis.[118] Coins of the Roman mint may by this time have reached the provinces, and inspired local die-cutters to give Agrippina II the attribute of Ceres. An unidentified mint in the province of Moesia-Thrace honored the new Augusta in a coin devoted entirely to her by the simple expedient of copying the *carpentum sestertii* of Agrippina I, but with a new inscription on the obverse that identifies the subject of the portrait as the daughter rather than the mother: AGRIPPINA[E] GERMANICI F CAESARIS AUG, "To Agrippina, the daughter of Germanicus and wife of the

[116] Trillmich, 1978, 76–77.

[117] Banti-Simonetti, *CNR* 16, 82–86 nos. 24–32; *RIC* 1², 130, no. 117; *BMCRE* 1, 197–198, nos. 234–235, pl. 34, fig. 3. The titles of Claudius give the date of A.D. 50–51. *RPC* 2223, p. 380.

[118] Banti-Simonetti, *CNR* 16, 77–81 nos. 18–22; *RIC* 1², 130 no. 119, pl. 17; *BMCRE* 1, 197, nos. 231–233, pl. 34, fig. 2. *RPC* 2621, p. 438.

Augustus."[119] In this case the primary motive of the designers was probably convenience: they wanted to honor a woman named Agrippina, and a good model was available, albeit in honor of a different person by that name, but they might also have been aware of the elder Agrippina's importance in the public presentation of her daughter. It was through her mother that Agrippina II could trace her all-important link to the deified Augustus, and Claudius was again honoring Agrippina I with an issue of *sestertii* (figure 85) designed to remind Romans of her status as a tragic martyr of the tyranny of Tiberius, while quietly omitting the embarrassing fact that she had also been the mother of Caligula.[120]

Corinth, finally, honored Agrippina II on several issues of *asses*. Here, as on the issues from Moesia-Thrace, she appears alone, without any other member of the imperial family, an honor she never received from the Roman mint where her likeness invariably appeared on the reverses of coins of Claudius or Nero. Most of the reverses on these local issues have nothing to do with the Augusta; they represent gods of local importance.[121] A reverse of Venus in a chariot could conceivably have special importance in relation to the emperor's wife, and another reverse that represents a male in a toga with a draped female who seems to have the attributes of *Salus* (health) could refer to the happy new beginning that the marriage of Claudius and Agrippina II supposedly represented, but it may be unwise to read too much significance into these choices of reverse type. There is one important exception, however, probably datable to the year A.D. 54 when Claudius adopted Nero: the reverse consists of two full-length male figures, both clad in the toga and so unmistakably Roman men, who extend their hands to one another.[122] These are probably Nero and his adoptive brother Britannicus, to judge from the inscription on a similar reverse of Claudius's coins from the same mint.

The obverse inscription that accompanies Agrippina II's portrait

[119] Banti-Simonetti, *CNR* 16, 45–46 nos. 1, 1/1; Von Kaenel, 1984, 141–144, pl. 24, figs. 25–31.
[120] Trillmich, 1978, 78–79.
[121] Banti-Simonetti, *CNR* 16, 49–52 nos. 1–19. Reverses, type I: *Genius* of the colony; type II: Poseidon in *biga* drawn by hippocamps; type III: Venus in chariot drawn by a nereid and a triton; type IV: Helios in quadriga; type V: togate figure with patera in one hand; type VI: male togate figure with a patera and a female figure with a serpent (possibly *Salus*). *RPC* 1190, 1193, 1196, 1198, p. 255.
[122] Banti-Simonetti, *CNR* 16, 58 no. 20. *RPC* 1183, p. 254. Coin with Claudius: *RPC* 1182, p. 254.

is quite informative. The other issues from Corinth simply named her "AGRIPPINA AUGUSTA," sometimes abbreviated as "AGRIP-PINA AUG," but this one calls her "IUL AGRIPP AUG [MATER] CAESARIS," Julia Agrippina Augusta the Mother of Caesar.

Throughout her marriage to Claudius, the coins both of Rome and of the provinces corroborate the information of the historians that Agrippina II not only wielded an unprecedented degree of influence with the *princeps*, but enjoyed unprecedentedly public recognition. The Roman coins of her son's principate demonstrate the next phase of the process. (Figures 131–132) The very first issue of A.D. 54 (figure 131) has a rather awkward obverse composition, but one that demonstrates the effort of the coin designer to grapple with an unusual situation. The portraits of Nero and Agrippina II both appear on the obverse, facing one another, so that neither will seem subordinate in importance to the other.[123] The lack of space forces the die-cutters to cram the figures into the circle of the flan so that they almost touch noses, like children in a staring contest, an understandable difficulty in view of the lack of precedents for such a composition. Not since the second triumvirate had a Roman man and woman, Marc Antony and Octavia Minor, appeared in such a confronted arrangement (figures 9–10), and those coins did not come from Rome but from one of Antony's mints, on the one occasion when Octavia Minor had merited this special honor by helping to arrange a treaty between her brother and her husband.

In the *aurei* and *denarii* of A.D. 54, (figure 131) Nero's bust is on the viewer's left, the proper right of the composition, a position that could imply precedence, since the Latin language is written from left to right and literate people accustomed to this method of writing tend to read images in the same order. But the inscriptions surrounding the flan gives Agrippina II's names and titles, in the nominative voice, while Nero's, in the dative, are relegated to the reverse. The reverse design consists of an oak crown, one of the insignia of imperial power, which encloses another inscription, "EX.S C," "by decree of the Senate," meaning presumably that the wreath is one of the honors that the Senate has voted to him. Both imperial figures receive honors on this coin, but there is an obvious effort to balance them as equally as possible.

---

[123] Banti-Simonetti, *CNR* 16, 106–115 nos. 13–29, 123–129 nos. 45–59; *RIC* 1² 150, nos. 1–3, pl. 17; *BMCRE* 1, 200 nos. 1–3, pl. 38, figs. 1–3.

In the following year, A.D. 55, Agrippina II still appears on the obverses of gold and silver coins from the Roman mint, but this time in jugate portraits that assign her to the position behind Nero.[124] (Figure 132). Her titles now appear on the reverse, while Nero's occupy the obverse. The reverse type, however, still emphasizes Agrippina II's greatest source of official prestige as priestess of Divus Claudius. Claudius and another male figure, probably the deified Augustus (the only other emperor to that date who had received consecration) appear side by side in a chariot drawn by four elephants, the sort of vehicle that used to carry the portrait of the Deified Augustus and later, those of Drusilla and of Livia, into the Circus Maximus during the ceremonies that preceded public games.[125] Claudius would of course have received a similar honor after his own consecration. The surrounding inscription identifies Agrippina II as "AGRIPP AUG DIVI CLAUD NERONIS CAES MATER," "Agrippina Augusta the wife of the Deified Claudius and mother of Nero Caesar." This inscription and image together efficiently remind the viewer both of the dazzling public spectacle associated with the late emperor's cult and of his widow's special connection to it. These coins did not replace the earlier issue, which was probably still in abundant circulation at the time of their release, but represented a more artistically successful solution to the problem of representing the emperor and his mother as partners in power.[126]

By the following year, Agrippina II's portrait and name vanish from the coins of the Roman mint, never to return. Provincial cities were either somewhat slower to learn of the estrangement of Nero and his mother or less offended by the powerful position of a woman, because Caesarea in Cappodocia continued to represent Agrippina II on the obverses, and Nero on the reverses, of *drachmae* and *didrachmae* datable from A.D. 54 to 56.[127] In some of these coins, she appears bareheaded while Nero wears the laurel wreath, but in others, she wears both a veil over her head and a crescent diadem. The latter could belong to any number of female deities, but combined with the veil it could suggest an identification specifically with Juno-Hera,

[124] Banti-Simonetti, *CNR* 16, 99–105 nos. 1–12 and 116–121 nos. 30–42; *RIC* 1², 150 nos. 6–7, pl. 17. *BMCRE* 1, 201 nos. 7–8, pl. 38, figs. 4–5.
[125] Suet. *Claud.* 11.2; Scullard, 1979, 254–256.
[126] Barrett, 1996, 167.
[127] Banti-Simonetti, *CNR* 16, 129–138 nos. 60–77.

wife of the supreme god of the Greco-Roman pantheon and an appropriate object of identification for the widow of a deified emperor who appears in more than one extant statue as Jupiter.[128] Both attributes however have fairly broad meanings, and could also suggest an association with *"Pietas,"* equally appropriate for a priestess.[129]

Agrippina II: the Sculptural Portraits

In public sculpture, the sheer volume of Agrippina II's surviving portraits and the number of types during her lifetime attest to her visibility in a series of roles, first as sister, then as wife and finally as the mother of emperors. Five types can be identified with relatively little difficulty, although some controversy lingers about the identity of the first one, datable to the time of Caligula. (Figures 107–110). Some observers have identified it as one of Caligula's other two sisters, while some prefer to recognize it as Messalina.[130] My own arguments for accepting the identification as Agrippina II have been discussed above in Chapter 5, but in my opinion the decisive argument is Trillmich's observation that not only do a large number of replicas (at least eight) survive but that they display a variety of styles that suggest production over a period of some years. Of the possible candidates, only Agrippina II would have warranted the re-copying of an earlier portrait type a decade or so after its creation, when

---

[128] Statues of Claudius as Jupiter:

A) Vatican, Sala Rotondo. Stone, 1985, 381, pl. 86, fig. 2; Niemeyer, 1968, 107, no. 95, pl. 34, fig. 1; Helbig⁴ 1, no. 45, pp. 37–38; Lippold, *Vatican* 3¹, 137–39, no. 550.

B) Olympia Museum, inv. λ 125. Rose, 1997, 147–149, no. 80, pl. 191; Hitzl, 1991, 38–43 no. 2, 62–63, 67–68, pls. 8–13, 14.a.b; 38.b; 40.a; Stone, 1985, 381–84, pl. 82, fig. 2; Niemeyer, 1968, 107 no. 96 pl. 34, fig. 2.

[129] "PIETAS" appears with these attributes on a *dupondius* of Drusus II, A.D. 22–23, that some interpret as a portrait of Livia or some other woman of the Julio-Claudian family, but which I believe to be a purely ideal type. Mikocki, 1995, 27–28, 166 no. 109, pl. 26; *BMCRE* 1, 133 no. 98 pl. 24.7; *RIC* 1² 97 no. 43, pl. 11.

[130] Poulsen, *Portraits* 1, 97 under no. 61, mentions some of the replicas of this type and identifies them as a portrait of Agrippina II from the time before her marriage to Claudius. Trillmich, 1983, 21–37, advances additional arguments in favor of this identification. Polaschek, 1972, 201–210, identifies them as "a sister of Caligula," but does not attempt to decide which one. Boschung, *JRA* 1993, 71–73 no. W, and Mikocki, 1995, 45, 186, no. 240, pl. 12, prefer the identification as Messalina.

she returned from exile, enjoyed a period of great popularity even
before her marriage to Claudius, and eventually became the emperor's
wife.[131] An unusual number of these replicas are cameos or small
works in semiprecious stone, the sort of luxury object that would
belong to a private owner as a way of discreetly displaying, for a
select audience, his or her support for a contender for power in the
imperial family, as Agrippina II was in the years between her return
from exile and the fall of Messalina.[132] (Figure 133).

The following type, probably created at the time of her marriage
to Claudius, was short-lived, surviving in only two replicas, and
appears to have been a rough-and-ready solution to the problem of
recarving Messalina's portraits into Agrippina II's.[133] (Figures 118–119).
In these, her hair consists of scallop-shaped loops flattened onto the
scalp. But by far the two most abundantly replicated portraits are
her so-called "Ancona" (figures 134–137) and "Milan" (figures 105–106)
types, which may have existed contemporaneously, since the latter
may be simply a more ornamental variant on the former. In both
of these portraits, the Augusta still parts her hair in the middle and
wears it in a looped queue down the nape of her neck, as she did
in the Providence-Schloss Fasanerie type (figures 107–110) and the

---

[131] Trillmich, 1983, 26–37, list of extant replicas p. 27.

[132] Megow, 1987, 301–304 nos. D33–D39 (as Drusilla). Among the most securely
identifiable replicas of this type in semi-precious materials are:

A) British Museum inv. 3946, green chalcedony head, h. 9 cm., w. 5.4 cm.
Wood, 1995, 466, figs. 11–13; Megow, 1987, 301 no. D33, pl. 19, figs. 2, 6–8;
20.1; Trillmich, 1983, 27 no. 4, pl. 5, figs. 3–4; Polaschek, 1972, 201, figs. 2, 7, 11.

B) Cambridge, Fitzwilliam Museum inv. GR 166–1937, fragment of a head in
green chalcedony, h. 4.7 cm., w. 4.3 cm. Megow, 1987, 301–2 no. D34, pl. 19,
figs. 3–5; Trillmich, 1983, 27 no. 2, pl. 5.2.

C) Paris, Bibliothèque Nationale, Cabinet des Médailles inv. 280, sardonyx cameo,
h. 5.5 cm., w. 4.1 cm. Megow, 1987, 302 no. D36, with full literature, pl. 16.3;
Trillmich, 1983, 24–26, pl. 4, fig. 1; Polaschek, 1972, 210 no. B.b.

D) Paris, Bibliothèque Nationale, Cabinet des Médailles inv. 277, sardonyx cameo,
h. 6.9 cm., w. 5.3 cm., bust of a woman, draped, facing left, above a cornucopiae
from which emerges the bust of a child. In the background, a small female bust
wearing a helmet (Minerva? Dea Roma? Portrait?) Wood, 1995, 467–468, fig. 14;
Wood, 1992, 230–232, fig. 11; Megow, 1987, 303–4, no. D.39, with full literature;
Trillmich, 1983, 22–26, pl. 2; Polaschek, 1972, 174, 206. My two earlier publications discuss in more detail the controversies surrounding the identification of this
gem and the portrait type to which it belongs, and my reasons for accepting the
identification as Agrippina the Younger.

[133] Fittschen-Zanker 3, 6–7 n. 4, "Typus I Neapel-Parma," a and b. The two
replicas are Parma, Museo Nazionale inv. 830, from the imperial group at Velleia,
and Naples, Museo Nazionale di Archeologia, inv. 6242. See Chapter 5 for discussion, and Chapter 5 note 114 for full references.

Naples-Parma portrait (figures 118–119), but now her hair flows in smooth waves outward from the part for a short distance, then breaks into a mass of curls on each side of her face. These curls give her a resemblance, most probably fully intentional, to her mother, but in the portraits of Agrippina I, the curls appeared to be natural, escaping by "accident" from the waves of the coiffure. In the portraits of Agrippina II, on the contrary, these are neatly coiffed ringlets arranged in three or four parallel rows on each side of the face that probably required long and patient labor by a number of lady's maids. This coiffure was probably far more difficult to create than the fashion that Agrippina II and Drusilla wore during the principate of Caligula: that earlier fashion was elaborate and artificial, but required only the use of the curling iron for the hair on the sides of the head, and then a series of "spit curls" around the face, formed from the short wisps left over. If the Claudian portraits faithfully represent an actual fashion, Agrippina II and her ladies' maids could have created the new coiffure in one of two ways: by cutting some of her hair short in front and curling the short locks into artificial ringlets, or by attaching an artificial hairpiece across the crown, as Flavian and Trajanic-era women undoubtedly later did. No one person could grow enough hair for the coiffure represented in portraits like the celebrated Busta Fonseca of the Capitoline Museum; these women clearly drew their own hair back into turbans or queues of braids at the back of the head, then attached the high crests of curls in front separately, like a tiara.[134] In either case, the coiffure required effort and expense. Agrippina II obviously considered the fashion worth the trouble—quite possibly, because it assimilated her appearance to that of her mother, who along with Germanicus figured prominently in Claudian propaganda of these years.

The "Milan type" (figures 105–106) differs from the "Ancona" (figures 134–137) in adding one more, much smaller fringe of curls below the hairline along the forehead, perhaps a remnant of the earlier coiffure from her portraits at the time of Caligula. The larger mass of curls partially covers the ears, which in the Ancona type are completely exposed. If the mass of curls around the face is in fact an attached hairpiece, these smaller curls may represent her own

---

[134] Rome, Museo Capitolino, inv. 434, marble bust, h. 47.5 cm; of ancient part (head and neck) 39 cm., of head alone 28 cm. Fittschen-Zanker 3, 53–54 no. 69, pls. 86, 87, with earlier literature.

hair emerging from under it. In either case, it appears to be an
extra embellishment that copyists could omit or include as time and
money allowed. In all these portraits, unlike in her two earlier types,
she wears shoulder locks, usually two on each side. In this respect,
copyists may have enjoyed some freedom of personal judgment, since
a few replicas, such as the Vatican statue illustrated here (figures
134–135) appear to represent the locks as soft and loosely waved
strands, but the great majority of replicas show two tightly curled
corkscrew curls adhering smoothly to the neck (figures 136–137).[135]

This coiffure survived into the early years of Nero's principate,
continuing to appear on monuments datable to the period after his
accession, such as one of the reliefs of the Sebasteion at Aphrodisias
(figure 142). At the time of Nero's accession in 54, however, one
more sculptural type seems to have been created for her, the so-
called Stuttgart type (figures 138–140), which shows a slight increase
in age, since her face is now somewhat plumper and more mature.
Here, there is no smooth area of waves on each side of the central
part: the curls begin immediately on each side. This coiffure unmistakably appears on some specimens of Agrippina's coin portraits from
the years 54 and 55 (figure 132, e.g.), unlike those from the lifetime
of Claudius in which die-cutters painstakingly represented the smooth
area of hair alongside the part and above the curls (figures 121, 122,
130). The evidence of these Neronian coins, therefore, justifies the
dating of the Stuttgart type to the end Claudius's principate or the
beginning of Nero's.

In the eponymous replica in Stuttgart (figure 138), a work of very
high quality, there is also a new flamboyance in the interpretation
of the shoulder-locks, since the coils of hair are a little looser, and
parts of them carved free of the neck.[136] Several of the replicas include a crescent diadem. This is not a new honor for Agrippina II,
since replicas of her Ancona type sometimes also show this ornament (figures 136–137), but a handsome head in Copenhagen (figures
139–140) combines the diadem with a veil over the back of the

---

[135] Vatican, Museo Chiaramonti 2084, head mounted on a statue of Hygeia to
which it does not belong. Life-size; h. of statue 183 cm. Most of the neck is restored,
but the softly waved locks of hair along the neck begin above the break and do
not appear to be recut. Fittschen-Zanker 3, 7, no. 5, n. 4, Typus III g, Beilage
3c–d; Amelung, *Vatican* 1, 351–352 no. 62 pl. 37.

[136] Fittschen-Zanker 3, 7 no. 5, n. 4, "Typus IV Stuttgart;" Hausmann, 1975,
33–34 no. 8, figs. 21–23, 25.

head, and gives her the rare honor of life-size representation in a very expensive material, black granite, that is far more difficult to carve than marble.[137] The torso to which this head belonged has recently been identified in a fragment from the Claudianum in Rome. The complete statue represented Agrippina at the height of her short-lived glory as priestess of her deified husband. Its present condition suggests one more honor to the Augusta, as well: the curls immediately above the forehead are worked with great care and survive almost completely intact, but those between the forehead and the diadem have been chiseled away. The pristine condition of the face, and the neat cutting that left the curls in front intact suggests that this was no act of vandalism or accidental breakage, but a preparation of the stone for some attachment, most probably a garland. The corn-ear crown of Ceres with which she had appeared in so many coin profiles seems the most likely such addition. When this attribute was added is impossible to know: the head may have been designed from the start to include an attachment in another material, in which case the second and third rows of curls back from the forehead would never have been carved, and the surface simply prepared for an attachment. If the head was modified at some later date, however, the only possible time, given Agrippina II's fall from favor in the years after Nero's accession, would have been after the coup that drove Nero from power, when her reputation might have been rehabilitated.

Agrippina II probably did not sit for a new portrait in A.D. 54. The creator of this type is more likely to have invented it by modification of the existing Claudian prototypes of the "Ancona" and "Milan" groups, from which it deviates in only a few essential features. The fact that patrons felt a need for distinctively new portraits of the Augusta reflects a recognition of her new status as priestess of a deified emperor and mother of his successor; Livia's portrait type with the middle part came into being under much the same

---

[137] Ny Carlsberg Glyptotek cat. 634, I.N. 753, basalt head, h. 30 cm. Poulsen, *Portraits* 1, 97 no. 62, pls. 104–105; Fittschen-Zanker 3, 7 no. 5, n. 4, "Typus IV Stuttgart." Belli Pasqua, 1995, 74 no. 12 and 82–84 no. 26.

Examples of the Ancona portrait type with a diadem:

Ny Carlsberg Glyptotek cat. 636, I.N. 755, marble head, h. 36 cm., Fittschen-Zanker 3, 7 no. 5, n. 4, "Typus III Ancona" b; Poulsen, *Portraits* 1, 96–97, no. 61 pls. 102–103.

Museo Nazionale Romano inv. 56965, marble head, h. 23 cm. *MNR Sculture* 1⁹, 153–55, no. R110; Fittschen-Zanker 3, 7 no. 5, n. 4, "Typus III Ancona" n; Felletti-Maj, 1953, 66 no. 110.

circumstances. The well-established Ancona type probably continued in use as well, however, and the replicas of that type that represent her wearing a diadem may date to the years after Nero's accession.

Without archaeological information about context, the dates of these replicas cannot be fixed more closely than A.D. 50–A.D. 55 or 56, but whether they date to her husband's or her son's principate, these diademed versions of her portrait merit special attention. A handsome marble head of the "Ancona type" in Copenhagen (figures 136–137), made for insertion into a statue, shows her wearing not only a diadem but one decorated with elaborate openwork patterns of lotuses and palmettes.[138] A crescent diadem could belong to almost any of the major goddesses, but a *stephane* ornamented with flowers seems to have belonged in particular to the Greek Persephone, the Latin Proserpina, whose images appear with this attribute on Italian soil at least as early as the fifth century B.C.[139] Flowers, with their self-evident meaning of youth and new life, were especially appropriate for the mythological daughter, but since the images of Demeter and Kore often deliberately parallel one another, the attribute would be appropriate for Demeter-Ceres as well. Antonia Minor's Baia statue wore such an attribute (figures 64–66), in a syncretic image that combined attributes of Venus with the statuary type of the Kore Albani, and Livia wore it in the statue that represented her as Ceres-Fortuna, but the only living woman before Agrippina II to be so honored in extant sculpture was her sister Drusilla, in the portrait now in the Von Hessen collection (figures 114–115).[140] The battered and weathered condition of this head has destroyed most of the diadem, but the pattern of drill channels that created the open-work floral pattern is still visible. The later recutting of the head indicates that the diadem was part of the original composition, to which another attribute, probably an *infula*, was later attached in plaster at the time of her death and deification. The diadem, then, must have been an attribute to which Drusilla was entitled while still alive, and accords well with what we know of her assimilation to Kore in the statue from Caere now in the Vatican. (Figures 111–113). In the

---

[138] Copenhagen, Ny Carlsberg Glyptotek cat. 636, references above, n. 137.

[139] Persephone wears such a stephane on at least three of the types of tablets from the votive deposits at Locri: see Zuntz, 1971, 164–168; Langlotz, 1963, 271, pls. 71, 72; Carratelli, 1996, 701–2, nos. 166.IV–166.VI.

[140] See Chapter 5, note 97.

later portraits of her sister Agrippina II, likewise, the flowered diadem of Demeter-Kore seems consistent with the campaign of propaganda that aggressively identified her on coinage with Ceres.

In this guise she appears on a panel of the Sebasteion probably datable to the lifetime of Claudius (figure 141), and she appears again as Fortuna on another panel of the same monument, but this one obviously a few years later, after Nero's accession (figure 142). The Sebasteion, a long double-storied portico leading to a Roman-style temple, was a large and ambitious work that must have taken many years to complete.[141] It is hardly surprising, then, that the sculptured panels that decorate it do not reflect any one agenda at one time but span a period of years. Internal evidence, as Smith has rightly noted, indicates that the two reliefs on which Agrippina II appears are not the work of the same hands or the same time. In the earlier panel, Claudius is the focus of the composition, standing frontally in the center in heroic nudity while two draped figures on each side turn their attention toward him. One is a headless male figure in the toga, probably a personification of the Roman Senate or People, but the other is a portrait of Agrippina II in her Milan type. She clasps the right hand of Claudius with her own, and holds aloft a bouquet of corn ears with her left, an attribute that identifies her directly with Ceres, as does the figure type: the drapery, essentially, is that of the "Kore of Praxiteles" statuary type, and the pose of the figure matches that prototype in every detail except the gesture of the right arm, which must here be modified to allow her to clasp her husband's hand. Although the local patrons of Aphrodisias recognized the importance of the Augusta, their willingness to honor her had economic limits. They did not pay the best available portrait sculptor to carve her face, since the portrait head of Claudius on the same panel is of recognizably far higher quality than the rather stiff and mechanical reproduction of her image.

By the time Nero became emperor, local patrons had gained an increased respect for the status of the Augusta, if their respect can be measured financially: on the panel on which the young Nero

---

[141] Rose, 1997, 164–69, no. 105; Smith, 1987, 90.

Claudian panel: Aphrodisias depot, marble relief, h. 160 cm., w. 170 cm. (top) and 164 cm. (bottom), d. 43 cm. Rose, 1997, pl. 204; Mikocki, 1995, 39, 180 no. 202 with earlier literature; Smith, 1987, 106–110 pls. 8–9.

Neronian panel: Aphrodisias depot, marble relief, h. 172 cm., w. 142.5 cm. at bottom, d. 37.5 cm. Rose, 1997, pl. 207; Smith, 1987, 127–132, pls. 24–26.

appears in a general's armor, it is Agrippina II, with the attributes
this time of Fortuna, who places the imperial oak crown on his head,
a gesture that implies seniority and superior rank. (Figure 142). Her
face, in the simpler but more elegantly executed "Ancona type," is
a work of far higher quality than the replica of her "Milan type"
on the earlier panel, skillfully blending idealization with recognizable
fidelity to her official types. The face here almost approximates a
Classical oval, but still shows the characteristic forms of her forehead, eyebrows, mouth and chin. Unlike the earlier panel, in which
her expression is blank and stolid, the portrait here subtly characterizes her through the firm set of her lips, despite the classical seren-
ity of the expression. Her face and that of Nero, this time, are
probably the work of the same portrait specialist, and the panel's
composition balances the two in symmetrical stances, rather than
giving one figure a central place in a group of three, as the Claudius
panel did. The panel, although far more successfully realized, is comparable in the scrupulously equal balance of the figures to the *aurei*
and *denarii* of A.D. 54 from the Roman mint (figure 131).

The number of portraits of Agrippina II that must date to the
principate of Nero is impressive, and seem to suggest that production of them continued up to the time of her death, since the survival of these objects implies the original existence of many more.
There are at least four extant replicas of the Stuttgart type, which
appears to be a Neronian period creation, as well as replicas of her
earlier portrait types that artistic and archaeological context date to
the principate of her son. The Sebasteion relief of Agrippina II
crowning Nero (figure 142) is one such work, while the beautiful
statue of Agrippina II from Olympia (figures 105–106) may represent her as the priestess of her deified husband. The literary record
documents that Nero stripped her of her bodyguard, drove her from
her residence in Rome, and generally used any means at his disposal to deprive her of power, and yet there is also good reason to
believe that whether Nero liked it or not, she did continue to exercise some control over his actions until the very end of her life.

Posthumous portraits of Agrippina II are, for obvious reasons,
quite rare, since few would dare to honor the memory of a woman
officially condemned as an enemy of the emperor. Long after her
death, however, and that of Nero, at least one imperial patron paid
very public and extraordinary honor to her. The colossal portrait
bust of Agrippina II (figures 143–144) that came to light in the ruins

of the forum of Trajan appears to have been mounted in a tondo frame, and therefore to have taken the form of an *imago clipeata*, a portrait in the form of a shield.[142] This was one of the most honorific forms that a portrait could assume, and enjoyed special sacrosanctity. In the atrium of a private house, such portraits would be mounted near the tops of walls, and could not be removed even if the house changed ownership.[143] Trajan's forum appears to have followed that arrangement in a public space, creating a national ancestral gallery like the sort that one could see in the atria of traditional Roman houses, but on a grandiosely large scale, with some sixty colossal clipeate portraits of imperial figures, arranged along the attics of the colonnades on each side of the forum.[144] To include in such a setting a woman who had been executed on imperial orders and posthumously condemned for her supposed treason was an extraordinary choice, probably motivated primarily by a desire to rebuke the tyranny of Nero and to contrast with it the *pietas* of Trajan. Since the sculptural program of the forum survives only in fragments, we can only speculate whether other prominent victims of tyrannical emperors, such as Claudia Octavia, might have been similarly honored. But would Trajan, a shrewd statesman, and Apollodoros of Damascus, a designer of true genius, have permitted the inclusion in such a setting of a woman whom the general public remembered as Tacitus portrays her? Possibly Agrippina II's memory enjoyed some sympathy due to the circumstances of her death, but it is possible also that people remembered her with increasing affection after her moderating influence on Nero's conduct had vanished, bringing an end to the five good years, the "*quinquennium Neronis*" that Trajan himself explicitly praised as an era of good government.[145]

This Trajanic Agrippina II is a remarkable creation, recognizably reproducing her characteristic features, but following none of her lifetime portrait types directly. Any competent sculptor with a large enough piece of stone can achieve colossal scale, but it is a rarer talent to endow such an object with true presence, as this artist has

---

[142] Rome, Mercati Traiani, marble head, h. 85 cm., of face, 57 cm. Packer, 1997, 1, 59, 381–82 no. 191 on marble head, with full earlier references, p. 381 no. 190 n. 1 on isotopic analysis of marble; Kreikenbom, 1992, 204 no. III.73, pl. 16b; Wood, 1988, 424–25, figs. 15–16; Fittschen-Zanker 3, 6–7 no. 5, pl. 6.

[143] Winkes, 1979, 481–84.

[144] Packer, 1997, 1, 59, 423.

[145] Barrett, 1996, 238–240.

done. Artistically and in its impact on the viewer, the colossal tondo is the equal of the portrait of the deified Livia known as Juno Ludovisi (figures 50–51), a work that long fascinated modern viewers for reasons entirely separate from its antiquarian significance as the image of a goddess or of some historical woman.[146] The modeling of the face of the colossal Agrippina II is sensitive, although the hard edges that outline and define features like the mouth and eyes allow it to read clearly from a distance, and the facial expression combines the characteristically firm set of Agrippina's lips with a pensive quality appropriate to a portrait of a woman whom people might now regard as a political martyr. The better portraits of her mother Agrippina I offered precedents for the devices that sculptors use here to characterize Agrippina II. The coiffure is a unique variation on those of her lifetime portrait types, most closely resembling the "Ancona" and "Milan" types, but departing freely from them: there is a broad area of smooth waves on each side of the central part, as in her Claudian portraits, that emphasizes the breadth of her low forehead and enhances the characteristically square form of her face, then two tiers of ringlets on each side of the face and a row of short corkscrew-curls above them. Three more short corkscrew-curls hang over the cheeks in front of each ear, while four descend from behind the ears to the shoulders on each side.

The sculptor has taken advantage of the space that the scale makes available to elaborate Agrippina II's curls and hanging locks into a fanciful decorative pattern of his own making, but by calling the viewer's attention to these features with his imaginative treatment, he may have another purpose in mind as well. The proliferation of corkscrew curls behind the ears enhances the resemblance of this posthumous and heroized portrait to Classical images of Demeter, such as the Demeter of Knidos, and the Eirene of Ploutos (figures 98–99). Agrippina II's identification with Demeter/Ceres, "rich-haired Demeter," had been widely accepted during her lifetime, and earlier portraits of her with the attributes of the melancholy, maternal goddess would probably still have existed in the era of Trajan, but the artist of this portrait, rather than simply attach the attributes of the goddess to the portrait, has introduced evocative Classicizing elements into the likeness itself.

---

[146] See Von Heintze, 1957, 3–10; Rumpf, 1941, 34–35. For complete references, see Chapter 2, n. 178.

Agrippina II: the Glyptic Images

Large works of marble statuary and relief were intended for the eyes of the general public, and for dissemination throughout the empire. Small-scale but highly luxurious objects like cameos reached a smaller but more select audience, one whose opinion was vitally important to the imperial family. Agrippina II figures on some of the most impressive and iconographically rich of such gems to survive from the Julio-Claudian period. Some private patron, for example, evidently chose to elaborate on the theme of the coins on which Agrippina II wore the corn-ears of Ceres, by commissioning a gem that represented Claudius and Agrippina II as Triptolemos and Ceres in a dragon-drawn chariot, scattering the blessings of prosperity to their grateful subjects.[147] Neither portrait is particularly well-executed here, and that of Agrippina II in particular shows her with an oddly flat face and narrow head, making her nose appear longer but less projecting than most of her sculptural types. This is of course a small and free-hand replica of her "Ancona" type, but could conceivably betray a change in meaning: the woman could have originally been Messalina, recut to represent Agrippina II. Such an identification for Messalina would not be at all surprising, given the early and enduring popularity of identification of imperial wives and mothers with Ceres, and the importance of the Eleusinian cult to Claudius in particular. The same imagery persisted into the early years of Nero's principate, when the emperor and his mother again appeared as Triptolemos and Ceres on an agate vessel.[148]

One of the earliest cameos of Agrippina II as imperial wife, to judge from the use of her Caligulan portrait type, is a cameo now in the Bibliothèque Nationale (figure 133), in which her portrait bust rests on a cornucopiae from which the figure of a child emerges. In the background behind her is a small bust of Minerva, which some have read as emerging from another cornucopiae that is foreshortened behind her right shoulder. In its present state, however, the gem reveals no trace of a second cornucopiae, and the evidence for

[147] Paris, Bibliothèque Nationale, Cabinet des Médailles inv. 276, sardonyx cameo, h. 8.3 cm., w. 7.6 cm. Mikocki, 1995, 39, 180 no. 203 with full earlier literature, pl. 9; *LIMC* 4, 905, no. 176, s.v. "Demeter/Ceres" (S. De Angeli); Megow, 1987, 207–8 no. A86, pl. 27.3.
[148] Lindner, 1984, 111, pl. 24, fig. 2; *LIMC* 4[1] 902 no. 138, s.v. "Demeter/Ceres" (S. De Angeli); Mikocki, 1995, 180–181 no. 205.

its existence consists only of an early drawing that may take imaginative liberties with the object.[149] By far the most common practice when cornucopiae appear in pairs is to place them parallel to the picture-plane rather than at foreshortened angles. When two such cornucopiae support portrait busts, a symmetrical arrangement can then suggest the equality of the figures represented. This same device has appeared on coin types that honor the children of Drusus II and of Claudius, and will appear on the great Gemma Claudia in Vienna (figure 95). The composition of the latter suggests what the original form of the Paris cameo might have been, since the Paris gem has evidently been damaged and recut at least once in its existence: the portrait of Agrippina II might have faced another bust, possibly of Claudius, that rested on a similar cornucopiae facing in the opposite direction, possibly supporting the image of another child. If the child on the extant part of the gem is Nero, as seems likely, then a bust of Britannicus might have balanced him on the other side. This reconstruction of the gem, obviously, must remain speculative, but it is certain that Agrippina II does appear here with at least one child of the imperial family, and that the gem honors her specifically for her fecundity.

The great Gemma Claudia (figure 95) was most probably a wedding gift to Claudius and Agrippina II from some élite patron eager to express his approval for the official line of propaganda, in which the match brought glory to the emperor by uniting his line more closely with that of his popular brother Germanicus and of Agrippina I, both regarded as martyrs to the tyranny of Tiberius, and a couple whose children were directly descended through their mother from the Deified Augustus.[150] Here, the living and the dead couples face each other in pairs of jugate busts, each of which emerges from a cornucopiae that join at the tips, while between the two pairs the imperial eagle of Rome looks up toward Claudius but turns its torso toward Germanicus. The whole composition rests on a mass of captured armor, the spoils of victory of Germanicus's own campaigns and of those in Britain that had taken place under the auspices of Claudius as emperor. Claudius, the living ruler and the only one of

---

[149] Fuchs, 1990, 109–110. For my response, see Wood, 1992, 231.

[150] Vienna, Kunsthistorisches Museum 19, inv. IX a 63. Sardonyx cameo, h. 0.12 m., w. 0.152 m. Major recent publications: Mikocki, 1995, 182 no. 214, pl. 23; Megow, 1987, 200–201, no. A81, with full literature, pls. 31, 32, figs. 1,2,4; Oberleitner, 1985, 55–57.

the two brothers actually to achieve the status of *princeps*, takes pride of place on the left, the side that one reads first when reading left to right, and wears the oak crown and aegis of Jupiter. Germanicus wears the elements of military rank that he deserved as a triumphant general, the laurel crown and military paludamentum fastened on the shoulder with a large brooch.

The women may be relegated to the background, but the gem cutter has carefully represented enough of their faces and coiffures to render their likenesses unmistakable, and has given both of them divine attributes. Agrippina II wears the turret crown and corn-ear garland, thus appearing in the guise of a goddess of fertility, but this time specifically Cybele, or a syncretic Cybele-Ceres. The Asiatic goddess had special significance for Romans as the protector of their city against foreign enemies.[151] Cybele's cult had been brought to Rome during the second Punic war for specifically that purpose. Agrippina I, opposite, wears a crested helmet and laurel wreath. The most obvious association is with Minerva, but here as in so many other cases, the identification of the virgin goddess with the mother of nine children makes an awkward fit. Both her helmet and her daughter's turret crown, however, are polysemic attributes that could simultaneously conjure up a variety of associations in the mind of an educated viewer, who when seeing the two attributes together like this might think of place personifications like Dea Roma. Agrippina I could thus embody specifically the city of Rome, while the attributes of Agrippina II have broader associations.[152] The new wife of Claudius might then embody the well-being of the entire Roman empire.

As in the much earlier coins of Antony and Octavia Minor that were discussed in the first chapter, the jugate portraits of Germanicus and Agrippina I display the almost irresistible tendency of an artist, when representing two parallel profiles, to assimilate the appearances of the subjects to one another. The lines of the couple's straight foreheads and slightly arched noses are virtually identical, and their chins and throats have a similar shape, although the gem-cutter has scrupulously indicated the difference between Germanicus's mouth, with its Claudian overbite, from Agrippina I's, which does not have this orthodontic problem. The eyes of the two show an even more

---

[151] Livy 29.10.4–6; Dion Hal. *AntRom* 2.19.4–5.
[152] Hölscher, 1988, 529–31, fig. 5.

striking similarity, since these features are obviously somewhat con-
ventionalized: both have large, round and widely opened eyes, the
orbital folds of which are indicated by a shallowly incised line parallel to the edge of the upper lid. This gem cutter was quite capable of representing eyes differently, as the face of Claudius reveals:
his eye is smaller and more deeply set, with a fleshy fold hooding
the outer corner. The eye of the younger Agrippina, on the other
hand, follows the same convention as those of her parents, emphasizing her resemblance to both of them.

Undoubtedly the most spectacular glyptic monument on which
Agrippina II appears, finally, is the Grande Camée de France, the
largest extant work of Roman cameo carving, and probably, like the
Gemma Claudia, a lavish gift to the imperial family, possibly this
time on the occasion of Claudius's adoption of Nero (figure 145).[153]
The complex composition of this gem has engendered numerous
conflicting interpretations, but painstaking scholarship over the years
has at last established at least plausible identifications for many of
the major figures. Although controversies inevitably remain, there is
broad consensus on the general meaning of the iconographic program, despite some differences of opinion about whether the gem
was contemporaneous with the events portrayed or, as I believe, created decades after the fact. There is no need to add here to the
many excellent studies that have examined the work in exhaustive
detail and reviewed the relevant scholarship; what matters most for
the present purposes are the roles of three generations of women
who appear in the middle register.

The occasion represented, in an allegorical form that allowed the
artist some freedom with chronology, must have taken place between
the death of Drusus II, who appears in the heavens in a clearly
recognizable likeness, and that of Livia, who appears just as clearly
in the world of the living: in other words, between A.D. 23 and
A.D. 29.[154] The gem itself, however, is probably no earlier than the
marriage of Claudius and Agrippina II, who appear together as a

---

[153] Paris, Bibliothèque Nationale, Cabinet des Médailles inv. 264, sardonyx cameo,
h. 31 cm., w. 26.5 cm. Major recent references: Winkes, 1995, 145 no. 71; Megow,
1987, 202–206 no. A 85 with full earlier literature, pl. 32, figs. 5–10 and pl. 33;
Mikocki, 1995, 21, 157–58 no. 45; Jucker, 1976, 211–250; Bartman, 1998 and forthcoming. Bartman prefers a date during the principate of Tiberius, contemporaneous
with the events represented.

[154] Boschung, 1989, 64–65.

couple at the right side of the central register. The portrait of Agrippina II is a careful and accurate replica of her Ancona type in which every standard detail of her coiffure and physiognomy is present.[155] Claudius and Agrippina II appear at first glance to be rather minor and subsidiary figures, displaced from the center of the composition by two other pairs of imperial men and women, but the entire program of the work demonstrates the transmission of lawful authority through the dynasty, from the deified Augustus to Tiberius, from Tiberius to his original heir Germanicus, then (I believe) to the older sons of Germanicus who should have succeeded Tiberius had they lived, and finally (Caligula being discreetly omitted) to Claudius, the brother and son-in-law of Germanicus, who will eventually pass on the principate to Nero, great-grandson of Augustus and grandson of Germanicus.

The interpretation that I believe to be most convincing is the one that Megow presents, following Jucker in most important respects. At the bottom of the gem is a register of captured barbarian prisoners, who represent the military triumphs on which members of the dynasty have established their claim to power. Above it is a larger field in which the figures form two distinct registers: some hover above in the heavens, and therefore appear to be deceased and deified, or at least heroized, members of the family. The others, in the middle of the cameo, are firmly anchored to a ground-line and therefore are presumably still alive. Overhead, the deified Augustus in the rayed crown of the sun-god rides to heaven on the back of a male personification in stereotypically "eastern" costume who carries a globe, while two other members of the Julio-Claudian family who have presumably also died approach him from left and right. The figure on the viewer's left, a man in military costume who apparently ascends to heaven unassisted, has been identified beyond serious dispute as Drusus II, the son of Tiberius, easily recognizable here by his distinctively large, projecting nose and sloping forehead.[156] The other, who rides a winged horse and is escorted before Augustus by a little winged Eros, obviously enjoys greater distinction in this context. Megow and Jucker identify this figure as Drusus I, and the man standing in front of Tiberius as his son

---

[155] Jucker, 1976, 232–33, 241–42.
[156] Jucker, 1976, 213–214.

Germanicus.[157] In this one respect, however, I respectfully disagree
with Jucker's otherwise magisterial study of the gem, since his comparison of the figure with portraits of Drusus I is less compelling
than its resemblance to portraits of Germanicus.[158] Drusus I, his sons
and his grandsons would naturally have shown a family resemblance
that makes certainty difficult, but the gem-cutter has taken pains to
emphasize the short, compact face and square jaw of this man, features that are more prominent in the portraits of Germanicus than
of his father.

During his lifetime and afterward, likenesses of Germanicus were
often paired with those of his adoptive brother in compositions that
stressed the equality of the two heirs, although here it appears that
one of the two is, as Orwell would have said, more equal than the
other. If the man on the Pegasus is Germanicus, however, then the
man standing in front of Tiberius must be someone else. The same
figure could appear twice if the scenes were to be read as a con-
tinuous narration, but the organization of this gem is very different
from that of Roman sarcophagi, or of the columns of Trajan and
of Marcus Aurelius, in which there is a clearly legible flow of action
from left to right, and in which the reappearing figure of the hero
is always clearly identifiable as the same person. Here, figures in the
two registers interact, suggesting a simultaneous occurrence, and the
gem-cutter has been at some pains to differentiate the face of the
standing man from that of the man on the winged horse. The young
man before Tiberius has a family resemblance to Germanicus, to be
sure, but his face is a little fleshier, the point of his chin somewhat
larger, and he wears a soft, downy beard—not the clipped stubble
of a soldier, but the sort of beard that a young man would allow
to grow before ceremonially shaving for the first time. This figure,
then, would most logically be Nero I, the oldest son of Germanicus
(and, most significantly, the namesake of the living stepson of Claudius
after his adoption), at the moment when it seemed as though Tiberius
would name him as the next heir to power. Shortly after the death
of his own son Drusus II, Tiberius presented Nero I and Drusus III
to the Senate. The presence of Drusus II above these figures, slightly
lower in position than Augustus and the man on the winged horse,

---

[157] Megow, 1987, 204; Jucker, 1976, 218–219, 228–229.
[158] Jucker 1976, 228–229, figs. 5 and 6. On the iconography of Drusus II and
Germanicus on this gem, see Boschung, 1989, 64–65.

seems to indicate that he has just arrived in the heavens, and that the scene below is taking place a short time after he has died.

Whether the man on the winged horse is Drusus I or Germanicus, however, and whether the man before Tiberius is Germanicus or his son Nero I, the basic meaning remains much the same: the rightful heirs to power are the descendants of the divine Augustus, through Germanicus and Agrippina I. Despite the fact that neither Germanicus nor his two older sons lived to assume the imperial purple, the lawful heirs to the empire are the children of Germanicus, of whom Agrippina II is now the sole survivor, and his only grandchild Nero. (The embarrassing interlude of Caligula, the only child of Germanicus actually to hold power, is discreetly glossed over!) If my interpretation is correct, then Claudius and Agrippina II joyously witness the apotheosis of Germanicus, which takes place directly above their heads, as power passes to his children, but again, the apotheosis of Claudius's own father and Agrippina II's grandfather would make equally good sense in the context.

In the center of the cameo, Tiberius sits with the attributes of Jupiter, extending toward the chosen heir his right hand, which holds the *lituus* of a priest. As *pontifex maximus* of the state religion, Tiberius has spiritual as well as political authority in his choice for the succession. Beside the emperor is his mother Livia, whose identification has never been seriously disputed, wearing the coiffure with a middle part and a looped queue rather than a chignon at the nape of her neck.[159] Here, she holds in her hand the poppies and corn ears of Ceres, with whom Livia's association was by now extremely familiar. By the time when this gem was made, it was also an identification that her great-granddaughter Agrippina II prominently shared in her coin portraits (figures 121–122). Among earthly beings, Tiberius and Livia are the most important of the pairs in this register, to whom authority flows downward from the deified Augustus over their heads. The pair in front of them is second in rank, but parallel to them in that they too, in my opinion, represent a mother and her son. The standing woman has been extensively recut, and now appears to wear the hairstyle fashionable in the mid-third century A.D., but her profile, with the high forehead, slightly arched nose, long

---

[159] Winkes, 1995, 44–50, esp. p. 49, and 1982, 131–38. On the Boston cameo that shows this coiffure see also Megow, 1987, 256–57 no. B19, pl. 10.5; Mikocki, 1995, 169 no. 129 pl. 29.

rectangular jaw and firm chin support the widely accepted identification of her as Agrippina I, the mother of Nero I, on whose head
she places a helmet. Agrippina II sits behind Livia, on a lower chair
carefully differentiated from the Deified Augusta's more impressive
throne. Nonetheless, Agrippina II's chair has impressively decorative
griffin arm-rests. Claudius, in full armor, stands beside her, and it
is he who looks and gestures upward most dramatically to the figures
in the heavens, while the military trophy over his left shoulder reminds
us that he enjoys not only the reflected glory of his dead and heroized relatives, but has had military accomplishments of his own to
celebrate. Agrippina II also looks upward, although with a quieter
gesture and thoughtful expression.[160]

Although Claudius and Agrippina II do not occupy the middle of
the composition, they help to frame it: balancing them on the other
side is a little boy, also in armor, attended by a female figure. This
female defies identification with any historical personage: like the
figure who bears the deified Augustus aloft and the figure in eastern costume who sits on the ground between the thrones of Agrippina II and of Livia, she is not a portrait but an ideal personification,
probably representing *Providentia*, or "Forethought"—the wisdom, presumably, that led Augustus to put the line of succession in place that
will lead to this child.[161] The shape of her profile, in which the forehead and nose form one straight line and the chin is heavy and
rounded, conforms to Classical canons of ideal beauty. In one respect,
however, her treatment is quite unusual, in that the hair around her
face, instead of being swept back in natural waves, forms two tiers
of ringlets rather similar to those of Agrippina II, who faces her
from the opposite side of the gem. She does not wear a contemporary Julio-Claudian coiffure, since the hair at her nape is looped up
simply into the fillet that encircles her head, rather than forming a
chignon or hanging queue, but the curls assimilate her to the living
Augusta, and this allusion must be intentional. Before the later recutting deformed the central group, Agrippina I surely also wore curls
around her face, probably in regular rows, as her hair tends to be
represented in coins and gems. These three females, then, Agrippina I, Agrippina II, and *Providentia*, would have formed a repeating

---

[160] Jucker, 1976, 232–233, 241–242. Jucker suggests that her pose is deliberately
modeled on that of a Sibyl.
[161] Megow, 1987, 203; Jucker, 1976, 246–47.

pattern of curly-haired women across the middle register, just as the three standing male figures in armor, the heir in front of Tiberius, Claudius, and the child on the viewer's left, form a repeating pattern of male figures, all of whom are in line of succession to imperial power. The round-faced boy in front of *Providentia*, prominently and frontally presented to the viewer, is almost certainly Agrippina II's son Nero, the ultimate beneficiary of the line of dynastic succession that the gem diagrams.[162] Nero, of course, had not been born yet in A.D. 23, but his presence, like the representation of Claudius and Agrippina II as a couple, is a chronological liberty that prophecies the future of the dynasty, with the benefit, of course, of the gem-cutter's hindsight.

The Grande Camée de France represents not only the apotheosis of Germanicus and the glorification of his descendants, but the high-water mark of glory for the Julio-Claudian women in propagandistic art. Three of them appear together here, demonstrating along with the men the bloodlines that justify the position of the most recent heir. During most of the principate of Nero, women of the ruling family drop into artistic oblivion, as the women of his family become political liabilities to the emperor. One wife died on his orders, another allegedly at his hands, and his marriage to the third was too brief to allow her to obtain much prominence in public monuments. Poppaea received deification and public honor after her death, but the only likeness of her recognizable in official art is the little figure on one issue of coins from the Roman mint (figure 146). Profiles intended to represent Poppaea appear on coins of Alexandria, and on those of at least one other unidentified mint in the Greek-speaking east, identified by the inscription as "ΠΟΠΠΑΙΑ ΣΕΒΑΣΤΗ," "Poppaea Augusta."[163] These coins are probably not very reliable for Poppaea's physical features, but at least record that she wore the same type of coiffure as Agrippina II during the principates of Claudius and Nero: a broad area of curls covers the side of the head, a long, loosely waved lock falls forward to the shoulder, and a looped queue, fastened low on the nape, hangs down her neck.

A head in the Museo Nazionale Romano of a woman wearing a crescent diadem and a coiffure that shares these features has been

---

[162] Megow, 1987, 203–205; Jucker, 1976, 237.
[163] Bernoulli, 1882–84, 2¹, 417, pl. 35.19; Cohen, 1880, 1, 314–315 nos. 1–3.

proposed as a possible image of Nero's second wife.[164] In favor of
this hypothesis is the resemblance of her rather pudgy face to Nero's
adult portrait types, since a wife's appearance could be assimilated
to that of her husband. The diadem suggests, although it does not
prove, imperial status, and the fanciful version of the coiffure, which
now consists of rows of curls rolled up from the scalp rather than
ringlets that adhere to the contours of the skull, seems to confirm a
Neronian date. Von Heintze has identified a portrait in Schloss Fasanerie as a portrait of the same woman, but the latter work cannot
be a replica of the same prototype, since the hair on the sides of
the head forms waves flattened against the scalp, rather than curls.[165]
The similarities of the features are indeed striking, but until and unless a true replica of either of the two portraits should come to light,
the identity and imperial status of both must remain unproven. Private
funerary portraits could apotheosize their subjects with attributes like
the crescent diadem, and the diademed head in Rome could well
be a private portrait from Nero's time. Statilia Messalina, as mentioned above, remains to be identified in any extant works of art.

A dynasty depends for its survival on the existence of a smooth
mechanism for the transferral of power from one generation to the
next. The lack of any consistent and indisputable method for selecting an heir plagued the Julio-Claudians throughout their period of
power, and led to the many vicious power struggles within the family. Throughout that period, the increasingly bold representation of
women of the family in public art as part of a propagandistic effort
to justify the current emperor's status, or his choice of heir, reflects
the increasing need over the generations to emphasize bloodlines and
distinguished descent, and parallels the development of the principate into a monarchical system. The disappearance of women from
the public art of Nero, on the other hand, is surely symptomatic of,
though not by any means the only cause of, the collapse and demise
of the dynasty.

---

[164] *MNR Sculture* 1¹, 286–87 no. 178 (Virginia Picciotti-Giornetti); Felletti-Maj,
1953, 76 no. 131; Helbig⁴ 3, 225–26, no. 2308 (Helga von Heintze).
[165] Von Heintze, *Fulda*, 35–37 no. 25, pls. 42, 43, 117a.

CHAPTER SEVEN

CONCLUSIONS

The works of portraiture that this volume has surveyed do not display any one coherent style or progression of styles, if we consider
only their visual form. On the contrary, the likenesses of women
who were contemporaries and rivals for public influence, such as
Livilla I and Agrippina I, strikingly demonstrate the variety of formal
devices from which portraitists could choose, depending on the wishes
of their patrons and the personae that the subjects were attempting
to convey. Replicas of many portrait types, moreover, demonstrate
that copyists felt no obligation to follow the style or mood of the
officially disseminated type if a local patron preferred to present an
imperial figure more flamboyantly or perhaps more soberly than the
prototype did. This freedom of interpretation is most obvious in the
portraits of Livia, but the phenomenon appears as well in the likenesses of other women, especially those whose images continued to be
powerful political symbols after their deaths, and were adapted and
modified over a period of time. One such woman was Agrippina I;
we can observe the phenomenon to a lesser degree in the portraits
of her daughter, the deified Drusilla, despite the brief duration of her
cult, and even to some extent in the one securely datable posthumous
portrait of Agrippina II from after the fall of Nero.

If the styles of the works under study cannot be neatly summarized,
however, their political messages and their display of overt honors
to their subjects demonstrate a clear trajectory. From the scarce and
problematic portraits of Octavia Minor, whom her brother first skillfully exploited as a public symbol in his rivalry with Antony, but
whom he still had to present in public with cautious reticence, we
see a steady increase in the public visibility of these women and the
institutionalization of their status as members of a hereditary dynasty.
First and foremost, every woman owed her place in the public image
of her family to her fertility, real or anticipated, as an ancestress or
as a mother of future emperors. Yet a few of the most prominent
of these women conspicuously failed to fulfill this dynastic imperative:
Livia, although the mother of two sons who were viable heirs to

power, produced no children with Augustus; Octavia Minor's only son died young, and Drusilla died childless. In these cases, many patrons, both imperial and private, seem to have sensed no irony or contradiction in celebrating them as symbolic, rather than as literal, mothers, a phenomenon that should alert us to the fact that Roman families valued their women for more than their reproductive function. From the time of Livia onward, the ability of these women to intercede with their husbands in matters of official policy was a matter of public knowledge, and apparently of widespread public approval. In many cases, these women may have been honored with public representation in statuary or coins, or in private settings with cameo gems or small-scale images in lararia, precisely because they had exercised that influence to the benefit of the patrons of the images.

Every principate from that of Augustus onward marks a new "first" in honors to women: under Augustus, statues of women of the imperial family appeared in public places, and living women were represented in the historical reliefs of a major public monument; under Tiberius, a recognizable portrait likeness of a woman first appeared on coinage of the mint of Rome, albeit without an identifying inscription, and a woman was first openly identified in inscriptions and in visual iconography with a major goddess, Ceres Augusta. During the principate of Caligula, not only did the living women of the family receive a number of unprecedented honors, such as inclusion with the emperor in oaths of allegiance and the full status of honorary Vestal Virgins, but one deceased woman, Agrippina I, was the first to receive an issue of coinage dedicated entirely to her, while another, Drusilla, became the first Roman woman to be deified. Claudius added a second *diva*, his grandmother Livia, to the state pantheon, and made his fourth wife, Agrippina II, the first living woman since Livia to hold the title of Augusta, as well as the first living woman ever to appear in recognizable portrait likenesses with identifying inscriptions on coins of the Roman mint. Finally, under Nero, Agrippina II went on to share the obverses of coins with her son, in formats that suggested near equality of power. As noted at the end of the previous chapter, however, that high point of political prominence was followed by her disastrous fall from grace, after which the women of Nero's family sink to a much more modest and subordinate level in public art, although Poppaea still appears on some coins, and is known to have been honored with some public statuary as well as with a grandiose state funeral.

In subsequent dynasties, however, although no woman ever again achieves the prominence of an Agrippina II, the precedents of the Julio-Claudian period seem to have exerted some influence both on the real powers of imperial women and on the ways in which the visual arts publicly recognized their positions. Julia Flavia, the daughter of Titus, appeared during her lifetime on coins that associated her with Ceres, the goddess with whom Livia had been most widely identified, and who remained by far the most popular divine figure for association with imperial women. Julia Flavia's portrait on some of the obverses of these coins, significantly, bears a more than casual resemblance to those of Livia's "adoption" portrait type, the type that had first appeared on coinage of the Roman mint under the guise of *Salus Augusta* (figure 34): Julia, despite the changes in fashion that dictate a full mass of curls around the face, wears a small, low chignon on the back of her head in many of these coins, and smoothly combed waves on the side of the head behind the area of curls, an arrangement that gives her profile the same general shape as Livia's "*Salus*" profiles.[1] Later, after Julia's death, the *carpentum sestertii* that honored Livia in A.D. 22 and Agrippina the Elder during the principate of Caligula obviously served as prototypes for the sestertii that recorded Julia Flavia's deification: again, the reverses of *sestertii* bear the image of a decorated *carpentum* drawn by mules, in a format closely similar to that of the earlier issues.[2] Domitian's motives for consecrating his niece were probably much like those of Caligula when he deified Drusilla: neither Julia Flavia nor Drusilla had produced heirs, but each was honored for her unfulfilled potential as a mother of future emperors. Julia Flavia, like Drusilla before her, was closely associated with Venus in coinage and sculpture, both during her lifetime and after her death and deification.[3] The poet Martial

[1] *BMCRE* 2, 278 nos. 253, pl. 5, fig. 5, and 278 no. 254. The same slightly old-fashioned coiffure appears on some of Julia Flavia's other issues as well, e.g. *BMCRE* 2, 279 no. 256, with a reverse of Vesta. For the parallels to Livia's portraits, Daltrop, Hausmann and Wegner, 1966, 54.
[2] *BMCRE* 2, 402–403 nos. 458–463, pl. 80, fig. 3.
[3] Mart. *Epigrams* 6.13.5–8.
Coins of Julia Flavia with reverses of Venus: *BMCRE* 2, 247, 140–143, pl. 47, figs. 15 and 16. Sculptural portraits of Julia Flavia with the coiffure of a Hellenistic Venus:

hailed the deified Julia as a protective fate watching over the wel-
fare of her family and safeguarding the fertility of its living members, as she spun the golden life-thread of Domitian's unborn son.[4]

Nor was Julia Flavia the only Flavian woman to receive consecration: Vespasian's daughter Domitilla, who had died before her father
became emperor, was similarly honored and represented on coins.
The deification of women, which Seneca had once scornfully dismissed as the folly of Caligula, had become not only acceptable to
the Roman public but a good way for a family of modest social origins to acquire some imperial luster.[5] The *sestertii* that record Domitilla's
divine honors are even more directly modeled on the *carpentum sestertii*
of Agrippina I than are those of Julia Flavia; even the wording of
the inscription, MEMORIAE DOMITILLAE, follows the identical
formula.[6] The representation of women on coinage of the Roman
mint and in public statuary remains commonplace in every succeeding
dynasty, as does the addition of divine attributes to the portraits of
these women, and the adaptation for their likenesses of statuary types
based on Classical or Hellenistic prototypes that originally represented
the major Olympian goddesses.

The Julio-Claudian emperors were not, in many cases, the most
skilled practitioners of public relations. Augustus was a master at
manipulating public opinion, but none of his successors matched his
ability, and some, like Caligula and Nero, were disastrously incompetent at understanding what the public could and could not accept.
The survival during the Flavian and subsequent dynasties of the
iconography that honors imperial women could hardly have derived
from any nostalgia for the recent past. Rather, the visual imagery
that honors both Drusilla and Julia Flavia, as young women who

---

Vatican, Braccio Nuovo no. 78, marble bust, h. 94 cm., of head 39 cm. Amelung,
Vatican 1, 95, no. 78, pl. 12.

Copenhagen, Ny Carlsberg Glyptotek cat. 657, I.N. 1264, marble head, h. 56
cm. Poulsen, *Portraits* 2, 1974, 46–47 no. 11, pls. 19–20; Daltrop, Hausmann and
Wegner, 1966, 58, 115, 118, pl. 45; *LIMC* 8[1], 217 no. 285, 8[2] pl. 155 no. 285,
s.v. "Venus" (E. Schmidt).

[4] Mart. *Epigrams* 6.3.5–6.

[5] On the deification of Domitilla: Stat. *Silv.* 1.1.94–98; Daltrop, Hausmann and
Wegner, 1966, 60–62; coins of Diva Domitilla *BMCRE* 2, 246 nos. 136–138, pl. 47,
11–13; 249 no. 148 pl. 48.1; 251, nos. 14–15; 270–271 nos. 226–229, pl. 51, 8
and 9; 312 no. 68 pl. 61.11. For an earlier, satirical reference to the deification of
Drusilla, Sen. *Apocol.* 1; attitudes toward the deification of women had obviously
changed by Statius's time.

[6] *BMCRE* 2, 270–271 nos. 226–229, pl. 51, figs. 8 and 9.

died untimely deaths and became *divae*, or that presents Plotina as an *exemplum* of chastity and matronly respectability, like the early portraits of Livia, must have succeeded because the imagery appealed to strongly held popular emotions and sentiments about the appropriate role of a woman in an elite family. That role was of course, and inevitably, defined by a society that was both patriarchal and strongly hierarchical: a woman's primary value to society was reproductive, her virtues defined by loyalty to the men of her family. On the other hand, by no possible stretch of the imagination were women like Octavia, Livia, and the Agrippinae, elder and younger, disenfranchised or powerless; their familial roles provided them with a means to exercise their wills, and to receive public approval in many cases for doing so. To what extent women of more humble circumstances shared an equivalent level of power in the spheres of their family's political activities and business affairs is difficult to ascertain. The images of imperial women give us reason to suspect, however, that although Roman society expected women to accept a subordinate role to that of men, women of will and intelligence found ways within the structure of that society to empower themselves.

APPENDIX

GENEALOGY AND NOMENCLATURE

The family tree of the Julio-Claudian dynasty is far too complex to diagram in full on a single page. Many of its members had multiple marriages, with offspring by several spouses, and many marriages took place for dynastic purposes between cousins of the family's two main branches. The following charts demonstrate the immediate relationships of each of the women whose images have been discussed at any length in the preceding chapters; where lines of descent intersect, but space does not allow a full elaboration, I have given cross references to other charts that will supply more complete information. Children who died in infancy have been omitted from the tables except for those that figured prominently in dynastic propaganda before their deaths, as for example Germanicus II, one of the twin sons of Drusus II and Livilla I, and Claudia Augusta, the daughter of the emperor Nero.

Roman nomenclature can be both confusing and repetitive. In the interests of space and clarity, I have usually referred to all historical figures in the text by the best known abbreviations of their names, or familiar nicknames: so, for example, the emperor whose actual name was Gaius Julius Caesar Germanicus but is far better known by his childhood nickname "Caligula" has been called "Caligula" or "Gaius 'Caligula'" in the text. In the genealogical tables, persons with the same name but of different generations will be identified by Roman numerals: Agrippina I, and Agrippina II, and Drusus I and Drusus II, e.g., while siblings with the same name will be differentiated in the standard Roman manner by the designations "major" and "minor:" for example, Antonia Major and Antonia Minor. The following is a list of the forms of the names that will be used for the major figures discussed here, and of their full names and identities:

Agrippa: Marcus Vipsanius Agrippa, b. 64 or 63 B.C., d. 12 B.C. General and prominent political figure during the principate of Augustus, husband of Julia I, father of Vipsania Agrippina, Gaius Caesar, Lucius Caesar, Agrippa Postumus, Julia II and Agrippina I.

Agrippa Postumus: Marcus Vipsanius Agrippa Postumus, b. 12 B.C., d. A.D. 16, son of Agrippa and Julia I.

Agrippina I: Vipsania Agrippina, b. ca. 14 B.C., d. A.D. 33, daughter of Agrippa and Julia I, wife of Germanicus, mother of Nero I, Drusus III, Caligula, Agrippina II, Drusilla I, Livilla II, and 3 other children, 2 of whom died in infancy and one in early childhood.

Agrippina II: Julia Agrippina, b. A.D. 15, d. A.D. 59, daughter of Germanicus and Agrippina I, wife of Gnaeus Domitius Ahenobarbus and later of the emperor Claudius, mother of the emperor Nero.

Antonia Major: Antonia Major, b. 39 B.C., d. ?, daughter of Antony and Octavia Minor, wife of Lucius Domitius Ahenobarbus, mother of Gnaeus Domitius Ahenobarbus, Domitia, and Domitia Lepida.

Antonia Minor: Antonia Minor, b. 36 B.C., d. A.D. 37, daughter of Antony and Octavia Minor, wife of Drusus I, mother of Germanicus, the emperor Claudius, and Livilla I.

Antony: Marcus Antonius, b. ca. 83 B.C., d. 30 B.C., triumvir and rival for power of Octavian, husband of Fulvia and father by her of Marcus Antonius and Iullus

Antonius; later husband of Octavia Minor, and father by her of Antonia Major and Antonia Minor; and finally married (although the marriage was not acknowledged by Roman law) to Cleopatra VII of Egypt, father by her of Alexander Helios, Cleopatra Selene, and Ptolemy Philadelphus.

Augustus: Gaius Julius Caesar Octavianus Augustus, b. 63 B.C., d. A.D. 14, emperor 31 B.C.–A.D. 14, known as Octavian prior to 27 B.C., son of G. Octavius and Atia, adopted son of Gaius Julius Caesar, father of Julia I.

Britannicus: Tiberius Claudius Britannicus, b. A.D. 41, d. A.D. 55, son of the emperor Claudius and Messalina, brother of Claudia Antonia and Claudia Octavia, adopted brother of the emperor Nero.

Caligula: Gaius Julius Caesar Germanicus, A.D. 12–41, emperor 37–41, son of Germanicus and Agrippina I, brother of Nero I, Drusus III, Agrippina II, Drusilla I and Livilla II, father of Drusilla II.

Claudia Antonia: Claudia Antonia, b. A.D. 27, d. A.D. 66, daughter of the emperor Claudius and Aelia Paetina.

Claudia Augusta: b. A.D. 63, d. four months later in A.D. 63, daughter of the emperor Nero and Poppaea.

Claudia Octavia: Claudia Octavia, b. A.D. 40 or 42, d. A.D. 62, daughter of the emperor Claudius and Messalina.

Claudius, Emperor: Ti. Claudius Caesar Augustus Germanicus, b. 10 B.C., d. A.D. 54, son of Drusus I and Antonia Minor, father of Claudia Antonia, Claudia Octavia, and Britannicus.

Drusilla I: Julia Drusilla, b. ca. A.D. 16 (date and order of birth uncertain), d. A.D. 38, first or second daughter of Germanicus and Agrippina I, sister of Caligula.

Drusilla II: Julia Drusilla, b. A.D. 39, d. A.D. 41, daughter of Caligula and of Milonia Caesonia.

Drusus I, often called Drusus Major: Nero Claudius Drusus, b. 38 B.C., d. 9 B.C., son of Ti. Claudius Nero and Livia Drusilla, husband of Antonia Minor, father of Germanicus, the emperor Claudius, and Livilla I.

Drusus II, often called Drusus Minor: Drusus Julius Caesar, b. 13 B.C., d. A.D. 23, son of the emperor Tiberius and Vipsania Agrippina, husband of Livilla I, father of Tiberius Gemellus, Germanicus II and Julia III.

Drusus III: Drusus Julius Caesar, b. A.D. 7, d. A.D. 33, son of Germanicus and Agrippina I, older brother of Caligula.

Gaius Caesar: Gaius Caesar, b. 20 B.C., d. A.D. 4, son of Agrippa and Julia I, adopted son of Augustus.

Germanicus: born Nero Claudius Germanicus, later adopted by Tiberius as Germanicus Julius Caesar, b. 15 B.C., d. A.D. 19, son of Drusus I and Antonia Minor, husband of Agrippina I, father of Nero I, Drusus III, Caligula, Agrippina II, Drusilla I, and Livilla II.

Germanicus II: Germanicus Julius Caesar, b. A.D. 19, d. A.D. 23, son of Drusus II and Livilla II, twin brother of Tiberius Gemellus.

Julia I: Julia, b. 39 B.C., d. A.D. 14, daughter of Augustus and Scribonia, wife of Marcellus, then of Agrippa, and finally of Tiberius, mother of Gaius Caesar, Lucius Caesar, Agrippa Postumus, Julia II and Agrippina I.

Julia II: Julia, b. 19 or 18 B.C., d. A.D. 28, daughter of Agrippa and Julia I.

Julia III: Julia, b. A.D. 3 or 4, d. A.D. 43, daughter of Drusus II and Livilla I.

Livia: Livia Drusilla, known from A.D. 14 onward as Julia Augusta, b. 58 B.C., d. A.D. 29, daughter of M. Livius Drusus Claudianus and Alfidia, wife first of Tiberius Claudius Nero and later of Augustus, mother by her first husband of Drusus I and of the emperor Tiberius.

Livilla I: Claudia Livia Julia, b. ca. 13 B.C., d. A.D. 31, daughter of Drusus I and Antonia Minor, wife of Drusus II, mother of the twins Tiberius Gemellus and Germanicus II, and of Julia III.

Livilla II: Julia Livilla, b. A.D. 18, d. A.D. 42, daughter of Germanicus and Agrippina, sister of Caligula.

Lucius Caesar: Lucius Caesar, b. 17 B.C., d. A.D. 2, son of Agrippa and Julia I, adopted son of Augustus.

Marcellus: Marcus Claudius Marcellus, b. 42 B.C., d. 23 B.C., son of Gaius Claudius Marcellus and Octavia Minor.

Messalina (sometimes spelled "Messallina"): Valeria Messalina, b. ca. A.D. 25, d. A.D. 48, daughter of Domitia Lepida and M. Valerius Messala Barbatus, third wife of Claudius, mother of Claudia Octavia and Britannicus.

Nero I: Julius Caesar Nero, b. ca. A.D. 6, d. A.D. 31, eldest son of Germanicus and Agrippina I, brother of Caligula.

Nero, Emperor: born L. Domitius Ahenobarbus, adopted by Claudius as Nero Claudius Caesar, b. A.D. 37, d. A.D. 68, emperor A.D. 54–68, son of Gn. Domitius Ahenobarbus and Agrippina II.

Octavia: Octavia Minor, b. ca. 70 B.C., d. 11 B.C., daughter of G. Octavius and Atia, sister of Augustus, wife of Gaius Claudius Marcellus and later of Antony, mother of Marcellus, Claudia Marcella Major, Claudia Marcella Minor, Antonia Major and Antonia Minor.

Poppaea: Poppaea Sabina, later Poppaea Sabina Augusta, b. A.D. 32, d. A.D. 65, daughter of T. Ollius and Poppaea Sabina, second wife of Nero, mother of Claudia Augusta.

Tiberius, Emperor: Tiberius Caesar Augustus, b. 42 B.C., d. A.D. 37, emperor A.D. 14–37, son of Tiberius Claudius Nero and Livia Drusilla, adopted son of Augustus, father of Drusus II.

Tiberius Gemellus: Tiberius Julius Caesar Gemellus, b. A.D. 19, d. A.D. 37, son of Drusus II and Livilla I, twin brother of Germanicus II.

CHART NO. 1: FAMILY TREE OF OCTAVIA MINOR

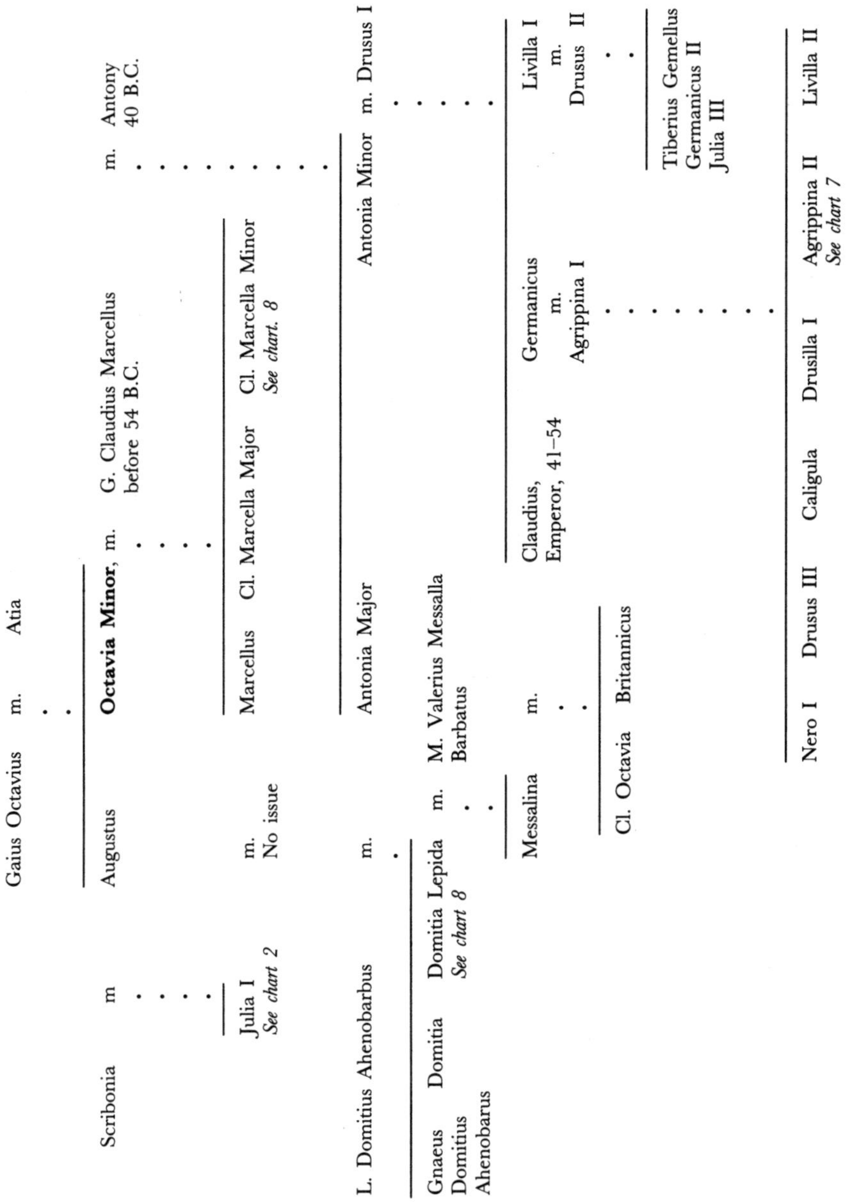

Gaius Octavius m. Atia

Scribonia m Augustus **Octavia Minor**, m. G. Claudius Marcellus m. Antony
before 54 B.C. 40 B.C.

Julia I
See chart 2

m.
No issue

Marcellus Cl. Marcella Major Cl. Marcella Minor
See chart 8

L. Domitius Ahenobarbus Antonia Major m. Antonia Minor m. Drusus I

Gnaeus Domitia Domitia Lepida m. M. Valerius Messalla
Domitius See chart 8 Barbatus
Ahenobarus

Messalina m. Claudius, Germanicus Livilla I
Emperor, 41–54 m. m.
Agrippina I Drusus II

Cl. Octavia Britannicus

Tiberius Gemellus
Germanicus II
Julia III

Nero I Drusus III Caligula Drusilla I Agrippina II Livilla II
See chart 7

CHART NO. 2: FAMILY TREE OF JULIA F. AUGUSTI (JULIA I)

Scribonia   m.   **Julia I**   Augustus   m.   Livia   m.   Drusus I   m.   Antonia Minor   m.   Ti. Claudius Nero

Marcellus m. Agrippa   Tiberius,   Germanicus   Claudius   Livilla I m. Drusus II
No issue   m. **Julia I**   Emperor,
                                 No issue   41–54

Gaius   Lucius   Agrippa   Julia II   Agrippina I   Tiberius Gemellus
Caesar Caesar   Postumus   Germanicus II
                                                                                                         Julia III

Nero I   Drusus III   Caligula   Drusilla I   Drusilla I   Livilla II   Agrippina II   m.   Cn. Domitius Ahenobarbus

                                                                        Nero, emperor 54–68

CHART 3: FAMILY TREE OF LIVIA DRUSILLA, LATER KNOWN AS JULIA AUGUSTA

M. Livius Drusus Claudianus   m.   Alfidia

Scribonia   m.   Augustus   m.   Livia   m.   Ti. Claudius Nero
No issue

Julia
(See chart 2)

Tiberius, m. Vipsania Agrippina   Drusus I   m.   Antonia Minor
Emperor 14–37

Drusus II   m.   Livilla I   Claudius, Emperor 41–54   Germanicus m. Agrippina I

Tiberius Gemellus
Germanicus II
Julia III

Gn. Domitius Ahenobarbus   m.   Agrippina II   Drusilla I   Livilla II   Nero I   Drusus III   Caligula

Nero, Emperor

CHART 4: FAMILY TREE OF ANTONIA MINOR

Antony   m.   Octavia Minor
(See Chart 1)

Domitius Ahenobarbus m.   Antonia Major   **Antonia Minor**   m.   Drusus I

Gn. Domitius
Ahenobarbus,
Father of Nero
See charts 3, 7

Domitia   Domitia Lepida
m. M. Valerius
Messalla Barbatus
See chart 8

Messalina   m.   Claudius
Emperor,
41–54

Livilla I, m. Drusus II
See chart 3

Tiberius Gemellus,
Germanicus Julius Caesar
Julia III

Germanicus, m. Agrippina I

Agrippina II,
m.
Gn. Domitius
Ahenobarbus

Drusilla I   Livilla II   Nero I   Drusus III   Caligula

Britannicus   Claudia Octavia   m.   Nero, Emperor

No issue

CHART 5: FAMILY TREE OF VIPSANIA AGRIPPINA

Julia, f. Augusti   m.   Agrippa   m.   Attica

See chart 2

Asinius Gallus   m.   Vipsania Agrippina   m.   Tiberius, Emperor 14–37

C. Asinius Pollio
M. Asinius Agrippa
Asinius Gallus   Livilla I   m.   Drusus II
Cn. Asinius
Asinius Saloninus
Ser. Asinius Celer

Tiberius Gemellus, Germanicus II, Julia III

CHART 6: FAMILY TREE OF CLAUDIA LIVIA JULIA (LIVILLA I)

Livia   m.   Ti. Claudius Nero   Octavia Minor   m.   Antony

Vipsania Agrippina   m.   Tiberius Emperor, 14–37   Drusus I   m.   Antonia Minor   Antonia Major

Drusus II   m.   Livilla I   Claudius, Emperor   Germanicus   m.   Agrippina I
See charts 1–4

Tiberius Gemellus,
Germanicus Julius Caesar
Julia III

CHART 7: FAMILY TREE OF AGRIPPINA I AND HER DAUGHTERS
AGRIPPINA II, DRUSILLA I AND JULIA LIVILLA (LIVILLA II)

Scribonia   m.   Augustus   m.   Livia   m.   Ti. Claudius Nero
                                      No issue

             Julia f. Augusti m. M. Agrippa   Drusus I   Tiberius, Emperor 14–37
                                                     m. Antonia Minor   m. Vipsania Agrippina (see
                                                     See chart 4   chart 5)

Gaius   Lucius   Agrippa Postumus   Julia II   Agrippina I   m.   Germanicus
Caesar   Caesar

Milonia Caesonia   m.   Caligula   Nero I   Drusus III   Drusilla I   Livilla II   Agrippina II
                                                                                          m. Gn. Domitius
                                                                                          Ahenobarbus, father of
                                                                                          Nero. Second marriage
                                                                                          to Claudius without
                                                                                          issue.

             Drusilla II   Claudia Octavia   m.   Nero, Emperor   m.   Poppaea
                                                                      No issue

                                                                                                     Claudia Augusta

CHART 8: VALERIA MESSALINA AND HER DAUGHTER CLAUDIA OCTAVIA

C. Claudius Marcellus m. Octavia Minor m. . . . . . Antony

Marcellus Cl. Marcella Major Cl. Marcella Minor m. M. Valerius Barbatus Antonia Minor *See chart 4* Antonia Major m. . . . . . L. Domitius Ahenobarbus

M. Valerius Messalla Barbatus m. . . . . . Domitia Lepida Domitia Gn. Domitius Ahenobarbus, m. Agrippina II *See charts 3, 4, 7*

Claudius, Emperor m. . . **Messalina**

Britannicus **Claudia Octavia** m. Nero, Emperor No issue

ABBREVIATIONS

For all standard journals and reference works, including some catalogues such as those of the Capitoline Museums and of the coins in the British Museum, the abbreviations used here will be those listed in "Editorial Policy, Notes for Contributors, and Abbreviations," *AJA* 95 (1991) 1–16. All works will be cited in the notes by author's last name and year of publication; the full references can be found in the bibliography. For certain frequently cited works, and for works in which the date of publication alone does not give sufficient identification, the following abbreviations will be used.

Amelung, *Vatican* 1: Walther Amelung, *Die Skulpturen des Vaticanischen Museums* Vol. 1, Berlin, 1903, reprint Berlin and New York: De Gruyter, 1995.

Amelung, *Vatican* 2: Walther Amelung, *Die Skulpturen des Vaticanischen Museums* Vol. 2, Berlin, 1908, reprint Berlin and New York: De Gruyter, 1995.

Baia: Multiple authors. *Baia: Il ninfeo imperiale sommerso di Punta Epitaffio*. Naples: Edizione Banca Sannitica, 1983.

Banti-Simonetti, *CNR*: Alberto Banti and Luigi Simonetti, *Corpus Nummorum Romanorum*. Florence: A. Banti, 1972–, 18 vols.

BMCRE: Harold Mattingly. *Coins of the Roman Empire in the British Museum*. London: the British Museum, 1923, reprinted with revisions 1975.

Boschung, *Augustus* 1993: Boschung, Dietrich. *Die Bildnisse des Augustus, Das römische Herrscherbild* pt. 1 v. 2. Berlin: Mann, 1993.

Boschung, *JRA* 1993: Boschung, Dietrich. "Die Bildnistypen der iulisch-claudischen Kaiserfamilie: ein kritischer Forschungsbericht." *JRA* 6, 1993, pp. 39–79.

Caere 2: Fuchs, Michaela, Paolo Liverani, Paola Santoro. *Caere 2: Il teatro e il ciclo statuario giulio-claudio*. Ed. Paola Santoro. Rome: Consiglio Nazionale delle Ricerche, 1989.

Von Heintze, *Fulda*: Von Heintze, Helga. *Die antiken Porträts in Schloss Fasanerie bei Fulda*. Mainz am Rhein: von Zabern, 1968.

De Kersauson, *Louvre* 1: de Kersauson, Kate. *Catalogue des portraits romains* 1: *Portraits de la République et d'époque Julio-Claudienne*. Paris: Editions de la Réunion des musées nationaux, 1986.

Kleiner, *Sculpture* 1992: Kleiner, Diana E.E., *Roman Sculpture*. New Haven and London: Yale University Press, 1992.

Lippold, *Vatican* 3^1: Lippold, Georg. *Die Skulpturen des Vaticanischen Museums* Vol. 3^1. Berlin: Reimer, 1936.

Lippold, *Vatican* 3^2: Lippold, Georg. *Die Skulpturen des Vaticanischen Museums* Vol. 3^2. Berlin: Reimer, 1956.

MNR Sculture: *Museo Nazionale Romano: Le sculture*, ed. Antonio Giuliano. Rome: De Luca, 1979–.

Polaschek, *Antonia*, 1973: Polaschek, Karin. *Studien zur Ikonographie der Antonia Minor*. Rome: Bretschneider, 1973.

Polaschek, *Porträttypen*, 1973: Polaschek, Karin. *Porträttypen einer Claudischen Kaiserin*. Rome: Bretschneider, 1973.

Poulsen, *Portraits* 1: Poulsen, Vagn. *Les portraits romains* 1: *République et dynastie Julienne*. Copenhagen, 1962.

RIC: Harold Mattingly and C.H.V. Sutherland, *Roman Imperial Coinage*, Vol. 1, 2nd edition, London Spink, 1984.

Rose, *AJA* 1990: Rose, C. Brian. "'Princes' and Barbarians on the Ara Pacis," *AJA* 94, 1990, 453–467.

Rose, *JRA* 1990: Rose, Charles Brian. "The supposed Augustan arch at Pavia (Ticinum) and the Einsiedeln 326 manuscript." *JRA* 3, 1990. 163–168.

Roselle, 1990: Multiple authors, *Un decennio di ricerche a Roselle. Statue e ritratti*, exhibition catalogue. Florence: Edizioni Zeta, 1990.

RPC: Andrew Burnett, Michel Amandry and Pere Pau Ripollès, *Roman Provincial Coinage*. London: British Museum Press, and Paris: Bibliothèque Nationale de France, 2nd edition, 1998.

Tölle-Kastenbein, *AM*, 1974: Tölle-Kastenbein, Renate. "Juno Ludovisi: Hera oder Antonia Minor?" *AM* 89 (1974) pp. 241–253, pls. 91–96.

Tölle-Kastenbein, *Samos*, 1974: Tölle-Kastenbein, Renate. *Samos XIV: Das Kastro Tigani, die Bauten und Funde griechischer, römischer und byzantinisher Zeit*. Bonn: Rudolf Habelt Verlag, 1974.

Winkes, "Bildnistypen," 1988: Winkes, Rolf. "Bildnistypen der Livia." *Ritratto ufficiale e ritratto privato: Atti della II Conferenza Internazionale sul Ritratto Romano*. Roma: Consiglio Nazionale delle Richerche, 1988, 555–561.

Winkes, "Spanish Image," 1988: Winkes, Rolf. "A Spanish Image of Livia." *Revue des Archéologues et Historiens d'art de Louvain*, 21, 1988, 75–78.

BIBLIOGRAPHY

N.A., *A History of the Hispanic Society of America, Museum and Library, 1904–1954*. New York: Hispanic Society, 1954.

Multiple authors. *Baia: Il ninfeo imperiale sommerso di Punta Epitaffio*. Naples: Edizione Banca Sannitica, 1983. Chapter on statuary group: Bernard Andreae, "Le sculture," pp. 49–72, pls. 122–174.

Multiple authors. *Un decennio di ricerche a Roselle: Statue e ritratti*. Florence: Edizioni Zeta, 1990.

Allen, Pauline. "Contemporary Portrayals of the Byzantine Empress Theodora (A.D. 527–548)." *Stereotypes of Women in Power: Historical Perspectives and Revisionist Views*. Ed. Barbara Garlick, Suzanne Dixon and Pauline Allen. Greenwood Press: New York, Westport, CT and London, 1992, 93–103.

Amedick, Rita. "Die Kinder des Kaisers Claudius: zu den Porträts des Tiberius Claudius Britannicus und der Octavia Claudia." *RM* 98, 1991, 373–395, pls. 95–104.

Amelung, Walther, *Die Skulpturen des Vaticanischen Museums*. Vols. 1 and 2. Berlin, 1903 and 1908, reprinted New York: De Gruyter, 1995.

Anderson, Maxwell. "The Portrait Medallions of the Imperial Villa at Boscotrecase," *AJA* 91, 1987, 127–135.

Andreae, Bernard. *Odysseus: Archäologie des europäischen Menschenbildes*. Frankfurt: Societäts-Verlag, 1982.

Anti, Carlo. *Il Regio Museo Archeologico nel Palazzo Reale di Venezia*. Rome: Libreria dello Stato, 1930.

Anti, Carlo. "Un nuovo ritratto di Agrippina Maggiore." *AfrIt* 2, 1928, 3–16, pls. 1–3.

Arias, Paolo Enrico. "Analisi Critica delle Statue/The Critical Analysis of the Statues," *Gli Eroi Venuti dal Mare/Heroes from the Sea*. Rome: Gangemi, 1986.

Arias, Paolo Enrico. "Nuovi Contributi all'iconografia di Ottavia Minore." *RM* 54, 1939, 76–81, pls. 18–22.

Aurenhammer, Maria. "Römische Porträts aus Ephesos." *Ritratto ufficiale e ritratto privato: Atti della II Conferenza Internazionale sul Ritratto Romano*. Roma: Consiglio Nazionale delle Richerche, 1988, 123–130.

Aurigemma, Salvatore. "Sculture del Foro Vecchio di Leptis Magna raffiguranti la Dea Roma e principi della casa dei Giulio-Claudi." *AfrIt* 8, 1940, pp. 1–92.

Balsdon, J.P.V.D. *Roman Women*. New York: The John Day Company, 1962.

Balty, Jean Charles. "Groupes statuaires impériaux et privés de l'époque julio-claudienne." *Ritratto ufficiale e ritratto privato: Atti della II Conferenza Internazionale sul Ritratto Romano*. Roma: Consiglio Nazionale delle Richerche, 1988, pp. 31–46.

Balty, Jean Charles. "Il 'gruppo' giulio-claudio del foro di Béziers." *Lo Sguardo di Roma*, exhibition catalogue. Rome, Acquario di Roma, 15 Feb.–25 Apr. 1996.

Balty, Jean Charles. "Style et facture: notes sur le portrait romain du IIIe siècle du notre ère," *RA* (1983), 301–315.

Balty, Jean Charles, and Daniel Cazes. *Portraits Impériaux de Béziers. Le groupe statuaire du forum*. Toulouse: Musée Saint-Raymond, 1995.

Banti, Alberto, and Luigi Simonetti, *Corpus Nummorum Romanorum*. Florence: A. Banti, 1972–, 18 vols.

Barker, E.R. *Buried Herculaneum*. London: A. and C. Black, 1908.

Barrett, Anthony A. *Agrippina: Sex, Power and Politics in the Early Empire.* New Haven and London: Yale University Press, 1996.

Barrett, Anthony A., *Caligula: the Corruption of Power.* New Haven: Yale University Press, 1990.

Bartels, Heinrich. *Studien zum Frauenporträt der augusteischen Zeit: Fulvia, Octavia, Livia, Julia.* Munich: Feder Verlag, 1963.

Bartman, Elizabeth. "Beyond *I, Claudius*: the Roman Empress Livia." Lecture presented at the Detroit Institute of Arts, March 10, 1998, for the Archaeological Institute of America, typescript supplied to me by the author.

Bartman, Elizabeth. *Portraits of Livia: Imaging the Imperial Woman in Augustan Rome.* Cambridge: Cambridge University Press, forthcoming November 1998. Some pages of the ms. have been supplied to me by the author.

Belhomme, M. "Sculptures antiques pour le musée de Toulouse." *Memoires de la société archéologique du midi de la France* 5 (1841–1847), 277–295.

Belli Pasqua, Roberta, *Sculture di età Romana in "Basalto".* Rome, L'Erma di Bretschneider, 1995.

Bernoulli, J.J. *Römische Ikonographie.* 3 vols. Berlin-Stuttgart: W. Spemann, 1882–1884, reprinted Hildesheim: G. Olms, 1969.

Bianchi-Bandinelli, Ranuccio. *Leptis Magna.* Milan: Mondadori, 1964.

Bieber, Margarete. *Ancient Copies: Contributions to the History of Greek and Roman Art.* New York: New York University Press, 1977.

Bieber, Margarete. *The Sculpture of the Hellenistic Age,* rev. ed. New York: Columbia University Press, 1961.

Bieber, Margarete. *The Statue of Cybele.* Malibu: The J. Paul Getty Museum, 1968.

Blome, Peter. "Zur Umgestaltung griechischer Mythen in der römischen Sepulkralkunst. Alkestis-, Protesilaos- und Proserpinasarkophage." *RM* 85 (1978), 435–445.

Blümel, Carl. *Katalog der Sammlung antiker Skulpturen* V: *Römische Kopien Griechischer Skulpturen des vierten Jahrhunderts v.Chr.* Berlin, 1938.

Blümel, Carl. *Römische Bildnisse.* Berlin: Verlag für Kunstwissenschaft, 1933.

Boardman, John. *Greek Sculpture: the Classical Period.* London: Thames and Hudson, 1985.

Boddington, Ann. "Sejanus. Whose Conspiracy?" *AJPhil,* 84, 1963, 1–16.

Bol, Renate. "Beobachtungen zur Porträtgruppe aus dem Metroon in Olympia." *Ritratto ufficiale e ritratto privato: Atti della II Conferenza Internazionale sul Ritratto Romano.* Roma: Consiglio Nazionale delle Richerche, 1988, pp. 141–147.

Bol, Renate. "Ein Bildnis der Claudia Octavia aus dem olympischen Metroon." *JdI* 101, 1986, pp. 289–306.

Bonacasa, Nicola. *Ritratti Greci e Romani della Sicilia.* Palermo : Fondazione I. Mormino del Banco di Sicilia, 1964.

Bonfante, Larissa. "Daily Life and Afterlife," *Etruscan Life and Afterlife.* Detroit: Wayne State University Press, 1986, 232–278.

Boschung, Dietrich. *Die Bildnisse des Augustus, Das römische Herrscherbild* pt. 1 v. 2. Berlin: Mann, 1993.

Boschung, Dietrich. *Die Bildnisse des Caligula, Das römische Herrscherbild* 4 pt. 1. Berlin: Mann, 1989.

Boschung, Dietrich. "Die Bildnistypen der iulisch-claudischen Kaiserfamilie: ein kritischer Forschungsbericht." *JRA* 6, 1993, pp. 39–79.

Burnett, Andrew, Michel Amandry and Pere Pau Ripollès, *Roman Provincial Coinage.* London: British Museum Press, and Paris: Bibliothèque Nationale de France, 2nd edition, 1998.

Busignani, Alberto. *Die Heroen von Riace: Statuen aus dem Meer.* Frankfurt/Berlin/Vienna: Propyläen, 1982, translation of *Gli Eroi di Riace,* Florence: Sansoni, 1981.

Caffarelli, Ernesto Vergara, and Giacomo Caputo. *Leptis Magna,* ed. R. Bianchi-Bandinelli. N.p.: Arnoldo Mondadori Editore, 1964.

Calza, Raissa. *Scavi di Ostia 5¹: I ritratti.* Rome: Istituto Poligrafico dello Stato, 1964.
Calza, Raissa. *Scavi di Ostia 9: I ritratti romani dal 160 circa alla metà del III secolo D.C.* Rome: Istituto Poligrafico dello Stato, 1977.
Caputo, Giacomo, and Gustavo Traversari, *Le sculture del teatro di Leptis Magna.* Rome: Bretschneider, 1976.
Carratelli, G.P. ed., *The Western Greeks,* exhibition catalogue, Palazzo Grassi, Venice, March-December 1996. Venice: Bompiani, 1996.
Cazes, Daniel. "1844: Une Importante découverte archéologique à Béziers." Toulouse: Musée Saint-Raymond, 1994.
Clavel, Monique. *Béziers et son territoire dans l'antiquité.* Paris: Les Belles Lettres, 1970.
Clinton, Kevin. "The Eleusinian Mysteries: Roman Initiates and Benefactors, Second Century B.C. to A.D. 267." *ANRW* 2.18.2 (1989), 1499–1539.
Cohen, Henry. *Description historique des monnaies frappés sous l'empire romain 1.* Paris and London: MM. Rollin & Feuardent, 1880.
Conlin, Diane Atnally. "The Reconstruction of Antonia Minor on the Ara Pacis." *JRA* 5 (1992) 209–217.
Crawford, Michael H. *Roman Republican Coinage.* 2 vols. Cambridge University Press, 1974.

Daltrop, Georg, Ulrich Hausmann and Max Wegner, *Die Flavier. Das römische Herrscherbild* Part 2 vol. 1, Berlin, 1966.
Dareggi, Gianna. "Il ciclo statuario della 'Basilica' di Otricoli: la fase Giulio-Claudia." *BdA* 67 ser. 6, 1982, 1–36.
De Grazia-Vanderpool, Catherine. "Fathers and Daughters: Julia f. Augusti." Presented at the annual meetings of the AIA, Dec. 28, 1993.
De Grazia-Vanderpool, Catherine. "Roman Portraiture: the Many Faces of Corinth," *Corinth* XX, forthcoming 1999.
Deiss, J.J. *Herculaneum: Italy's Buried Treasure.* 2nd ed. New York: Harper and Row, 1985.
Dobbins, John J. "Problems of Chronology, Decoration and Urban Design at Pompeii," *AJA* 98, 1994, 629–694.

Eck, Werner. "Das *S.c. de Cn. Pisone patre* und seine Publikation in der Baetica," *Cahiers du Centre Glotz* 4, 1993, 189–208.
Eck, Werner, Antonio Caballos, Fernando Fernández. *Das senatus consultum de Cn. Pisone patre,* Vestigia 48. Munich: Beck, 1996.
Elsner, John. "Cult and Sculpture: Sacrifice in the Ara Pacis Augustae." *JRS* 81 (1991), 50–61.
Ehrenberg, Victor, and A.H.M. Jones. *Documents Illustrating the Reigns of Augustus and Tiberius.* 2nd ed. Oxford: Clarendon Press, 1955.
Erhart, K. Patricia. "A New Portrait Type of Octavia Minor. (?)" *J. Paul Getty Museum Journal,* 1980, 117–128.
Erhart, K. Patricia. "A Portrait of Antonia Minor in the Fogg Art Museum and its Iconographical Tradition." *AJA* 82, 1978, 193–212.
Espérandieu, Emile. *Receuil general des bas reliefs de la Gaule Romaine I.* Paris: Imprimerie nationale, 1907.

Felletti-Maj, Bianca Maria. *Museo Nazionale Roman: I ritratti.* Rome: Libreria dello Stato, 1953.
Ferrill, Arther. "Augustus and his Daughter: a Modern Myth." *Studies in Latin Literature and Roman History* 2, ed. Carl Deroux. *Collection Latomus* 168. Brussels, 1980, 332–346.
Fittschen, Klaus. *Die Bildnistypen der Faustina Minor und die Fecunditas Augusta.* Abh.Gött. 126 se. 3. Göttingen: Vandenhoeck and Ruprecht, 1982.
Fittschen, Klaus. "Zur Datierung des Mädchenbildnisses vom Palatin und einiger anderer Kinderporträts der mittleren Kaiserzeit." *JdI* 106, 1991, 297–309, pls. 65–76.

Fittschen, Klaus. *Katalog der antiken Skulpturen in Schloss Erbach. Archäologische Forschungen* 3. Berlin: Mann, 1977.

Fittschen, Klaus, and Paul Zanker. *Katalog der römischen Porträts in den Capitolinischen Museen und den anderen kommunalen Sammlungen der Stadt Rom* 3, *Kaiserinnen und Prinzessinnenbildnisse, Frauenporträts*. Mainz am Rhein: Verlag Philipp von Zabern, 1983.

Flory, Marleen. "*Abducta Neroni Uxor*: the Historiographical Tradition on the Marriage of Octavian and Livia." *Transactions of the American Philological Association* 118 (1988), pp. 343–359.

Flory, Marleen. "Livia and the History of Public Honorific Statues for Women in Rome." *TAPA* 123 (1993), 287–308.

Flory, Marleen. "*Sic exempla parantur*: Livia's Shrine to Concordia and the Porticus Liviae," *Historia* 33 (1984), 309–330.

Flower, Harriet I. *Ancestor Masks and Aristocratic Power in Roman Culture*. Oxford: Clarendon Press, 1996.

Flower, Harriet I. Book review of Werner Eck, Antonio Caballos, Fernando Fernández. *Das senatus consultum de Cn. Pisone patre*, Vestigia 48. Munich: Beck, 1996, *BMCR* 97.7.22.

Freedberg, David. *The Power of Images*. Chicago: University of Chicago Press, 1989.

Frel, Jiři. *Roman Portraits in the Getty Museum*. Exhibition catalogue, Philbrook Art Center, April 26–July 12, 1981.

Freyer-Schauenburg, Brigitte. "Io in Alexandria." *RM* 90, 1983, pp. 35–49, pls. 23–29.

Freyer-Schauenburg, Brigitte. "Die Kieler Livia." *Bonner Jahrbuch* 182 (1982), 209–224.

Frischer, Bernard. *The Sculpted Word*. Berkeley and Los Angeles: University of California Press, 1982.

Frova, Antonio, ed. *Scavi di Luni: Relazione preliminare delle campagne di scavo 1970–1971*. Rome: L'Erma di Bretschneider, 1973.

Fuchs, Michaela, Paolo Liverani, Paola Santoro. *Caere 2: Il teatro e il ciclo statuario giulio-claudio*. Ed. Paola Santoro. Rome: Consiglio Nazionale delle Ricerche, 1989.

Fuchs, Michaela. "Frauen um Caligula und Claudius: Milonia Caesonia, Drusilla und Messalina." *AA* 1990, 107–122.

Fuchs, Siegfried. "Deutung, Sinn, und Zeitstellung des Wiener Cameo mit den Fruchthornbüsten," *RM* 51, 1936, 212–237.

Fuchs, Siegfried. "Neue Frauenbildnisse der frühen Kaiserziet." *Die Antike*, 14, 1938, pp. 255–280.

Fullerton, Mark D. "The *Domus Augusti* in Imperial Iconography of 13–12 B.C." *AJA* 89 (1985), 473–483, pls. 55–57.

Furnée van Zwet, L. "Fashion in Women's Hair Dress in the First Century of the Roman Empire." *BABesch*. 31, 1956, pp. 1–22.

Galinsky, Karl. *Augustan Culture: an Interpretative Introduction*. Princeton: Princeton University Press, 1996.

Galinsky, Karl. "Venus, Polysemy, and the Ara Pacis Augustae." *AJA* 96 (1992), 457–75.

García y Bellido, Antonio. *Esculturas Romanas de España y Portugal*. Madrid: Consejo Superior de Investigaciones Científicas, 1949.

Gardner, Jane F. *Women in Roman Law and Society*. Bloomington and Indianapolis: Indiana University Press, 1991.

Giorgio Giacosa, *Ritratti di Auguste*. Trans. Ross Holloway as *Women of the Caesars*. Milan: Edizioni Arte e Moneta, 1974.

Giuliano, Antonio. *Catalogo dei ritratti Romani del Museo Profano Lateranense*. Vatican City: Tip. Poliglotta Vaticana, 1957.

Giuliano, Antonio, ed. *Museo Nazionale Romano: Le sculture*. Rome: De Luca, 1979–.

Giuliano, Antonio, ed. *La collezione Boncompagni-Ludovisi*. Venice: Marsilio, 1992.

Goethert, Klaus-Peter. "Zur Einheitlichkeit der Statuengruppe aus der Basilika von Velleia." *RM* 79, 1972, pp. 235–287.

Gonzalez, J. "Tabula Siarensis, Fortunales Siarenses et Municipia Civium Romanorum." *Zeitschrift für Papyrologie und Epigraphik* 55, 1984, pp. 55–100.

Grant, Michael, trans. *Tacitus: The Annals of Imperial Rome*. Harmondsworth: Penguin, 1971.

Greifenhagen, Adolf. "Neue Beobachtungen an alten Stücken der Antikenabteilung." *Berliner Museen: Berichte aus den staatlichen Museen der Stiftung preussischer Kulturbesitz*, n.f. 14, 1964, 32–36.

Griffin, Miriam T. *Nero: the End of a Dynasty*. London: Batsford, 1984.

Grimm, Günter. "Zum Bildnis der Iulia Augusti." *RM* 80, 1973, 279–282, pls. 86–87.

Gross, Walter Hatto. *Iulia Augusta. Der Akademie der Wissenschaften in Göttingen: Philologisch-Historische Klasse*, 3rd series, no. 52. Göttingen: Van den Hoeck and Ruprecht, 1962.

Grueber, H.A. *Coins of the Roman Republic in the British Museum*. 3 vols. London: British Museum, 1910 (reprint 1970).

De Grummond, Nancy. "Pax Augusta and the Horae on the Ara Pacis Augustae." *AJA* 94 (1990), 663–677.

Hafner, German. "Zum Augustus-Relief in Ravenna." *RM* 62, 1955, pp. 160–173.

Hafner, German. *Späthellenistische Bildnisplastik*. Berlin: Mann, 1954.

Hallett, Judith. *Fathers and Daughters in Roman Society*. Princeton: Princeton University Press, 1984.

Hanfmann, George M.A. *Roman Art*. New York and London: Norton, 1975.

Hanson, Christine, and Franklin P. Johnson. "On Certain Portrait Inscriptions." *AJA* 50, 1946, pp. 389–400.

Hanson, John Arthur. *Roman Theater Temples*. Princeton, New Jersey: Princeton University Press, 1959.

Harrison, Evelyn. *The Athenian Agora I: Portrait Sculpture*. Princeton: Princeton University Press, 1953.

Hartswick, Kim. "The Athena Lemnia Reconsidered." *AJA* 87, 1983, 335–346, pls. 42–46.

Hausmann, Ulrich. *Römerbildnisse*. Stuttgart: Würtemburgisches Landesmuseum, 1975.

Head, Barclay V. *Historia Nummorum: a Manual of Greek Numismatics*. London, 1910, reprint London: Spink and Son, 1963.

Heintze, Helga Von. *Die antiken Porträts in Schloss Fasanerie bei Fulda*. Mainz am Rhein: von Zabern, 1968.

Heintze, Helga Von. *Juno Ludovisi. Opus Nobile* 4. Bremen: Walter Dorn Verlag, 1957.

Higginbotham, James. "The Roman Villa at Sperlonga: An Architectural Reexamination." Presented at the annual meetings of the AIA in December, 1990. Abstract published *AJA* 95, 1991, 304.

Hitzl, Konrad. *Die Kaiserzeitliche Statuensausstattung des Metroon. Olympische Forschungen* 19. Berlin-New York: De Gruyter, 1991.

Houser, Caroline. *Greek Monumental Bronze Sculpture*. New York and Paris: Vendome Press, 1983.

Houser, Caroline. *Greek Monumental Bronze Sculpture of the Fifth and Fourth Centuries B.C.* Diss. Harvard, 1975; New York and London: Garland, 1987.

Hurwit, Jeffrey M. "The Death of the Sculptor?" *AJA* 101 (1997), 587–591.

Inan, Jale, and Elisabeth Rosenbaum. *Roman and early Byzantine portrait sculpture in Asia Minor*. London, Published for the British Academy by Oxford University Press, 1966.

Inan, Jale and Elisabeth Rosenbaum, *Römische und Frühbyzantinische Porträtplastik aus der Türkei: Neue Funde*. Mainz am Rhein: Philipp von Zabern, 1979.

Jucker, Hans. "Der grosse Pariser Kameo: eine Huldigung an Agrippina, Claudius und Nero." *JdI* 91, 1976, 211–250.
Jucker, Hans. "Die Prinzen auf dem Augustus-Relief in Ravenna." *Mélanges d'histoire et d'archéologie offerts a Paul Collart*. Lausanne: Dépositaire: Diffusion De Boccard, 1976, 237–267.
Jucker, Hans. "Die Prinzen des Statuenzyklus aus Veleia." *JdI* 92, 1977, 204–240.
Jucker, Hans. "Zum Carpentum-Sesterz der Agrippina maior." *Forschungen und Funde: Festschrift Bernhard Neutsch*. Ed. Fritz Krinzinger, Brinna Otto, Elisabeth Walde-Psenner. Innsbruck, 1980, 205–217.

Kaenel, Hans Markus Von. "Britannicus, Agrippina Minor und Nero in Thrakien." *SNR* 63 (1984), 127–150, pls. 20–27.
Kähler, Heinz. *Die Augustusstatue von Primaporta*. Cologne: M. DuMont Schauberg, 1959.
Kampen, Natalie. *Image and Status: Roman Working Women in Ostia*. Berlin: Mann, 1981.
Kaplan, Michael. "Agrippina Semper Atrox: a Study in Tacitus' Characterization of Women." *Studies in Latin Literature and Roman History* I, ed. Carl Deroux, *Collection Latomus* 164. Brussells, 1979, 410–417.
Kent, J.P.C. *Roman Coins*. London: Thames and Hudson, 1974.
De Kersauson, Kate. *Catalogue des portraits romains* 1: *Portraits de la République et d'époque Julio-Claudienne*. Paris: Editions de la Réunion des musées nationaux, 1986.
Kleiner, Diana E.E., and Susan Matheson, *I Claudia: Women in Ancient Rome*. Exhibition catalogue, Yale University Art Gallery, Sept. 6–Dec. 1, 1996, San Antonio Museum of Art, Jan. 3–Mar. 9, 1997, North Carolina Museum of Art, Apr. 6–June 15, 1997. Austin, TX: University of Texas Press, 1996.
Kleiner, Diana E.E. "Politics and Gender in the Pictorial Propaganda of Antony and Octavian," *Echos du Monde Classique/Classical Views*, 36 n.s. 11 (1992) pp. 357–367.
Kleiner, Diana E.E., *Roman Sculpture*. New Haven and London: Yale University Press, 1992.
Kleiner, Fred. *The Arch of Nero*. Rome: Bretschneider, 1985.
Kleiner, Fred. "The Sacrifice in Armor in Roman Art." *Latomus* 42, 1983, 287–302.
Klose Dietrich O.A. *Die Münzprägung von Smyrna in der römischen Kaiserzeit*. AMUGS 10. Berlin: De Gruyter, 1987.
Köckel, Valentin. *Porträtreliefs stadtrömischer Grabbauten. Beiträge zur Erschließung hellenistischer und kaiserzeitlicher Skulptur und Architektur* 12. Mainz am Rhein: Philipp von Zabern, 1993.
Koeppel, G.M. "The third man: restoration problems on the North Frieze of the Ara Pacis Augustae." *JRA* 5, 1992, 216–218.
Kokkinos, Nikos. *Antonia Augusta: Portrait of a Great Roman Lady*. London and New York: Routledge, 1992.
Koppel, Eva. *Die römische Skulpturen von Tarraco*. Berlin: De Gruyter, 1985.
Kraft, Konrad. "Der politische Hintergrund von Senecas Apocolocyntosis." *Historia* 15, 1966, 97–122.
Kreikenbom, Detlev. *Griechische und römische Kolossalporträts bis zum späten ersten Jahrhundert n.Chr. JdI-EH* 27. Berlin and New York: Walter de Gruyter, 1992.

Langlotz, Ernst. *Die Kunst der Westgriechen*. Munich: Hirmer, 1963.
Laubscher, Hans Peter. *Arcus Novus und Arcus Claudii, zwei Triumphbögen an der Via Lata in Rom*. Göttingen, 1976.
Levi della Vida, G. "Due iscrizioni imperiali neo-puniche di Leptis Magna." *AfrIt.* 6, 1935, 15–27.
Levick, Barbara. *Claudius*. London: B.T. Batsford, Ltd., 1990.
Lewis, R.G. "Some Mothers," *Athenaeum* 66, 1988, 198–200.
Lindner, Ruth. *Der Raub der Persephone in der antike Kunst, Beitrag zur Archäologie* 16, Würzburg: K. Triltsch, 1984.

Lippold, Georg. *Die Skulpturen des Vaticanischen Museums* Vols. 3^1 and 3^2. Berlin: Reimer, 1936 and 1956.

Liverani, Paolo. "Rilavorazioni antiche e moderne su sculture dei Musei Vaticani." *RendPontAcc.* 63, 1990–1991, pp. 163–191.

L'Orange, Hans Peter. *Apotheosis in Ancient Portraiture.* Oslo, H. Aschehoug; Cambridge, Mass., Harvard University Press, 1947, reprinted New Rochelle, N.Y.: Caratzas Brothers, 1982.

Macdonald, William L. *The Architecture of the Roman Empire* II: *An Urban Appraisal.* New Haven and London: Yale University Press, 1986.

Marella, Maria Luisa, "Di un ritratto di 'Ottavia'." *MemLinc* 3, 1942, 31–82, pls. 1–3.

Massner, Anne-Kathrein. *Bildnisangleichung: Untersuchungen zur Entstehungs- und Wirkungsgeschichte der Augustusporträts (43 v.Chr–68 n.Chr.) Das römische Herrscherbild* part 4, W.H. Gross ed. Berlin: Mann, 1982.

Mattingly, Harold. *Coins of the Roman Empire in the British Museum.* London: the British Museum, 1923, reprinted with revisions 1975.

Mattingly, Harold, and C.H.V. Sutherland, *Roman Imperial Coinage*, vol. 1, 2nd ed. London: Spink, 1984.

Mau, August. *Pompeii: its Life and Art.* Trans. F. Kelsey, 2nd ed. New York: the MacMillan Company, 1902, reprint New York: Caratzas, 1982.

Megow, Wolf-Rüdiger. "Zu einigen Kameen späthellenistischer und frühaugusteischer Zeit," *JdI* 100 (1985), 445–96.

Megow, Wolf-Rüdiger. *Kameen von Augustus bis Alexander Severus, AMUGS* 11. Berlin: De Gruyter, 1987.

Meriç, Recep, Reinhold Merkelbach, Johannes Nollé and Sencer Şahin, *Die Inschriften von Ephesos.* Bonn: Rudolf Habelt Verlag, 1981.

Michelucci, Maurizio. *Roselle: la Domus dei Mosaici.* Montepulciano, Siena: Editori del Grifo, 1985.

Mikocki, Tomasz. *Sub Specie Deae: Les impératrices et princesses romaines assimileés à des déesses: étude iconologique. RdA Suppl.* 14. Rome: Bretschneider, 1995.

Milkovich, Michael. *Roman Portraits.* Worcester, MA: Worcester Art Museum, 1961.

Möbius, Hans. "Zweck und Typen der römischen Kaiserkameen," *ANRW* II.12.3, 1975, 32–88.

Mørkholm, Otto. *Early Hellenistic Coinage.* Cambridge: Cambridge University Press, 1991.

Nicols, John. "Antonia and Sejanus." *Historia* 24 (1975), 48–58.

Niemeyer, Hans-Georg. *Studien zur statuarischen Darstellung der römischen Kaiser.* Berlin: Mann, 1968.

Oberleitner, Wolfgang. *Geschnittene Steine: Die Prunkkameen der Wiener Antikensammlung.* Vienna, Cologne and Graz: Hermann Böhlaus Nachf., 1985.

Packer, James. *The Forum of Trajan in Rome: a Study of the Monuments.* 3 vols. Berkeley : University of California Press, 1997.

Paglia, Camille. "Ice Queen, Drag Queen." *The New Republic* 214 (March 4, 1996), 24–26.

Pekáry, Thomas. *Das römische Kaiserbildnis in Staat, Kult und Gesellschaft.* Part 3 of *Das römische Herrscherbild,* M. Wegner, ed. Berlin, 1985.

Pietrangeli, C. "Giulia." *EAA* 3. Rome: Istituto Poligrafico dello Stato, 1960, 921.

Pijoan, J. *Antique Marbles in the Collection of the Hispanic Society of America.* New York: Hispanic Society of America, 1917.

Pfanner, Michael. "Über das Herstellung von Porträts." *JdI* 104 (1989), 157–257.

Polaschek, Karin. *Porträttypen einer Claudischen Kaiserin.* Rome: Bretschneider, 1973.

Polaschek, Karin. "Studien zu einem Frauenkopf im Landesmuseum Trier und zur weiblichen Haartracht der iulisch-claudischen Zeit." *TrZs* 35, 1972, 141–210.

Polaschek, Karin. *Studien zur Ikonographie der Antonia Minor*. Rome: Bretschneider, 1973.

Pollini, John. "The Cartoceto Bronzes: Portraits of a Roman Aristocratic Family of the Late First Century B.C." *AJA* 97 (1993), 423–446.

Pollini, John. "Gnaeus Domitius Ahenobarbus and the Ravenna Relief." *RM* 88, 1981, 117–140, pls. 31–42.

Pollini, John. "Man or God? Divine Assimilation and Imitation in the Late Republic and Early Principate." *Between Republic and Empire: Interpretations of Augustus and his Principate*. Berkeley: University of California Press, 1990, 334–357.

Pollini, John. *The Portraiture of Gaius and Lucius Caesar*. New York: Fordham University Press, 1987.

Pollini, John. "The Promulgation of the Image of the Leader in Roman Art." Presented Dec. 30, 1985, at the 87th annual meeting of the AIA. Abstract *AJA* 90 (1986), 217.

Pollini, John. "Time, Narrativity and Dynastic Constructs in Augustan Art and Thought," presented at the 88th general meeting of the Archaeological Institute of America, December, 1986, abstract published *AJA* 91 (1987), 298.

Pollitt, J.J. *The Art of Ancient Greece: Sources and Documents*. Cambridge: Cambridge University Press, 2nd ed., 1990.

Pomeroy, Sarah. *Goddesses, Whores, Wives and Slaves: Women in Classical Antiquity*. New York: Schocken Books, 1975.

Poulsen, Frederik. *Porträtstudien in norditalienischen Provinzmuseen*. Copenhagen: Kgl. Hof-Boghandel Bianco Lunos Bogtrykkeri, 1928.

Poulsen, Frederik. *Römische Privatporträts und Prinzenbildnisse*. Copenhagen: Munksgaard, 1939.

Poulsen, Vagn. "Drei antike Skulpturen im Residenzmuseum München." *Münchner Jahrbuch der bildenden Kunst* 19, 3rd ser., 1968, 9–28.

Poulsen, Vagn. "Nero, Britannicus, and Others: Iconographical Notes." *Acta Archaeologica* 22 (1951), 119–135.

Poulsen, Vagn. "Once More the Young Nero, and Other Claudians." *Acta Archaeologica* 25 (1954), 300–301.

Poulsen, Vagn. "Portraits of Claudia Octavia." *OpRom* 4 (1964), 107–111.

Poulsen, Vagn. *Les portraits romains* 1: *République et dynastie Julienne*. Copenhagen: Munksgaard, 1962.

Poulsen, Vagn. *Les portraits romains* 2. Copenhagen: Munksgaard, 1974.

Poulsen, Vagn. "Studies in Julio-Claudian Iconography." *Acta Archaeologica* 17 (1946), 1–48.

Pozzi, E. "L'Attività archeologica nella Soprintendenza di Napoli e Caserta." *Magna Grecia e Mondo Miceneo: Atti del ventiduesimo convegno di studi sulla Magna Grecia*. Taranto: Istituto per la Storia e l'Archeologia della Magna Grecia, 1983.

Protzmann, Heiner. "Antiquarische Nachlese zu den Statuen der sogenannten Lemnia Furtwänglers in Dresden." *Jahrbuch der Staatlichen Kunstsammlungen Dresden*, 1984, 7–22.

Purcell, Nicholas, "Livia and the Womanhood of Rome." *PCPS* n.s. 32 (1986), 78–105.

Queyrel, Francois. "Un portrait d'Agrippine l'Ancienne à Tenos," *BCH* 109 (1985), 615–618.

Reynolds, J.M., and J.B. Ward-Perkins, *The Inscriptions of Roman Tripolitania*. Rome and London: Published for the British School in Rome, 1952.

Richardson, Lawrence. *Pompeii: an Architectural History*. Baltimore: Johns Hopkins Press, 1988.

Richlin, Amy. "Julia's Jokes, Galla Placidia, and the Roman Use of Women as Political Icons." *Stereotypes of Women in Power: Historical Perspectives and Revisionist*

Views. Ed. Barbara Garlick, Suzanne Dixon, and Pauline Allen. New York, Westport, CT and London: Greenwood Press, 1992, 65–91.

Ridgway, Brunilde Sismondo. *Fifth Century Styles in Greek Sculpture*. Princeton: Princeton University Press, 1981.

Ridgway, Brunilde Sismondo. *Museum of the Rhode Island School of Design: Classical Sculpture*. Providence: Rhode Island School of Design, 1972.

Ridgway, Brunilde Sismondo. *Roman Copies of Greek Sculpture: The Problem of the Originals*. Ann Arbor: University of Michigan Press, 1984.

Ridgway, Brunilde. *The Severe Style in Greek Sculpture*. Princeton: Princeton University Press, 1970.

Robertson, Martin. *A History of Greek Art*. Cambridge: The University Press, 1975.

Rose, Charles Brian. *Dynastic Commemoration and Imperial Portraiture in the Julio-Claudian Period*. Cambridge: Cambridge University Press, 1997.

Rose, C. Brian. "'Princes' and Barbarians on the Ara Pacis," *AJA* 94 (1990), 453–467.

Rose, Charles Brian. "The supposed Augustan arch at Pavia (Ticinum) and the Einsiedeln 326 manuscript." *JRA* 3 (1990), 163–168.

Rosenbaum, Elisabeth. *A Catalogue of Cyrenaican Portrait Sculpture*. London: Oxford University Press, 1960.

Rowe, Greg. Book review of Nikos Kokkinos, *Antonia Augusta: Portrait of a Great Roman Lady*. London and New York: Routledge, 1992. *BMCR* 94.5.14.

Ruesch, Arnold. *Guida Illustrata del Museo Nazionale di Napoli*. Naples: Richter, 1911.

Rumpf, Andreas. *Antonia Augusta*. No. 5 of *Abhandlungen der Preußischen Akademie der Wissenschaften, Philosophisch-historische Klasse*. Berlin: Verlag der Akademie der Wissenschaften, 1941.

Saletti, Cesare. *Il Ciclo statuario della basilica di Velleia*. Milan: Casa Editrice Ceschina, 1968.

Saletti, Cesare. "Tre ritratti imperiali da Luni: Tiberio, Livia, Caligola." *Athenaeum* n.s. 51 (1973), 34–48.

Salviat, François. "À la découverte des empéreurs romains et de leur famille d'après les historiens et les portraits de Gaule narbonnaise," *Dossiers de l'Archéologie*, Paris, 41, 1980, 6–90.

Sande, Siri. "Die Aspasia-Herme und verwandte Bildnisse," *Acta Hyperborea* 4, *Ancient Portraiture: Image and Message*. Copenhagen, 1992, 43–58.

Sande, Siri. "Römische Frauenporträts mit Mauerkrone." *ActaAAHP* 5, (1985), 151–245.

Santoro L'Hoir, Francesca. "Tacitus and Women's Usurpation of Power." *Classical World* 88 (1994), 5–25.

Scott, Kenneth. *The Imperial Cult Under the Flavians*. Stuttgart-Berlin: W. Kohlhammer, 1936.

Scullard, H.H. *The Elephant in the Greek and Roman World*. Cambridge: Thames and Hudson, 1979.

Seinby, Eva Margarete, ed. *Lexicon Topographicum Urbis Romae*. 3 vols. Rome: Edizioni Quasar, 1993–1996.

Sensi, Luigi. "Ornatus e status sociale delle donne romane," *Annali della Facoltà di Lettere e Filosofia* ser. 7, *Studi Classici-Perugia* 18 (1980–81), 55–102.

Serra-Ràfols, J. de C. "Sobre un hallazgo y una publicación recientes," *Cuadernos de Arqueologia e Historia de la Ciudad Ayuntamiento de Barcelona*. Museo de Historia de la Ciudad. Vol. 6, 1964.

Sichtermann, Helmut, and Guntram Koch. *Griechische Mythen auf römischen Sarkophagen*. Tübingen: Wasmuth, 1975.

Simon, Erika, *Ara Pacis Augustae*. Tubingen: Wasmuth, 1967.

Small, Alastair M. "A New Head of Antonia Minor and its Significance." *RM* 97 (1990), 217–234, pls. 60–66.

Smith, R.R.R. "The Imperial Reliefs from the Sebasteion at Aphrodisias." *JRS* 77 (1987), 88–138.

Smith, R.R.R. "Roman Portraits: Honours, Empresses, and Late Emperors." *JRS* 75 (1985), 209–221.

Smith, R.R.R. *Hellenistic Royal Portraits*. Oxford: Oxford University Press, 1988.

Spaeth, Barbette Stanley. "The Goddess Ceres in the Ara Pacis Augustae and the Carthage Relief." *AJA* 98 (1994), 65–100.

Stähli, Adrian. "*Ornamentum Academiae*: Kopien griechischer Bildnisse in Hermenform." *Acta Hyperborea* 4, Ancient Portraiture: Image and Message. Copenhagen, 1992, 147–172.

Stone, Shelley C. "The Imperial Sculpture Group in the Metroon at Olympia." *AM* 100 (1985), 377–391, pls. 82–86.

Strong, Donald. *Roman Imperial Sculpture*. London: Tiranti, 1961.

Sutherland, C.H.V. *Roman Coins*. New York: Putnam, 1974.

Sutherland, C.H.V., and C.M. Kraay. *Catalogue of the Coins of the Roman Empire in the Ashmolean Museum*. Oxford, 1975.

Sydenham, Edward A. *The Coinage of the Roman Republic*. London: Spink and Son, Ltd. 1952.

Tansini, Raffaella. *I Ritratti di Agrippina Maggiore*. RdA Suppl. 15, Bretschneider: Rome, 1995.

Tölle-Kastenbein, Renate. *Samos XIV: Das Kastro Tigani, die Bauten und Funde griechischer, römischer und byzantinisher Zeit*. Bonn: Rudolf Habelt Verlag, 1974.

Tölle-Kastenbein, Renate. "Juno Ludovisi: Hera oder Antonia Minor?" *AM* 89 (1974), 241–253, pls. 91–96.

Torelli, Mario. *The Typology and Structure of Roman Historical Reliefs*. Ann Arbor: University of Michigan Press, 1982.

Touchette, Lori-Ann. "Roman Copies and Nineteenth Century Technique?" Presented at the meetings of the College Art Association of America, Feb. 22, 1991.

Traversari, Gustavo. *Museo Archeologico de Venezia: i ritratti*. Rome: Istituto Poligrafico dello Stato, 1969.

Traversari, Gustavo. *Sculture del V–IV Secolo A.C. del Museo Archeologico di Venezia*. Venice, 1973.

Treu, Georg. *Olympia* III. Berlin: A. Asher & Co., 1897.

Trillmich, Walter. "Beobachtungen am Bildnis der Agrippina Maior oder: Probleme und Grenzen der 'Typologie.'" *MM* 25, 1984, 135–158, pls. 27–35.

Trillmich, Walter, "Ein Bildnis der Agrippina Minor von Milreu/Portugal." *MM* 15, 1974, 184–202, pls. 35–46.

Trillmich, Walter. *Familienpropaganda der Kaiser Caligula und Claudius*. AMUGS 8. Berlin: De Gruyter, 1978.

Trillmich, Walter. "Zur Formgeschichte von Bildnis-Typen." *JdI* 86 (1971), 179–213.

Trillmich, Walter. "Der Germanicus-Bogen in Rom und das Monument für Germanicus und Drusus in Leptis Magna." *Estudios sobre la Tabula Siarensis, Anejos de Archivo Español de Arqueología*. C.S.I.C. Madrid, 1988, 51–60.

Trillmich, Walter. "Julia Agrippina als Schwester des Caligula und Mutter des Nero," *Hefte des Archäologischen Seminars der Universität Bern*, 9 (1983), 21–37, pls. 2–7.

Vermeule, Cornelius. *Greek and Roman Sculpture in America*. Los Angeles: University of California Press, 1980.

Vermeule, Cornelius C. "Notes on a New Edition of Michaelis: Ancient Marbles in Great Britain," *AJA* 59 (1955), 129–150.

Vierneisel-Schlörb, Barbara. *Klassische Skulpturen des 5. und 4. Jahrhunderts v.Chr*. Munich, Antikensammlung: C.H. Beck, 1979.

Vinson, Martha. "Domitia Longina, Julia Titi and the Literary Tradition." *Historia* 38 (1989), 431–50.

Vollenweider, Marie-Louise. *Catalogue raisonné des sceaux, cylindres, intailles et camées*. Geneva: Musée d'art et d'histoire de Genève, 1967.

Vollenweider, Marie-Louise. *Die Porträtgemmen der römischen Republik.* Mainz: Von Zabern, 1974.

Vollenweider, Marie-Louise. *Die Steinschneidekunst und ihre Künstler in spätrepublikanischer und augusteischer Zeit.* Baden-Baden: Bruno Grimm, 1966.

Walters, Henry Beauchamp. *Catalogue of the Engraved Gems and Cameos, Greek, Etruscan and Roman, in the British Museum.* London: The British Museum, 1926.

Wegner, Max. *Gordianus III bis Carinus. Das römische Herrscherbild,* part 3, vol. 3. Berlin, 1979.

Wegner, Max. *Hadrian, Plotina, Marciana, Matidia, Sabina. Das römische Herrscherbild,* part 2, Vol. 3. Berlin, 1956.

Wegner, Max. *Die Herrscherbildnisse in antoninischer Zeit, Das römische Herrscherbild* 2 pt. 4. Berlin, 1939.

West, Robert. *Römische Porträt-Plastik.* Munich, 1933.

Winkes, Rolf. "Bildnistypen der Livia." *Ritratto ufficiale e ritratto privato: Atti della II Conferenza Internazionale sul Ritratto Romano.* Roma: Consiglio Nazionale delle Richerche, 1988, 555–561.

Winkes, Rolf. "Der Kameo Marlborough: ein Urbild der Livia." *AA* 1982, 131–138.

Winkes, Rolf. *Livia, Octavia, Julia.* Louvain-la-Neuve and Providence: Art and Archaeology Publications, 1995.

Winkes, Rolf. "Pliny's Chapter on Roman Funeral Customs in the Light of *Clipeatae Imagines,*" *AJA* 83 (1979), 481–484.

Winkes, Rolf. "A Spanish Image of Livia." *Revue des Archéologues et Historiens d'art de Louvain,* 21 (1988), 75–78.

Winkler, Lorenz. *Salus: vom Staatskult zur politischen Idee, eine archäologische Untersuchung.* Vol. 4 of *Archäologie und Geschichte,* ed. Tonio Hölscher. Heidelberg: Verlag Archäologie und Geschichte, 1995.

Wood, Susan. "Alcestis on Roman Sarcophagi," *AJA* 82 (1978), 499–510.

Wood, Susan. "Alcestis on Roman Sarcophagi: Postscript," *Roman Art in Context,* ed. E. D'Ambra (Englewood Cliffs, N.J.: Prentice Hall, 1993), 96–99.

Wood, Susan. "Diva Drusilla Panthea and the Sisters of Caligula." *AJA* 99 (1995), 457–482.

Wood, Susan. "Forgotten Women in the Imperial Portrait Group from Béziers," *Archaeological News* 20–21 (1996–97), 1–19.

Wood, Susan, "*Memoriae Agrippinae*: Agrippina the Elder in Julio-Claudian Art and Propaganda." *AJA* 92 (1988), 409–426.

Wood, Susan. "Messalina, wife of Claudius: Propaganda successes and failures of his reign." *JRA* 5 (1992), 219–234.

Wood, Susan. "Mortals, Empresses and Earth Goddesses: Demeter and Persephone in Public and Private Apotheosis." Presented at the Yale University Art Gallery, Nov. 2, 1996, forthcoming in *I Claudia II: Papers from the Colloquium.*

Wrede, Henning. *Consecratio in Formam Deorum: Vergöttlichte Privatpersonen in der römischen Kaiserzeit.* Mainz am Rhein: Von Zabern, 1981.

Zanker, Paul. *Forum Augustum: das Bildprogramm.* Tübingen: Wasmuth, 1968.

Zanker, Paul. *Forum Romanum: die Neugestaltung durch Augustus.* Tübingen: Wasmuth, 1972.

Zanker, Paul. *The Power of Images in the Age of Augustus.* Trans. Alan Shapiro. Ann Arbor: the University of Michigan Press, 1988.

Zuntz, Gunter. *Persephone: Three Essays on Religion and Thought in Magna Graecia.* Oxford: Clarendon Press, 1971.

MUSEUM CATALOGUES AND REFERENCE WORKS, BY LOCATION OF COLLECTION:

Berlin:
Blümel, Carl. *Katalog der Sammlung antiker Skulpturen* V: *Römische Kopien Griechischer Skulpturen des vierten Jahrhunderts v.Chr.* Berlin: Verlag für Kunstwissenschaft, 1938.
Blümel, Carl. *Römische Bildnisse.* Berlin: Verlag für Kunstwissenschaft, 1933.
Copenhagen:
Poulsen, Vagn. *Les portraits romains* 1: *République et dynastie Julienne.* Copenhagen, 1962.
Poulsen, Vagn. *Les portraits romains* 2. Copenhagen: Munksgaard, 1974.
Cyrene:
Rosenbaum, Elisabeth. *A Catalogue of Cyrenaican Portrait Sculpture.* London: Oxford University Press, 1960.
Schloss Erbach:
Fittschen, Klaus. *Katalog der antiken Skulpturen in Schloss Erbach. Archäologische Forschungen* 3. Berlin: Mann, 1977.
Schloss Fasanerie bei Fulda:
Heintze, Helga Von. *Die antiken Porträts in Schloss Fasanerie bei Fulda.* Mainz am Rhein: von Zabern, 1968.
London, British Museum:
Grueber, H.A. *Coins of the Roman Republic in the British Museum.* 3 vols. London: British Museum, 1910 (reprint 1970).
Mattingly, Harold. *Coins of the Roman Empire in the British Museum.* London: the British Museum, 1923, reprinted with revisions 1975.
Walters, Henry Beauchamp. *Catalogue of the Engraved Gems and Cameos, Greek, Etruscan and Roman, in the British Museum.* London: the British Museum, 1926.
Munich Glyptothek:
Vierneisel-Schlörb, Barbara. *Klassische Skulpturen des 5. und 4. Jahrhunderts v. Chr.* Munich, Antikensammlung: C.H. Beck, 1979.
Naples, Museo Nazionale di Archeologia:
Ruesch, Arnold. *Guida Illustrata del Museo Nazionale di Napoli.* Naples: Richter, 1911.
Oxford, Ashmolean Museum:
Sutherland, C.H.V., and C.M. Kraay, *Catalogue of Coins of the Roman Empire in the Ashmolean Museum,* Part 1. Oxford: Clarendon Press, 1975.
Paris, Musée du Louvre:
De Kersauson, Kate. *Catalogue des portraits romains* 1: *Portraits de la République et d'époque Julio-Claudienne.* Paris, 1986.
Providence, Rhode Island:
Ridgway, Brunilde Sismondo. *Museum of the Rhode Island School of Design: Classical Sculpture.* Providence, 1972.
Rome, Capitoline Museums:
Fittschen, Klaus, and Paul Zanker. *Katalog der römischen Porträts in den Capitolinischen Museen und den anderen kommunalen Sammlungen der Stadt Rom* 3, *Kaiserinnen und Prinzessinnenbildnisse, Frauenporträts.* Mainz am Rhein: Verlag Philipp von Zabern, 1983.
Rome, Museo Nazionale Romano:
Felletti-Maj, Bianca Maria. *Museo Nazionale Romano: I ritratti.* Rome: Libreria dello Stato, 1953.
Museo Nazionale Romano: Le sculture, ed. Antonio Giuliano. Rome: De Luca, 1979–
La collezione Boncompagni-Ludovisi. Giuliano, Antonio, ed. Venice: Marsilio. 1992.
Rome, Vatican:
Amelung, Walther. *Die Skulpturen des Vaticanischen Museums* Vols. 1 and 2, Berlin, 1903 and 1908, reprinted New York: De Gruyter, 1995.
Lippold, Georg. *Die Skulpturen des Vaticanischen Museums,* Vols. 3^1 and 3^2. Berlin: Reimer, 1936 and 1956.

Giuliano, Antonio. *Catalogo dei ritratti romani del Museo Profano Lateranense*. Vatican City, 1957.
Sicily:
Bonacasa, Nicola. *Ritratti Greci e Romani della Sicilia*. Palermo: Fondazione I. Mormino del Banco di Sicilia, 1964.
Spain and Portugal:
García y Bellido, Antonio. *Esculturas Romanas de España y Portugal*. Madrid: Consejo Superior de Investigaciones Científicas, 1949.
Tarragona:
Koppel, Eva. *Die römische Skulpturen von Tarraco*. Berlin: De Gruyter, 1985.
Turkey:
Inan, Jale, and Elisabeth Rosenbaum. *Roman and early Byzantine portrait sculpture in Asia Minor*. London, Published for the British Academy by Oxford University Press, 1966.
Inan, Jale and Elisabeth Rosenbaum, *Römische und Frühbyzantinische Porträtplastik aus der Türkei: Neue Funde*. Mainz am Rhein: Philipp von Zabern, 1979.
Venice:
Anti, Carlo. *Il Regio Museo Archeologico nel Palazzo Reale di Venezia*. Rome: Libreria dello Stato, 1930.
Traversari, Gustavo. *Museo Archeologico de Venezia: i ritratti*. Rome: Istituto Poligrafico dello Stato, 1969.
Traversari, Gustavo. *Sculture del V–IV Secolo A.C. del Museo Archeologico di Venezia*. Venice, 1973.
Worcester, MA:
Milkovich, Michael. *Roman Portraits*. Worcester, MA: Worcester Art Museum, 1961.

INDEX

Page references are indicated by numbers in regular font; references to photographs and captions are indicated in bold-face.

I. *Proper Names of Persons and Deities*

II. *Geographical Names and Ancient Provenances*

III. *Museums, Monuments and Modern Locations:*

IV. *General Index:*

Cistophoros (pl. Cistophoroi): 44, 47–8, 51, 63, **2, 3**

Classical style and works of sculpture: 18, 19, 23, 73, 97–8, 99, 118, 122, 128, 134, 174–75, 198, 225–29, 243, 244, 245, 280, 302, 312, 318, **97, 98, 99, 100**

Classicizing style: 97–8, 99, 115, 140, 226–27, 302, 312

Claudius, Divus, temple of: 266–68

Clementia: 79

Clipeus Virtutis: 79

Coiffure: 18–19, 20, 22, 23, 24–5, 41, 45, 59–60, 91, 93–4, 118, 119–20, 125–26, 127–28, 130–31, 132, 133, 151, 156–57, 162–63, 166, 169, 170–71, 172, 173, 174–75, 186, 190–91, 192, 193, 197, 198, 200, 201, 218–20, 222, 226–28, 229–30, 234, 236, 239–40, 241, 244, 246–47, 276, 277–78, 280, 282, 283–84, 288–89, 296–97, 307, 309, 311, 312–13

Colony, status of: 251

Colossal scale: 110–112, 121–23, 128–29, 131, 133–35, 170, 302, 303–304

Columns, sculpture: 310

Concordia: 77, 78, 161, 210, 266, 282

Concrete: 24

Condemnation of memory: *see* "*damnatio memoriae*"

Conspiracy theories: 84–86

Constantia, representation of: 156

CONSTANTIAE AUGUSTI coin series of Antonia Minor: 155–57

Consul: 45

Contrapposto: 122, 164

Copying methods: 23, 104, 192

Copyist(s): 6, 20, 23, 24, 25, 26, 92, 107, 110, 127, 141, 164, 174, 175, 186, 200, 251, 301–302, 315

Corinthian capitals: 24

Corn-ear crown: 112–13, 122–24, 149, 154–55, 156, 290, 299, 305, 307

Cornucopiae: 116, 129, 156, 180, 196, 210, 282, 305–308, **48, 56, 79**

Corona Civica: *see* "Oak crown"

Costume: 17, 20, 24, 25, 87, 113, 115, 120, 122, 125, 128, 140, 160, 164, 165–66, 169, 215, 241, 242–43, 307, 309, 312–13

Crescent diadem: 125, 126, 129–30,

132, 133, 135, 166, 170, 223, 224, 231–32, 234, 235, 240, 241, 242, 294, 298–99, 300, 313, **45, 46, 47, 48, 49, 50, 51, 52, 64, 65, 66, 93, 94, 101, 102, 102, 104, 114, 115, 116, 117, 136, 137, 139, 140, 142**

Cult statue: 19, 77, 127, 129, 135, 172

Curule chair: *see* "*sella curulis*"

Cyclops: 166–67

Damnatio memoriae: 30, 74, 128, 148, 152, 181, 193, 194, 195, 273–74, 279, 285

Deconstructionist interpretations: 26

Deification: 34, 75, 84, 92, 113–14, 127–38, 172, 175–76, 209, 213, 231–32, 241–42, 245, 250, 266–67, 272, 281, 309–310, 313, 316, 317

Demeter Kourotrophos: 199, 290

Denarius, pl. denarii: 46, 65, 66, 67, 88, 152–53, 154–57, 163, 291, 293–94, 302, 313, **7, 20, 55, 122**

Didrachm: 275, 294, **120**

Diva Augusta, title of: 88–9, 112, 127–38, 250

Divorce: 36, 37, 76, 178–79, 182, 212, 213, 255

Doryphoros of Polykleitos: 98

Drachma (pl. drachmae): 46, 294

Drill, sculptural use of: 23, 123, 125, 126–27, 128, 129, 130, 132, 134, 135, 167–68, 170, 201, 219–20, 221, 242, 245, 277, 284, 300

Dupondius, pl. dupondii: 49–51, 88, 89, 109–10, 120, 153–54, 157, 163, 209, 210–11, **57, 81, 83**

Eagle, symbol of imperial Roman power: 306

Elephant-drawn chariot: 250, 294

Eleusinian goddesses: *see* "Demeter," "Kore," "Persephone," "Proserpina"

Eleusinian mysteries: 92–3, 243, 290

Eleusis relief: 243

Equestrian order: 82

Euergetism: 13, 77, 150

Exposure of infants: 7, 83

Fayum Type of Livia: 15, 94–5, 97, 118, 192, **22, 23, 35, 36, 37, 38**

Feminism, feminists: 4, 8, 10

Feminization: 86, 205–206

Tyche: *see* "Fortuna"
Typology: 16, 91–2

Univira: 76, 143

Valetudo: 82.
Velletri Type of Octavia Minor: 52–4, 55, 58–9, 60, 61, 62, 73, **11, 12, 13, 14, 15**
Vestal Virgins: 82, 148, 209, 210, 212, 225, 241, 254, 316
Victory, personification of: 41–4
Virginity: 288
Viriplaca, cult of: 12
Virtus: 79, 153
Vitta: 98, 159, 224

Wilton House type of Antonia Minor: 157–70, 173, 175, 188, 191, 197, 251, **59, 60, 61, 62, 63, 64, 65, 66, 68**
Winged horse: 276, 287, 309–310, **145**
Witchcraft: 146
Witch-hunts: 182
Wolf: 198

"Youthful-idealized" portraits of Antonia Minor: 171
Youthful-realistic portrait type of Antonia Minor: *see* "Leptis-Malta type"

LIST OF ILLUSTRATIONS AND PHOTO CREDITS

1: *Aureus* of C. Numonius Vaala, 43 or 40 B.C., Rome, with bust of Victory on obverse that appears to have portrait-like face, tentatively identified as Fulvia. Actual size. London, British Museum RR Rome #4215, copyright British Museum.

2: *Cistophoros* of Antony, 40–ca. 35 B.C., Pergamon, bust of Octavia with emblems of Dionysiac cult on reverse. Actual size. Munich, Staatliche Münzsammlung, museum photo.

3: *Cistophoros* of Antony, 40–ca. 35 B.C., Miletus, jugate portrait of Antony and Octavia on obverse. Actual size. Munich, Staatliche Münzsammlung, museum photo.

4: *Aureus* of Antony, 40 B.C., city of origin unknown, with reverse portrait of Octavia, unique specimen, also known as the De Quelen Aureus. Enlarged. Staatliche Museen zu Berlin—Preußisscher Kulturbesitz, Münzkabinett, museum photo.

5: *Aureus* of Antony, 40–ca. 35 B.C., city of origin unknown, with reverse portrait of Octavia. Actual size. London, British Museum, BMC East 144, copyright British Museum.

6: *Tetradrachm* of Cleopatra VII of Egypt, 55–30 B.C., Askalon. Actual size. London, British Museum, BMC Askalon 20. Copyright British Museum.

7: *Denarius* of Antony and Cleopatra, 32 B.C., Eastern mint, city of origin uncertain. Actual size. London, British Museum, copyright British Museum.

8: *Tetradrachm* of Antony and Cleopatra, 37–32, probably 37 B.C., Antioch. Actual size. New York, American Numismatic Society 1967.152.567, museum photo.

9: *Sestertius* of Antony, ca. 36–35 B.C., city of origin unknown, with obverse confronted portraits of Antony and Octavia. Actual size. New York, American Numismatic Society 1944.100.7100. Museum photo.

10: *Tressis* of Antony, ca. 36–35 B.C., city of origin unknown, obverse of Octavia facing jugate portraits of Antony and Octavian, London, British Museum, illustration after Grueber, *BMCRR* 2 p. 515, copyright British Museum.

11: Octavia, ca. 35–11 B.C. after an original probably of 35 B.C., from Velletri, marble, h. 39.5 cm., Rome, Museo Nazionale Romano inv. 121221. Photo DAI Rom. Inst. Neg. 40.1170, reproduced by permission of the Deutsches Archäologisches Institut, Rome.

12: 3/4 view of Figure 11. Photo DAI Rom. Inst. Neg. 40.1172, reproduced by permission of the Deutsches Archäologisches Institut, Rome.

13: Profile of Figure 11. DAI Rom. Inst.Neg. 40.1180, reproduced by permission of the Deutsches Archäologisches Institut, Rome.

14. Octavia, ca. 35–11 B.C., replica of Velletri type, from Smyrna, marble, h. 23.5 cm. Athens, National Museum no. 547. Photograph courtesy of the Hellenic Republic Ministry of Culture.

15: Left profile of Figure 14. Photograph courtesy of the Hellenic Republic Ministry of Culture.

16: "Octavia (?)," ca. 35–11 B.C., marble, h. 14 cm., of face 10.6 cm. Eichenzell, Schloss Fasanerie cat. 13. Photo: DAI Rom. Inst. Neg. 67.1131, reproduced by permission of the Deutsches Archäologisches Institut, Rome.

17: Profile of Figure 16, DAI Rom. Inst. Neg. 67.1133, reproduced by permission of the Deutsches Archäologisches Institut, Rome.

18: Variously identified as "Octavia," "Julia," or "Vipsania Agrippina," ca. 12 B.C.–A.D. 37, probably ca. A.D. 23, from Béziers, marble, h. 35 cm. Toulouse, Musée Saint Raymond inv. 30 004, museum photo.

19: Profile of Figure 18. Museum photo.

20: *Denarius* of C. Marius Tro., 13–12 B.C., Rome, reverse with of busts of Gaius Caesar, Julia, and Lucius Caesar. Enlarged. Staatliche Museen zu Berlin—Preußischer Kulturbesitz, Münzkabinett, museum photo.

21: Bronze coin of Livia and Julia, ca. 20 B.C.–2 B.C., Pergamon. Actual size. London, British Museum Mysia 249. Copyright British Museum.

22: Livia, Fayum type, ca. A.D. 4–14, from Arsinoë, Egypt, marble, h. 39 cm., Copenhagen, Ny Carlsberg Glyptotek, cat. 615, museum photo, copyright Jo Selsing.

23: Profile view of Figure 22. Museum photo, copyright Jo Selsing.

24: Livia, Albani-Bonn type, ca. 27 B.C.–A.D. 14, Louvre, MA 1233, basalt, h. 33.4 cm., Paris, Musée du Louvre, photo Musée du Louvre, M. and P. Chuzeville.

25: Profile view of Figure 24. Photo Musée du Louvre M. and P. Chuzeville.

26: Livia, Marbury Hall type, marble, ca. 35 B.C.–A.D. 14, h. of head 23.3 cm. Neck restored. Rome, Museo Nazionale Romano inv. 572. Photo DAI Rom. Inst. Neg. 78.1936, reproduced by permission of the Deutsches Archäologisches Institut, Rome.

27: Profile view of Figure 26. Photo DAI Rom. Inst. Neg. 78.1937, reproduced by permission of the Deutsches Archäologisches Institut, Rome.

28: "Livia (?)," variant portrait type with braids around head, ca. A.D. 41–54, from Istanbul, marble, h. 42 cm. Copenhagen, Ny Carlsberg Glyptotek inv. 748. Museum photo, copyright Jo Selsing.

29: Profile view of Figure 28. Museum photo, copyright Jo Selsing.

30: Ara Pacis Augustae, south frieze, detail: Livia. 13–9 B.C., Rome, marble relief, h. of panel 160 cm. Photo Barbara Malter, Archivio Fotografico dei Musei Capitolini.

31: Ara Pacis Augustae, east frieze, goddess or personification (Pax Augusta?). 13–9 B.C., Rome, marble relief, h. 157 cm. Photo DAI Rom. Inst. Neg. 86.1448, reproduced by permission of the Deutsches Archäologisches Institut, Rome.

32: Livia, provincial variant, ca. 27 B.C.–A.D. 14, from Neuilly-le-Real, bronze, h. 21 cm., of head 10 c.m. Paris, Musée du Louvre, inv. Br 28. Photo Musée du Louvre, M. and P. Chuzeville.

33: Profile view of Figure 32. Photo Musée du Louvre, M. and P. Chuzeville.

34: *Dupondius* of Tiberius, A.D. 22/23, Rome, reverse of *Salus Augusta* with portrait features of Livia. Actual size. New York, American Numismatic Society, museum photo.

35: Livia, variant on Fayum type, A.D. 23, from the Old Forum of Leptis Magna, marble, h. 68 cm. Tripolis Museum. Photo Antonio P. Ortolan, after Aurigemma, 1940, courtesy of the American Academy in Rome.

36: Tiberius and Livia as "Ceres Augusta," A.D. 14–29, sardonyx cameo, h. 5.5 cm. Florence, Museo Archeologico inv. 177, photo courtesy of the Soprintendenza Archeologica per la Toscana.

37: Livia as Priestess of the Deified Augustus, A.D. 14–29, Fayum type, from Otricoli, marble, h. 211 cm. Vatican, Sala dei Busti inv. 637, photo Musei Vaticani, Archivio Fotografico XXXIV.13.81.

38: Livia as Ceres-Fortuna, Fayum type, statue ca. A.D. 14–29, detail of head, marble, h. 253 cm. Paris, Louvre, MA 1242, photo Musée du Louvre M. et P. Chuzeville.

39: Livia, adoption type, ca. A.D. 14–23, from Béziers, marble, h. 50 cm. Toulouse, Musée Saint Raymond, inv. 30 006, museum photo.

40: Profile view of Figure 39. Museum photo.

41: Livia as Cybele and priestess of the Deified Augustus, A.D. 14–29, sardonyx cameo, h. 9 cm., w. 6.6 cm. Vienna, Kunsthistorisches Museum, inv. IXa95. Museum photo.

42: Livia as Venus, with bust of Augustus (?) or Tiberius as child (?), probably A.D. 14–29, turquoise cameo, h. 3.1, w. 3.9 cm. Boston Museum of Fine Arts, inv. 99, museum photo, reproduced by permission of the Boston Museum of Fine Arts.

43: Livia as Ceres Augusta, A.D. 35–36, from temple in theater of Leptis Magna, marble, h. 310 cm., Tripolis museum. Photo DAI Rom. Inst. Neg. 61.1723, reproduced by permission of the Deutsches Archäologisches Institut, Rome.

44: Livia as Ceres Augusta, probably ca. A.D. 29–37, marble, h. 199 cm., Paris, Louvre, inv. MA 1245, photo Musée du Louvre, M. and P. Chuzeville.

45: Livia, A.D. 37–41, from Velleia, marble, h. 224.5 cm., Parma, Museo Nazionale di Antichità inv. 1870 no. 146, 1952, no. 828, photo DAI Rom. Inst. Neg. 67.1593, reproduced by permission of the Deutsches Archäologisches Institut, Rome.

46: Detail of face of Figure 45. Photo DAI Rom. Inst. Neg. 67.1594, reproduced by permission of the Deutsches Archäologisches Institut, Rome.

47: Livia as Ceres, probably A.D. 41–54, marble, h. of bust 79 cm., of head 26.3 cm., Rome, Museo Capitolino inv. 121, photo DAI Rom. Inst. Neg. 79.1572. Reproduced by permission of the Deutsches Archäologisches Institut, Rome.

48: Livia as Ceres/Fortuna, probably A.D. 41–54, from Pozzuoli, marble, h. 215 cm., Copenhagen, Ny Carlsberg Glyptotek inv. N. 1643. Museum photo, copyright Jo Selsing.

49: Detail of face of Figure 48. Museum photo, copyright Jo Selsing.

50: Deified woman, probably Livia (so–called "Juno Ludovisi"), probably A.D. 41–54, marble, h. 116 cm., Rome, Museo Nazionale Romano, Palazzo Altemps, inv. 8631, photo courtesy of Art Resource/Alinari.

51: Profile view of Figure 50, photo courtesy of Art Resource/Alinari.

52: Relief of the Deified Augustus and Livia, Germanicus, and a figure of controversial identification, probably A.D. 41–68, marble, h. 140 cm. Ravenna, Museo Nazionale. Photo DAI Rom. Inst. Neg. 54.306, reproduced by permission of the Deutsches Archäologisches Institut, Rome.

53: Ara Pacis Augustae, south frieze, showing members and associates of the imperial family, including (left to right) Agrippa; a child of controversial identification, probably a client of Agrippa belonging to a provincial royal family; Livia; Tiberius; Antonia Minor; Germanicus as a child, and Drusus I. 13–9 B.C., Rome, marble relief, h. 160 cm. Photo: DAI Rom. Inst. Neg. 72.2403, reproduced by permission of the Deutsches Archäologisches Institut, Rome.

54: Detail of figure 53, face of Antonia Minor, Archivio Fotografico Musei Capitolini.

55: *Denarius* of Antonia Minor, A.D. 41–54, Rome, reverse of *Sacerdos Divi Augusti.* Actual size. London, British Museum RE Claudius 114. Copyright British Museum.

56: *Aureus* of Antonia Minor, A.D. 41–54, Rome, reverse of *Constantiae Augusti.* Actual size. London, British Museum RE Claudius 109. Copyright British Museum.

57: *Dupondius* of Claudius, A.D. 41, Rome, with reverse portrait of Antonia Minor. Actual size. London, British Museum RE Claudius no. 166. Copyright British Museum.

58: *Sestertius* of Claudius, A.D. 41, Rome, with reverse portrait of Drusus I. Actual size. London, British Museum RE Claudius, no. 157. Copyright British Museum.

59: Antonia Minor, A.D. 23, from the Old Forum of Leptis Magna, marble, life-size, h. of head 30 cm. Photo DAI Rom. Inst. Neg. 61.1772, reproduced by permission of the Deutsches Archäologisches Institut, Rome.

60: Antonia Minor, probably A.D. 14–37, marble, h. of bust in present condition 53.4 cm., of head and neck 28 cm., of head from chin to occiput 23 cm. Cambridge, Arthur M. Sackler Museum, Harvard University Art Museums, museum photo.

61: Profile view of Figure 60. Museum photo.

62: Antonia Minor, after A.D. 37, probably A.D. 41–54, marble, h. 203 cm., Paris, Musée du Louvre, inv. MA 1228, photo Musée du Louvre, M. and P. Chuzeville.

63: Detail of face of Figure 62, photo Musée du Louvre, M. and P. Chuzeville.

64: Antonia Minor, A.D. 41–48, from the imperial nymphaeum at Baia, marble, h. 155 cm. Baiae, Castello Aragonese. Foto Marburg, C408.009.

65: Detail of face of Figure 64. Foto Marburg, C408.011.

66: Profile view of Figure 65. Foto Marburg C408.013.

67: So-called "Antonia Minor," more probably a private citizen, 12 B.C.–A.D. 37, Béziers, marble, h. 25 cm. Toulouse Musée Saint Raymond inv. 30 005, museum photo.

68: Antonia Minor, probably ca. A.D. 37, marble head on bust to which it does not belong, h. of face from chin to top of fillet 17.85 cm. University of Alberta Museum, inv. 981.28. Photo courtesy of the Department of History and Classics, University of Alberta, Canada.

69: Claudia Octavia, A.D. 41–48, from the imperial nymphaeum at Baia, marble, h. 120 cm. Baiae, Castello Aragonese. Foto Marburg C407.993.

70: Detail of face of Figure 69, Foto Marburg C407.995.

71: Profile view of Figure 69. Foto Marburg C407.997.

72: "Vipsania Agrippina (?)," A.D. 23, from the Old Forum of Leptis Magna, marble, h. 37 cm. Tripolis Museum. Photo: Antonio P. Ortolan, after Aurigemma, Figure 45, courtesy of the American Academy in Rome.

73: Profile view of Figure 72. Photo Antonio P. Ortolan, after Aurigemma, Figure 46, courtesy of the American Academy in Rome.

74: Livilla I (?) or Livilla II (?), portrait of the "Leptis-Malta type," either A.D. 23 or A.D. 37–38, from the Old Forum of Leptis Magna, marble, h. 22.5 cm. Tripolis Museum. Photo Antonio P. Ortolan, after Aurigemma, courtesy of the American Academy in Rome.

75: Profile view of Figure 74. Photo Antonio P. Ortolan, after Aurigemma, courtesy of the American Academy in Rome.

76: Livilla I (?) or Livilla II (?), "Leptis-Malta type," either A.D. 14–31 or A.D. 37–41, marble, h. 66 cm., of head and neck 32 cm. Vatican, Ingresso, Ambulacro, inv. 103, photo Musei Vaticani, Archivio Fotografico XXXIV.35.46.

77: Profile view of Figure 76, photo Musei Vaticani, Archivio Fotografico XXX.2.59.

78: Livilla I with her twin sons Tiberius Gemellus and Germanicus II, A.D. 19–23, sardonyx cameo, h. 6.1 cm., w. 5.0 cm., Paris, Bibliothèque Nationale, Cabinet des Médailles, inv. 243, museum photo, reproduced by permission of the Bibliothèque Nationale de France.

79: Livilla I and her twin sons Tiberius Gemellus and Germanicus II, A.D. 19–23, sardonyx cameo, h. 7.6 cm., w. 6.0 cm. Staatliche Museen zu Berlin, Preussischer Kulturbesitz, Antikensammlung inv. 11096, museum photo.

80: *Sestertius* of Agrippina I, A.D. 37–41, Rome, with reverse of *carpentum*. Actual size. New York, American Numismatic Society, museum photo.

81: *Dupondius* of Germanicus, A.D. 37, Rome. Actual size. New York, American Numismatic Society 1957.172.1523, museum photo.

82: *Sestertius* of Caligula, A.D. 37, Rome, with reverse figures of Agrippina II, Drusilla, and Livilla II. Actual size. London, British Museum, photo copyright British Museum.

83: *Dupondius* of Nero I and Drusus III, A.D. 37–38, Rome. Actual size. London, British Museum, photo copyright British Museum.

84: Bronze *as*, A.D. 38, Apamea in Bithynia, with obverse figure of Agrippina I as *Pietas*, and reverse of Livilla II, the deified Drusilla, and Agrippina II. Actual size. Staatliche Münzsammlung, Munich, museum photo.

85: *Sestertius* of Claudius, 41–54 A.D., Rome, with reverse portrait of Agrippina I. Actual size. Cambridge, Mass., Arthur M. Sackler Museum, Harvard University Art Museums, Gift of George Davis Chase, Class of '89, 1942.176.116. Museum photo.

86: Agrippina I, A.D. 23, from the Old Forum of Leptis Magna, marble, life-size (precise measurement not available). Tripolis Museum. Photograph: DAI Rom. Inst. Neg. 61.1730, reproduced by permission of the Deutsches Archäologisches Institut, Rome.

87: Agrippina I, principate of Caligula, A.D. 37–41, from Velleia, marble, h. 209 cm. Parma, Museo Nazionale di Antichità, inv. 829. Photo DAI Rom. Inst. Neg. 67.1585, reproduced by permission of the Deutsches Archäologisches Institut, Rome.

88: Detail of face of Figure 87. Photo DAI Rom. Inst. Neg. 67.1586. reproduced by permission of the Deutsches Archäologisches Institut, Rome.

89: Agrippina I, probably A.D. 14–33, from Pergamon, marble, h. 37.5 cm., of head 21 cm. Istanbul, National Archaeological Museum, photo courtesy of the Deutsches Archäologisches Institut, Istanbul, neg. no. 64/66.

90: Profile of Figure 89, photo courtesy of the Deutsches Archäologisches Institut, Istanbul, neg. no. 64/67.

91: Agrippina I, probably datable principate of Caligula, A.D. 37–41, marble, h. of ancient part 31 cm., of head 24 cm. Rome, Musei Capitolini inv. 421, photo Barbara Malter, Archivio Fotografico Musei Capitolini.

92: Profile view of Figure 91, photo Barbara Malter, Archivio Fotografico Musei Capitolini.

93: Agrippina I, statue, detail of face, probably datable to principate of Claudius, A.D. 41–54, from Tindari, Sicily, marble, h. 210 cm., of head and neck, 37 cm. Palermo, Museo Nazionale di Archeologia inv. 698, photo DAI Rom. Inst. Neg. 88.1156, reproduced by permission of the Deutsches Archäologisches Institut, Rome.

94: Profile view of Figure 93. Photo DAI Rom. Inst. Neg. 88.1155, reproduced by permission of the Deutsches Archäologisches Institut, Rome.

95: Gemma Claudia, with confronted jugate portraits of Claudius and Agrippina II (left) and Germanicus and Agrippina I (right), A.D. 49, sardonyx cameo, h. 12 cm. Vienna, Kunsthistorisches Museum inv. IX.A.63. Museum photograph.

96: Agrippina I, probably datable principate of Claudius, ca. A.D. 41–54, sardonyx cameo, h. 4.5 cm., w. 3.5 cm. London, British Museum, museum photograph, copyright British Museum.

97: Elgin Caryatid, 421–405 B.C., from the Erechtheion, Athens, marble, h. 231 cm. London, British Museum, inv. 407, copyright British Museum.

98: Demeter, original Greek sculpture of the fourth century B.C., from Knidos, marble, 152.3 cm. London, British Museum, inv. 1300, museum photograph, copyright British Museum.

99: Eirene of Kephisodotos, Roman copy after an original of the early 4th century B.C., marble, h. 199 cm. Munich Glyptothek inv. 219, 1, photograph by blow up, reproduced courtesy of the Staatliche Antikensammlung und Glyptothek, Munich.

100: Apollo of Kassel, detail of face: Roman copy after an original of the 5th century B.C. (?), marble, h. of statue 197 cm. Kassel, Museum Schloß Wilhelmshöhe, museum photo, reproduced by permission of the museum.

101: Head variously identified as Agrippina I, Claudia Octavia, or Agrippina II, principate of Claudius, A.D. 49–54, marble, h. 48 cm. Vatican, Museo Chiaramonti inv. 1480. Photo courtesy of Archivio Fotografico, Monumenti, Musei e Gallerie Pontificie, no. XXX–21–28.

102: Profile view of Figure 101. Photo courtesy of Archivio Fotografico, Monumenti, Musei e Gallerie Pontificie, no. XXX–21–29.

103: Head variously identified as Agrippina I, Claudia Octavia, or Agrippina II, probably A.D. 54–59, from Olympia, marble, h. 35.5 cm. Olympia Museum, 147. Photograph: DAI Ath. neg. Ol.2163, reproduced by permission of the Deutsches Archäologisches Institut, Athens.

104: Profile view of Figure 103. Photograph: DAI Ath. Neg. Ol–2164, reproduced by permission of the Deutsches Archäologisches Institut, Athens.

105: Agrippina II, Milan type, probably ca. A.D. 54–59, Olympia, marble, h. 203 cm., of head 26.5 cm. Photo: DAI Athens Neg. 86.59, reproduced by permission of the Deutsches Archäologisches Institut, Athens.

106: Detail of face of Figure 105. Photo DAI Ath. Neg. 79/815, reproduced by permission of the of the Deutsches Archäologisches Institut, Athens.

107: Agrippina II, Providence–Schloss Fasanerie type, A.D. 37–38, white marble, set on bust of colored marble to which it does not belong, h. of head 30.5 cm. Providence, Museum of the Rhode Island School of Design, museum photo, reproduced by permission of the museum.

108: Profile view of Figure 107, museum photo, reproduced by permission of the museum.

109: Agrippina II, Providence-Schloss Fasanerie type, A.D. 37–38, marble, h. 32.2 cm. Eichenzell, Schloss Fasanerie bei Fulda, photo DAI Rom. Inst. Neg. 67.1185, reproduced by permission of the Deutsches Archäologisches Institut, Rome.

110: Profile view of Figure 109, photo DAI Rom. Inst. Neg. 67.1188, reproduced by permission of the Deutsches Archäologisches Institut, Rome.

111: Drusilla, A.D. 37–38, modified after her death in A.D. 38, from the Julio-Claudian family group in or near the theater of Caere, marble, h. 204 cm., of head 25 cm. Vatican, Museo Gregoriano Profano inv. 9952, museum photo.

112: Detail of face of Figure 111, museum photo.

113: Profile view of face of Figure 111, museum photo.

114: Drusilla, A.D. 37–38, modified after her death in A.D. 38, marble, h. 32.2 cm., of face, 19.5 cm. Collection of Prince Heinrich von Hessen, photo DAI Rom. Inst. Neg. 67.1192, reproduced by permission of the Deutsches Archäologisches Institut, Rome.

115: Profile view of Figure 114, photo DAI Rom. Inst. Neg. 67.1194, reproduced by permission of the Deutsches Archäologisches Institut, Rome.

116: Diva Drusilla, A.D. 38–41, marble, life-size. Munich Glyptothek, inv. 316, museum photo.

117: Profile view of Figure 116, museum photo.

118: Agrippina II, Parma-Naples type, A.D. 49, from imperial group at Velleia, marble, h. 203 cm. Parma, Museo Nazionale di Antichità, inv. 830. Photo: DAI Rom. Inst. Neg. 67.1590, reproduced by permission of the Deutsches Archäologisches Institut, Rome.

119: Detail of head of Figure 118. Photo DAI Rom. Inst. Neg. 67.1591, reproduced by permission of the Deutsches Archäologisches Institut, Rome.

120: Silver *didrachm*, A.D. 41–48, Caesarea in Cappadocia, with obverse portrait of Messalina, and reverse type of the three children of Claudius: Claudia Octavia, Britannicus and Claudia Antonia. Actual size. London, British Museum, Messalina and Claudius 242, copyright British Museum.

121: *Aureus* of Claudius, A.D. 49–54, Rome, with reverse portrait of Agrippina II. Actual size. New York, American Numismatic Society 1954.256.6, museum photo.

122: *Denarius* of Agrippina II, A.D. 49–54, Rome, with reverse portrait of Nero. Actual size. London, British Museum, Claudius no. 82, copyright British Museum.

123: Messalina with the child Britannicus, A.D. 41–48, found near Rome, marble, h. 195 cm. Paris, Musée du Louvre, MA 1224, photo Musée du Louvre, Documentation Photographique de la Reunion des Musées Nationaux.

124: Detail of face of Figure 123, photo Musée du Louvre, Documentation Photographique de la Reunion des Musées Nationaux.

125: Profile view of Figure 124, photo Musée du Louvre, Documentation Photographique de la Reunion des Musées Nationaux.

126: Messalina, A.D. 41–48, marble head, h. 29.3 cm. Dresden Albertinum, inv. 358, museum photo.

127: Profile view of Figure 126, museum photo.

128: Claudia Octavia? (Sometimes identified as Messalina). Principate of Claudius, A.D. 41–54; if it represents Claudia Octavia at time of marriage to Nero, A.D. 53. Marble, h. 29 cm. Vatican, Museo Chiaramonti, inv. 1814. Photo Musei Vaticani Archivio Fotografico XXXV 8–51.

129: Profile view of Figure 128. Photo Musei Vaticani Archivio Fotografico XXX1–15–76.

130: Silver *tetradrachm*, A.D. 50–54, Ephesus, obverse with jugate portrait of Claudius and Agrippina II. Actual size. London, British Museum, Claudius no. 231, museum photo, copyright British Museum.

131: *Aureus* of Nero and Agrippina II, A.D. 54, Rome, with confronted obverse portraits. Actual size. London, British Museum RE Nero no. 1, copyright British Museum.

132: *Aureus* of Nero and Agrippina II, A.D. 55, Rome, with jugate obverse portraits. Actual size. New York, American Numismatic Society, 1967.153.219, museum photo.

133: Agrippina II, bust of Nero emerging from the cornucopiae to her left, probably A.D. 49, sardonyx cameo, h. 6.9 cm., w. 5.3 cm. Paris, Bibliothèque Nationale de France, Cabinet des Médailles, museum photo.

134: Agrippina II, statue of Ancona type, A.D. 49–54, marble, h. 183 cm. Vatican, Museo Chiaramonti, inv. 2084. Museum photo.

135: Detail of face of Figure 134. Museum photo.

136: Agrippina II, Ancona type with diadem, A.D. 49–54, marble, h. 36 cm. Copenhagen, Ny Carlsberg Glyptotek cat. 636. Museum photo, copyright Jo Selsing.

137: Profile view of Figure 136. Museum photo, copyright Jo Selsing.

138: Agrippina II, Stuttgart type, A.D. 54–59, marble, h. 40.5 cm., of head, 22.8 cm. Stuttgart, Würtemburgisches Landesmuseum, Arch. 68/2, museum photo.

139: Agrippina II, Stuttgart type, A.D. 54–59, basalt, h. 30 cm. Copenhagen, Ny Carlsberg Glyptotek, cat. 634, museum photo, copyright Jo Selsing.

140: Profile view of Figure 139. Museum photo, copyright Jo Selsing.

141: Panel from the Sebasteion at Aphrodisias with figures of Agrippina II (Milan type), Claudius, and a togate personification, A.D. 49–54, marble relief, h. 160 cm, w. at top 170 cm., at bottom 164 cm., d. 43 cm. Aphrodisias Museum, photograph reproduced courtesy of New York University, Institute of Fine Arts, Aphrodisias Archive.

142: Panel from the Sebasteion of Aphrodisias with figures of the emperor Nero as a young man and of Agrippina II (Ancona type), probably A.D. 54–55, no later than A.D. 59, marble, h. 172 cm., w. 142.5 at bottom, d. 37.5 cm. Aphrodisias Museum, photograph reproduced courtesy of New York University, Institute of Fine Arts, Aphrodisias Archive.

143: Agrippina II, posthumous portrait, A.D. 113–118, from *imago clipeata* in the Forum of Trajan, marble, h. 85 cm, of face 57 cm. Rome, Mercati Traiani, photo Barbara Malter, Archivio Fotografico Musei Capitolini.

1: *Aureus* of C. Numonius Vaala, 43 or 40 B.C., Rome, with bust of Victory on obverse that appears to have portrait-like face, tentatively identified as Fulvia. Actual size. London, British Museum RR Rome #4215.

2: *Cistophoros* of Antony, 40 ca. 35 B.C., Pergamon, bust of Octavia with emblems of Dionysiac cult on reverse. Actual size. Munich, Staatliche Münzsammlung.

3: *Cistophoros* of Antony, 40 - ca. 35 B.C., Miletus, jugate portrait of Antony and Octavia on obverse. Actual size. Munich, Staatliche Münzsammlung.

4: *Aureus* of Antony, 40 B.C., city of origin unknown, with reverse portrait of Octavia, unique specimen, also known as the De Quelen Aureus. Enlarged. Staatliche Museen zu Berlin – Preußisscher Kulturbesitz, Münzkabinett.

5: *Aureus* of Antony, 40 - ca. 35 B.C., city of origin unknown, with reverse portrait of Octavia. Actual size. London, British Museum, BMC East 144.

6: *Tetradrachm* of Cleopatra VII of Egypt, 55-30 B.C., Askalon. Actual size. London, British Museum, BMC Askalon 20.

7: *Denarius* of Antony and Cleopatra, 32 B.C., Eastern mint, city of origin uncertain. Actual size. London, British Museum.

8: *Tetradrachm* of Antony and Cleopatra, 37-32, probably 37 B.C., Antioch. Actual size. New York, American Numismatic Society 1967.152.567.

9: *Sestertius* of Antony, ca. 37-35 B.C., city of origin unknown, with obverse confronted portraits of Antony and Octavia. Actual size. New York, American Numismatic Society 1944.100.7100.

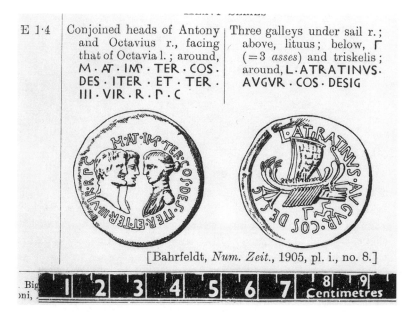

| E 1·4 | Conjoined heads of Antony and Octavius r., facing that of Octavia l.; around, M · AT · IM͡P · TER · COS · DES · ITER · ET · TER · III · VIR · R · P · C | Three galleys under sail r.; above, lituus; below, Γ (= 3 *asses*) and triskelis; around, L · ATRATINVS · AVGVR · COS · DESIG |

[Bahrfeldt, *Num. Zeit.*, 1905, pl. i., no. 8.]

10: *Tressis* of Antony, ca. 37-35 B.C., city of origin unknown, obverse of Octavia facing jugate portraits of Antony and Octavian, London, British Museum, illustration after Grueber, *BMCRR* 2 p. 515.

11. Octavia, ca. 35-11 B.C. after an original probably of 35 B.C., from Velletri, marble, h. 39.5 cm., Rome, Museo Nazionale Romano inv. 121221.

12: 3/4 view of Figure 11.

13: Profile of Figure 11.

14. Octavia, ca. 35-11 B.C., replica of Velletri type, from Smyrna, marble, h. 23.5 cm.
Athens, National Museum no. 547.

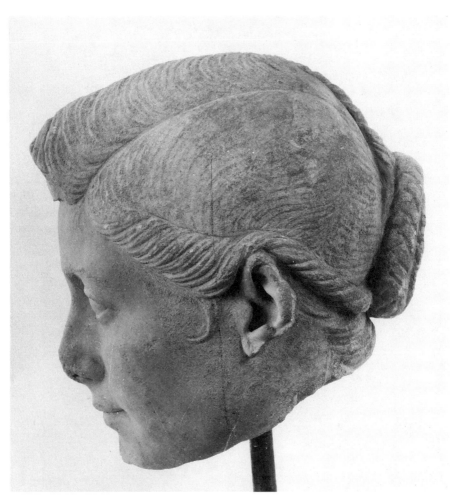

15: Left profile of Figure 14.

16: "Octavia (?)," ca. 35-11 B.C., marble, h. 14 cm., of face 10.6 cm. Eichenzell, Schloss Fasanerie cat. 13.

17: Profile of Figure 16.

18: Variously identified as "Octavia," "Julia," or "Vipsania Agrippina," ca.12 B.C. -
A.D. 37, probably ca. A.D. 23, from Béziers, marble, h. 35 cm. Toulouse, Musée
Saint Raymond inv. 30 004.

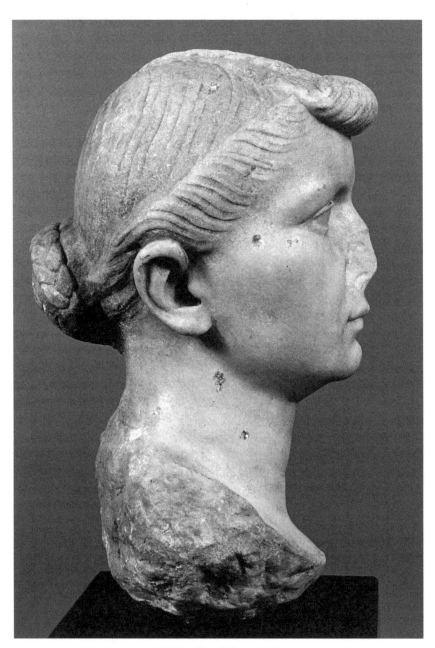

19: Profile of Figure 18.

20: *Denarius* of C. Marius Tro., 13-12 B.C., Rome, reverse with of busts of Gaius Caesar, Julia, and Lucius Caesar. Enlarged. Staatliche Museen zu Berlin – Preußischer Kulturbesitz, Münzkabinett.

21: Bronze coin of Livia and Julia, ca. 20 B.C. - 2 B.C., Pergamon. Actual size. London, British Museum Mysia 249.

22: Livia, Fayum type, ca. A.D. 4-14, from Arsinoë, Egypt, marble, h. 39 cm., Copenhagen, Ny Carlsberg Glyptotek, cat. 615.

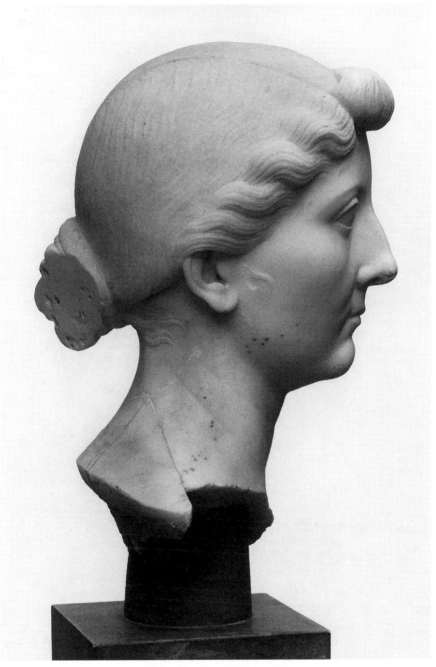

23: Profile view of Figure 22.

24: Livia, Albani-Bonn type, ca. 27 B.C. - A.D. 14, Louvre, MA 1233, basalt, h. 33.4 cm., Paris, Musée du Louvre.

25: Profile view of Figure 24.

26: Livia, Marbury Hall type, marble, ca. 35 B.C. - A.D. 14, h. of head 23.3 cm. Neck restored. Rome, Museo Nazionale Romano inv. 572.

27: Profile view of Figure 26.

28: "Livia (?)," variant portrait type with braids around head, ca. A.D. 41-54, from Istanbul, marble, h. 42 cm. Copenhagen, Ny Carlsberg Glyptotek inv. 748.

29: Profile view of Figure 28.

30: Ara Pacis Augustae, south frieze, detail: Livia. 13-9 B.C., Rome, marble relief, h. of panel 160 cm.

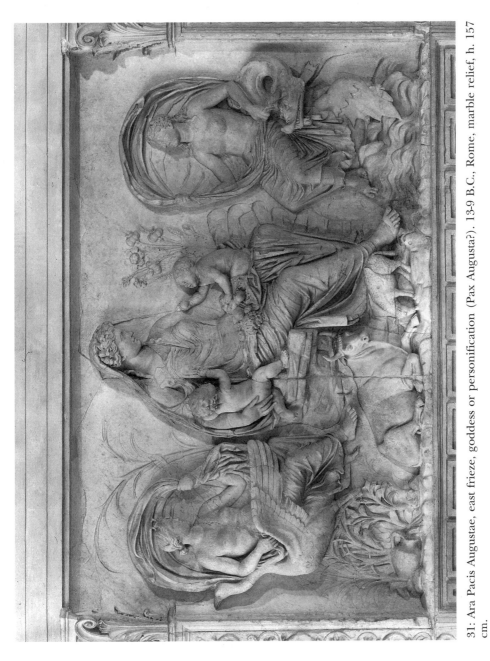

31: Ara Pacis Augustae, east frieze, goddess or personification (Pax Augusta?). 13-9 B.C., Rome, marble relief, h. 157 cm.

32: Livia, provincial variant, ca. 27 B.C. - A.D. 14, from Neuilly-le-Real, bronze, h. 21 cm., of head 10 cm. Paris, Musée du Louvre, inv. Br 28.

33: Profile view of Figure 32.

34: *Dupondius* of Tiberius, A.D. 22/23, Rome, reverse of *Salus Augusta* with portrait features of Livia. Actual size. New York, American Numismatic Society.

35: Livia, variant on Fayum type, A.D. 23, from the Old Forum of Leptis Magna, marble, h. 68 cm. Tripolis Museum.

36: Tiberius and Livia as "Ceres Augusta," A.D. 14-29, sardonyx cameo, h. 5.5 cm.
Florence, Museo Archeologico inv. 177.

37: Livia as Priestess of the Deified Augustus, A.D. 14-29, Fayum type, from Otricoli, marble, h. 211 cm. Vatican, Sala dei Busti inv. 637.

38: Livia as Ceres-Fortuna, Fayum type, statue ca. A.D. 14-29, detail of head, marble, h. 253 cm. Paris, Louvre, MA 1242.

39: Livia, adoption type, ca. A.D. 14-23, from Béziers, marble, h. 50 cm. Toulouse, Musée Saint Raymond, inv. 30 006.

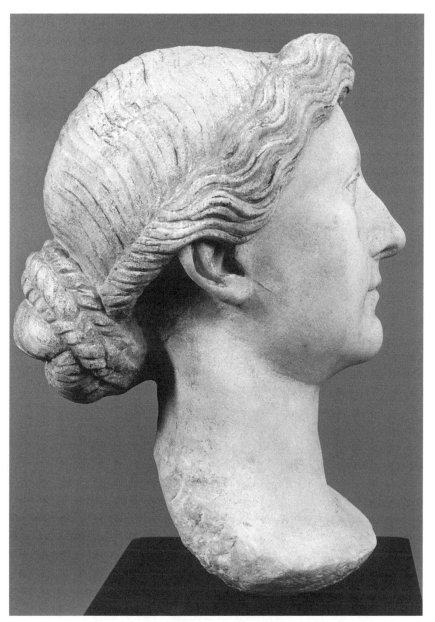

40: Profile view of Figure 39.

41: Livia as Cybele and priestess of the Deified Augustus, A.D. 14-29, sardonyx cameo, h. 9 cm., w. 6.6 cm. Vienna, Kunsthistorisches Museum, inv. IXa95.

42: Livia as Venus, with bust of Augustus (?) or Tiberius as child (?), probably A.D. 14-29, turquoise cameo, h. 3.1, w. 3.9 cm. Boston Museum of Fine Arts, inv. 99.

43: Livia as Ceres Augusta, A.D. 35-36, from temple in theater of Leptis Magna, marble, h. 310 cm., Tripolis museum.

44: Livia as Ceres Augusta, probably ca. A.D. 29-37, marble, h. 199 cm., Paris, Louvre, inv. MA 1245.

45: Livia, A.D. 37-41, from Velleia, marble, h. 224.5
cm., Parma, Museo Nazionale di Antichità inv. 1870
no. 146, 1952, no. 828.

46: Detail of face of Figure 45.

47: Livia as Ceres, probably A.D. 41-54, marble, h. of bust 79 cm., of head 26.3 cm., Rome, Museo Capitolino inv. 121.

48: Livia as Ceres/Fortuna, probably A.D. 41-54, from Pozzuoli, marble, h. 215 cm., Copenhagen, Ny Carlsberg Glyptotek inv. N.1643.

49: Detail of face of Figure 48.

66

50: Deified woman, probably Livia (so-called "Juno Ludovisi"), probably A.D. 41-54, marble, h. 116 cm., Rome, Museo Nazionale Romano, Palazzo Altemps, inv. 8631.

51: Profile view of Figure 50.

52: Relief of the Deified Augustus and Livia, Germanicus, and a Figure of controversial identification, probably A.D. 41-68, marble, h. 140 cm. Ravenna, Museo Nazionale.

53: Ara Pacis Augustae, south frieze, showing members and associates of the imperial family, including (left to right) Agrippa; a child of controversial identification, probably a client of Agrippa belonging to a provincial royal family; Livia; Tiberius; Antonia Minor; Germanicus as a child, and Drusus I. 13-9 B.C., Rome, marble relief, h. 160 cm.

54: Detail of Figure 53, face of Antonia Minor.

55: *Denarius* of Antonia Minor, A.D. 41-54, Rome, reverse of *Sacerdos Divi Augusti*. Actual size. London, British Museum RE Claudius 114.

56: *Aureus* of Antonia Minor, A.D. 41-54, Rome, reverse of *Constantiae Augusti*. Actual size. London, British Museum RE Claudius 109.

57: *Dupondius* of Claudius, A.D. 41, Rome, with reverse portrait of Antonia Minor. Actual size. London, British Museum RE Claudius no. 166.

58: *Sestertius* of Claudius, A.D. 41, Rome, with reverse portrait of Drusus I. Actual size. London, British Museum RE Claudius, no. 157.

59: Antonia Minor, A.D. 23, from the Old Forum
of Leptis Magna, marble, life-size, h. of head 30
cm.

60: Antonia Minor, probably A.D. 14-37, marble, h. of bust in present condition 53.4 cm., of head and neck 28 cm., of head from chin to occiput 23 cm. Cambridge, Arthur M. Sackler Museum, Harvard University Art Museums.

61: Profile view of Figure 60.

62: Antonia Minor, after A.D. 37, probably A.D.
41-54, marble, h. 203 cm., Paris, Musée du Louvre,
inv. MA 1228.

63: Detail of face of Figure 62.

64: Antonia Minor, A.D. 41-48, from the imperial
nymphaeum at Baia, marble, h. 155 cm. Baia, Castello Aragonese.

65: Detail of face of Figure 64.

66: Profile view of Figure 65.

67: So-called "Antonia Minor," more probably a private citizen, 12 B.C. - A.D. 37, Béziers, marble, h. 25 cm. Toulouse Musée Saint Raymond inv. 30 005.

68: Antonia Minor, probably ca. A.D. 37, marble head on bust to which it does not belong, h. of face from chin to top of fillet 17.85 cm. University of Alberta Museum, inv. 981.28.

69: Claudia Octavia, A.D. 41-48, from the imperial
nymphaeum at Baia, marble, h. 120 cm. Baia, Castello
Aragonese.

71: Profile view of Figure 69.

70: Detail of face of Figure 69.

72: "Vipsania Agrippina (?)," A.D. 23, from the Old Forum of Leptis Magna, marble, h. 37 cm. Tripolis Museum.

73: Profile view of Figure 72.

74: Livilla I (?) or Livilla II (?), portrait of the "Leptis-Malta type," either A.D. 23 or A.D. 37-38, from the Old Forum of Leptis Magna, marble, h. 22.5 cm. Tripolis Museum.

75: Profile view of Figure 74.

76: Livilla I (?) or Livilla II (?), "Leptis-Malta type," either A.D. 14-31 or A.D. 37-41, marble, h. 66 cm, of head and neck 32 cm. Vatican, Ingresso, Ambulacro, inv. 103.

77: Profile view of Figure 76.

78: Livilla I with her twin sons Tiberius Gemellus and Germanicus II, A.D. 19-23, sardonyx cameo, h. 6.1 cm., w. 5.0 cm., Paris, Bibliothèque Nationale, Cabinet des Médailles, inv. 243.

79: Livilla I and her twin sons Tiberius Gemellus and Germanicus II, A.D. 19-23, sardonyx cameo, h. 7.6 cm., w. 6.0 cm. Staatliche Museen zu Berlin, Preussischer Kulturbesitz, Antikensammlung inv. 11096.

80: *Sestertius* of Agrippina I, A.D. 37-41, Rome, with reverse of *carpentum*. Actual size. New York, American Numismatic Society.

81: *Dupondius* of Germanicus, A.D. 37, Rome. Actual size. New York, American Numismatic Society 1957.172.1523.

82: *Sestertius* of Caligula, A.D. 37, Rome, with reverse Figures of Agrippina II, Drusilla, and Livilla II. Actual size. London, British Museum.

83: *Dupondius* of Nero I and Drusus III, A.D. 37-38, Rome. Actual size. London, British Museum.

84: Bronze *as*, A.D. 38, Apamea in Bithynia, with obverse Figure of Agrippina I as *Pietas*, and reverse of Livilla II, the deified Drusilla, and Agrippina II. Actual size. Staatliche Münzsammlung, Munich.

85: *Sestertius* of Claudius, 41-54 A.D., Rome, with reverse portrait of Agrippina I. Actual size. Cambridge, Mass., Arthur M. Sackler Museum, Harvard University Art Museums, Gift of George Davis Chase, Class of '89, 1942. 176.116.

86: Agrippina I, A.D. 23, from the Old Forum of
Leptis Magna, marble, life-size (precise measurement not available). Tripolis Museum.

87: Agrippina I, principate of Caligula, A.D. 37-41, from Velleia, marble, h. 209 cm. Parma, Museo Nazionale di Antichità, inv. 829.

88: Detail of face of Figure 87.

89: Agrippina I, probably A.D. 14-33, from Pergamon, marble, h. 37.5 cm., of head 21 cm. Istanbul, National Archaeological Museum.

90: Profile of Figure 89.

91: Agrippina I, probably datable principate of Caligula, A.D. 37-41, marble, h. of ancient part 31 cm., of head 24 cm. Rome, Musei Capitolini inv. 421.

92: Profile view of Figure 91.

93: Agrippina I, statue, detail of face, probably datable to principate of Claudius, A.D. 41-54, from Tindari, Sicily, marble, h. 210 cm., of head and neck, 37 cm. Palermo, Museo Nazionale di Archeologia inv. 698.

94: Profile view of Figure 93.

95: Gemma Claudia, with confronted jugate portraits of Claudius and Agrippina II (left) and Germanicus and Agrippina I (right), A.D. 49, sardonyx cameo, h. 12 cm. Vienna, Kunsthistorisches Museum inv. IX.A.63.

96: Agrippina I, probably datable principate of Claudius, ca. A.D. 41-54, sardonyx cameo, h. 4.5 cm, w. 3.5 cm. London, British Museum.

97: Elgin Caryatid, 421-405 B.C., from the Erechtheion, Athens, marble, h. 231 cm. London, British Museum, inv. 407.

98: Demeter, original Greek sculpture of the fourth century B.C., from Knidos, marble, 152.3 cm. London, British Museum, inv. 1300.

99: Eirene of Kephisodotos, Roman copy after an original of the early 4th century B.C., marble, h. 199 cm. Munich Glyptothek inv. 219, 1.

100: Apollo of Kassel, detail of face: Roman copy after an original of the 5th century B.C. (?), marble, h. of statue 197 cm. Kassel, Museum Schloß Wilhelmshöhe.

101: Head variously identified as Agrippina I, Claudia Octavia, or
Agrippina II, principate of Claudius, A.D. 49-54, marble, h. 48 cm.
Vatican, Museo Chiaramonti inv. 1480.

102: Profile view of Figure 101.

103: Head variously identified as Agrippina I, Claudia Octavia, or Agrippina II, probably A.D. 54-59, from Olympia, marble, h. 35.5 cm. Olympia Museum Λ 147.

104: Profile view of Figure 103.

106: Detail of face of Figure 105.

105: Agrippina II, Milan type, probably ca. A.D. 54-59, Olympia, marble, h. 203 cm., of head 26.5 cm.

107: Agrippina II, Providence-Schloss Fasanerie type, A.D. 37-38, white marble, set on bust of colored marble to which it does not belong, h. of head 30.5 cm. Providence, Museum of the Rhode Island School of Design.

108: Profile view of Figure 107.

109: Agrippina II, Providence-Schloss Fasanerie type, A.D. 37-38, marble, h.
32.2 cm. Eichenzell, Schloss Fasanerie bei Fulda.

110: Profile view of Figure 109.

111: Drusilla, A.D. 37-38, modified after her death in A.D. 38, from the Julio-Claudian family group in or near the theater of Caere, marble, h. 204 cm., of head 25 cm. Vatican, Museo Gregoriano Profano inv. 9952.

112: Detail of face of Figure 111.

113: Profile view of face of Figure 111.

114: Drusilla, A.D. 37-38, modified after her death in A.D. 38, marble, h. 32.2 cm., of face, 19.5 cm. Collection of Prince Heinrich von Hessen.

115: Profile view of Figure 114.

116: Diva Drusilla, A.D. 38-41, marble, life-size. Munich Glyptothek, inv. 316.

117: Profile view of Figure 116.

118: Agrippina II, Parma-Naples type, A.D. 49, from imperial group at Velleia, marble, h. 203 cm. Parma, Museo Nazionale di Antichità, inv. 830.

119: Detail of head of Figure 118.

120: Silver *didrachm*, A.D. 41-48, Caesarea in Cappadocia, with obverse portrait of Messalina, and reverse type of the three children of Claudius: Claudia Octavia, Britannicus and Claudia Antonia. Actual size. London, British Museum, Messalina and Claudius 242.

121: *Aureus* of Claudius, A.D. 49-54, Rome, with reverse portrait of Agrippina II. Actual size. New York, American Numismatic Society 1954.256.6.

122: *Denarius* of Agrippina II, A.D. 49-54, Rome, with reverse portrait of Nero. Actual size. London, British Museum, Claudius no. 82.

123: Messalina with the child Britannicus, A.D. 41-48, found near Rome, marble, h. 195 cm. Paris, Musée du Louvre, MA 1224.

124: Detail of face of Figure 123.

125: Profile view of Figure 124.

126: Messalina, A.D. 41-48, marble head, h. 29.3 cm. Dresden Albertinum, inv. 358.

127: Profile view of Figure 126.

128: Claudia Octavia? (Sometimes identified as Messalina). Principate of Claudius, A.D. 41-54; if it represents Claudia Octavia at time of marriage to Nero, A.D. 53. Marble, h. 29 cm. Vatican, Museo Chiaramonti, inv. 1814.

129: Profile view of Figure 128.

130: Silver *tetradrachm*, A.D. 50-54, Ephesus, obverse with jugate portrait of Claudius and Agrippina II. Actual size. London, British Museum, Claudius no. 231.

131 *Aureus* of Nero and Agrippina II, A.D. 54, Rome, with confronted obverse portraits. Actual size. London, British Museum RE Nero no. 1.

132: *Aureus* of Nero and Agrippina II, A.D. 55, Rome, with jugate obverse portraits. Actual size. New York, American Numismatic Society, 1967.153.219.

133: Agrippina II, bust of Nero emerging from the cornucopiae to her left, probably A.D. 49, sardonyx cameo, h. 6.9 cm., w. 5.3 cm. Paris, Bibliothèque Nationale de France, Cabinet des Médailles.

134: Agrippina II, statue of Ancona type, A.D. 49-54, marble, h. 183 cm. Vatican, Museo Chiaramonti, inv. 2084.

135: Detail of face of Figure 134.

136: Agrippina II, Ancona type with diadem, A.D. 49-54, marble, h. 36 cm. Copenhagen, Ny Carlsberg Glyptotek cat. 636.

137: Profile view of Figure 136.

138: Agrippina II, Stuttgart type, A.D. 54-59, marble, h. 40.5 cm., of head, 22.8 cm.
Stuttgart, Würtemburgisches Landesmuseum, Arch. 68/2.

139: Agrippina II, Stuttgart type, A.D. 54-59, basalt, h. 30 cm. Copenhagen, Ny Carlsberg Glyptotek, cat. 634.

140: Profile view of Figure 139.

141: Panel from the Sebasteion at Aphrodisias with Figures of Agrippina II (Milan type), Claudius, and a togate personification, A.D. 49-54, marble relief, h. 160 cm, w. at top 170 cm., at bottom 164 cm., d. 43 cm. Aphrodisias Museum.

142: Panel from the Sebasteion of Aphrodisias with Figures of the emperor Nero as a young man and of Agrippina II (Ancona type), probably A.D. 54-55, no later than A.D. 59, marble, h. 172 cm., w. 142.5 at bottom, d. 37.5 cm. Aphrodisias Museum.

143: Agrippina II, posthumous portrait, A.D. 113-118, from *imago clipeata* in the Forum of Trajan, marble, h. 85 cm, of face 57 cm. Rome, Mercati Traiani.

144: Profile view of Figure 143.

145: Grande Camée de France, A.D. 49-54, sardonyx cameo, h. 31 cm., w. 26.5 cm. Paris, Bibliothèque Nationale de France, Cabinet des Médailles.

146: *Aureus* of Nero, A.D. 62-65, Rome, with reverse of Nero and Poppaea, inscription AUGUSTUS AUGUSTA. Actual size. New York, American Numismatic Society.

SCHOLARS' LIST

*Through its Scholars' List Brill aims to make available
to a wider public a selection of its most successful
hardcover titles in a paperback edition.*

Titles now available are:

AMITAI-PREISS, R. & D.O. MORGAN, *The Mongol Empire and its Legacy.*
2000. ISBN 90 04 11946 9, price USD 29.90

COHEN. B., *Not the Classical Ideal.* Athens and the Construction of the Other
in Greek Art. 2000. ISBN 90 04 11712 1, price USD 39.90

GRIGGS, C.W., *Early Egyptian Christianity* from its Origins to 451 CE.
2000. ISBN 90 04 11926 4, price USD 29.90

HORSFALL, N., *A Companion to the Study of Virgil.* 2000.
ISBN 90 04 11870 5, price USD 27.90

JAYYUSI, S.K., *The Legacy of Muslim Spain.* 2000.
ISBN 90 04 11945 0, price USD 54.90

RUTGERS, L.V., *The Jews in Late Ancient Rome.* Evidence of Cultural
Interaction in the Roman Diaspora. 2000.
ISBN 90 04 11928 0, price USD 29.90

TER HAAR, B.J., *The Ritual and Mythology of the Chinese Triads.*
Creating an Identity. 2000. ISBN 90 04 11944 2, price USD 39.90

THOMPSON, T.L., *Early History of the Israelite People* from the Written &
Archaeological Sources. 2000. ISBN 90 04 11943 4, price USD 39.90

WOOD, S.E., *Imperial Women.* A Study in Public Images, 40 BC – AD 68
2000. ISBN 90 04 11950 7, price USD 34.90

YARBRO COLLINS, A., *Cosmology & Eschatology in Jewish & Christian
Apocalypticism.* 2000. ISBN 90 04 11927 2, price USD 29.90

———